Implementing and Enforcing EU Criminal Law

Implementing and Enforcing EU Criminal Law

Theory and Practice

Ivan Sammut and Jelena Agranovska (Eds.)

eleven
international publishing

Published, sold and distributed by Eleven International Publishing
P.O. Box 85576
2508 CG The Hague
The Netherlands
Tel.: +31 70 33 070 33
Fax: +31 70 33 070 30
e-mail: sales@elevenpub.nl
www.elevenpub.com

Sold and distributed in USA and Canada
Independent Publishers Group
814 N. Franklin Street
Chicago, IL 60610
USA
Order Placement: (800) 888-4741
Fax: (312) 337-5985
orders@ipgbook.com
www.ipgbook.com

Eleven International Publishing is an imprint of Boom uitgevers Den Haag.

ISBN 978-94-6236-983-2

© 2020 The authors | Eleven International Publishing

TABLE OF CONTENTS

FOREWORD

This book is the result of an academic project, funded by the Hercules Programme of the European Commission to study legislation dealing with crimes against the financial interest of the EU awarded to the Department of European and Comparative Law within the Faculty of Laws of the University of Malta. The study deals with the notion of criminal law at the European Union level as well as the relationship between the EU legal order and the national legal order. The focus of the study is on the development of EU criminal legislation aimed at protecting the financial interests of the EU, with a focus on cybercrime, fraud and public spending. It starts with the current legal basis in the TFEU, followed by the development of EU legislation in the area as well as the legislation of relevant bodies, such as EPO, OLAF and EUROPOL. The study tackles how this legislation is being received by the national legal orders, whereby 11 EU Member States are selected based on size, geography and legal systems. These Member States are France, Ireland, Croatia, Estonia, Germany, Italy, Malta, Spain, Latvia, Greece and Poland. A comparative study is made between those sections of EU criminal law dealing with the financial interests of the EU in these Member States to analyse the current legislation and propose future developments. The study, which is led by the editors based at the University of Malta, approaches the subject from a European perspective. Besides the European perspective, the study focuses on national case studies, followed by a comparative analysis.

LIST OF ABBREVIATIONS

AFA	French Anti-Corruption Agency
AFCOS	Anti-Fraud Coordination Services
AG	Advocate General
AML	Anti-Money Laundering
BZSt	German Federal Tax Office (Bundeszentralamt für Steuern)
CARIN	Camden Asset Recovery Inter-Agency Network
CFI	Court of First Instance
CFSP	Common Foreign & Security Policy
CJEU	Court of Justice of the European Union
CMLRev	Common Market Law Review
CNLF	*Comité National de Lutte Contre la Fraude*
COCOLAF	Advisory Committee for the Coordination of Fraud Prevention
COM	Communication
CP	*Codice Penale* – Italian Criminal Code
CPP	Code of Penal Procedure
CUP	Cambridge University Press
DDoS	Distributed Denial of Service
DGDDI	*Direction Générale des Douanes et des Droits Indirects*
DGFiP	*Direction Générale des Finances Publiques*
DNLF	*Délégation Nationale à la Lutte contre la Fraude*
EAW	European Arrest Warrant
EBLR	European Business Law Review
EC	European Community
ECB	European Central Bank
ECJ	European Court of Justice
ECON	The Committee on Economic and Monetary Affairs
ECR	European Court Report
ECtHR	European Court of Human Rights
EEC	European Economic Community
EEW	European Evidence Warrant
EFTA	European Free Trade Area
ELJ	European Law Journal
ELRev	European Law Review
EMU	Economic Monetary Union
EP	European Parliament
EPC	Estonian Penal Code
EPL	European Private Law
EPPO	European Public Prosecutor's Office
EU	European Union
EUI	European University Institute
FD	Framework Decision
FinCEN	U.S. Treasury's Financial Crimes Enforcement Network
FIU	Financial Intelligence Unit
GEMI	General Commercial Register
GSIS	General Secretariat of Information Systems

IAID	Internal Audit and Investigations Department
IALS	Institute of Advanced Legal Studies (London)
IBOAs	Institutes, Bodies, Offices and Agencies of the EU
ICLQ	International Comparative Law Quarterly
ICT	Information and Communication Technology
IOCTA	Internet Organised Crime Threat Assessment
JHA	Justice & Home Affairs
JIT	Joint Investigative Team
KNAB	Latvian Bureau for Prevention and Combating of Corruption
LCL	Latvian Criminal Law
LCPL	Latvian Criminal Procedure Law
LEA	Law Enforcement Agency
LIBE	Civil Liberties, Justice and Home Affairs
MJ	Maastricht Law Journal
MLR	Modern Law Review
MS	Member States
OCRFDF	*Office général pour la répression de la grande délinquance financière*
OECD	Organisation for Economic Cooperation & Development
OJ	Official Journal
OLAF	EU Anti-Fraud Office
OMC	Open Method of Coordination
OUP	Oxford University Press
PC	Polish Criminal Law
PCAC	Permanent Commission Against Corruption
PIF	Directive (EU) 2017/1371 of the European Parliament and of the Council of 5 July 2017 on the fight against fraud to the Union's financial interests by means of criminal law
RAF	*Rote Armee Fraktion*
SAM	State Aid Modernisation
SEA	Single European Act
SMEs	Small & Medium-Sized Enterprises
TEC	Treaty European Community
TEU	Treaty European Union
TFEU	Treaty on the Functioning of the European Union
UCLAF	*Unité de Coordination de la Lutte Anti-Fraude*
UNCAC	United Nations Conventions Against Corruption
VAT	Value-Added Tax

Contributors

AGRANOVSKA Jelena

Jelena is a lecturer in European and Comparative Law within the Faculty of Laws, University of Malta. Before joining the University of Malta in 2016, she had received the degrees of PhD at King's College London, LL.M. in European and International Law at London Metropolitan University and LL.B. at the Moscow State University. Her PhD thesis focused on the EU Member States' compliance with judgments of the CJEU on so-called 'golden share' cases. Jelena's academic interests lie broadly in the areas of EU law, corporate law and the law of the Internal Market. Her research often takes a transnational, European or comparative perspective and applies an interdisciplinary approach to law. Before joining the University, Jelena worked with an environmental NGO as EU policy researcher and as an in-house counsel with a Latvian software development company.

BORG Shaun James

Shaun James Borg is a practising lawyer who graduated from the University of Malta. He obtained his Bachelor of Laws degree in 2014 and furthered his studies by completing the Diploma of Legal Procurator and Diploma of Notary Public in the following two years. His Doctor of Laws thesis, submitted in 2018, was titled 'Digital Privacy and Data Protection in the EU: The Proposed EU Regulation on Privacy and Electronic Communications'. The dissertation centred on a critical analysis of the proposed 'e-privacy regulation', specifically in light of the then-emergent GDPR regime. Shaun was awarded the Professor David J. Attard Best Doctor of Laws Thesis Award in recognition of academic excellence achieved in the Doctor of Laws Thesis (2017-2018). Following the successful completion of the Doctor of Laws course, Shaun maintained a keen interest in legal writing and research and contributed to the writing of a paper on cybercrime in the EU with a special focus on Directive 2017/1371. At present, he works within the financial services sector as a lawyer, where issues related to EU and ICT law regularly intersect, especially with regard to data protection and anti-money laundering. He also serves as an examiner on the Board of Examiners of Bachelor of Laws (Honours) dissertations.

BRIÈRE Chloé

Chloé Brière holds a PhD in law delivered jointly by the Université Libre de Bruxelles and the University of Geneva in September 2016. She holds an LL.M. in European law (College of Europe, Bruges, 2009-2010) and a Master 2 in European economic law (Sciences Po Paris, University of Strasbourg). After working for two years as an academic assistant in the legal department of the College of Europe, she joined the Institute for European Studies as a PhD researcher in July 2012. She has been a member of the GEM PhD School, Erasmus Mundus Joint Doctorate 'Globalisation, the EU & Multilateralism' since September 2013. After holding positions at the Dublin City University and UNODC, she is, since October 2018, 'Chargé de recherches F.R.S. – F.N.R.S / Post-doctoral researcher' at the Université Libre de Bruxelles. In this framework, she conducts extended research on the external relations of the EU in criminal matters.

CARUANA Mireille

Mireille Caruana is a lecturer in the Department of European and Comparative law within Faculty of Laws, of the University of Malta. Previously, she was employed within the same University as a research assistant for various research projects coordinated by the Department of Information Policy and Governance, Faculty of Media and Knowledge Science in the University of Malta. She has dedicated much of her academic career to date to information policy and governance with a particular focus on European technology law. Her PhD research at the University of Bristol (2008/2014) is about data protection. Previously Mireille read for an LL.M. in Computer and Communications Law at Queen Mary University of London (2007-2008). Before moving to the UK in 2006, she read for the degrees of Doctor of Laws (LL.D) and Magister Juris in European and Comparative Law at the University of Malta. She has taught various undergraduate and postgraduate courses in Malta. More recently, she lectured computer science students at the University of Bristol on law and information technology.

ĐURĐEVIĆ Zlata

Zlata Đurđević is a tenured professor of law at the University of Zagreb and the president of the Croatian Association of Criminal Sciences and Praxis. She specializes in criminal procedure, human rights, European and international criminal law and psychiatric law. She is teaching at the University of Luxembourg and at the European Law Faculty in Ljubljana. She obtained her LL.M. in criminal law and PhD from the University of Zagreb and holds an M.Phil. degree in criminology from the University of Cambridge. She passed the judicial state exam in 1994. In 2010 she was a visiting professor at UC Berkeley, School of Law where she taught criminal law aspects of the European Convention on Human Rights. For two years (2014-2016) she was a senior research scholar at the Yale Law School conducting research titled 'Towards a European Criminal Procedure: Integration at the Expense of Human Rights'. She is a member of the Executive Committee of the International Organization of Penal Law (AIDP), a contact point for Croatia in the European Criminal Law Academic Network (ECLAN) and a president of the Croatian Association of European Criminal Law. She has served many times in a consultancy capacity to governmental, judicial, public and non-governmental organizations in fields ranging from human rights to compliance with international and European law. She partnered in numerous international projects related to defence rights in criminal proceedings, the establishment of the European Public Prosecutor Office and the rights of mentally disabled persons. She was a president of the drafting committee for a new Croatian criminal procedural code in 2013. She has written over 60 publications and presented at over 80 national and international conferences.

ENGELHART MARC

Marc Engelhart is a senior researcher at the Max Planck Institute for Foreign and International Criminal Law in Freiburg i. Br. (Germany). He is head of the section for business and economic criminal law since 2012 and of the Max Planck Research Group on 'The Architecture of Public Security Regulation' since 2015. His main research focus is on business and economic criminal law, European and international criminal law, the law of criminal procedure, security studies and comparative criminal law. He has published extensively in these fields, including monographs and edited books. He works as an expert for German, foreign and international institutions. Marc Engelhart was also admitted to the German bar in 2006 and has been a practising lawyer since then. From 2009 to 2011, he worked at an international corporate law firm in Stuttgart (Germany). He is a specialist in economic crimes, corporate wrongdoing and compliance. Marc Engelhart completed his studies at the University of Freiburg (Germany) and at the University of Edinburgh (United Kingdom) from 1999 to 2003. He completed his legal studies with the first state examination in law in Germany. From 2003 to 2005, he completed his training in the judicial service, serving part of it as a trainee in the German Federal Ministry of Justice in Berlin (Germany). From 2003 to 2009, he held a research position at Max Planck Institute for Foreign and International Criminal Law and was responsible for the German section. There he finished his doctoral thesis on 'Sanktionierung von Unternehmen and Compliance' (corporate criminal liability and compliance), which was distinguished with the Otto Hand Medal and Otto Hahn Award in 2011 and honoured with the prize of the 'Wirtschaftsstrafrechtliche Vereinigung' (the German economic criminal law association) in 2012. From February 2014 to February 2015, Marc Engelhart was a visiting scholar at the Institute for Criminology (University of Cambridge, United Kingdom) and at the Centre for Criminology (University of Oxford, United Kingdom).

FILLETTI STEFANO

Stefano Filletti graduated with a Bachelor of Laws, Diploma of Notary Public and Doctor of Laws from the University of Malta. He furthered his studies in international law and law of the seas at the International Maritime Law Institute (IMO) where he was awarded a Masters of Law Degree with distinction. As a Chevening Scholar, he read law at the University of Oxford where he was awarded a Masters of Law Degree in Criminal Law (M.Jur) with distinction. He was also awarded a Doctor of Philosophy (PhD) Degree from the University of Malta. He is a resident lecturer at the University of Malta in criminal law and also a visiting lecturer at the International Maritime Law Institute (IMO). He is the co-editor of the *New Journal of European Criminal Law* published by Intersentia, co-editor of the *Mediterranean Journal of Human Rights* published by the Faculty of Laws at the University of Malta, and co-editor of the journal *Law and Practice* published by the Chamber of Advocates (Malta). Filletti also acts as an advisor to both private and public entities and has held various posts. He heads the Maltese delegation to the Council of Europe – European Committee on Crime Problems (CDPC). Filletti is also the Head of the Department of Criminal Law within the Faculty of Laws at the University of Malta.

GINTER JAAN

Jaan Ginter is a criminology professor at the University of Tartu Law School. He has done research and has taught at the Law School since 1979. Ginter received his first law degree from the University of Tartu in 1979, PhD from the Institute of Criminology (Moscow) in 1986 and LL.M. from Columbia University (New York City) in 1993. He is serving as the European Criminal Law Academic Network (ECLAN) contact point for Estonia. His research and writing encompass criminology, the judicial system, ethics, criminal law and procedure (including international and European criminal law and procedure). He is the author of 11 monographs, 19 articles published in journals indexed or abstracted in international databases or as a part of collections of articles published an international science publishing houses, 20 other academic papers, five conference abstracts and eight other publications (textbooks, legal commentaries, etc.). He is experienced at working in a European and global dimension, such as being a rapporteur for Latvia and Malta at the Council of Europe GRECO workgroup and being a member of different workgroups focusing on cooperation in criminal matters between the EU Member States.

GIUFFRIDA FABIO

Fabio Giuffrida is a researcher in EU criminal law at the Faculty of Law, Economics and Finance of the University of Luxembourg. In this capacity, he was the coordinator of a research project concerning the admissibility of evidence collected by OLAF in criminal proceedings. Fabio completed his Master of Laws at the University of Catania (Italy), where he also attended the *Scuola Superiore di Catania*, a higher education institution that provides university students with additional courses. After graduation, he worked as a trainee lawyer in Italy and was admitted to the Italian Bar in October 2016. In 2014, he served a three-month internship at the Italian Desk of Eurojust and, in 2015, he spent a couple of months as a trainee in the Serious and Organized Crime – Fraud Unit of Europol. In 2015, Fabio was admitted to a PhD programme in EU criminal law at Queen Mary University of London (QMUL). During his PhD, he worked as a research assistant in an EU-funded research project ('EUPenTRAIN – Preparing the Environment for the EPPO: Fostering Mutual Trust by Improving Existing Common Legal Heritage and Enhancing Common Legal Understanding') and in the CEPS (Centre for European Policy Studies) & QMUL Task Force on 'The Future of EU, UK and US Cooperation in Criminal Justice and Police Cooperation'. He has published widely on matters related to EU criminal law, including the protection of the Union's financial interests, the consequences of the EPPO's establishment on national criminal justice systems and on the Area of Freedom, Security and Justice, the *Taricco* case of the Court of Justice, and the impact of Brexit on EU police and judicial cooperation in criminal matters. He also co-authored an article on the effects of the ECtHR's (European Court of Human Rights) judgments ascertaining violations of substantive criminal law on Italian final decisions.

GRASSO GIOVANNI

Giovanni Grasso is a professor of criminal law at the Law Faculty of the University of Catania, where he also teaches a module on European criminal law. He was the Director of the Specialization School for Legal Professions at the same University (2009-2017) and is the president of the *Centro di Diritto Penale Europeo* (Centre for European Criminal Law) of Catania. He is the contact point for Italy for the European Criminal Law Academic Network (ECLAN) and a member of the Scientific Committee of the Siracusa International Institute for Criminal Justice and Human Rights. Since January 2017, he is judge of the Constitutional Court of Bosnia and Herzegovina. From March 1996 to December 2003, he was a member of the Human Rights Chamber for Bosnia and Herzegovina. Between 1998 and 2002, he was vice-president of the Chamber and president of the II Panel. Professor Grasso served as a judge from November 1976 to October 1986. He worked as an investigating judge in Milan before being posted at the Legislative Office of the Italian Ministry of Justice, where he was responsible for legal reform initiatives related to criminal law and criminal procedure. Professor Grasso is a member of the Catania Bar since 1986 and is entitled to practice before higher courts since 1990. Between 2014 and 2018, he was a member of the Defence Counsel of the Municipality of Catania. Professor Grasso was a member of the EU-funded *Corpus Juris* project on the protection of the Union's financial interests (1997-2000) and has published extensively in the field of Italian and European criminal law, including a monograph on crimes committed by omission and another on the impact of EU criminal law on national criminal justice systems. He is also one of the co-authors of a renowned commentary on the Italian criminal code.

NOWAK CELINA

Prof. Dr Celina Nowak holds a Masters' degree of the Warsaw University and a postgraduate diploma of the Université de Paris I – Panthéon-Sorbonne. She received her PhD (based on a thesis Corruption in the Polish criminal law in the light of international instruments) in 2007 and her habilitation in law (based on a book on the influence of globalisation on the Polish criminal law) in 2015 in the Institute of Law Studies of the Polish Academy of Sciences. She currently holds a position of Director of the Institute of Law Studies of the Polish Academy of Sciences. Prof. Celina Nowak's research interests focus in particular on criminal law, comparative criminal law, international & transnational criminal law, European criminal law. She has published various articles and chapters in edited books in Polish, English and French. She is also the author of two monographs and editor and co-editor of ten more. She has taken part in many comparative law research and consultancy projects in Poland and abroad.

O'NEILL RUAIRI

Ruairi O'Neill is a lecturer at the Centre of English and European Law at the University of Warsaw, where he has taught since 2008. He obtained an honours degree in law at the National University of Ireland, Galway and his LL.M. in European Law at the Radboud University Nijmegen. As an academic, he lectures and conducts research on private and commercial law issues as well as European Union law relating to free movement, cross-border private law, EU fundamental rights and, more recently, Brexit. He is also a barrister and Denning Scholar of the Honourable Society of Lincoln's Inn. He advises law firms in Poland and across Central Europe on local and EU procedural and substantive law issues relating to disputes in both Ireland and England and Wales. He runs a charity in Poland that specializes in the utilization of EU grants in the field of justice aimed at improving both the general quality of the court services and the application of EU law in national courts in Central and Eastern Europe.

RODRÍGUEZ MARTÍN PABLO

Pablo Martín Rodríguez obtained his Law Degree (1994) and PhD (2000) at the University of Granada. He was a Jean Monnet Fellow at the Robert Schuman Centre of Advanced Studies of the European University Institute (Florence, 2005-2006) and visiting scholar at Cornell Law School (Ithaca, 2012). Former deputy dean and chair Jean Monnet of the University of Almería (2008-2014), he is currently director of the Department of Public International Law and International Relations of the University of Granada. He is the sole author and/or co-editor of several books on public international law and European Union law. He has published many articles in peer-reviewed scientific journals such as the *Columbia Journal of European Law, Journal of World Trade, European Constitutional Law Review, Cahiers de Droit Européen, Revue des Affaires Européens, Revista de Derecho Comunitario Europeo, Revista Española de Derecho Europeo, Revista Española de Derecho Constitucional, Revista Española de Derecho Internacional* or *Revista General de Derecho Europeo.*

SAMMUT IVAN

Ivan Sammut is the Head of Department of European and Comparative Law at the Faculty of Laws of the University of Malta, where he has taught and researched since 2005. Before joining the University as an academic, he practised law in Malta and acted as a consultant in EU law. He was also employed with the European Commission for two years. He also acts a freelance EU law consultant with various local law firms and has authored several reports for the European Commission, among others. As a practising lawyer in Malta, his practice specializes in EU law. He has been a senior lecturer and a coordinator of a Jean Monnet module dealing with EU legal drafting and translation since 2013. He has considerable experience in the translation of EU documents and also holds an MA in Translation Studies from the University of Birmingham in the UK. He graduated BA in Law and European Studies in 1999 and Doctor of Laws in 2002 from the University of Malta. He was called to the Maltese bar in 2003. Subsequently, he read for LL.M. in European Legal Studies from the College of Europe in Bruges (Belgium), and a Magister Juris in European & Comparative law from the University of Malta. In 2010 he successfully defended his PhD thesis, which is in the area of European private law, at the University of London. His teaching and research interests focus in particular on the EU Internal Market legislation, justice and home affairs law, competition law, European private law from a comparative perspective and European private international law. He has published various articles in Malta and in international peer-reviewed journals such as the *European Private Law Review.* Dr Sammut is also the author of a monograph entitled 'Constructing Modern European Private Law – A Hybrid System' published by CSP in the UK.

TURMO ARACELI

Araceli Turmo is an Assistant Professor *(Maître de Conférences)* in EU Law at the University of Nantes, France. She completed her PhD at the Université Panthéon-Assas (Paris II). Her doctoral thesis on *Res Judicata* in European Union Law was published by Bruylant in 2017. It aims to prove that the ECJ has constructed an autonomous, complex doctrine of *res judicata*, specific to EU law, and distinct from concepts such as *ne bis in idem* or *stare decisis*. Her main areas of research are European Union procedural law, European citizenship, fundamental rights, and the AFSJ, in particular, European criminal law and asylum policy. Recent papers focus on the topics of the conflicting EU and ECHR standards for *ne bis in idem*, the European Public Prosecutor and infringement proceedings.

VOUROS EFSTRATIOS

Estratios Vouros is a graduate of the Law School of the University of Athens. He has been a practising lawyer for more than 30 years, having been admitted to the Athens Bar Association in 1988, and a lawyer practising before the Supreme Courts of Greece since 1997. He has extensive knowledge of civil, labour, commercial and corporate law, covering a wide range of subject matter. His particular fields of interest include pharmaceutical law, labour law, real estate and building contracts, as well as public procurement. He is currently the legal advisor of the Panhellenic Association of Pharmaceutical Wholesalers. Furthermore, he specializes in providing full legal support for medium-sized corporations, consulting on matters such as commercial agreements, corporate restructuring and labour law. He also has extensive experience in consulting for construction companies, as well as corporations or individuals wishing to invest in real property. He is fluent in English and also speaks German.

XANTHAKI HELEN

Helen Xanthaki, UCL, is the dean of Postgraduate Laws Studies of the University of London, a visiting professor at Queen Mary University of London, a senior associate research fellow at the Sir William Dale Centre for Legislative Studies at the Institute of Advanced Legal Studies of the University of London, and the president of the International Association for Legislation. Helen was one of the authors of the third phase of Corpus Juris, the is the author of reports on OLAF for the Commission and the European Parliament, and the coordinator of more than 20 EU-wide comparative studies on aspects of EU criminal law. Her current research is on the effectiveness of EU legislation, and she uses EU criminal law instruments as case studies.

Introduction

Ivan Sammut & Jelena Agranovska

The European Union is a constitutional system founded by the European Union Treaties and governed by the principle of conferral. Article 5(2) of the Treaty on European Union (TEU) explains the principle of conferral in a straightforward way by stating that: *the Union shall act only within the limits of the competences conferred upon it by the Member States in the Treaties to attain the objectives set out therein*. This is very similar to the original Article 4 of the European Economic Community (EEC) which provided that the institutions should act within the limits of the powers conferred on them. The biggest question regarding criminal law is to determine what effect been conferred upon the EU by the Member States. This argument brings about a discussion on the spillover of competence as intended by European integration. The EEC originally started as a common market and eventually evolved into an economic union that is the Internal Market after the Maastricht Treaty, and eventually, new competences such as environmental protection, social policy and criminal law started mushrooming in subsequent treaty amendments.

The evolution of the EU's criminal competence is quite complex. One can start by looking at the context in which the Court of Justice of the European Union (CJEU) accepts implied powers in the field of criminal law. Criminal competence has them all up by several different means. The two principal means involve treaty revision and the interpretation of existing treaty provisions by the CJEU. However, following the Lisbon amendments, one can argue that while there is competence in criminal law at the EU level, the Member States are still much in control especially when it comes to the actual enforcement of criminal law. Hence, the European Union has specific competence conferred upon it by the Member States to take initiatives in the field of criminal law, yet its actual enforcement is entirely in the hands of the Member States, as the EU lacks any central enforcement mechanism. To make it even more complicated, other aspects of criminal law and procedures are still entirely within the competence of the Member States, and there is very little to no effort to ensure that the EU's initiatives fit well with the rest of the particular Member State's law mechanisms and enforcement. In some EU law, even EU's Internal Market legislation, one can have criminal principles or criminal legislation interacting with Internal Market principles. One can recall the famous

Dassonville case[1] dealing with the importation of whisky into Belgium, where the CJEU, following a reference from the Belgian court, decided that criminal law cannot be used to put actual or potential barriers to the flow of goods between the Member States. Hence the evolution of EU law results in the marriage between criminal law introduced at the EU level and national law, a marriage which may or may not work, as is discussed in this work.

When dealing with European criminal law, one should not forget that it is in the interest of both the European Union and its Member States that there is adequate protection from crimes that are against the financial interest of the European Union. The European Union's budget is raised and collected from the European citizens' taxes. Distributed to the Member States, this revenue allows further investment at a national level making the national economy grow even further, thus enhancing the Internal Market. When the EU realized that billions of euros per year are lost to criminals who undertake illicit activity, it vowed to do something concrete. If this money is pocketed by criminals due to fraudulent actions, money laundering, corruption and all sorts of other illicit behaviours which attack the funds of the European Union and the potential growth and improvement of the EU's market are substantially reduced. The side effect is that ordinary people lose trust and confidence in the concept of a 'European Union'. Identifying this problem to eliminate these matters paves the beginning of a winding path towards eradicating the problem.

Although the Member States do criminalize most of the crimes mentioned above and have ratified international conventions dealing with this matter, it occurred to the EU that this was not enough. This, in turn, made the EU believe that combating crime can only be successful through the use of criminal law because, in itself, criminal law – using sanctions – is not only punitive but also acts as a deterrent. As a reaction to this, the Area of Freedom, Security and Justice practically opens the Treaty on European Union (TEU)[2] by securing for the European citizens an area of freedom, security and justice while ensuring the prevention and combating of crime. This is also stressed in Title V of the TFEU which places European criminal law at a supranational level, symbolizing that nowadays the latter is at the top of the Union's agenda. Furthermore, through the competence that the EU acquired under the Lisbon Treaty, it started working towards harmonizing certain definitions of offences and sanctions in an attempt to have a level playing ground within its territory to deter such crimes.

The Lisbon Treaty has provided the tools to further European policies through criminal law. This work studies the tools which have been provided through the Lisbon Treaty about European criminal law using which crimes are criminalized because they

---

1   Judgment of the Court of 11 July 1974, *Procureur du Roi v. Benoît and Gustave Dassonville.* Reference for a preliminary ruling: Tribunal de première instance de Bruxelles – Belgium. Case 8-74. *European Court Reports 1974-00837* ECLI identifier: ECLI:EU:C:1974:82.
2   Article 3(2) TEU.

negatively affect the financial interests of the European Union. After a brief introduction to the legal basis and crimes against the financial interests of the EU, the work focuses on inter-agency cooperation and cybercrime. This is followed by several case studies from 11 Member States selected based on their size, geographical position and legal tradition. The work is concluded by a comparative exercise.

1   EU Law and Criminal Law

The Legal Basis

Ivan Sammut

1.1   Introduction

The European Union started as a common market, and following the Maastricht Treaty in 1993, it evolved into an economic union. As an economic union, one would not expect that the legal basis ventures into other fields besides the economic field. However, the Maastricht Treaty went beyond the economic concepts that were originally found in the European Economic Community (EEC) Treaty. In fact, the Treaty on European Union (TEU) encompassed a three-pillar structure with different modes of governance. While the traditional community pillar was supranational in nature, the second pillar, the common and foreign security policy (CFSP) and the third pillar, justice and home affairs (JHA), were mainly intergovernmental, varying in different degrees from each other. European criminal law can mainly trace its modern origins to the third pillar.

The evolution of the institutional framework of EU criminal law has been a gradual process. Although the major legislative developments have taken place in the last two decades and through the case law of the CJEU, steps for enhancing cooperation between the Member States in criminal matters outside the Treaty framework appeared in the early 1970s. One can mention, for example, the TREVI framework. This cooperation was a network of law enforcement officials meeting on an informal basis to discuss action on counterterrorism issues. TREVI was an informal structure with no clear legal framework, and it operated outside the then community law. In the 1980s, this was expanded to include new areas of cooperation such as drugs and organized crime, which are areas of common interest to the Member States.

With the development of the EU's Internal Market, it had become evident in cases brought before the CJEU in Luxembourg that the focus of the EU on economic matters did not stop EU's actions from having criminal law implications or from being associated with criminal choices in the Member States. The cause for the abolition of internal frontiers in the Internal Market, which became a major objective in the 1980s and the early 1990s, can be taken as a step forward in creating a spillover effect of law and policy to broader issues in the market, including criminal law. For example, one can mention the spillover effect that resulted from the abolition of internal frontiers and the goal of the free movement of persons. The birth of the Schengen Agreement, which then evolved into a Schengen Convention and eventually into the Schengen acquis, created the need for further cooperation in EU criminal matters. The Palma Document,[1] whose conclusions were endorsed by the Madrid European Council in 1989 following the publication in 1985 of the white paper on the completion by the Internal Market, led to a new impetus in the evolution of criminal law. The Palma Document leads to the achievement of an area without frontiers that involve, as necessary, the approximation of laws. Adding that the abolition of the internal borders affects a whole range of matters, including combating terrorism, the trafficking enforcement cooperation and judicial cooperation, this background led to the eventual creation of the third pillar.

1.2 EUROPEAN CRIMINAL LAW PRE-LISBON

As it been explained in the previous section, the first significant step in the evolution of European criminal law happened with the Maastricht amendments. In Maastricht, the provisions relating to EU criminal law were included in Title VI of the EU Treaty entitled 'Provisions on cooperation in the fields of justice and home affairs'. This marked the first time the union established competence in the field of JHA including judicial cooperation in criminal matters, customs cooperation, and police cooperation to prevent and combat terrorism, unlawful drug trafficking and other serious forms of international crimes. This was complemented by the establishment of the European Police Office (Europol).

However, the third pillar remained mainly intergovernmental in nature, and this meant that the traditional community method, where the European Commission representing the Union has the sole right to initiate policy and both the Council of Ministers representing the Member States as well as the European Parliament representing the peoples of Europe could not apply to these new competencies. As a result, very little, except cooperation where the Member States wanted, could be achieved. The operation of the third pillar demonstrated the weaknesses and limits of the compromise reached in Maastricht by the Member States. Legislative production was scarce and mainly took the form of conventions, which are all extremely cumbersome to ratify. Several joint actions were adopted, some of them providing definitions of key concepts of EU criminal law such as organized crime, but the legal status was unclear, and their implementation prospects were questionable.

As a result, a mere half a decade after the entry into force of the Maastricht Treaty, the Member States came up with the adoption of the Amsterdam Treaty. The deficiencies of the third pillar were discussed in the intergovernmental conference leading to the adoption of the Amsterdam Treaty. The indifferent national approaches to these matters did not stop the adoption of considerable changes to the third pillar in

---

1   P. A. Weber-Panariello, *The Integration of Matters of Justice and Home Affairs into Title VI of the Treaty on European Union. A Step Towards More Democracy?* EUI Working Paper RSC No. 92/32, Florence EUO up, 1995, p. 5.

Amsterdam. The Maastricht third pillar areas of immigration, asylum, borders and civil law were 'communitarized', forming part of Title IV of the EC Treaty, and the third pillar was now renamed 'Provisions on the police and judicial cooperation in criminal matters'. This was revamped and strengthened. The Amsterdam amendments, subject to some limited changes by the Treaty of Nice, in particular regarding the role of Eurojust and enhanced cooperation, form the basis of the institutional framework of the third pillar pre-Lisbon.

Another important development following the Amsterdam Treaty was the incorporation of the Schengen acquis into the then European Community Treaty. The institutional developments in the third pillar brought about in Amsterdam must be taken in the context of the express reference to the development of the Union as an AFSJ as a Union objective. The inclusion of this objective, which is also visible in both Title IV of the EC Treaty and Title VI of the EU Treaty (the remaining third pillar dealing with criminal matters), is significant in that it forms the framework within which EU action on justice and home affairs, including criminal law, are interpreted. Intergovernmental elements in the third pillar remained in Amsterdam, although the role of the Union institutions was, in general, enhanced in comparison with Maastricht. With regards to decision making, unanimity in the Council remains for the vast majority of third pillar law. The European Parliament, while in an enhanced position in comparison with Maastricht, continues to have an extremely limited role. The European Parliament is merely consulted in the adoption of framework decisions, decisions and conventions. This means that the Member States retain considerable leverage in this area and hence the Member States are firmly in control of the evolution of European criminal law.

To the above discussion, one can add that the Amsterdam Treaty also included a passerelle provision,[2] reformulated so that the Council may decide unanimously after consulting the European Parliament to transfer action in the areas mentioned in Article 29 TEU to Title IV of the EC Treaty. The Commission, which has also embarked on a series of court challenges contesting the legality of the choice of third pillar legal basis for EU criminal law harmonization instruments, proposed the use of this provision after the rejection of the Constitutional Treaty. The Constitutional Treaty had largely abolished the third pillar and had hence communitarized criminal matters. This concept was then taken up by the Lisbon amendments.

1.3   European Criminal Law after the Lisbon Treaty

The Lisbon amendments that entered into force in December 2009 finally brought about the communitarization of the remaining third pillar by abolishing the pillar structure in the amended European Community Treaty, now renamed Treaty on the Functioning of

---

2   *See* Article K9 of the Maastricht Treaty.

the European Union (TFEU). This is what governs European criminal law today. Article 67 TFEU – which is the article which opens Title V – establishes the main goals of the Union regarding the area of freedom, security and justice. This article establishes that the Union shall be an area of freedom, security and justice to ensure a high level of security by combating and preventing crime. In attempting to reach such an aim, the Union shall implement measures for cooperation between police and judicial authorities as well as adopt the principle of mutual recognition for criminal judgments.

The main legal base is Article 82 TFEU, which deals with criminal procedure. Under this article, a distinction can be drawn between paragraphs 1 and 2. Under Article 82 paragraph (1), the legislator establishes that cooperation in the criminal law field shall take place using mutual recognition between judges[3] and through the approximation of laws of the Member States. It shall be ensured that judgments are recognized throughout the Union and that jurisdictional conflicts between the Member States are circumvented. Under the second paragraph, the Treaty speaks about particular procedures which take place during a specific trial and the Union is given the competence to adopt minimum rules[4] on the rights of the individual during the criminal procedure, the rights of victims and the admissibility of evidence.

In an attempt to make clear what 'minimum rules' are, the third subparagraph of paragraph 2 talks about the fact that the Member States are prohibited from adopting legislation which affords less protection to the individuals than that prescribed in the minimum rules themselves. However, this does not impede the Member States from imposing standards which go beyond the minimum established by the Union. In adopting these minimum rules, national legal traditions and systems are to be taken into consideration. The most stringent requirement of them all is that the minimum rule is to be undertaken only "to the extent necessary to facilitate mutual recognition of judgments and judicial decisions ... with a cross border dimension",[5] as much research would have to be conducted in satisfaction of the fact that it truly is essential to promote the mutual recognition of judgments.

Article 82(2) TFEU is subject to what is commonly called 'the emergency brake procedure';[6] nevertheless, if there are at least nine Member States which still want to push the draft directive to success, this can be done using enhanced cooperation.[7] Given that matters which fall within the scope of paragraph 2 of Article 82 TFEU are

---

3   Article 82 TFEU is to be contrasted with Article 74 TFEU which regards cooperation between civil servants rather than between judges.

4   The 'minimum rules' are the main elements which are to be adopted by the European Parliament and the Council by means of the ordinary legislative procedure.

5   Article 82(2) TFEU.

6   The 'emergency brake' illustrates a practical example where the Union strikes a balance between wanting to work efficiently yet it also leaves room for the interests of the Member States. In this case, the 'emergency brake' can be made use of when the draft directive according to Article 82(2) goes against the Member State's criminal justice system.

7   Enhanced cooperation is found in Articles 20(2) and 329(1)TFEU.

subject to the emergency brake, it is to be distinguished from paragraph 1 of this same article which does not allow for the emergency brake procedure. The first thing to point out is that paragraph 1 speaks of *'measures'* while paragraph 2 mentions *'directives'* to be adopted to facilitate judicial cooperation in criminal matters. Paragraph 1 establishes that the principle of mutual recognition is the basic principle for judicial cooperation in criminal matters. On the other hand, paragraph 2 provides the procedure as to how mutual recognition of judgments is to be made easier, i.e., through the adoption of minimum rules. Also, measures adopted under paragraph 1 to facilitate cooperation between judicial authorities of the Member States do not deal with the substantive aspect of the procedural laws as this falls under paragraph 2. Paragraph 1 is the legal basis upon which the European Evidence Warrant (EEW)[8] has been adopted, because the EEW speaks of the transfer of evidence and not the admissibility of evidence. The same line of thought follows for the European Arrest Warrant (EAW)[9] which speeds up the process of arresting the person in the executing Member State and surrendering him to the issuing state; freezing orders;[10] the mutual recognition of financial penalties and confiscation orders;[11] the transfer of prisoners; the mutual recognition of criminal sentences; prior convictions and probation and pre-trial orders; mutual assistance and the transfer of information relating to criminal records.

Article 83 TFEU deals with substantive criminal law where European Union intervention is unrelated to mutual recognition. Instead, this article creates two legal bases by providing a division between core and traditional criminal law and furthermore, it gives reasons why the approximation of criminal laws is essential at the Union level, namely due to having a cross-border dimension, the nature or impact of such offences and the particular need to combat crimes on a frequent basis.[12]

Under Article 83(1) TFEU, harmonization will take place to adopt minimum rules[13] – through the ordinary legislative procedure – concerning the definition of certain

---

8 Council Framework Decision 2008/978/JHA of 18 December 2008 on the European evidence warrant for the purpose of obtaining objects, documents and data for use in proceedings in criminal matters [2008] OJ L350/72.

9 European Arrest Warrant Decision.

10 Council Framework Decision 2003/577/JHA of 22 July 2003 on the execution in the European Union of orders freezing property or evidence [2003] OJ L196/45.

11 Council Framework Decision 2005/214/JHA of 24 February 2005 on the application of the principle of mutual recognition to financial penalties [2005] OJ L76/16.

12 Article 83 TFEU.

13 Hans G. Nilsson, 'How to Combine Minimum Rules with Maximum Legal Certainty?' (2011) 14 *Europarättslig Tidskrift* 665, 669 'minimum rules' are described as a decision *'on the constituent elements of a criminal conduct'* which shall have a harmonizing and unifying effect.

offences and sanctions[14] "of particularly serious crimes". The rationale for providing an exhaustive list of these crimes is that the latter have a cross-border element and are severe enough that require the intervention of the Union to be combated against on common ground. Such crimes are money laundering, corruption, computer crime, organized crime, terrorism, trafficking in human beings and sexual exploitation of women and children, illicit drugs trafficking and illegal arms trafficking.[15]

By Article 83(2) TFEU,[16] if it is proved that the approximation of national criminal laws is essential for there to be the effective implementation of Union policy, then directives establishing minimum rules as to the definition and sanctions of crimes which do not fall under paragraph 1 shall be adopted. Thus, a separate legal basis is provided for the adoption of traditional criminal law under Article 83(2) TFEU. For there to be the adoption of a directive under Article 83(2) TFEU, three requirements need to be satisfied, namely two procedural and a substantive one. For the procedural requirements to be satisfied, there has to be the previous harmonization in the policy field within which the Union intends to criminalize, and the directives have to be adopted using ordinary or extraordinary legislative procedure.

A difference that can be pointed out between these two subparagraphs is that paragraph 1 gives a list of the crimes which fall within its scope and therefore, it can be argued *a contrario sensu*, that subparagraph 2 of Article 83 TFEU is not limited in scope to some crimes, as if this were to be the case, then once again the legislator would have provided a list. The relationship between these two paragraphs is that each paragraph is to be regarded as a *lex specialis* concerning the other paragraph, meaning that the scope of paragraph 1 could not be extended to cover those offences which fall within the scope of paragraph 2 of Article 83 TFEU and vice versa.[17] One thing in common is that both paragraphs envisage the adoption of minimum rules defining the sanctions that are to be applied to the crimes which fall within the scope of each paragraph.

The emergency brake is a procedure introduced by the Lisbon Treaty with the aim of keeping the interests of the Member States in the big picture and therefore, allowing the States to intervene and pull this brake if the measures adopted under Article 82(2) and Article 83(1)&(2) affect "fundamental aspects of its criminal justice system".[18] After pulling the brake, the draft directive is to be referred to the European Council, and in

---

14 The definitions of '*criminal offence*' and '*sanction*' are to be described in the particular directive adopted under Article 83(1) TFEU. When it comes to the definition of '*sanction*', the legislative capacity of the Union here is very wide as it can include a detailed article regarding the penalty imposed, dealing with – just to mention a few – imprisonment, the least number of years of imprisonment that a national court could impose, fines, community service, *etc.*

15 In giving an exhaustive list of crimes which need to fulfil certain requirements, the competence under the Lisbon Treaty is more restrictive when compared to the situation under the former third pillar. In fact, according to the TFEU, only these ten crimes are considered as being '*serious*'.

16 Article 83(2) TFEU is a new provision which was not to be found in previous treaties.

17 Steve Peers, 'EU Criminal Law and the Treaty of Lisbon' (2008) *European Law Review* 507.

18 Article 82(3) TFEU & Article 83(3) TFEU.

consequence, the ordinary legislative procedure would be frozen for a maximum of four months. Within four months of the draft directive having been referred to the European Council, the latter shall discuss the draft itself and the objection which pushed the Member States to actually pull the brake. It shall then either "terminate the suspension of the ordinary legislative procedure"[19] if consensus is reached with the consequence that the ordinary legislative procedure would carry on. However, it might be the case that there is disagreement in the Council and there are not at least nine Member States which wish to further the draft proposal using enhanced cooperation, which would result in the draft proposal being suspended indefinitely. If on the other hand, there is disagreement, but there is a minimum of nine Member States which wish to carry on with the draft directive using enhanced cooperation,[20] the Member States concerned shall inform the European Parliament, the Commission and the Council. This does not mean that the latter nine or more Member States are free to adopt any measure, meaning they cannot cooperate beyond the scope of the draft Directive because the Treaty does not give a free hand. Moreover, the Member States which wish to join the enhanced cooperation at a later date are allowed to do so, as long as the measures adopted are the ones which would have been taken up within the framework of enhanced cooperation.

The emergency brake needs to be differentiated from those instances in Article 86 TFEU and Article 87(2) TFEU where enhanced cooperation can still be taken up by at least nine Member States following that unanimity is not reached in the Council. In the last two articles, it is not stated as to why the representatives of the Member States in the Council would have vetoed the measures in question. To this extent, it can be stated that a veto can be availed of by the Member States without any particular reason. On the other hand, the emergency brake as mentioned under Articles 82(3) and 83(3) TFEU can only be employed if the draft directive necessarily affects the criminal justice system of that particular state.

The emergency brake should be used with caution in the sense that the Member States should take into account not just their national criminal justice systems but also that such a procedure will ultimately lead to a fragmentation of the criminal justice policy at the Union level,[21] resulting in two parallel realities, because the draft adopted following enhanced cooperation would be applicable to those Member States which have actually taken the draft further, yet at the same time the European Union legal regime would be applicable to all of the Member States including those who adopted the draft via enhanced cooperation. This shows further the importance that the phrase "fundamental

---

19   *Ibid.*
20   For further information on 'enhanced cooperation' refer to Articles 329, 330, 331 TFEU.
21   Maria Fletcher and Robin Lööf with Bill Gilmore, *EU Criminal Law and Justice,* Edward Elgar, Cheltenham, 2008, p. 42.

aspects of its criminal justice system"[22] is not interpreted too widely because this could stifle progress.

Crime prevention has been taken to a different level with the coming into force of the Lisbon Treaty due to a new legal basis – Article 84 TFEU – which exclusively deals with the prevention of crime to the exclusion of harmonization of laws of the Member States. Such an article aims to combat crime even before it takes place as this proves to be more effective. By Article 84 TFEU,

> The European Council invites the Member States and the Commission to actively promote and support crime prevention measures focussing on prevention of mass criminality and cross border crime affecting the daily life of our citizens.[23]

Moreover, the European Council invites for there to be a proposal for the setting up of the Observatory for the Prevention of Crime whose tasks would be to

> collect, analyse and disseminate knowledge on crime, including organised crime (including statistics) and crime prevention, to support and promote Member States and Union institutions when they take preventive measures and to exchange best practice.[24]

The work carried out within the European Crime Prevention Network should be used by the Observatory for the Prevention of Crime.

The Lisbon Treaty provides for the first time a legal basis – Article 86 TFEU – upon which the European Union can set up the European Public Prosecutor's Office (EPPO) using regulations to combat "crimes affecting the financial interests of the Union".[25] Thus, it can be stated from the outset that the European Public Prosecutor will deal with crimes *against* the Union and not necessarily any crime which is committed *within* the Union. The regulations that shall be adopted shall determine

> the general rules applicable to the European Public Prosecutor's Office, the conditions governing the performance of its functions, the rules of procedure applicable to its activities, as well as those governing the admissibility of

---

22 Articles 82(3) TFEU & Article 83(3) TFEU.
23 The Stockholm Programme – https://eur-lex.europa.eu/legal-content/EN/TXT/PDF/?uri=CELEX:52010X G0504(01)&from=EN, accessed 15 July 2019.
24 *Ibid.*
25 Article 86(1) TFEU.

evidence, and the rules applicable to the judicial review of procedural measures taken by it in the performance of its functions.[26]

However, no clue is given as to how these issues will be regulated. The creation of the Office of the European Public Prosecutor shall take place using the special legislative procedure,[27] i.e., in this field, the Union has retained unanimity. However, in the case that consensus is not reached, a possibility is provided for the adoption of the Office through enhanced cooperation if at least nine Member States agree to the latter's establishment.

Following the Lisbon amendments, Article 86 TFEU, the competences of the European Public Prosecutor shall be to investigate, prosecute[28] and bring to justice the perpetrators of, and accomplices in, offences against the Union's financial interests. Also, paragraph 2 gives the power to the European Public Prosecutor to choose the forum where the proceedings will take place. This choice of forum has to be a competent court of the Member States. Paragraph 4 of Article 86 TFEU provides for the possibility of an extended jurisdiction of the European Public Prosecutor – to be arrived at unanimously – to cover not only "crimes affecting the financial interests of the Union", but also "serious crime having a cross-border dimension". It follows therefore, that the mandate of the European Public Prosecutor is broad; however, this, in turn, raises some questions as to whether this extension of jurisdiction can take place when the Office of the European Public Prosecutor would have been established by all of the Member States, yet only a small group of the Member States wish to extend the powers of the office in question. This would result in a two-speed office. Secondly, could such extension take place when the European Public Prosecutor would have been established using enhanced cooperation?

Finally, one can also make reference to Article 325 TFEU which does not fall under the chapter on judicial cooperation in criminal matters, account of which is still to be taken because through such an article, the Union is given an unprecedented legal basis to adopt measures to deter and counter fraud and any other illegal activities which affect the Union's financial interests. Through the use of the words "act as a deterrent",[29] "prevention of and fight against fraud"[30] and "effective and equivalent protection" it can be realized that the inclination of this article tends towards criminal law, for these

---

26   Article 86(3) TFEU.
27   Article 86(1) TFEU.
28   It is indicative that the European Public Prosecutor has the final decision as to whether to prosecute the offence or not.
29   Article 325(1) TFEU.
30   Article 325(4) TFEU.

concepts are used in the latter's field. Thus, the main aim of this article is the protection of the Union's money through the adoption of criminal law.[31]

It seems that the legislator here has enacted a dovetailed action because, at a national level, Member States are to fight fraud against the Union's financial interests in the same way as they would fight it if it were affecting their national financial interests. This is called the 'assimilation principle'. Secondly, the European Parliament and Council shall legislate against fraud to prevent and combat it. Thus, it can be stated that Article 325 TFEU is a legal basis for the harmonization of criminal law both of the national and European level as long as the measures adopted prevent and fight fraud that affects the financial interests of the Union.

The fact that Article 325 TFEU is constituted as the provision which deals with the financial interests of the Union automatically makes it distinct from Article 83 TFEU because there need not be the conditions that the crime has to be serious with a cross-border element. Also, it slips from the emergency brake procedure, thus allowing for a greater success of the adoption of the measure. In conclusion, the potential of such an article is very beneficial for the fight against European Union fraud, especially because if it is combined with Article 86 TFEU, it would enhance the European Public Prosecutor's scope.

1.4   The Role of the CJEU

As the legal basis of the third pillar is mainly intergovernmental, the EU's institutions, in general, play a limited role in the evolution of European criminal law. One of the most significant limitations is the Commission's power to institute infringement proceedings against the Member States. The role of the CJEU has been strengthened in comparison with Amsterdam but remains subject to significant limitations. The Court's third pillar jurisdiction is delineated by Articles 46(b) and 35 TFEU.[32] The Court does have jurisdiction to give preliminary rulings on the validity and interpretation of framework decisions and decisions on the interpretation of conventions and on the validity and interpretation of the measures implementing them. However, such jurisdiction is subject to acceptance by the Member States and not all Member States have declared acceptance so far. Before Lisbon, there were also limitations in cases of preliminary reference; however, now Article 267 TFEU also applies to these legal bases discussed earlier on in this paper. The court has jurisdiction to review the legality of union law on the grounds of lack of competence, infringement of an essential procedural

---

31   In fact, Article 325 TFEU serves as a legal basis for the Commission, 'On the fight against fraud to the Union's financial interests by means of criminal law' (Proposal) COM (2012) 363/2 final.

32   A. Arnull, 'Taming the Beast? The Treaty of Amsterdam and the Court of Justice', in O'Keeffe and Twomey (eds.), *Legal Issues After Amsterdam Treaty*, OUP, Oxford, pp. 109-122.

requirement, infringement of the Treaty or any rule of law relating to its application or misuse of powers. The standing is however limited to the Member States, the European Commission, the Council of Ministers and the European Parliament under Article 263 TFEU.

Although the CJEU has limited jurisdiction, there have been some landmark judgments that have helped shape European criminal law. The leading judgment is the case of *Pupino* dealing with the doctrine of direct effect in this area of law.[33] For the first time, the CJEU has confirmed that EU framework decisions can be applied in national criminal courts. On 16 June 2005, the CJEU issued a groundbreaking judgment stating that a Council framework decision concerning police and judicial cooperation in criminal matters must be respected in a national criminal court case. The case before the Court concerned an Italian nursery school teacher accused of maltreating her five-year-old charges. Under Italian law, there was no procedure allowing the young victims to give evidence in private – they would have to appear before the full court (except in sexual offence cases). However, an EU framework decision does provide for special procedures for the protection of minors in such a case.

Under the EU Treaty, framework decisions adopted under the third pillar have no direct effect, i.e., they cannot usually be directly invoked by individuals in national courts. However, the CJEU pointed out that framework decisions are 'binding' on Member States in that they have a bearing on the interpretation of national law. The CJEU went on to say that, in this case, "the Italian court is required to interpret (national law) as far as possible in a way that conforms to the wording and purpose of the framework decision". In this case, this meant allowing vulnerable victims to be protected when giving testimony.

The above shows that the CJEU, in spite of its limited jurisdiction, can still play an essential role in the evolution of European criminal law. It is also respectful of the degree of integration that states signatory to the Amsterdam treaty wished to achieve in criminal matters. Through court activism, the CJEU design dissociates the envisaged degree of integration in Amsterdam from the needs to ensure the effective achievement of Union objectives. This is an example of how the CJEU continues to play an important role in the evolution of this field.

1.5   THE CONCEPT OF MUTUAL RECOGNITION

The concept of mutual recognition has been primarily adopted and used in the Internal Market as an integration tool. Because it proved to be fruitful, it is now the cornerstone

---

33   Judgment of the Court (Grand Chamber) of 16 June 2005. Criminal proceedings against Maria Pupino. Reference for a preliminary ruling: Tribunale di Firenze – Italy. Police and judicial cooperation in criminal matters – Articles 34 EU and 35 EU – Framework Decision 2001/220/JHA – Standing of victims in criminal proceedings – Protection of vulnerable persons – Hearing of minors as witnesses – Effects of a framework decision. Case C-105/03. Reports of Cases 2005 I-05285.

principle in the area of freedom, security and justice – another area of integration. The principle of mutual recognition derives from the idea of a common area of justice encompassing the territory of the Member States of the Union, within which there would be free movement of judgments. More concretely, it signifies that when a decision has been handed down by a judicial authority which has competence under the law of the Member State in which it is situated, by the law of that State, the decision becomes fully and directly effective throughout the territory of the Union. The competent authorities in the Member States in the territory where the decision may be enforced have "to assist in the enforcement of the decision as if it were a decision handed down by a competent authority in that State".[34]

With the application of mutual recognition, judges are put at the centre stage because they are granted further enforcement capacity of judgments, orders and warrants which have been handed down by a national judicial authority other than the one in which recognition is sought, with limited grounds for refusal of enforcement. In simpler words, mutual recognition of sovereign acts implies that the requested Member State is obliged to accept another Member State's judgments as if they were delivered by the former Member State's courts and even further, enforce such judgments. This way, judgments take effect in the Member States other than the one in which they were delivered.

The European Commission recognizes that mutual recognition is to be achieved using trust[35] and approximation of national laws. Mutual trust implies that the requested state has confidence that the delivered judgment complies with the law and respects individual's rights while on the other hand, the requesting state trusts that the judgment will be executed correctly. In a remark on mutual trust between the Member States, the European Court of Justice stated that:

> the [Member] States have mutual trust in their criminal justice systems, and each of them recognises the criminal law in force in the other [Member] States even when the outcome would be different if its own criminal law were applied.[36]

---

34 Council of the European Union, 'Evaluation report on the fourth round of mutual evaluations "Practical application of the European Arrest Warrant and corresponding surrender procedures between Member States" report on Belgium' No. 16454/2/06, www.asser.nl/upload/eurowarrant-webroot/documents/cms_eaw_id1358_1_CouncilDoc.16454.2.06%20Rev%202.pdf, accessed 15 July 2019.

35 Commission, 'Mutual Recognition of Judicial Decisions in Criminal Matters and the Strengthening of Mutual Trust between Member States' (Communication) COM (2005) 195 final, 6.

36 Joint Cases C-187/01 and C-385/01 *Oberlandesgericht Köln (Germany) and the Rechtbank van eerste aanleg te Veurne (Belgium) v. Gözütuk and Brügge* [2003] ECR I-1378, para. 33.

From this, it follows that the most significant consequence mutual recognition has had is that legislative divergences between the Member States are not seen any longer as a form of hindrance. On the contrary, there is a common area of enforcement.

Nevertheless, it is to be pointed out that states have surrendered part of their sovereign power when dealing with the implementation of decisions within their territory. In fact, those that oppose the introduction of mutual recognition in the criminal law field argue that this principle causes problems at a constitutional level due to the well-known maxim *nullum crimen sine lege*, yet there is a list of 32 offences which does not admit the dual criminality principle[37] and thus the executing Member State still has to surrender or arrest the person even though under its national laws, no crime would have been committed. Moreover, the reason that mutual recognition should be dealt with caution is that it could lead to an opposite scenario where any judgment, decision or order which is coming from any one of the other Member States has to be accepted when it might be the case that it should not be accepted unless specific requisites comply.

Finally, mutual recognition is to be contrasted to the principle of cooperation between states. The principle of cooperation entails that a state is requested to assist another state with an aspect of the latter's criminal justice system. The requested state's decision to assist the other state depends on its justice system, although refusal for such cooperation has been limited using treaties. However, with mutual recognition, the decision taken by the issuing state is enforced in the requested state's legal system.

A form of ranking between the mutual recognition and approximation of laws was introduced in the Hague Programme,[38] where it was stated that approximation of laws is to be used to ensure mutual trust and mutual recognition of judicial decisions and judgments. The Stockholm Programme establishing that once again followed this reasoning:

> Further action is needed on the closer alignment of substantive law in relation to certain serious crimes, generally of cross-border nature, which requires common definitions and penalties. Alignment[39] here will help to extend mutual recognition and, in some cases, almost completely abolish the grounds for a refusal to recognise other Member States' judgments,[40]

---

37   Council Framework Decision 2002/584/JHA of 13 June 2002 on the European Arrest Warrant and the surrender procedures between Member States [2002] OJ L190/1 (European Arrest Warrant Decision), Article 2(2).

38   Council, The Hague Programme: Strengthening Freedom, Security and Justice in the European Union [2005] OJ C53/1.

39   In accordance with Nadja Long, 'Harmonisation of Substantial Criminal Law in the European Union – The concepts of "serious crime" and "particularly serious crime"' (2011) 18(1) *Law and European Affairs* 159, 161; although the word 'alignment' has been used here, it is to be taken to mean 'approximation'. 'Alignment' has only been used in the Stockholm Programme.

40   Commission, 'An Area of Freedom, Security and Justice Serving the Citizen' (Communication) COM [2009] 262 final.

which in turn confirms what has been primarily established under the Tampere Programme. Thus, an approximation of laws is a tool which should facilitate the better functioning of mutual recognition.

1.6 CONCLUSION

Looking at EU criminal law, one is faced with a significant body of law that is surely affecting most aspects of criminal justice. A starting point for any inquiry into the nature of EU criminal law must be by looking at the existing legal framework. Even though the Member States may have failed to consider the potential theoretical and conceptual implications of their actions, this does not rule out the possibility that these actions have, in effect, resulted in the reconceptualization of criminal justice. Therefore, a question that may be asked is whether, as a result of the significant acquis of the AFSJ, we are now faced with the *de facto* reconceptualized pan-EU system of criminal justice. If the legislator fails to provide the theoretical context, such a context needs to be deduced from the legislation itself. The case studies provided later on in this work will serve as examples of how EU criminal law is being implemented in this context in the selected Member States.

2   An Open Method of Coordination (OMC) for European Criminal Law?

Ivan Sammut

2.1   Introduction

The European Union may be perceived as a multi-level governance system in which a European private law can be established both by harmonization and by the OMC. In areas where EU law has been less intrusive traditionally, such as European criminal law one can argue for the use of an open method of coordination (OMC). The term 'governance' is very versatile. It is used in connection with several contemporary social sciences, especially economics and political science. It originates from the needs of economics (as regards corporate governance) and political science (as regards state governance) for an all-embracing concept capable of conveying diverse meanings not covered by the traditional term 'government'. Referring to the exercise of power overall, the term 'governance', in both corporate and state contexts, embraces action by executive bodies, assemblies (e.g., national parliaments) and judicial bodies (e.g., national courts and tribunals). The term 'governance' corresponds to the so-called post-modern form of economic and political organizations. According to the political scientist Roderick Rhodes, the concept of governance is currently used in contemporary social sciences with at least six different meanings: the minimal State, corporate governance, new public management, good governance, social-cybernetic systems and self-organized networks.[1] The European Commission established its own concept of governance in the White Paper on Governance,[2] in which the term 'European governance' refers to the rules, processes and behaviour that affect how powers are exercised at the European level, particularly as regards openness, participation, accountability, effectiveness and coherence. These five 'principles of good governance' reinforce those of subsidiarity and proportionality.

---

1   R. Rhodes, 'The New Governance: Governing without Government' (1996), 44 *Political Studies* 652.
2   COM (2001) 428 final.

Table 2.1 The further Europeanization of criminal law requires a multi-level mode of governance confirming the traditional supranational community method mode of governance with intragovernmental innovative methods such as OMC/soft-law

Mode of Governance	Method	Tools
Traditional supranational mode	The community method – the Commission has the exclusive right to propose legislation while the Council and EP decide together	Harmonization UnificationCodification/ Consolidation
Proposed intergovernmental mode	Innovative methods such as OMC, soft-law, formalized networks/institutions	Cooperation Standardization/ Unification

2.2 GOVERNANCE

The EU must draft new governance techniques that prove effective, efficient and most importantly, democratically accountable in the context of multi-level regulation and considerable diversity in national legal systems. The traditional methods used by nation-states in fixing those settlements of fundamental values in private law through the enactment of codes and respect for the evolution of judicial precedents must be adapted and even wholly revised to be relevant to the multi-governance structure of the EU. The governance system of a multi-level pluralistic EU requires new methods for the construction of this union of shared fundamental values which would respect cultural diversity and the innovative modes of governance mentioned above.

While the Treaty of Amsterdam provided for the increased momentum in the development of private law in the European field, one must not lose sight of the fact that we are now in the age of globalization. The action of strong political and economic forces, the ease of travel, the development of communication technologies and the advent of the Internet are contributing to the convergence of national societies in a shift from territorial to functional differentiation at the world level.[3] The field of law, particularly private law, is also becoming 'globalized'. The diverse sectors of the new 'world society' are developing their own legal frameworks, thereby displacing the importance of state-produced law and legal centralism.

Parallel to the process of globalization, another significant phenomenon, which erodes the importance of national boundaries and the conception of the state as the centre of the

---

3   G. Teubner, 'Global Bukwina: Legal Pluralism in the World Society', in G. Teubner (ed.), *Global Law without a State,* Dartmouth, 1997, p. 3 *et seq.*

legal order, is taking place in certain geographical areas.[4] It is the process of regional integration, with a maximum exponent in the EU. This is witnessing the gradual transformation of European sovereign states into new political entities without historical precedents, breaking the traditional dualism of states and international organizations. There is a considerable transfer of sovereignty from the state to the EU level so that the EU can no longer be characterized as an instrument for implementing the will of the Member States. Indeed the Member States play a central role in the decision-making process at the European level, but they do so in a constitutional-legal context which they do not fully control. EU law is gradually developing into an autonomous, distinct and independent supranational legal order, possessing primacy over the law of the Member States, the provisions of which are directly applicable to the nationals of the Member States.

2.3   The OMC Method

There are several innovative modes of governance which can be tested to examine how they can influence the development of European criminal law and take it to new dimensions. However, one of the most important ones is OMC. The reason for choosing the OMC as the main mode to test the hypothesis is due to it being the most flexible and policy-oriented mode that provides very concrete mechanisms to address the balance between the need to respect diversity among Member States, and the unity and meaning of common EU action. The OMC is a collection of mechanisms previously developed under the broad 'soft-law' tradition in the EU, such as collective recommendations, review, monitoring and benchmarking. Sometimes it is contended that the OMC offers nothing new when compared with soft-law.[5] However, this work intends to prove that the matter is otherwise and innovative modes of governance such as the OMC are a very valid mode in which to examine the future potential of European criminal law especially in bringing the different European legal families together.[6]

Today the OMC is eminently a legitimizing discourse. It provides the EU's policy-makers with a common vocabulary and a legitimizing project – to make Europe the most competitive and knowledgeable society in the world. As a legitimizing discourse, open coordination enables policy-makers to deal with the new tasks in policy areas that are either politically sensitive or in any case not amenable to the classic community method. The result is that practices that up to a few years ago would simply have been labelled as 'soft-law', new policy instruments, and benchmarking are now presented as

4   T. Wilhelmsson, 'Jack-in-the-Box Theory of European Community Law', in Erikson and Hurri (eds.), *Dialectic of Law and Reality*, 1999, p. 437 *et seq.*, at p. 447.
5   S. Borrás and K. Jacobsson, 'The Open Method of Co-ordination and New Governance Patterns in the EU' (2 April 2004) 11 *Journal of European Public Policy* 185-208.
6   *See* P. F. Kjaer, *Between Governing and Governance*, Hart Publishing, Oxford, 2010, p. 104.

'applications', if not 'prototypes' of 'the' method.[7] The reality is that the method varies markedly across policy areas. This work focuses on how the open method can influence the challenges presented to European criminal law and examines whether developments in private law can go beyond what may appear to be achievable in the foreseeable future.

Naturally, as attested earlier in the introduction to this chapter, European criminal law is so complex that any analysis involving only one mode of governance would be incomplete. The OMC is certainly one of the most important innovative modes of governance for the reasons already outlined, but a successful analysis would be incomplete without the examination of other innovative modes of governance. The innovative modes of governance contribute to the redefinition of some important institutional choices concerning European criminal law and allow for the overcoming of the binary allocation scheme of legislative competence between the EU and the Member States. Innovative modes of governance provide new coordination mechanisms across the Member States and between them and the EU to improve the process of implementation and reduce inadequacies.[8]

The OMC has developed over time so that its precise procedures have been delineated gradually. The notion of an OMC first materialized in the conclusions of the Lisbon Summit in March 2000.[9] Such a method was already envisaged in the procedures for coordinating national economic policy under the Economic Monetary Union (EMU) established under the Maastricht Treaty, and in the employment chapter of the Amsterdam Treaty. In Lisbon, the Portuguese Presidency successfully gave a name to this new method, while linking it to the new agenda for socio-economic development which was the fruit of a political compromise aligning the visions of both the right-wing and left-wing parties. The main procedures of this method are common guidelines to be translated into national policy, combined with periodic monitoring, evaluation and peer review organized as mutual learning processes and accompanied by indicators and benchmarks as a means of comparing best practices.[10]

The OMC may be analysed as a multi-level process of governance, comprising at least four levels. First, the European Council agrees on the general objectives to be achieved and offers general guidelines. Then the Council of Ministers selects quantitative and/or qualitative indicators for the evaluation of national practices. These indicators are selected upon a proposal by the Commission or other independent bodies and agencies. This is followed by the adoption of measures at the national or regional level, given the

---

7   S. Borrás and K. Jacobsson, *op. cit.* at p. 187.

8   F. Cafaggi and H. Muir-Watt (eds.), *Making European Private Law – Governance Design*, Edward Elgar: Cheltenham and Northampton 2008, *op. cit.* at p. 289.

9   V. Hatzopoulos, 'Why the Open Method of Coordination is Bad for You: A Letter to the EU' (May 2007) 13(3) *European Law Journal* 309-342 at p. 311.

10 *Ibid.*, p. 312.

achievement of the set objectives in pursuit of the indicators chosen.[11] These were usually referred to as the 'National Action Plans' or NAPs. The process is completed with mutual evaluation and peer review between the Member States, at the Council level. Since its official launch in 2000, it has been proposed as a new way of governance in several different fields such as immigration, environment and innovation, research and development, among others.

Proposals to apply the OMC to European criminal law can be made in the context of addressing problems arising from the lack of competence, but even more important to accommodate the goal of harmonization with that of preserving legal diversity, in its institutional and cultural forms.[12] It is important to underline that those proposals were aimed at enforcing the weakest modes of the European chain: monitoring the process of implementation of European criminal law and governing the differences at the Member State level, not only those in existing laws amenable to harmonization, but also and perhaps more importantly, those stemming from the use of directives harmonizing different fields.[13] This brings the discussion to the point where one can analyse how the OMC has contributed or could contribute to the development of European criminal law.

While the term OMC was formally launched in Lisbon in 2000 as a mode of governance, it had existed earlier, though it was not formally recognized as such. Certainly, one can examine any role the OMC may have played in the development of European criminal law through analysing both the formal and informal attempts. However, given the fact that the OMC may be more useful when a clear legal base is absent, it is worth examining it as a mode of governance in comparison with the more traditional soft-law approach. Given the nature of European criminal law and, in particular, the significance of private law-making by an individual or collective actors, it is clear that major adjustments should be made to the current OMC methodologies, especially with regard to the relatively weak involvement of private actors.[14] Soft-law can include recommendations and opinions as they have no binding force as well as a variety of other instruments which may include resolutions and declarations, action programmes and plans, decisions of the representatives of the Member States meeting in Council and guidelines issued by the institutions as to how they exercise their powers and inter-institutional arrangements.[15] Professor Chalmers explains that these measures all come under the generic 'soft-law'.[16] Referring to Professor Snyder, he explains that

---

11 E. Szyszczak, 'Experimental Governance: The Open Method of Coordination' (2006) 12(4) *European Law Journal* 486, at p. 494.
12 F. Cafaggi, 'The Making of European Private Law: Governance Design', in F. Cafaggi and H. Muir-Watt (eds.), *Making European Private Law – Governance Design, op. cit.* at p. 344.
13 *Ibid.*, p. 344.
14 *See Ibid.*, p. 344.
15 D. Chalmers et al., *European Union Law – Text and Materials*, Cambridge University Press, Cambridge, 2006, p. 137.
16 *Ibid.*, p. 137.

these are rules of conduct, which in principle have no legally binding force but which nevertheless may have practical effects.[17] Table 2.2 highlights the differences between the OMC and traditional soft-law and can also serve as a critique for the OMC as a methodology to be used in the development of European criminal law.

Table 2.2   Differences between the OMC and traditional soft-law

The Open Method of Coordination	Traditional Soft-law
Intergovernmental approach: the Council and the Commission have dominant roles	Supranational approach: the Commission and the CJEU have dominant roles
Political monitoring at the highest level	Administrative monitoring
Clear procedures and interactive process	Weak and *ad hoc* procedures
Systematic linking across policy areas	No explicit linking of policy areas
Interlinking EU and national public action	No explicit linking of EU/national levels
Seeks the participation of social factors	Does not explicitly seek participation
Aims at enhancing learning processes	No explicit goal of enhancing learning is stated

One can identify at least seven different points that mark the distinction between the two. Firstly, the essentially intergovernmental-oriented approach oriented to the OMC differs from the previous supranational-oriented approach to soft-law in the EU. The Council and the Commission both play an important role in the innovative mode of governance while the CJEU has played a decisive role in including soft-law as a source of a non-binding but decisive form of regulation in the *acquis*. In contrast, this Court has no role to play in the OMC. The CJEU will play a role when it is hard-law. This idea is reinforced by the second difference: the OMC involves a high level of political participation.[18] While good legislation involves a bottom-up approach in its formulation, hard legislation is always enacted top-down at the end. The OMC can thus reconcile these two approaches.

Thirdly, the clear procedural mechanism and the high-level political participation entail more mutual commitments and peer pressure mechanisms than the *ad hoc* and weak procedures of previous soft-law mechanisms. Fourthly, while soft-law has previously been used mostly *ad hoc* within the confines of particular policy areas, the OMC has the goal of strategically bridging policy areas and orientating policies towards a common goal. The OMC seeks to strategically bridge policy areas in a double horizontal way, by linking national policies with each other, and by linking functionally different policies at the EU level. Finally, similar to the practices of the OECD, the innovative

---

17   F. Snyder, 'The Effectiveness of European Community Law: Institution, Processes, Tools and Techniques' (1993) 56 *MLR* 19, 32.
18   S. Borrás and K. Jacobbson, *op. cit.* at p. 189.

method of governance is designed to support learning as it builds on and encourages mutual cooperation and the exchange of knowledge and experiences.[19]

The OMC enables common objectives to be agreed on while leaving the choice of means to the individual Member States or other entities responsible for the achievement of policy goals. The OMC has contributed to the elaborate monitoring methods, benchmarking and adjustments, all of which are required in the area of European criminal law.[20] Some criticisms have been directed towards its openness to private actors and its top-down nature while other critics have addressed effectiveness, especially about the sanctioning system. Deeper critiques concern its compatibility with the rule of law.[21] However, in spite of its advantages and disadvantages with regard to its viability to contribute towards the development of European criminal law, neither the OMC and the innovative modes of governance nor the traditional community method may be used without resort to the tools that can be used for the Europeanization of private law.

European criminal law operates in the frame of a complex multi-level system whose structure is quite complex. It should not be described by juxtaposing uniform market values at the EU level and differentiated cultural and moral values at the Member State level. From this perspective, governance would be perceived only as an institutional response to cultural differences, associated with national identities to make them compatible with the creation of the Internal Market. One of the other issues to be examined in this context is the improvement in legislative design. Legislation needs better design and coordination. With respect to law-making, improvements can be made to achieve better coordination among different Commission directorates at the stage of legislative initiatives as well as linguistic improvements in translations of legislative documents.[22]

2.4   CONCLUSION – A NEW MODE OF GOVERNANCE FOR EUROPEAN CRIMINAL LAW

It may be argued that the EU suffers from a political and democratic deficit. Its system of governance appears to be best suited to the task of managing a single market, an economic community guided by the narrow objectives of efficiency and free markets. Numerous issues at the European level are, in reality, political questions that demand democratic decision-making procedures. The context of this debate is that there is a

---

19   *Ibid.*, p. 189.
20   *See* W. Van Gerven, 'Bridging Private Laws Closer, Bridging (Private) Laws Closer to Each Other at the European Level', in F. Cafaggi (ed.), *The Institutional Framework of European Private Law*, OUP, Oxford, 2006, p. 63.
21   *See* W. Scheuerman, 'Democratic Experimentalism or Capitalist Synchronisation? Critical Reflections on Directly-deliberative Poliarchy' 17 *Canadian Journal of Law and Jurisprudence* 101-128.
22   F. Cafaggi, *op. cit.* at p. 333.

technocratic 'yes' to increase the powers of Europe confronted by a popular 'no vote' as happened in the first Irish referendum on the Lisbon Treaty. While the development of European criminal law is not directly a central issue in the constitutional process of reforming the EU Treaties, and it is not necessarily linked with the constitutional development of the EU, it will somehow also be influenced by it. One important reason for this is that the development of European criminal law has gone beyond the limits traditionally attributed to the Internal Market.

Some political scientists such as Moravesik look on the one hand at intergovernmentalism and on the other hand at neo-functionalism as the two main competing schools of thought that help to explain European integration.[23] However, it can be argued that a significant challenge comes from a new school of thought that portrays the EU as a 'multi-level system of governance'.[24] This theory highlights the erosion of the nation-state but denies the transformation to a new European super-state. The concept of governance is flexible enough to capture the *sui generis* characteristics of an emerging European polity and leave open the question of exactly where the European system lies on the scale between the traditional nation-state and the looser forms of international cooperation. In parallel, the theory also helps with the conceptualization of 'integration' as a contingent political process and is, therefore, better equipped than functionalism in dealing with the interests and strategies that engage and are pursued by both institutional and governmental actors on one side and by private actors such as academics on the other side. This holds for both the national and supranational levels.

Thus the 'multi-level system of governance' is a good theory to understand the development of European criminal law. First, the multi-level approach appears to be compatible with certain specific features of the present situation of European private law, which includes the conservation of the core elements of the national system together with the imposition by the EU of several private law instruments designed for Internal Market building. One could also mention the openness of the European legal system to international cooperation in its regulatory activities as well as in its efforts to facilitate private law relations. Secondly, this approach also has the advantage of being able to conceptualize 'governance' as independent from and beyond the formalized nation-states and Union structures. This is compatible with the erosion of the powers of the nation-state on the one hand and the growth of regulatory powers at a European level on the other hand. Thirdly, this analytical framework also allows the interdependence of legal integration and disintegration to be articulated and characterized as a dual and simultaneous development. This allows for the building up

---

23 *See* Moravesik, 'Preferences and Power in the European Community: A Liberal Inter-governmentalist Approach' (1993) 31 *JCMS* 473-524.

24 *See* Marks, Hooghe and Blank, 'European Integration Since 1980s State Centric Versus Multi-level Governance' (1996) 34 *JCMS* 343-378.

of a framework for economic and social regulation, which is very beneficial for the Internal Market and likewise cuts the ties between national markets and their traditional institutional environments.[25]

An important analytical feature of multi-level governance portrays the EU as a non-state and a non-hierarchal system. One can perhaps use the term 'deliberative supranationalism'.[26] This term does not only accept the open-mindedness or contingency of the integration process but is itself based on two intuitions. The first is that it builds upon legal theories which ground the laws' validity on the institutions of the traditional constitutional state. The second takes the notion of 'deliberation' further, no longer grounding supranationalism in formal international law or technocratic traditions, but in the establishment of external and tampering deliberative processes between states as institutional actors and societies.

An important factor which would influence the extent to which the European criminal law could develop is the conceptualization that supranational constitutionalism is an alternative to the model of the constitutional nation-state. This has to respect that state's constitutional legitimacy but at the same time clarify and sanction the commitments arising from its interdependence with equally democratically legitimized states. Supremacy requires the identification of rules and principles, ensuring the coexistence of different constituencies and the compatibility of the objectives of these constituencies with the common concerns that they may share. European private law, as in the rest of EU law, has to lay down a legal framework which structures political deliberation about these issues.

However, while the extent of the nation-state element's readiness to give way to European supranationalism is far from clear, it is well known that there is an ongoing transformation of the 'Community of Constitutional States' into a real and visible 'European Union'.[27] This *de facto* process is legalized by European law and constrained by the Treaty rules. Thus constitutional development is highly relevant to private law. Therefore one might ask where this relevance is leading to.

To answer this question, one must state what the Community and now the Union has done and continues to do to the national legal systems. It inserts new individual freedoms into them and thus strengthens the realm of private autonomy. It imposes new duties upon traders and assigns inalienable minimum rights to the consumers. So it establishes transnational regulatory frameworks to which national institutions of private law must adapt themselves. These interventions in the national system not only determine the social space allocated to the market but also set the limits and restrict techniques which might be used to identify and correct market failures. European interventions are

---

25   C. Joerges et al. (ed.), *Integrating Scientific Expertise into Legal Decision-making* (1997) pp. 295-323. at p. 299.
26   C. Joerges et al. (ed.), *op. cit.* pp. 300-319.
27   C. Joerges, *op. cit.* at p. 303.

concerned with those asymmetries in private relationships which legal systems have traditionally affirmed or sought to cure. Therefore, when seen in the perspective of deliberative theories of liberal democracy, the constitutional dimension of issues, such as the delineation of the realm of private autonomy and the protection of basic and inalienable rights, is simply irrefutable.[28]

The constitutional dimension partly overlaps with the institutional dimension, although the two are far from coextensive.[29] The institutional dimension of European criminal law is built around the different roles of European and national institutions. This includes the mode of cooperation and, to a more limited extent, competition between the legislators, courts and regulators. It brings the governance perspective to the centre stage. It broadens the perspective on competence, often focused on the alternative between existence and inexistence, by concentrating on the different modes through which the creation of the 'private law infrastructure' of a common market can be established. Special attention has to be given to the notion of private autonomy as a substantive principle of European private law. The role of private autonomy may vary from one system to another, and recurring arguments in favour of harmonization have been related to the differences concerning mandatory rules in the Member States and the problems they may cause for the creation of the integrated European market. The same reason could be applied to international private law rules.[30] Such circumstances could weaken the rationale for unification and limit harmonization to mandatory rules only.

A final note about the institutional dimension of European criminal law concerns the issue of language. The choice of one language to create new common rules and its subsequent translation into 20 or more languages does not address the comparative issue that has caused so many problems for the transposition of directives. Multilingualism is not a solution in itself. An adequate institutional framework for European criminal law needs to be supported by a comparative analysis engaging not only an evaluation of the effects associated with the use of multilingualism to pursue harmonization and preserve differentiation, but also an evaluation of the impact of harmonized rules in national and regional legal systems that maintain their own legal and everyday vocabularies.[31]

---

28 *See Ibid.,* pp. 304-305.
29 P.F. Kjaer, *op. cit.* at p. 15.
30 H. Muir Watt, 'The Challenge of Market Integration for European Conflicts Theory', in A. Hartkamp et al. (eds.), *Towards European Civil Code*, Kluwer, The Hague, 3rd ed., 2004, p. 191.
31 F. Cafaggi, 'Introduction', in F. Cafaggi (ed.), *The Institutional Framework of European Private Law*, OUP, Oxford, 2006, p. 21.

3   Crimes Against the Financial Interest of the EU

Ivan Sammut

3.1   Introduction to Substantive EU Criminal Law

One of the essential items on the Union's agenda in the fight against crime is the protection of the Union's budget. This affects billions of euros per year.[1] As a result, it is in the EU's and Member States' interest to fight corruption. The EU itself has adopted the 'Convention on the protection of the financial interests of the European Communities'[2] marking the first attempt by the Union in protecting its budget from fraud through criminal law,[3] i.e., the Europeanization of criminal law, accessed through the 'United Nations Convention against Corruption'.[4] The different legal systems of the Member States make fighting crime within the EU more difficult than it already is because each system admits different sanctions, time limits for criminal offences, rules for the collection of evidence and investigation powers. Combined with the difficulty which currently exists within the Union regarding the fact that no proper definitions are given for these European core crimes which affect the finances of the EU, the need was felt to retaliate to crime in a different and a more effective manner by dedicating articles to it in the Lisbon Treaty. The purpose of this paper is to give a general synopsis of how the EU combats crimes against its financial interests.

3.2   A Focus on Fraud and Corruption

The EU's tools in the fight against corruption and fraud have been reinforced through the introduction of the Lisbon Treaty using Articles 86 and 325 TFEU. Article 325 TFEU urges the Member States to fight against fraud and any other action which negatively affects the financial interests of the Union. The Commission adopted a communication

---

1   Fighting corruption in the EU (Communication) COM (2011) 308 final.
2   Council Act of 26 July 1995 drawing up the Convention on the protection of the European Communities' financial interests OJ C 316.
3   This Convention is very frequently referred to as the 'PIF Convention'. A definition of 'fraud' was formulated for this purpose and there was agreement as to when to prosecute if a crime against the Union's financial interests was committed.
4   Council Decision 2008/801/EC of 25 October 2008 on the conclusion, on behalf of the European Community, of the United Nations Convention against Corruption [2008] OJ L287.

'On the protection of the financial interests of the European Union by criminal law and by administrative investigations – an integrated policy to safeguard the taxpayers' money'.[5] With millions of euros claimed by criminals in various financial crimes, the EU cannot allow a patchy situation where it is the Member States which have to decide whether and how to protect the EU's budget. In its attempt to counter fraud and corruption, the EU has undertaken various actions to protect the economy.

Legislation dealing with anti-corruption measures is already in place, but it may not be enough, or certainly, lots of improvements are needed. At the heart of such legislation, there is the Framework Decision 2003/568/JHA on combating corruption in the private sector,[6] which deals with the problem of bribery. However, its transposition has not been smooth. Nevertheless, recent actions have been undertaken by the EU, primarily such as its accession to the 'United Nations Convention against Corruption'.[7] Furthermore, fuelled by the absence of any type of surveillance of anti-corruption policies and the lack of commitment by the Member States in their collaboration in the fight against corruption, the Commission has been urged time and again[8] particularly by the Stockholm Programme to monitor the efforts undertaken by the European Union and the Member States in their fight against corruption affecting the Union's money. In the attempt to respond to this cry, a reporting system has been established,[9] i.e., the Anti-Corruption Report.

The Anti-Corruption Report monitors the current framework, its application and implementation in the Member States, ultimately resulting in an overview of the advancements made by the Member States and the Union itself in this field. The fight against corruption cannot stop at the drawing up of such a report, but rather this report should be used to draft policies which are effective and target problems which are still persistent, notwithstanding what is already being done. Most importantly, this report should also be able to help assess whether there is a need to approximate national criminal laws dealing with corruption to facilitate investigations and proceedings between the Member States. The Anti-Corruption Report can be combined with the EU's participation in GRECO as benefits could be better reaped if both work together and alongside each other. This participation has been very much emphasized in the

---

5   Commission, 'On the protection of the financial interests of the European Union by criminal law and by administrative investigations – an integrated policy to safeguard taxpayers' money' (Communication) COM (2011) 293 final.
6   Council Framework Decision 2003/568/JHA of 22 July 2003 on combating corruption in the private sector [2003] OJ L192/54.
7   Council Decision 2008/801/EC of 25 October 2008 on the conclusion, on behalf of the European Community, of the United Nations Convention against Corruption [2008] OJ L287.
8   Commission, 'Establishing an EU Anti-Corruption reporting mechanism for periodic assessment' (Commission Decision) COM (2011) 3673 final.
9   Fighting Corruption Communication.

report drafted by the Commission.[10] Special emphasis has been given to the fact that this collaboration would not only mean that a better approach towards corruption would be taken but also that the recommendations put forward by the Stockholm Programme would be lived up to. Finally, although it does not provide the ultimate answer to eradicate corruption within the EU, it will provide a better insight into the problem through the collection of facts, figures and the examination of the impact which current legislation has on mitigating corruption.[11] Furthermore, the collateral effect of this report will result in urging the Member States to do their best in implementing legislation and living up to it.

Article 325 TFEU obliges both the Commission and the Member States to adopt measures to counter fraud which affect the Union's financial interests, and the Commission Communication on the Anti-Fraud Strategy[12] deals precisely with this matter. This newly introduced strategy – which is directed at Union institutions – aims to prevent, investigate and identify fraud, provide sanctions which deter criminals from committing such crime against the Union and recover assets considered as proceeds of crime. Given that the Anti-Fraud Strategy is directed at the Union institutions, the importance of OLAF and the contribution the latter will have can easily be understood. The importance of the Anti-Fraud Strategy lies in the fact that measures are not only directed at the Member States but also at the European Union institutions, tackling the issue that fraudsters could operate from within the institutions themselves. It recognizes the fact that fraud could take place from within the core of the Union and seeks to deal with such a problem. This proves that the European Union is committed to approaching the problem of fraud from all directions.

The EU has tried to defend its budget from corruption and fraud through several avenues as has been pointed out above. However, this is not yet giving the desired results which the EU aspires for and which the taxpayers deserve, especially because each Member State adopts its own rules and laws in its fight against fraud, which in turn results in non-equivalent protection across the Union. Therefore, the Union needs to tap into European criminal law as a possible and potential avenue to eradicate fraud.

The main aim of the directive 'On the fight against fraud to the Union's financial interests by means of criminal law'[13] is to ensure that the differences between the legal systems of the Member States of the EU are down to a minimum by implementing common minimum denominators regarding definitions of crimes, punishments and

---

10 Commission, 'On the modalities of the European Union participation in the Council of Europe Group of States against corruption (GRECO)' (Report) COM (2011) 307 final.

11 R. Stefanuc, 'Corruption or How to Tame the Shrew within the European Union Stick: The New Anti-corruption Initiative of the European Commission' (2011) 12 *ERA Forum*, www.springerlink.com.ejournals. um.edu.mt/content/f0578j2l28070787/fulltext.pdf, accessed 15 July 2019.

12 Commission, 'On the Commission Anti-Fraud Strategy' (Communication) COM (2011) 376 final.

13 Commission, 'On the fight against fraud to the Union's financial interests by means of criminal law' (Proposal) COM (2012) 363/2 final (Fighting Fraud through Criminal Law).

time limits.[14] Owing to this, criminals are not able to take any advantage of the discrepancies which emerge between the national legal systems, with the result that they are restricted in their movement across borders. Hindering criminals from taking advantage of the differences emanating from the legal systems of the Member States contributes to the fight against huge sums of money dished out from the taxpayers going into the criminals' pockets.

One of the ways proposed in trying to proximate this gap is by providing definitions of fraud-related offences which affect the financial interests of the EU; namely, definitions are given for corruption,[15] misappropriation[16] and public officials.[17] However, the proposal does not stop here because the incitement, aiding, abetting and attempt of these latter crimes are also criminalized.[18] Furthermore and once again in an attempt to ensure consistency throughout the European territory, a minimum threshold for imprisonment for these crimes is also provided so that there would be a common denominator for the sanctions prescribed at the national level.[19] The ultimate aim is that there is a common front in deterring fraud all over the EU affecting the same Union. This directive clearly indicates the EU's intention to Europeanize criminal law as that is the only way to seriously deter crime against its monies due to the fact that by means of criminal law, sanctions are provided.

3.3   MONEY LAUNDERING

The crime of money laundering is the aftermath of a prior, separate offence which would have generated the illicit money which is now sought to be laundered in some sector of the economy. The aim of money laundering is to mask the origin of the money. The Third Anti-Money Laundering Directive[20] stipulates that the Member States are to prohibit money laundering. Member States are urged to make sure that professional and financial institutions which might come into contact with persons who might have the intention to launder money and any other property which is the result of crime have to inform the relevant authorities. Thus, these professionals and financial institutions have to evaluate the people with whom they come into contact and analyse the risk that

---

14 European Commission, 'EU criminal law will protect taxpayers' money against fraudsters' (11 July 2012), http://ec.europa.eu/justice/newsroom/criminal/news/120711_en.htm, accessed 26 August 2018.
15 Fighting Fraud through Criminal Law, Art. 4(3).
16 Fighting Fraud through Criminal Law, Art. 4(4).
17 Fighting Fraud through Criminal Law, Art. 4(5).
18 Fighting Fraud through Criminal Law, Art. 5.
19 Fighting Fraud through Criminal Law, Art. 8 with a minimum imprisonment of at least 6 months and a maximum imprisonment of at least 5 years.
20 Council Directive 2005/60/EC of 26 October 2005 on the prevention of the use of the financial system for the purpose of money laundering and terrorist financing OJ L309/15.

they might be involved in money laundering.[21] Customer due diligence measures are also to be conducted by professionals[22] when they are establishing business ties with their clients. It can immediately be noticed that the directive's scope does not limit itself to just financial service providers. The Third Anti-Money Laundering Directive urges for constant monitoring of suspicious transactions and of people who might not act in an ordinary manner as requested by their profession. The fact that the directive adopts the risk-based approach shows a shift in monitoring from the public authorities to the private sector. Ultimately, the directive is focused on preventing money laundering as much as possible, and that is why it imposes obligations on the private sector to analyse their clients well.

The EU launched a proposal for a directive titled 'On the prevention of the use of the financial system for the purpose of money laundering and terrorist financing'.[23] Fuelled by the need to stay abreast of the anti-money laundering procedures in light of the fact that criminals constantly make use of the latest and most sophisticated technology to launder financial proceeds, the aim to be achieved by such proposal is to strengthen the Internal Market by simplifying the current legal system and better address the crime of money laundering for the benefit of all of the Union by countering the latest innovations adopted by criminals. It is also understood that the adoption of anti-money laundering procedures at a Union level is the best approach to effectively and truly counter this offence. This avoids the possibility of the Member States adopting national measures in order to safeguard their financial system which could not have the main aim of safeguarding all of the Internal Markets but rather be more focused on tackling the problem at a national level.

Another proposal was submitted on 5 July 2016 and referred jointly to Parliament's Committees on Economic and Monetary Affairs (ECON) and on Civil Liberties, Justice and Home Affairs (LIBE). This proposal would amend the fourth Anti-Money Laundering Directive, which was adopted on 5 June 2015 and is due to enter into force in 2017. The terrorist attacks of late 2015 had already prompted a review of the anti-money laundering framework when, in April 2016, the Panama Papers created a new sense of urgency to act in a related field.

The action plan for strengthening the fight against terrorist financing, presented by the Commission in February 2016, contains a number of measures aimed at addressing

---

21   This is referred to in the directive as the 'risk-based approach'.
22   The professionals which the directive makes reference to include lawyers, notaries, accountancy firms, real estate firms and company service providers.
23   Commission, 'On the prevention of the use of the financial system for the purpose of money laundering and terrorist financing' (Proposal) COM (2013) 45 final (Proposal for the Prevention of Money Laundering) which amalgamates and repeals Commission Directive 2006/70/EC of 1 August 2006 laying down implementing measures for Directive 2005/60/EC of the European Parliament and of the Council as regards the definition of 'politically exposed person' and the technical criteria for simplified customer due diligence procedures and for exemption for grounds of a financial activity conducted on an occasional or very limited basis [2006] OJ L214/29.

problems that became even more evident after the recent terrorist attacks. The following five problems have been identified: i) suspicious transactions involving high-risk third countries are not efficiently monitored due to unclear and uncoordinated customer due diligence requirements; ii) suspicious transactions made through virtual currencies are not sufficiently monitored by the authorities, which are unable to link identities and transactions; iii) current measures to mitigate money laundering/terrorist financing risks associated with anonymous prepaid instruments are not sufficient; iv) Financial Intelligence Units have limitations in the timely access to – and exchange of – information held by obliged entities; v) Financial Intelligence Units lack access or have delayed access to information on the identity of holders of bank and payment accounts.[24]

The protection of the financial aspect of the Union through criminalizing money laundering is essential for the better functioning of the Internal Market and to be able to freeze and confiscate proceeds of crime rather than allowing loopholes in the legislation for such proceeds to be channelled in the licit economy mainly through recourse to the gambling sector, investing in real estate, the banking system and through other financial systems. In doing so, the European Commission would be implementing what has been recommended in the Stockholm Programme, i.e., securing for the citizens of the European Union a safe and secure Union by targeting money laundering among other policy areas.

Article 83(1) TFEU pinpoints 'money laundering' as one of those crimes where minimum rules as to its definition may be adopted; however, unfortunately, no holistic definition of the term 'money laundering' has yet been adopted, even in the directive. However, the Commission has already shown its intention to supplement the proposed directive by providing a harmonized definition of the crime of money laundering basing itself on Article 83(1) TFEU.[25] Harmonization of this definition would prove to be essential as it would hinder the criminals from taking advantage of the divergent definitions currently existing under the Member States' legal systems which allows them to move freely from one jurisdiction to another with the intent to launder money gained illegitimately. With a common definition across the European territory, the Member States would be in a better position to identify particular acts which amount to money laundering and therefore cross-border cooperation would be more straightforward. In addition, since Article 83(1) TFEU would be used, the EU would also have the competence to determine what types of sanctions are to be awarded.

In 2018, the Council adopted a new anti-money laundering directive. This directive introduces new criminal law provisions which will disrupt and block access by criminals

---

24 www.europarl.europa.eu/RegData/etudes/BRIE/2016/587354/EPRS_BRI(2016)587354_EN.pdf, accessed 15 July 2019.

25 Commission, DG Home Affairs, Proposal to harmonise the criminal offence of money laundering in the EU (Roadmap) October 2012, http://ec.europa.eu/governance/impact/planned_ia/docs/2013_home_006_money_laundering_en.pdf, accessed 15 July 2019.

to financial resources, including those used for terrorist activities. The new rules include establishing minimum rules on the definition of criminal offences and sanctions relating to money laundering. Money laundering activities will be punishable by a maximum term of imprisonment of at least four years, and judges may impose additional sanctions and measures (e.g., temporary or permanent exclusion from access to public funding, fines, etc.). Aggravating circumstances will apply to cases linked to criminal organizations or for offences conducted in the exercise of certain professional activities. They also include the possibility of holding legal entities liable for certain money laundering activities which can face a range of sanctions (e.g., exclusion from public aid, placement under judicial supervision, judicial winding-up, etc.). Also, the new rules remove obstacles to cross-border judicial and police cooperation by setting common provisions to improve investigations. For cross-border cases, the new rules clarify which Member State has jurisdiction, and how those Member States involved cooperate, as well as how to involve Eurojust.[26]

3.4   CRIME AND EMU

The protection of the euro currency is fundamental because counterfeiting of the money goes against a power which only appertains to the state. People, in general, have to have the assurance that the money they use or receive as a means of payment is not false. Counterfeiting badly affects not only the countries where the money is being counterfeited but also the state whose money is being counterfeited. In the case of the EU, all of the Member States which have adopted the euro are negatively affected.[27] Moreover, the euro is a currency which is used in a large geographical area; not just by the Member States within the EU which have adopted the currency but also in other third countries.

As a result of the introduction of Framework Decision 'On increasing protection by criminal penalties and other sanctions against counterfeiting in connection with the introduction of the Euro',[28] the Member States have been obliged to punish the offence of counterfeiting. The latter legislation clearly defines under Article 3(1) the conduct that is being criminalized and furthermore, delineates the meaning of 'currency'.[29] In

---

26   https://www.consilium.europa.eu/en/press/press-releases/2018/10/11/new-rules-to-criminalise-money-laundering-activities-adopted/, accessed 15 July 2019.

27   Ciro Grandi, 'The Protection of the Euro against Counterfeiting' (2004) 12(2) *European Journal of Crime, Criminal Law and Criminal Justice*, http://web.ebscohost.com.ejournals.um.edu.mt/ehost/pdfviewer/pdfviewer?sid=d1df75a1-dbe6-4f83-8046-da6398b1e1b4%40sessionmgr14&vid=4&hid=27, accessed 15 July 2019.

28   Council Framework Decision 2000/383/JHA of 29 May 2000 on increasing protection by criminal penalties and other sanctions against counterfeiting in connection with the introduction of the euro [2000] OJ L140 (Euro Counterfeiting Decision), Art. 3.

29   Euro Counterfeiting Decision, Art. 1.

providing a clear description of the counterfeiting offence, the European Union has lived up to the principle of *lex certa*.[30] It has been made sure that combating counterfeiting is adequately taken care of through criminal law mainly by means of "effective, proportionate and dissuasive criminal penalties".[31] When the offence concerns the making or altering of the currency itself, imprisonment of not less than eight years is the punishment to be awarded.[32]

Given that it is the EU which is accountable for suppressing the crime of counterfeiting of the euro, there was the adoption of a regulation titled 'Laying down measures necessary for the protection of the Euro against counterfeiting'.[33] Among these measures, the most important point is the fact that information regarding counterfeiting of the euro is to be collected, processed and passed on to the European Central Bank such that this data can be studied with the aim that more knowledge is gathered on this particular crime. Moreover, credit institutions which get hold of counterfeit currency are obliged to hand them over to the competent national authorities.[34]

However, notwithstanding the above-mentioned actions undertaken by the Union, more deterrence is required by ensuring that homogenous criminal sanctions are adopted throughout all of the Member States. In countering this crime, it is essential that all of the Member States adopt the same approach not only because all their economies are negatively affected, but also because such a crime is a manifestation of organized crime operating across several States. The only manner to have an efficient way of combating this crime is through the adoption of criminal law measures and sanctions which are coherent in all of the Union. The latter can be successfully achieved following the entry into force of the Lisbon Treaty because a better legal basis has been provided for the adoption of a directive dealing with counterfeit of means of payment under Article 83(1) TFEU.

Directive 2014/62/EU entered into force on 22 May 2014. This directive is meant to boost the protection of the euro against counterfeiting by criminal law measures. The directive replaces Framework Decision 2000/383/JHA and supplements and helps implement the 1929 Geneva Convention on the suppression of counterfeiting. The new measures include tougher sanctions for criminals and improved tools for cross-border

---

30 European Criminal Policy Initiative, 'The manifesto on European criminal policy in 2011', www.zis-online. com/dat/artikel/2009_12_383.pdf, accessed 15 July 2019.

31 Euro Counterfeiting Decision, Art. 6(1). In accordance with Towards an EU Criminal Policy, 9 *effectiveness* requires that the sanction is suitable to achieve the desired goal *i.e.* observance of the rules; *proportionality* requires that the sanction must be commensurate with the gravity of the conduct and its effects and must not exceed what is necessary to achieve the aim and *dissuasiveness* requires that the sanctions constitute an adequate deterrent for potential future perpetrators.

32 Euro Counterfeiting Decision, Art. 6(2).

33 Council Regulation 1338/2001 of 28 June 2001 laying down measures necessary for the protection of the euro against counterfeiting [2001] OJ L181/6.

34 *Ibid.*, Art. 6.

investigation. The directive obliges the Member States to punish: i) fraudulent making or altering of currency (production of counterfeits); ii) distribution of counterfeit currency; iii) making and possessing counterfeiting equipment; and iv) fraudulent making of notes and coins not yet issued. This directive sets the minimum standard for maximum penalties of imprisonment in the Member States – maximum penalty of at least eight years for production and at least five years for distribution of fake notes and coins. It ensures that special investigative tools that are used for organized crime cases can also be used in serious cases of counterfeiting, thus improving the quality of cross-border investigations. The directive makes it possible to analyse seized counterfeits earlier during judicial proceedings, which improves detection of counterfeit euros and prevents their circulation. Finally, it also requires the Member States to collect data on the number of counterfeiting offences, persons prosecuted and convicted, and transmit these data to the Commission.[35]

3.5   THE PROTECTION AGAINST THE FINANCIAL INTEREST OF THE EU (PIF) DIRECTIVE

The protection of the financial interests of the EU is a key element of the EU policy agenda. Such protection is aimed at strengthening and increasing the confidence of citizens and ensuring the sound financial management of EU funds, as well as supporting the actions of the European Anti-Fraud Office (OLAF) in combating fraud and irregularities in the implementation of the EU budget. There has been an increase in the number of legislative texts and recommendations dealing with the protection of the EU's financial interests. In July 2012, the European Commission submitted a proposal on the fight against fraud affecting the Union's financial interests by means of criminal law. The proposal was aimed at strengthening administrative and criminal law procedures to fight fraud against the Union's financial interests. The objective of what is known as the PIF Directive was to deter fraudsters, improve the prosecution and to sanction crimes against the EU budget, and facilitate the recovery of misused EU funds, thereby increasing the protection of EU taxpayers' money. The Council adopted a general approach at first reading on 6 June 2013. The European Parliament adopted its position on 16 April 2014. In a report issued on 25 March 2014, the European Parliament's Committees on Budget and Civil Liberties, Justice and Home Affairs expressed concern about the existing differences in the sanctioning of fraud between the Member States.[36]

---

35   https://ec.europa.eu/info/business-economy-euro/euro-area/euro/anti-counterfeiting/legislation-against-euro-counterfeiting_en, accessed 15 July 2019.

36   www.europarl.europa.eu/legislative-train/theme-area-of-justice-and-fundamental-rights/file-protection-of-the-union-s-financial-interests-(PIF-directive), accessed 15 July 2019.

National criminal proceedings appeared neither effective nor equivalent, and the degree of success in prosecution varied between the Member States. This led to the necessity of providing a strong and coordinated response to fraud and any other illegal activities affecting the financial interests of the Union. One can argue in favour of the establishment of minimum and maximum criminal sanctions to ensure a degree of consistency across the EU on sanctions concerning financial fraud. Such a step would discourage forum shopping on the part of money-launderers and fraudsters. On 25 April 2017, the Council adopted the PIF Directive. The directive provided common definitions of a number of offences against the EU budget. These offences included cases of fraud and other related crimes such as active and passive corruption, the misappropriation of funds and money laundering, among others.[37]

On 22 June 2017, the European Parliament approved the Council position at first reading and instructed its president to sign the act with the president of the Council and to forward its position to the Council, the Commission and national parliaments. The definition of the Union's financial interests contained in the directive covers infringements of the common VAT systems where they are linked to the territory of two or more Member States and involve losses totalling at least €10 million. The definition of criminal offences covers active and passive corruption, as well as the misuse of funds. Minimum penalties are laid down for natural persons, and limitation periods are established that make it possible for the law to apply over a sufficient time to ensure that infringements can be addressed in an effective way. The directive also introduces an obligation for the Member States, the Commission, the agencies and the Court of Auditors to cooperate. Finally, the directive lays down the legal basis for the powers of the European Prosecutor by defining its competences. The European Public Prosecutor's Office (EPPO) will be a decentralized prosecution office of the European Union with exclusive competence for investigating, prosecuting and bringing to judgment crimes against the EU budget. It will have uniform investigation powers throughout the Union based on and integrated into the national law systems of the Member States. The European Parliament welcomed the proposal for a regulation on the establishment of the EPPO and stressed the need to establish a consistent, complementary system for protecting the Union's financial interests. It also urged the Commission to provide a clear EU-level definition of the roles of the future EPPO, Eurojust and OLAF, delimiting their respective remits.[38]

Article 1 of the PIF Directive aims at establishing "minimum rules concerning the definition of criminal offences and sanctions with regard to combatting fraud and other illegal activities affecting the Union's financial interests". As far as the scope of application of the PIF Directive is concerned, Article 2, para. 2, read in conjunction with Article 3, para. 2, let. d, explicitly delimits the scope of application of the directive

---

37 *Ibid.*
38 *Ibid.*

in respect of VAT fraud. The question of whether VAT fraud should fall within the scope of the directive and, if so, to what extent, was one of the most debated questions during the negotiations, which almost led to the failure of the whole directive. The final inclusion of a limited number of VAT offences in the final text of the directive is the result of a compromise between the Council, on the one hand, and the Commission and the European Parliament on the other hand; a compromise was finally reached after the ruling of the Court of Justice in the *Taricco* judgment.[39]

The solution adopted is nevertheless not completely satisfactory. According to it, not all VAT fraud cases, but only the most serious offences against VAT fall within the scope of the PIF Directive.[40] In particular, the directive applies only to those offences which are the result of an intentional act or omission against the common VAT system, which is connected to the territory of two or more Member States and involves total damage of at least €10 million. Only the most serious forms of VAT fraud, such as VAT carousel fraud, missing-trader intra-EU fraud (MTIC fraud), VAT fraud carried out by organized crime structures, or cases above a certain threshold, are therefore included in this definition.

The scope of application of the PIF Directive is consequently narrower than that of the PIF Convention. Article 2 of the PIF Convention, as interpreted by the Court of Justice, covers, in fact, all the VAT fraud, and not only the most serious offences against the common VAT system. The added value of the PIF Directive is weakened by its limited scope of application, but it is also weakened by the extensive leeway left to the Member States in defining the offences affecting the financial interests of the Union. As regards VAT fraud, for instance, the concept of 'damage' is not defined in the directive and considering that it is a legal concept defined in different ways by the Member States, the definition of VAT fraud will vary to a considerable extent across the EU. Therefore, until an autonomous definition of this notion is given by the Court, the scope of the PIF Directive will depend on the way the Member States decide to implement it. The illustration above is but one example of how the directive leaves a considerable leeway to the Member States.[41]

From the considerations above, it can therefore be concluded that the objective pursued by the PIF Directive to create a comprehensive common legal framework for the offences affecting the Union's financial interests is fulfilled only to a minimum

---

39 Judgment of the Court (Grand Chamber) of 8 September 2015, Criminal proceedings against Ivo Taricco and Others Request for a preliminary ruling from the Tribunale di Cuneo Reference for a preliminary ruling – Criminal proceedings concerning offences in relation to value added tax (VAT) – Art. 325 TFEU – National legislation laying down absolute limitation periods which may give rise to impunity in respect of offences – Potential prejudice to the financial interest of the European Union – Obligation, for the national court, to disapply any provision of national law liable to affect fulfilment of the Member States' obligations under EU law, Case C-105/14.

40 www.europeanpapers.eu/en/europeanforum/directive-EU-2017/1371-on-fight-against-fraud-to-union-financial-interests, accessed 15 July 2019.

41 *Ibid.*

extent and that the large discretion left to the Member States in implementing it risks watering down the minimum harmonization envisaged by the directive.

The directive achieves only partially the objective of creating a uniform sanctioning regime regarding the offences affecting the financial interests of the Union. Article 7, para. 1, of the PIF Directive, merely repeats the formula generally adopted since the ruling of the CJEU in the *Greek Maize* case,[42] i.e., that the offences should be punished by means of effective, proportionate and dissuasive criminal sanctions; it does not describe either the level or the type of criminal sanctions that should be applied. Some indications about the type and level of criminal penalties to be adopted by the Member States are given in the next paragraphs of the same Article 7, where it is established that Member States should ensure that the offences referred to in the previous articles are punishable "by a maximum penalty which provides for imprisonment" and "by a maximum penalty of at least four years of imprisonment when they involve considerable damage or advantage". The meaning of the term 'considerable' is explained in the same article, which also specifies that the Member States "may also provide for a maximum sanction of at least four years of imprisonment in other serious circumstances defined in their national law". Thus, the definition of the circumstances which allow the adoption of a maximum sanction of at least four years of imprisonment depends once again on the national legislation implementing the PIF Directive.[43]

Regarding the level of sanctions, the directive has provided for a 'minimum-maximum sanction' of four years of imprisonment, but it has not set out minimum imprisonment terms for particularly serious offences, as proposed by the Commission in its initial proposal. The Commission's opinion is that

> economic crime – including fraud – is typically an area where criminal sanctions can have a particularly deterrent effect, as potential perpetrators can be expected to make a certain calculation of risks before deciding to engage in such criminal activities.[44]

The introduction of minimum sanctions was consequently "considered necessary to ensure that an effective deterrence all over Europe" could be achieved. The minimum threshold was fixed by the Commission at three months imprisonment since in its view it was a proportionate period in relation to the seriousness of the offences and it could

---

42 Judgment of the Court of 21 September 1989, *Commission of the European Communities v. Hellenic Republic*. Failure of a Member State to fulfil its obligations – Failure to establish and make available the Community's own resources. Case 68/88.

43 www.europeanpapers.eu/en/europeanforum/directive-EU-2017/1371-on-fight-against-fraud-to-union-financial-interests, accessed 15 July 2019.

44 *Ibid.*

ensure that a European Arrest Warrant was issued and executed. Nonetheless, the final text of the directive does not provide for minimum sanctions.

Therefore, from the analysis above it can be concluded that the minimum harmonization envisaged by the directive does not eliminate the diverging sanctioning regime currently in existence; it could, therefore, easily happen than the same offence is punished by three months' imprisonment in one Member State and by six years' imprisonment in another.[45]

3.6   The Role of OLAF and Other Bodies

The European Union has created a number of bodies or agencies with responsibilities in the field of criminal law. Some of these bodies (like Europol) have been established by Union legislation under the then third pillar. Others, like OLAF, have hybrid status. Other bodies such as the EU anti-terrorism coordinator fall mainly under the CFSP. This section of this paper focuses on how these bodies, in particular, OLAF (as it is the one mainly linked to crimes against the financial interest of the EU) challenge state sovereignty in criminal matters.

The European Union budget finances a wide range of programmes and projects which improve the lives of citizens across the EU and beyond. The improper use of funds provided by the EU budget or the evasion of the taxes, duties and levies which fund the EU budget directly harms European citizens and prejudices the entire European project. The European Anti-Fraud Office (OLAF) is the only EU body mandated to detect, investigate and stop fraud with EU funds. OLAF fulfils its mission by: a) carrying out independent investigations into fraud and corruption involving EU funds, so as to ensure that all EU taxpayers' money reaches projects that can create jobs and growth in Europe; b) contributing to strengthening citizens' trust in the EU institutions by investigating serious misconduct by EU staff and members of the EU institutions; c) developing a sound EU anti-fraud policy.[46]

OLAF can investigate matters relating to fraud, corruption and other offences affecting the EU financial interests concerning: a) all EU expenditure – the main spending categories are structural funds, agricultural policy and rural development funds, direct expenditure and external aid; b) some areas of EU revenue, mainly customs duties; c) suspicions of serious misconduct by EU staff and members of the EU institutions.[47]

---

45   *Ibid.*
46   https://ec.europa.eu/anti-fraud/about-us/mission_en, accessed 15 July 2019.
47   *Ibid.*

3.7 Conclusion – Practical Implications

The above sections show that the European Union launched policy and legislation with regard to crimes against the financial interests of the EU. Nevertheless, as it has been repetitively pointed out, while the EU deals with criminal law on the basis of mutual recognition by its Member States, it still remains completely within the domain of the Member States to determine how to enforce crimes against the financial interests of the EU from within their own national legal systems. As a result, the actual enforcement will invariably differ from one Member State to another. The integration between EU criminal law is a big challenge to both Member States and the European Union's institutions. Sometimes, Europeanization may not lead to the desired effect, and sometimes it may. The next chapters of this book will see how European criminal law can actually be workable in practice taking into account domestic issues and local challenges.

4 INTER-AGENCY COOPERATION IN THE PROTECTION OF THE EU'S FINANCIAL INTERESTS

Chloé Brière

4.1 INTRODUCTION

Protecting its financial interests has been a long-standing concern for the European Union, especially due to a certain gap in their protection by national authorities. The establishment of specialized European actors responds to the desire to reinforce their protection, and the establishment of a European Public Prosecutor's Office (EPPO), competent to investigate, prosecute and bring to judgment crimes affecting the EU's financial interests, shall give it a new impetus. It will notably stimulate inter-agency cooperation between the relevant European actors, especially between the EU Anti-Fraud Office (OLAF), the EU Agency for Criminal Justice Cooperation (Eurojust) and the EPPO. The present chapter offers a legal appraisal of the instruments applicable to these actors, which have been recently either adopted, amended or subject to legislative proposals, with a focus on the provisions regulating their mutual cooperation. It pinpoints the impact their different histories may have on such cooperation, as well as the necessity to identify a common field of action. The contribution then examines the new provisions regulating their cooperation to determine whether they shall offer a solid basis for future inter-agency cooperation in PIF matters, and concludes that although they do provide improvements, their implementation will have to be closely followed.

The European Union (EU) has been repeatedly presented as an intergovernmental organization with no comparison. After more than 60 years of European integration, the level of cooperation reached between the Member States is unprecedented, and the desire to build an ever-closer Union has led to the ambitious development of key policies. To reflect the distinctive nature of the European Union, several aspects of European integration are often stressed, such as the recognition of its legal personality, the attribution of exclusive competences for which Member States conferred parcels of their sovereignty to EU institutions or the role played by the Court of Justice of the EU (CJEU) in ensuring the effective implementation of EU law. Another aspect distinguishes the EU from other international organizations, namely the possibility to collect its own financial resources. These resources contribute to the EU budget, together with contributions from the Member States, which participate in the elaboration of the multi-annual financial framework and the priorities enshrined therein. The EU budget is crucial to finance the implementation of ambitious EU policies, and its importance has been further reinforced in the past decade, marked with financial crises and austerity policies implemented throughout the EU. In a context of scarce public resources, the EU budget and the funding programmes set up on its basis, such the European Cohesion Fund, the Common Agricultural Fund or the European Regional Fund, constitute key instruments for ensuring European economic growth and social welfare.

In such a context, the protection of the EU's financial interests has gained increasing importance. This is particularly true considering the importance of fraud affecting the EU's financial interests. The detected fraud amounted – just in 2017 – to €390.7 million,[1] and the level of undetected fraud remains unknown. Fraud and crime affecting the EU's financial interests thus remains a hidden white-collar crime, largely undetected, and yet very lucrative for those engaging in it. It is far from being a marginal phenomenon, as this activity is highly attractive to criminals, including those belonging to criminal organizations.[2]

Combating fraud and crime affecting the EU's financial interests is expressly foreseen in the EU treaties, and more particularly in Article 325 TFEU. The latter provision imposes a duty on all the Union's institutions, bodies, offices and agencies (IBOAs), and the Member States, to counter fraud and any other illegal activities affecting the EU's financial interests through measures which shall act as a deterrent and be such as to afford effective protection (Article 325(1) TFEU). The Member States comply with this duty through the actions of competent national authorities, in accordance with the organization of their criminal justice systems. Its implementation is furthermore closely monitored by the EU institutions. The CJEU has, for instance, repeatedly stressed its importance, including to prevent the application of national laws.[3] For the IBOAs, Article 325 TFEU imposes an obligation to accept the control of specialized actors, which have received specific competences and mandates to protect the EU's financial interests, and combat fraud and crime affecting them, and to fully cooperate with them in case of suspicious behaviours.

The OLAF is of particular importance, considering its 20 years' worth experience in investigating fraud, and the expertise it has acquired in this field. Other actors are also of

---

1 European Court of Auditors, Special Report 'Fighting fraud in EU spending: action needed', 2019, p. 16.
2 *See* for instance Price Waterhouse Coopers Belgium and Netherlands, *How does organised crime misuse EU funds?*, Study requested by the EP's Committee on Budgetary Control, May 2011,121 pages. *See also* Europol, SOCTA 2017, pp. 44-45. *See also* OLAF, The OLAF Report 2017, 2018, p. 20 and following.
3 CJEU, C-105/14, *Criminal Proceedings against Ivo Taricco and others*, 8 September 2015, ECLI:EU: C:2015:555; and CJEU, C-42/17, *Criminal Proceedings against M.A.S. and M.B.*, 5 December 2017, ECLI: EU:C:201:936. *See also* CJEU, C-612/15, *Criminal Proceedings against Nikolay Kolev and others*, 5 June 2018, ECLI:EU:C:2018:392.

relevance, especially the Eurojust, which has a mandate for supporting and coordinating cross-border prosecutions in PIF cases.[4] Finally, the EPPO has received competences for investigating, prosecuting and bringing to criminal judgment offences affecting the EU's financial interests. These three actors are called upon to play a key role in PIF matters, relying on the complementarity of their mandates, and their mutual cooperation in this field, which is essential to ensure the effective implementation of the objectives assigned to them.

In a study realized for the European Parliament in 2014 addressing inter-agency cooperation, shortcomings in the cooperation between OLAF and Eurojust were identified, and the authors stressed how the establishment of the EPPO would impact future inter-agency cooperation,[5] which required the clarification of the relations between these three actors.[6] Five years later, the legal framework has drastically changed: the eegulation establishing the EPPO[7] and the regulation on Eurojust[8] have been adopted, as well as a directive approximating the definition of PIF offences.[9] Furthermore, after an in-depth evaluation of Regulation 883/2013,[10] the main text regulating OLAF's work, a proposal for a regulation amending is currently negotiated,[11] and the European Parliament adopted in April 2019 its position at first reading.[12] These evolutions are an opportunity to define the respective tasks of each actor and provide a solid foundation for their smooth cooperation.

---

4   The EU Agency for Police Cooperation, Europol, has also a mandate to support cross-border police cooperation in PIF cases; however its role remains minimal, and it will thus not be included in the discussions.

5   Anne Weyembergh, Inés Armada and Chloé Brière, 'The Inter-agency Cooperation and Future Architecture of the EU Criminal Justice and Law Enforcement Area', Study realized for the LIBE Committee of the European Parliament, IPOL_STU(2014)510000_EN, November 2014, p. 48.

6   European Parliament, Resolution of 5 October 2016 on the EPPO and Eurojust (P8_TA(2016)0376), para. 9, see also European Parliament, Resolution of 12 March 2014 on the proposal for a Council Regulation on the establishment of the EPPO (P7_TA(2014)0234), para. 13.

7   Council Regulation (EU) 2017/1939 of 12 October 2017 implementing enhanced cooperation on the establishment of the European Public Prosecutor's Office ('the EPPO') [2017] OJ L 283/1.

8   Regulation (EU) 2018/1727 of the European Parliament and of the Council of 14 November 2018 on the European Union Agency for Criminal Justice Cooperation (Eurojust) [2018] OJ L 295/138.

9   Directive (EU) 2017/1371 of the European Parliament and of the Council of 5 July 2017 on the fight against fraud to the Union's financial interests by means of criminal law [2017] OJ L 198/29.

10 Regulation (EU, Euratom) No 883/2013 of the European Parliament and of the Council of 11 September 2013 concerning investigations conducted by the European Anti-Fraud Office (OLAF) (…) [2013] OJ L 248/1.

11 European Commission, Proposal for a Regulation of the European Parliament and of the Council amending Regulation (EU, Euratom) No 883/2013 concerning investigations conducted by the European Anti-Fraud Office (OLAF) as regards cooperation with the European Public Prosecutor's Office and the effectiveness of OLAF investigations, COM (2018) 338 final, 23 May 2018.

12 European Parliament, Legislative resolution of 16 April 2019 on the proposal for a regulation of the European Parliament and of the Council amending Regulation (EU, Euratom) No 883/2013 concerning investigations conducted by the European Anti-Fraud Office (OLAF) as regards cooperation with the European Public Prosecutor's Office and the effectiveness of OLAF investigations (COM(2018)0338 – C8-0214/2018 – 2018/0170(COD)), TA/2019/0383.

The present chapter will conduct a legal appraisal of their instruments and provisions organizing their work and their mutual cooperation, in order to assess whether they shall offer a solid basis for future inter-agency cooperation in PIF matters. It will be divided into three main parts. Firstly, the history of the three actors will be analysed, as it impacts on their expertise and experience in inter-agency cooperation (Section 4.2). The discussion will then move to their respective competences in protecting the EU's financial interests and the identification of a common field of action (Section 4.3). Finally, the changes brought in their legal frameworks will be evaluated (Section 4.4).

4.2 COOPERATION BETWEEN DIFFERENT STAGES OF EXISTENCE

Fraud and crime affecting the EU's financial interests constitute a burden for the EU budget, and its gravity is even more reinforced in the current context marked by scarce public resources. The decision to establish specialized actors active at the EU level to combat fraud and crime affecting the EU's financial interests has been instrumental in turning the protection of the EU's financial interests from a mere theoretical objective into an effective EU policy. The process of establishing specialized actors at the EU level, entrusted with precise tasks in a defined policy area, is not specific to the protection of the EU's financial interests. Yet the coexistence of actors of different generations, with different backgrounds and histories, makes it particularly interesting.

The first actor established to protect the EU's financial interests is the EU Anti-Fraud Office (OLAF), which was established in 1999 to replace UCLAF ('Unité de Coordination de la Lutte Anti-Fraude'). This unit had been created in 1988 as a service, part of the Secretariat General of the Commission, and initially reported to the President of the Commission.[13] It worked alongside national anti-fraud departments and provided the coordination and assistance needed to tackle transnational organized fraud. Its powers increased gradually and included the possibility to launch investigations on its own initiative, or the obligation for all Commission Departments to inform it of any suspected instance of fraud. However, the events which led to the resignation of the Santer Commission, i.e., accusations of misuse of power, corruption and fraud against several Commissioners, created pressures for a stronger actor. As a consequence, UCLAF was transformed into OLAF. This body structurally belongs to the Commission, but functionally it enjoys complete autonomy for certain missions (e.g., internal

---

13 E. Lambert Abdelgawald (ed.), *Dictionary of European actors*, Larcier, 2015.

investigations)[14] and possesses stronger investigative powers.[15] It is a body of the European Community, established under the first 'Community' pillar of the European Union, via a Commission decision based on Article 162 EC.[16] The text has been amended since then, and it has to be read together with other instruments, defining OLAF's investigative powers and/or mandates in specific sectors.[17] After an extensive evaluation of its legal framework, concluded in 2017, the Commission pinpointed the need to adapt in several ways OLAF's operation to the existence of the EPPO,[18] and thus published on 23 May 2018 a proposal for a regulation amending Regulation 883/2013. As of May 2019, the Council of the EU has initiated discussions on the text,[19] and the European Parliament adopted its proposed amendments to the text in April 2019.[20]

The idea of establishing a judicial cooperation unit emerged almost concomitantly to the establishment of OLAF. The idea was first brought up at the European Council meeting of Tampere in October 1999.[21] In 2000, a provisional judicial cooperation unit was formed under the name of Pro-Eurojust,[22] and with the 9/11 terrorist attacks serving as a catalyst, Eurojust was formally established in 2002.[23] In July 2008, a first text – Council Decision 2009/426/JHA[24] – amended Eurojust's constitutive instrument. The purpose was to enhance the operational capabilities of Eurojust, increase the exchange of

---

14   As indicated in M. Luchtman and J.A.E Vervaele, 'Summary of Main Findings and Overall Conclusions', in M. Luchtman and J.A.E Vervaele (eds.), *Investigatory Powers and Procedural Safeguards: Improving OLAF's Legislative Framework Through a Comparison with Other EU Law Enforcement Authorities (ECN/ESMA/ ECB)*, April 2017, p. 328.

15   'The Added Value of OLAF, A few thoughts on the evidential value of OLAF reports in criminal investigations and for the criminal justice authorities in Belgium', Speech given by Advocate-General Francis Desterbeck at the formal inaugural sitting of the Court of Appeal in Ghent on 1 September 2005, OLAF/838/05-EN.

16   Commission Decision of 28 April 1999 establishing the European Anti-fraud Office (OLAF), OJ L 136, 31 May 1999, p. 20.

17   *E.g.* Commission Regulation (EC) No 1848/2006 of 14 December 2006 concerning irregularities and the recovery of sums wrongly paid in connection with the financing of the common agricultural policy and the organization of an information system in this field [2006] OJ L 355/56; Council Regulation (EC) No 1224/2009 of 20 November 2009 establishing a Community control system for ensuring compliance with the rules of the common fisheries policy [2009] OJ L 343/1; and Council Regulation (EC) No 515/97 of 13 March 1997 on mutual assistance between the administrative authorities of the Member States and cooperation between the latter and the Commission to ensure the correct application of the law on customs and agricultural matters [1997] OJ L 082/1.

18   European Commission, Report on Evaluation of the application of Regulation (EU, EURATOM) No 883/2013 of the European Parliament and of the Council of 11 September 2013 concerning investigations conducted by OLAF, COM (2017) 0589 final, 2 October 2017, 10 pages.

19   For more details *see* https://eur-lex.europa.eu/legal-content/EN/HIS/?uri=CELEX:52018PC 0338&qid=1557932336309.

20   European Parliament legislative resolution, *see* above.

21   European Council, *Tampere Conclusions*, October 1999, Conclusion No. 46.

22   Eurojust, *Eurojust News – Eurojust 10th Anniversary*, Issue No. 6, February 2012, p. 1.

23   Council Decision 2002/187/JHA of 28 February 2002 setting up Eurojust with a view of reinforcing the fight against serious crime [2002] OJ L 63/1.

24   Council Decision 2009/426/JHA of 16 December 2008 on the strengthening of Eurojust (...) [2009] OJ L 138/14.

information between the interested parties, facilitate and strengthen cooperation between national authorities and Eurojust and establish relations with partners and third States.[25] The Lisbon Treaty, which contained a provision only devoted to Eurojust (Article 85 TFEU), prompted the need to update the legal framework governing Eurojust's activities. The European Commission put forward in July 2013 a proposal for a regulation on Eurojust.[26] The negotiations progressed smoothly, but although the Council adopted its general approach in 2015,[27] the negotiations on Eurojust were put on hold while those on the EPPO were not closed. The negotiations started again in October 2017 and were concluded in June 2018 with the political agreement reached between the Council and the European Parliament, later formally approved.[28] The text shall apply to Eurojust from 12 December 2019.

The idea of establishing a European Public Prosecutor's Office appeared in the late 1990s, yet its establishment has been successively announced, postponed and relaunched. In 1997, a group of academics under the leadership of Mireille Delmas-Marty presented the 'Corpus Juris for the protection of the EU's financial interests', which among other things proposed the creation of an EPPO.[29] At the time, Member States opposed the idea, which seemed premature. In 2001, the Commission relaunched the debate with the presentation of a green paper on the criminal law protection of the financial interests of the EC and the establishment of an EPPO.[30] Again, nothing concrete resulted from it. The EPPO came back to the agenda, but this time via EU primary law, with the insertion of a specific article (Article 86 TFEU) by the Lisbon Treaty, which grants the EU the competence to set up an EPPO. This provision served as the legal basis for a Commission Proposal for a Council Regulation on the establishment of the EPPO, published on 17 July 2013,[31] and subject to a special legislative procedure, i.e., unanimity in the Council and consent of the European Parliament. After the agreement

---

25 Eurojust, *op. cit.* at pp. 1-2.
26 Commission, Proposal for a regulation of the European Parliament and of the Council on the EU Agency for Criminal Justice Cooperation (Eurojust), 17 July 2013, COM (2013) 535, final 60 pages.
27 Council, Proposal for a Regulation on the European Union Agency for Criminal Justice Cooperation (Eurojust) – General Approach, 27 February 2015, Council doc. No. 6643/15. The Council is invited to reach a general approach "noting that a further mandate for discussion will be sought from COREPER regarding the EPPO related provisions when the draft EPPO Regulation is sufficiently advanced".
28 European Parliament legislative resolution on the proposal for a regulation of the European Parliament and of the Council on the European Union Agency for Criminal Justice Cooperation (Eurojust), 4 October 2018, P8_TA(2018)0379; and Council, 'Making Eurojust more efficient and effective', Press Release 609/18, 06/11/2018.
29 M. Delmas-Marty, *Corpus Juris, Introducing Penal Provisions for the Purpose of the Financial Interests of the European Union*, éditions Economica, 1997; M. Delmas-Marty and J.A.E. Vervaele (eds.), *The Implementation of the Corpus Juris in the Member States*, Intersentia, 2000.
30 Commission, COM (2001) 715 final, 11 December 2001.
31 Commision, Proposal for a Council Regulation on the establishment of the European Public Prosecutor's Office, COM (2013) 534 final, 17 July 2013.

on a first compromise text in January 2017[32] and the absence of unanimity in the Council, the European Council acknowledged in March 2017 the absence of unanimity and opened the way to the establishment of the EPPO via enhanced cooperation.[33] In April 2017, 16 Member States notified the three EU institutions of their intention to launch enhanced cooperation to establish the EPPO.[34] This further postponed the adoption of the text, as new negotiations were required to reflect this fundamental change. The Council finally adopted its general approach on the EPPO Regulation on 8 June 2017.[35] At that time, 20 Member States confirmed their participation in the establishment of this new EU body.[36] The EPPO's Regulation was finally adopted by the participating Member States in October 2017. Since then, new Member States have notified their participation: the Netherlands in May 2018[37] and Malta in June 2018,[38] and the EPPO now counts 22 participating Member States out of the 28 EU Member States. The EPPO shall be operational by October 2020, and the first steps towards its establishment are being taken.[39]

Retracing the history of OLAF, Eurojust and the EPPO allows us to pinpoint the specificities of the paths they followed. OLAF, as the successor of a unit established in the late 1980s under the Community regime, can be considered as the oldest and the most 'European' actor. Eurojust has been elaborated under the third pillar regime, and its transition to a post-Lisbon regime is not effective yet. The EPPO represents the most advanced form of cooperation in criminal matters, which benefits from the entry into force of the Lisbon Treaty. The diversity in their backgrounds and histories has an impact on their mutual cooperation. The recent changes in their respective legal frameworks might imply that in the coming years, the focus would be placed on ensuring their proper implementation. During this transition phase, the EU actors will also need to establish their legitimacy and the added value of their reforms, and to gain/maintain the trust of competent national authorities. It would be crucial to ensure that inter-agency cooperation and the definition of its new modalities are not lost sight of. Yet

---

32   Council, Proposal for a Regulation on the establishment of the European Public Prosecutor's Office – General approach, 31 January 2017, Council doc. 5445/17.

33   European Council, Conclusions of 9 March 2017.

34   Council, Press release, 'European public prosecutor's office: 16 member states together to fight fraud against the EU budget', 3 April 2017, doc. 184/17.

35   Council, Draft Regulation implementing enhanced cooperation on the establishment of the EPPO – Presidency text, 3 April 2017, Council doc. 7761/17.

36   The original participating Member States are: Austria, Belgium, Bulgaria, Croatia, Cyprus, Czech Republic, Estonia, Finland, France, Germany, Greece, Italy, Latvia, Lithuania, Luxembourg, Portugal, Romania, Slovenia, Slovakia and Spain.

37   Council, Doc. 9023/18 Cor 1, 22 May 2018 and Commission, Decision (EU) 2018/1094 of 1 August 2018 *[2018] OJ L 196/1.*

38   Notification in annex of Council doc. 12683/18, 5 October 2018 and Commission, Decision (EU) 2018/1103 of 7 August 2018 *[2018] OJ L 201/2.*

39   *See* for instance the publication of the vacancy for the European Chief Prosecutor, OJ C 418A [2018] 1.

these contextual factors will evolve over time, and other factors, more permanent, may further impact their mutual cooperation.

4.3   RESPECT FOR THEIR RESPECTIVE MANDATES OF A COMMON FIELD OF ACTION

The protection of the EU's financial interests has long suffered from the lack of interest of competent national authorities in investigating, prosecuting and bringing to judgment fraud and crime affecting the EU's finances. The establishment of specialized European actors is crucial to fill this gap, stimulate the interests of national authorities and *in fine*, ensure effective protection of the EU's financial interests. The three actors under scrutiny have received specific mandates, competences and powers that allow them to contribute within their respective scope of action to combating PIF fraud and crime.

The analysis of the provisions regulating the mandates and competences of OLAF, Eurojust and the EPPO reveals a complex picture marked by differences regarding the mandate of each actor, the competences and powers at their disposal and the nature of their work. Table 4.1 offers a schematic overview of their similarities and differences, and the analysis can be summarized as follows: *OLAF and the EPPO are two bodies specialized in the protection of the EU's financial interests, with operational powers to conduct investigations and prosecutions, whereas Eurojust, an agency with a broader mandate, provides support and assistance to national authorities.*

Table 4.1   Summary of the differences between OLAF, Eurojust and the EPPO

	OLAF	EUROJUST	EPPO
Different contexts and instruments of different generations	Created as a Community body under the first pillar of the TEU with a long history (UCLAF)	Created as a Union body in the field of EU criminal law under the regime of the third pillar	Created as a Union body in the field of EU criminal law after communitarization by the Lisbon Treaty
	Ongoing negotiations for a proposal for a regulation	The legal regime 'lisbonized' with the adoption of the Eurojust Regulation (2018)	
Different natures	**Part of the administrative track**	Part of the criminal justice track	Part of the criminal justice track

	OLAF	EUROJUST	EPPO
Material compe- tences	Irregularities affecting the EU financial interests (Regulation No 2988/95) + sectoral instruments (CAP, EU funds…)	List of 32 offences provided for in Annex 1 of its regulation, including among others crime against the financial interests of the Union + other offences if asked by national authorities	PIF offences as approximated by PIF Directive + possibility to extend its scope of competence (Article 86 (4) TFEU)
Types of tasks	In charge of carrying out administrative investigations + coordination of competent national authorities	In charge of supporting and strengthening coordination and cooperation between national investigating and prosecuting authorities in relation to serious crime	In charge of carrying out judicial investigations, prosecuting and bringing to judgment
Avail- able in- vestiga- tive powers	Investigative measures defined in Regulation 883/2013 (including on-the-spot checks and inspections and interviews), read together with other instruments New provisions are amending those enshrined in Regulation 883/2013 cur- rently negotiated	Possibility to request national authorities to undertake an investigation or prosecution of certain acts, take special investigative measures or take another measure justified for the investigation or prosecution (Article 4 (2) Eurojust Regulation)	Investigative measures as defined by EPPO Regulation with major references to national law (Article 30 EPPO Regulation)

According to the TFEU, the mission of Eurojust is to "support and strengthen coordination and cooperation between national investigating and prosecuting authorities in relation to serious crime affecting two or more Member States or requiring a prosecution on common bases" (Article 85(1) TFEU). In practice, Eurojust is a 'facilitator' of judicial cooperation, which intervenes to smoothen the effective functioning of judicial cooperation instruments (such as the European Arrest Warrant), to resolve legal issues arising in complex cases (such as *ne bis in idem* issues or conflicts of jurisdiction) and/or to stimulate the coordination of judicial authorities.[40] It has been compared to a 'control tower',[41] whose members will intervene when they notice the need to investigate in a coordinated manner cross-border and/or complex cases.

---

40   Eurojust, 2013 Annual Report, p. 14.
41   Sénat, *Europol et Eurojust, op. cit.*, p. 39.

Regarding the scope of its competence, Eurojust's mandate covers various types of serious crime, and in particular the list of 32 offences provided for in the annex of its regulation.[42] Crime against the EU's financial interests is included in this list and thus falls within the competence of Eurojust. Nevertheless, in practice, a crime against the EU's financial interest does not constitute the main field of action of Eurojust. For example, in 2017 it represented around 160 cases, whereas other forms of crime received more attention (almost 2000 cases of fraud opened,[43] around 1000 cases of money laundering or around 900 cases of drug trafficking).[44] Regarding its powers, Eurojust has been traditionally described as an agency without operational powers. The adoption of the regulation can be interpreted as potentially outdating such affirmation, as it confers embryonic operational powers to Eurojust, which will be able, once the regulation enters into force, to ask the competent authorities to undertake an investigation or prosecution of specific acts, a request which can be refused on limited grounds.[45] In contrast, OLAF and the EPPO are only competent to investigate in matters of the protection of the EU's financial interests, and their difference lies in the classification of the behaviours they are competent to address (administrative irregularities versus criminal offences).

In this regard, OLAF's main competence is to "conduct administrative investigations for the purpose of fighting fraud, corruption and any other illegal activity affecting the financial interests of the Union" (Article 1(4) Regulation 883/2013, not amended by the proposal under negotiations). OLAF is thus competent to conduct administrative investigations, defined as any inspection, check or other measure undertaken with a view to achieving the objectives set out in Article 1 and to establish, where necessary, the irregular nature of the activities under investigation (Article 2(4) Regulation 883/2013). The OLAF proposal provides for a precision, namely that "those investigations shall not affect the powers of the EPPO or of the competent authorities of the Member States to initiate criminal proceedings".[46] OLAF's material competence is to conduct such investigations when the EU budget is allegedly affected by illegal activities, in particular, EU expenditures and most of its revenues (e.g., custom duties,

---

42 Eurojust Regulation, Art. 3. Competent national authorities may also request Eurojust's assistance for other types of offences (Art. 3 (3)).

43 Although fraud may include fraud affecting the EU's financial interests, the report does not provide sufficient detail on this point. The author chose to exclude the cases of fraud from the PIF statistics, as fraud cases may cover various behaviours, not connected to PIF (*e.g.*, tax fraud, computer fraud, advanced fee fraud, misappropriation of corporate assets). See Eurojust News, Issue no 4, July 2011.

44 Eurojust, Annual Report 2017, p. 12: in 2017, 91 PIF cases were ongoing from previous years and 68 were new cases.

45 Eurojust Regulation, Art. 4(2) & (6).

46 Proposal OLAF Regulation, amendment proposed in Art. 2.

agricultural duties, etc.).[47] The investigative powers of OLAF are particularly extended. They are mainly defined in Regulation 883/2013, read together with other instruments, and particularly with Regulations 2185/96[48] and 2988/95.[49] Its powers include the possibility to conduct on-the-spot checks and inspections. These investigative measures can be conducted in the EU institutions, bodies, agencies and offices (internal investigations – Article 4 Regulation 883/2013), or in the premises of economic operators in the Member States, and eventually in third countries and in premises of international organizations (external investigations – Article 3 Regulation 883/2013). The Office can also interview a person concerned or a witness at any time during an investigation (Article 9 Regulation 883/2013), and it must – when conducting such interviews – respect certain procedural guarantees.[50] OLAF may play a role in the criminal response to crimes affecting the EU's financial interests, as it has the possibility to transfer its investigation report and related evidence to the national judicial authorities for the initiation of criminal proceedings under the national legislations. The OLAF proposal further extends its powers, notably by recognizing OLAF's right of immediate and unannounced access to any relevant information in internal investigations, the possibility to request oral information in both types of investigations or by clarifying the duty of Member States to transmit bank account information to OLAF. The text also reinforces the procedural guarantees applicable in the course of OLAF investigations and harmonizes, to a certain extent, the evidentiary value of OLAF's reports. The latter aspect is crucial, especially in light of its future cooperation with the EPPO.

The EPPO is responsible for "investigating, prosecuting and bringing to judgment the perpetrators of, and accomplices in, the criminal offences affecting the financial interests of the Union" (Article 4(1) EPPO Regulation). This indicates that the EPPO shall conduct criminal investigations, i.e., investigations whose final purpose is to determine the presence of a criminal offence, and the innocence or guilt of a person. Its material competence is provided for via a reference to the PIF Directive, which defines minimum rules on the offences affecting the Union's financial interests. The EPPO's material competence also includes offences regarding participation in a criminal organization whose activity is focused on committing any of the offences referred to in

---

47   M. Scholten and M. Simonato, 'EU Report', in M. Luchtman and J.A.E Vervaele (eds.), *Investigatory Powers and Procedural Safeguards: Improving OLAF's Legislative Framework Through a Comparison with Other EU Law Enforcement Authorities (ECN/ESMA/ECB)*, April 2017, p. 14.

48   Council Regulation (Euratom, EC) No 2185/96 of 11 November 1996 concerning on-the-spot checks and inspections carried out by the Commission in order to protect the European Communities' financial interests against fraud and other irregularities [1996] OJ L 292/2.

49   Council Regulation (EC, Euratom) No 2988/95 of 18 December 1995 on the protection of the European Communities financial interests [1995] OJ L 312/1.

50   *See* in this regard K. Ligeti, 'The protection of procedural rights of persons concerned by OLAF administrative investigations and on whether OLAF case reports can be admitted as criminal evidence', In-depth analysis for the CONT Committee, July 2017, PE 603.790, 36 pages.

the PIF Directive, and any other criminal offence which is inextricably linked to criminal conduct falling in the scope of offences defined in the PIF Directive (Article 22 EPPO Regulation). The material scope of the EPPO's competence has been restricted throughout the negotiations of the text: it is a competence shared with national authorities,[51] it is subordinated to certain seriousness thresholds, e.g., the importance of the damage (Article 25(2) and Article 25(3b)) or the sanctions concerned (Article 25 (3a)),[52] and specific rules apply to VAT-related fraud (Article 25(3)).[53] Some amendments have softened the restrictions imposed, such as the possibility for national authorities to consent to the EPPO's competence if it appears that the EPPO is better placed to investigate or prosecute (Article 25(4) EPPO Regulation) or the recognition of the EPPO's competence over ancillary offences (Article 22(3) EPPO Regulation). As a result, the outlines of the EPPO's material competence are particularly complex, which will, of course, impact its cooperation with its partners. As for its investigative powers, participating Member States are obliged to ensure that the European Delegated Prosecutors can rely on certain investigative measures, i.e., a common toolbox of measures, available for offences punishable by a maximum penalty of at least 4 years of imprisonment (Article 30(1) EPPO Regulation). In addition, they can order or request all investigative measures that are available under national law in similar national cases (Article 30(4) EPPO Regulation), and they can rely on a *sui generis* mechanism for ordering investigative measures in another Member State (Article 31 EPPO Regulation).[54]

The complexities inherent to the mandates, competences and powers of European actors are particularly reflected in the instruments organizing the work of OLAF, Eurojust and the EPPO. The legislator has granted them competences that are not necessarily limited to the protection of the EU's financial interests, and the measures at their disposal for such protection are far from being equivalent to those at the disposal of competent national authorities. More importantly, for their mutual cooperation, the identification of a common field of action is a necessity. It refers to situations/cases in which the complementarity of their mandates and competences can bring a clear added value. Such identification may have in the past appeared difficult, notably because of the distinction made between administrative and criminal proceedings in PIF cases, and it has been reflected in the limited cooperation between OLAF and Eurojust in the past, even though their exchange of information on PIF cases demonstrated its added value, regardless of their legal classification of the facts.[55]

---

51 *See* in contrast Art. 11 (4) of the Commission's Proposal which provided for an exclusive competence.
52 On this issue, *see* Anne Weyembergh and Chloé Brière, *Towards an EPPO,* study realized for the LIBE Committee, 2016, PE 571.399, p. 25.
53 *Ibid.*, p. 24. *See* Art. (3) 1 PIF Directive.
54 *Ibid.*, pp. 28-33.
55 Weyembergh and others, *op. cit.* at p. 42.

Furthermore, the identification of a common field of action has evolved over time, notably through the recognition of a certain continuum in the detection, investigation and prosecution of behaviours likely to affect the EU's financial interests. For instance, the proposal for a regulation on OLAF addresses in its preamble how elements pointing to possible criminal conduct ... may, in practice, be present in initial allegations received by the Office or may emerge only in the course of an administrative investigation opened by the Office on the grounds of suspicion of administrative irregularity.[56]

Another factor in favour of the recognition of a broader common field of action lies in the establishment of the EPPO via enhanced cooperation. This shall result in the need for the EPPO to call upon the assistance of Eurojust and OLAF in cases involving both participating and non-participating Member States. Similarly, in PIF cases involving only Member States not party to the EPPO, the cooperation between OLAF and Eurojust may find an added value, notably to ensure the complementarity and coordination between the criminal and administrative proceedings.

Finally, the negotiations on their respective instruments have been an opportunity to identify and further clarify the synergies and the complementarity between their mandates, competences and powers. This did not only increase awareness of the importance of their mutual cooperation, but it also resulted in the insertion of specialized provisions on the matter.

4.4 Towards a New Age of Inter-Agency Cooperation in PIF Matters?

The past five years have been marked by drastic changes in the architecture of the EU Area of Criminal Justice, especially in the field of the protection of the EU's financial interests. The arrival of the EPPO constitutes a profound change, as it brings into the scene an actor founded on vertical cooperation and recipient of operational competences at a supranational level to combat PIF crime. Its regulation contains extended provisions organizing its cooperation with its partners, something rendered even more necessary by its establishment via enhanced cooperation between 22 Member States.

In the course of the negotiations of the EPPO Regulation, but also during the negotiations of the Eurojust Regulation, the EU legislator has been aware of the importance of inter-agency cooperation. This is reflected by the insertion of specific provisions organizing the EPPO's cooperation with Eurojust (Article 100 EPPO Regulation) and OLAF (Article 101 EPPO Regulation). It is also particularly reflected by the legislator's decision to put on hold the negotiations of the draft Eurojust Regulation until the EPPO Regulation was finalized. This allowed the legislator to adopt a text taking into account the future establishment of the EPPO, reflecting the compromise reached, and containing specific provisions on the Eurojust-EPPO

---

56 OLAF Proposal, Preamble, Recital 6.

cooperation and defining the role of Eurojust in relation to the Member States not participating in the EPPO (Articles 3(1) & (2) Eurojust Regulation). And last but not least, it is reflected by the presentation of a proposal for a regulation amending OLAF's legal framework, currently under negotiation, which is expressly devoted to organizing its cooperation with the EPPO.

This is in sharp contrast with the situation applicable five years ago. As pinpointed in the 2014 study, at the time, the bulk of inter-agency cooperation was left for bilateral discussion between agencies and bodies, through the negotiation and conclusion of cooperation agreements, administrative arrangements and/or memoranda of understanding.[57] Such an approach presented clear limits. On several occasions, the process of giving substance to bilateral cooperation was particularly cumbersome. For instance, once it had appeared that a first text would remain a dead letter, a second instrument was adopted in an attempt to reinvigorate cooperation.[58] The EU legislator was then invited to insert more concrete provisions on inter-agency cooperation.

It is thus particularly welcome to note that all instruments adopted since 2014, namely the Regulations on Europol, Eurojust and the EPPO, contain more detailed and even mirroring provisions on inter-agency cooperation and exchange of information.[59] Those organizing the bilateral cooperation between OLAF and the EPPO on the one hand,[60] and Eurojust and the EPPO, on the other hand,[61] have already been examined extensively by scholars.

The first positive development is the recognition of a general duty to cooperate with its partners (including but not limited to EU agencies and bodies). This general duty is phrased carefully, stressing that such cooperation should take place "in so far as necessary for the performance of its tasks" and "in accordance with their respective mandates" (Article 99(1) EPPO Regulation, Article 47(1) Eurojust Regulation). Yet such general duty is not (yet) enshrined in OLAF's legal framework. Regulation 883/2013 contains a different wording as it refers to its cooperation with Eurojust as 'appropriate' and does not refer to the respective mandates of the actors'. The provisions regulating its

---

57   Weyembergh and others, *op. cit.* at p. 49.
58   *See* for instance on Europol-Eurojust cooperation, pp. 15-16, or Eurojust-OLAF cooperation, pp. 39-40.
59   C. Brière, *Do you Have a Hit ? The Exchange of Information between EU Criminal Justice Bodies and Agencies* (book chapter, provisional title), forthcoming.
60   Anne Weyembergh and Chloé Brière, 'Relations between the EPPO and Eurojust – Still a Privileged Partnership', in Willem Geelhoed, Lendert H. Erkelens and Aren W. H. Meij (eds.), *Shifting Perspectives on the EPPO*, T.M.C. Asser Press, Springer, 2018, pp. 171-186, and Jorge A. Espina Ramos, 'The Relationship between Eurojust and the EPPO', in Lorena Bachmaier Winter (ed.), *The EPPO, The Challenges Ahead,* Springer, 2018, pp. 87-102.
61   Anne Weyembergh and Chloé Brière, *The Future Cooperation between OLAF and the EPPO*, In-depth Analysis for the CONT Committee, 2017, 34 pages, or Andrea Venegoni, 'The New Frontier of PIF Investigations, The EPPO and Its Relationship with OLAF' (2017) EUCRIM, Issue 4, pp. 193-196.

cooperation with EPPO, currently under negotiation, do not correct this gap,[62] which may still be done when the negotiations on the text restart after the European elections.

The new instruments also support the smooth exchange of information, as provisions foresee that both Eurojust and OLAF have a duty to report to the EPPO any criminal conduct in respect of which it could exercise its competence (Article 25(1) EPPO Regulation). In addition, the instruments also provide for their indirect access to the EPPO's Case Management System (Article 50(5) Eurojust Regulation and Article 12g OLAF Proposal),[63] and the EPPO has access to their respective databases (Articles 100 (3) and 101(5) EPPO Regulation).

Beyond the mutual exchange of information, the establishment of the EPPO raised a series of interrogations, linked notably to the identification of its 'privileged' partner. This point is particularly sensitive and may influence inter-agency cooperation. The analysis of the provisions dealing with the cooperation between OLAF, Eurojust and the EPPO (Articles 100 and 101 EPPO Regulation, Articles 50 and 51(2) Eurojust Regulation, Article 13 Regulation 883/2013 and Articles 12c-12g, OLAF's Proposal) is particularly interesting in this regard.

The formulation of Article 86 TFEU, providing for the establishment of the EPPO 'from Eurojust', and the initial alternative scenarios regarding the structure of the EPPO and its links with Eurojust were interpreted as indicating that Eurojust would benefit from this privileged relationship. This interpretation was initially validated by the proposal presented by the Commission in 2013, which did contain a provision focusing on the EPPO-Eurojust cooperation, and was silent on the EPPO-OLAF cooperation. The text further provided that the EPPO would rely on Eurojust for administrative support (services of common interest – Article 50(6) Eurojust Regulation and Article 100(4) EPPO Regulation).

However, the difficulties encountered in the negotiation of the EPPO Regulation and its establishment via enhanced cooperation have impacted the cooperation between the EPPO and its partners. Eurojust has seen the provision regulating its cooperation with the EPPO being substantially shortened and its future cooperation remains in the EPPO Regulation envisaged as being focused on cases involving both the participating and non-participating Member States, and/or third countries (Article 100(2)b EPPO Regulation). The EPPO would indeed, in such cases, need to rely on Eurojust's expertise and experience in supporting cross-border judicial cooperation between competent national authorities, and the new EU body can – like competent national

---

62   Regulation 883/2013, Art. 13. Proposal, Art. 1(1) – addressing only the cooperation between OLAF and the EPPO through the complementarity of their respective mandates", EP's first reading – amendment 21 not addressing this issue.

63   The EP's first reading aims at reinforcing data protection rules when OLAF accesses the EPPO's CMS, by providing for a general proportionality requirement, and or the keeping of a log of all instances of access (amendment 116). Such provision has not been foreseen for the indirect access by the EPPO to OLAF and Eurojust CMS, or for Eurojust's access to the EPPO's CMS.

authorities – request the assistance of Eurojust. For 'residual' PIF cases, especially those involving only non-participating Member States, and cases for which the EPPO has no competence, or has decided not to organize its competence, Eurojust would be competent to provide its assistance, as it does in cases involving other types of crime (Articles 3(1) & (2) Eurojust Regulation).

This contrasts with the provisions organizing the EPPO-OLAF cooperation, especially in the light of the amendments to the OLAF's legal framework. In light of the respective mandates of the EPPO and OLAF in protecting the EU's financial interests, and the recognition of operational competences to both actors, their mutual cooperation has been given more substance. OLAF often appears as the 'sword arm' of the EPPO, notably for the administrative dimension of the EPPO's work and for the conduct of complementary administrative investigations in PIF cases. OLAF is mandated to provide its support to the EPPO, by providing information, analysis, expertise and operational support; facilitating the coordination of specific actions of the competent administrative authorities and bodies of the Union and by conducting administrative investigations (Article 101(3) EPPO Regulation). Such support shall be provided at the request of the EPPO, whose request shall contain a certain number of elements, such as the information about the EPPO's investigation, or the measure(s) that OLAF should perform (Article 12e OLAF Proposal).[64] In addition, OLAF may receive information about cases the EPPO chose to dismiss or cases in which the EPPO decided not to exercise its competence (Articles 39(4) and 101(4) EPPO Regulation). OLAF would also be competent to open complementary investigations with a view to facilitating the adoption of precautionary measures or of financial, disciplinary or administrative action (Article 12f OLAF Proposal). The European Parliament has proposed numerous amendments to this provision, adding for instance that the EPPO should give its explicit written consent to OLAF's opening a complementary investigation (amendments 111-114). The final wording of this provision is particularly sensitive, as it is necessary to avoid duplication of efforts while reflecting the complementarity of OLAF and the EPPO.

Defining who could be qualified as the EPPO's privileged partner is not so easy. Certain common characteristics can be identified, such as the reciprocal indirect access to the EPPO's CMS, or the holding of regular bilateral meetings between the European chief prosecutor and the president of Eurojust or the director-general of OLAF (amendment 117 OLAF and Article 100(1) Eurojust Regulation). The differences in the form and intensity of cooperation foreseen seem to derive more from the intention to reflect the key competences and tasks of each actor than from the desire to single out one actor as the EPPO's privileged partner.

However, one gap can be identified, namely the lack of attention devoted to the cooperation between OLAF and Eurojust. Despite the conclusion of two memoranda of

---

64 The European Parliament proposed amendments to the text, turning these elements into minimum requirements (amendment 109).

understanding, their cooperation remains fragmented. Neither the adoption of the Eurojust Regulation nor the negotiation of an amended OLAF Regulation have triggered changes in the provisions regulating their cooperation. This gap is problematic, for instance, in cases involving non-participating States for which the EPPO cannot request OLAF's support. Addressing this gap is another opportunity for the EU legislator to seize when finalizing the negotiations of the OLAF proposal.

4.5   CONCLUSION

The legal framework regulating inter-agency cooperation in the field of the protection of the EU's financial interests has undergone crucial changes in the past five years. These changes not only reflect the establishment of the EPPO and the need to provide for its cooperation with previously established actors, such as Eurojust and OLAF. They also reflect the intention of the EU legislator to not leave inter-agency cooperation to the agencies and bodies themselves. This is noticeable through the insertion of provisions which are more detailed and establish a 'minimum' of cooperation between actors, as well as through the embryo of democratic accountability foreseen.[65] The need to ensure consistency between these provisions may explain the delays in the adoption of certain instruments, such as the Eurojust Regulation, or the differentiated time frame for their negotiation and adoption. This choice allows for the insertion of mirroring provisions and the filling of certain gaps. Yet finalizing the adoption of a consistent legal framework remains an ongoing process.

Furthermore, the future adoption of an amended OLAF Regulation will not put an end to the discussions. The provisions contained in the Regulations on Eurojust, the EPPO and OLAF are most likely to be complemented by internal rules of procedure and/or working arrangements between the concerned actors. Further recommendations can thus be made to the EU institutions, especially the need to reflect upon a comprehensive approach to the protection of the EU's financial interests.

In this regard, it is welcome to note that "disrupting the capacity of organised criminal groups and specialists involved in excise fraud and Missing Trader Intra-Community Fraud" has been recognized as one of the eight priorities for the fight against organized and serious international crime between 2018 and 2021.[66] This insertion allows for the definition of common action plans involving the relevant EU agencies and bodies, as well as the coordination of operational activities among competent national authorities. Yet this may not be sufficient. The protection of the EU's financial interests probably deserves

---

65   *See* for instance Eurojust Regulation, Art. 53(6) and Art. 67; EPPO Regulation, Art. 7; and Regulation 883/2013, Art. 15(9).

66   Council, Draft Council conclusions on the continuation of the EU Policy Cycle 2018-2021, Council Doc. 8604/17, p. 8.

a specific mechanism involving a wider variety of actors, including OLAF, Eurojust and the EPPO, alongside other relevant entities. This is particularly necessary considering that the EPPO would need all the support it can get at the crucial stage of its establishment and that it would have to address the remaining lack of support from non-participating Member States. As an advanced form of cooperation in criminal matters, its first steps will be watched closely, including by malevolent eyes. The design and implementation of a comprehensive approach, defining common priorities for OLAF, Eurojust and the EPPO, would be a way to stimulate inter-agency cooperation from the very beginning of the EPPO's activities, and support clear improvements in the protection of the EU's financial interests. This could include joint strategic planning or the exchange and rotation of staff. A key aspect would also be a requirement to report jointly to interested EU institutions and actors, such as the Council of the EU, the European Parliament or the European Court of Auditors. Last, but not least, the definition of such a joint approach would mostly benefit national authorities competent in PIF matters. Rather than fearing to report a potential PIF case to the wrong actor, effective inter-agency cooperation would allow them to count on the help of other EU actors in identifying the most appropriate actor to assist them.

5   Cybercrime in the EU with a Special Focus on Directive 2017/1371/EU

The Threats Posed by Cybercrime to the EU's Financial Interest

Mireille Caruana & Shawn Borg

5.1   Introduction

The financial interests of the EU are afforded a high level of protection from potential risks thanks to various legislative acts. In this regard, Directive 2017/1371 aims to fight fraud through criminal legislation. This research paper focuses on computer fraud together with select 'computer as a target' offences (hacking and denial-of-service attacks) which may threaten the Union's financial integrity. Concerning the chosen 'computer as a target' offences, these are governed by Directive 2013/40/EU, which sets out to approximate the Member States' criminal law on attacks against information systems. In this paper, the link between the above-mentioned directives is highlighted, together with the importance of having coherence between the two. Playing a less central role to this research, the proposed directive combating fraud and counterfeiting of non-cash means of payment is also acknowledged. The overarching theme of this research paper will nonetheless centre on select cybercrime offences, especially in light of their potential to harm the EU's financial interests.

Cybercrime is a relatively recent mode of crime and broadly arises from the malicious use of information and communication technology (ICT) – which act or conduct constitutes the *actus reus* – coupled with the requisite criminal intent, or *mens rea*. The novelty of this category of offences invites rapidly developing crimes, in turn creating particular obstacles to legislators and law enforcement organizations alike. While criminal laws are enacted to criminalize specific acts and outline their respective punishment, such laws also serve as deterrents. One such instance of criminal legislation is currently underway throughout the European Union (EU) and concerns the protection of the Union's financial interests.

Under Article 83(1) of the Treaty on the Functioning of the European Union[1] (TFEU) the EU has the explicit competence to harmonize national criminal law in limited areas, with 'computer crime' being one area where the EU has the competence to act and

---

1   Consolidated Version of the Treaty on the Functioning of the European Union [2012] OJ C326.

"establish minimum rules concerning the definition of criminal offences and sanctions".[2] Despite the merits of previous efforts and, in particular, the 2001 Council of Europe Convention on Cybercrime[3] ('Convention on Cybercrime' or 'Convention'), further development to ensure a common approach of the Member States to criminal law in the area of attacks against information systems was considered to be required. The first legislative act to be passed in this area was the Council Framework Decision 2005/222/JHA[4] on attacks against information systems. This has since been replaced by Directive 2013/40/EU[5] as the main piece of legislation on cybercrime.

Directive 2013/40/EU has as its main objective the approximation of "the criminal law of the Member States in the area of attacks against information systems".[6] Among other crimes, this directive tackles the hereunder discussed two types of 'computer as a target' offences, more specifically, the "offences of illegal access to an information system [and] illegal system interference".[7] Directive 2013/40/EU replaces Council Framework Decision 2005/222/JHA, which was in turn negotiated and drafted in the early 2000s. The need to update the relevant criminal laws to cater for technological developments prompted the EU to refresh its stance on select 'computer as a target' offences through Directive 2013/40/EU. While the foundations created by Framework Decision 2005/222/JHA were maintained, the more recent directive provides for harsher punishments and criminalizes the use of so-called 'botnets'.[8] This is catered for in Recital (5) of the directive, where the creation of a 'botnet' is defined as:

> The act of establishing remote control over a significant number of computers by infecting them with malicious software through targeted cyber-attacks. Once created, the infected network of computers that constitute the botnet can be activated without the computer users' knowledge in order to launch a large-scale cyber-attack, which usually has the capacity to cause serious damage.[9]

Botnets may, therefore, play a pivotal role in the launching of a large-scale distributed denial-of-service (DDoS) attack. Indeed, while the perpetrator may own a multitude of systems from which to launch a DDoS attack, it is more likely for this offence to be carried out through the use of botnets. In this case, the crime would be constituted

---

2   *Ibid.*, Art. 83(1).
3   Council of Europe Convention on Cybercrime (European Treaty Series 185) [2001].
4   Council Framework Decision 2005/222/JHA on attacks against information systems [2005] OJ L69/67.
5   Directive 2013/40/EU of the European Parliament and of the Council on attacks against information systems and replacing Council Framework Decision 2005/222/JHA [2013] OJ L218/8.
6   *Ibid.*, Recital (1).
7   *Ibid.*, Recital (8).
8   *Op. cit.* Directive 2013/40/EU Recital (5).
9   *Ibid.*

firstly of illegal access to multiple systems, which would be infected with malicious software (malware)[10] and consequently would constitute a botnet. Once this network of infected systems is created, a DDoS attack may be launched from this botnet, thus creating the second stage of the crime: the illegal interference with the target system of the DDoS. Therefore, a number of crimes would have to be committed in the preparatory acts leading up to the execution of a DDoS attack.

Directive (EU) 2017/1371 on the fight against fraud to the Union's financial interests by means of criminal law,[11] referred to as the Protection of Financial Interests (PIF) Directive, finds its basis in Article 83(2) TFEU. This latter sub-article provides that:

> If the approximation of criminal laws and regulations of the Member States proves essential to ensure the effective implementation of a Union policy in an area which has been subject to harmonisation measures, directives may establish minimum rules with regard to the definition of criminal offences and sanctions in the area concerned.[12]

The PIF Directive creates such minimum levels of protection against criminal offences purporting to be committed against the EU's financial interests – an area which is the subject of extensive harmonization. Recital (13) of the PIF Directive provides that certain criminal offences which target the EU's financial interests are closely connected to the offences covered by Article 83(1) of the TFEU and other Union legislative acts based on this sub-article. Given the close relationship between the PIF Directive and these legislative acts, coherence between these legal instruments is thus to be ensured in the wording of the PIF Directive.[13]

Insofar as the financial interests of the EU are concerned, cybercrime is a commonly used and, unfortunately, rather effective means for the perpetration of such acts having an impact on the EU's financial security. The European Union Agency for Law Enforcement Cooperation (Europol), in their 2017 Internet Organised Crime Threat Assessment (IOCTA),[14] presented a detailed breakdown of the main developments and emerging threats in cybercrime for that year. Particularly, Europol cites extortion as being a common tactic for the consummation of financially motivated attacks, with "ransomware and Distributed Denial of Service (DDoS) attacks remaining priorities for

---

10   Such as viruses and worms.
11   Directive (EU) 2017/1371 of the European Parliament and of the Council of 5 July 2017 on the fight against fraud to the Union's financial interests by means of criminal law [2017] OJ L198/29.
12   *Ibid.*, Art. 83(2).
13   *Ibid.*, Recital (13). "Some criminal offences against the Union's financial interests are in practice often closely related to the criminal offences covered by Article 83(1) of the Treaty on the Functioning of the European Union (TFEU) and Union legislative acts that are based on that provision. Coherence between such legislative acts and this Directive should therefore be ensured in the wording of this Directive."
14   Europol, *Internet Organised Crime Threat Assessment (IOCTA) 2017* (2017).

EU law enforcement".[15] Thus, among the various other types of cybercrime assessed by Europol for the year 2017 (such as 'child sexual exploitation online' and 'online criminal markets'),[16] it follows that threats to the financial interests of the EU – among which one may count DDoS and ransomware attacks – are some of the foremost issues which the Union has to tackle. In light of the conclusions reached in the IOCTA 2017 paper, one may safely conclude that the adoption of the PIF Directive, which is to be transposed and applicable by the 6th of July 2019,[17] comes at an ideal point in time.

The research objective is to analyse the PIF Directive mainly with reference to Directive 2013/40 and, on a lesser scale, the proposed directive on combating fraud and counterfeiting of non-cash means of payment.[18] Ultimately, the relationship between the risks created by fraud and 'computer as a target' crimes to the EU's financial interests should be better appreciated. The research question of this paper concerns the extent to which, if at all, the objectives of the PIF Directive are supported by other EU directives such as Directive 2013/40 on attacks against information systems and the proposed directive on combating fraud and counterfeiting of non-cash means of payment, specifically with the aim of protecting the EU's financial interests against cybercrime.

In order to answer this research question, the specific crimes listed in the PIF Directive are narrowed down to limit the analysis to cybercrime, which may have a bearing on the Union's financial interests. Having a direct link to the PIF Directive, computer fraud is the first offence to be examined in light of the financial harm it may cause. 'Computer fraud' will be taken to encompass "any act using computers, the Internet, Internet devices, and Internet services to defraud people, companies or government agencies of money [or] revenue".[19] The 'computer as a target' offences of illegal access to information systems ('hacking'), and illegal data and/or system interference, in particular (distributed) denial-of-service attacks (DDoS), are chosen in view of their prominence as "genuine financially motivated risks".[20] These two crimes, while being less directly linked to the PIF Directive than fraud, are catered for under Directive 2013/40, which ought to be coherent with the PIF Directive as per Recital (13) of the latter legal instrument. An examination of these offences is undertaken to determine whether the PIF Directive and Directive 2013/40 effectively complement each other in their respective roles which, although separate and distinct, at times intersect. It is at this point where cybercrime and financial harm converge, thus highlighting the importance of having synergy between these two directives.

---

15 *Ibid.*, 10 para. 2.
16 *Ibid.*, 12.
17 *Op. cit.* Directive (EU) 2017/1371 Art. 17(1).
18 Proposal for a Directive of the European Parliament and of the Council on combating fraud and counterfeiting of non-cash means of payment and replacing Council Framework Decision 2001/413/JHA.
19 'Computer Fraud', *Computer Hope*, 15 September 2017, https://www.computerhope.com/jargon/c/computer-fraud.htm, accessed 19 September 2018.
20 Europol, *op. cit.* at *Internet Organised Crime Threat Assessment (IOCTA) 2017* 10 para. 2.

Of particular importance to this research paper is the acknowledgement on the part of the EU lawmaker in the sixth Recital to Directive 2013/40/EU, wherein it is acknowledged that:

> Large-scale cyber-attacks can cause substantial economic damage both through the interruption of information systems and communication and through the loss or alteration of commercially important confidential information or other data.[21]

Given the EU's recognition of the threats posed by hacking and DDoS attacks (in the form of Directive 2013/40/EU), it is appropriate to include the said directive within this paper insofar as the offences catered for under this directive may cause economic harm. Furthermore, DDoS attacks may be carried out through the use of botnets, thereby entailing the commission of hacking, data and system interference as separate acts which, when taken collectively, would amount to the offence of DDoS. With regard to the connection between the PIF Directive and Directive 2013/40/EU, the latter directive's aim of establishing harsher penalties for hacking and DDoS attacks ties in strongly with the former directive's objective of protecting the EU's financial interests. Although questions still remain as to the effectiveness of harsh penalties as a means of deterring would-be criminals, especially in the realm of cybercrime, one should also note that in the absence of better solutions, deterrence remains the most immediately available and viable response.

Julian King, EU Commissioner for the Security Union,[22] has stated that the IOCTA 2017 report has shown that online crime has become the "new frontier of law enforcement",[23] and that regardless of whether attacks are carried out for political or for financial gain, there exists a need for the EU to ensure that cybercrime "does not pay".[24] Directive 2017/1371 is positioned against this backdrop since it has as its main goal the "combatting [of] fraud and other illegal activities affecting the Union's financial interests, with a view to strengthening protection against criminal offences which affect those financial interests".[25] While Article 1 of the PIF Directive does not directly and explicitly mention cybercrime, this mode of carrying out offences has become

---

21   *Op. cit.* Directive 2013/40/EU Recital (6).
22   European Commission, 'Commissioner (2016-2019) – Julian King – Security Union', *European Commission*, https://ec.europa.eu/commission/commissioners/2014-2019/king_en, accessed 8 July 2018.
23   Europol, '2017, The Year When Cybercrime Hit Close to Home', *Europol*, 27 September 2017, https://www.europol.europa.eu/newsroom/news/2017-year-when-cybercrime-hit-close-to-home, accessed 8 July 2018.
24   *Ibid.*
25   *Op. cit.* Directive 2017/1371 Art. 1.

increasingly more attractive to criminals, as evidenced by the IOCTA 2017 paper, as well as indicated by other reports.[26]

In an effort to counter the increase in reported cybercrime, the EU is stepping up its legislative efforts in order to combat such criminal activity. The PIF Directive, in this regard, focuses exclusively on the need for the EU to protect its financial interests, as will be detailed below.

5.2   The Remit of Directive 2017/1371 – Whose 'Financial Interests'?

The 'financial interests' of the EU may be interpreted in a vast manner. These interests could range from the personal financial interest of each and every EU citizen to the budget of EU organizations and institutions, while also covering anything in between. This broad spectrum would be very difficult to regulate with a single legal instrument; therefore, the PIF Directive homes in on a specific portion of the above-mentioned spectrum of financial interests. While the personal financial interests of EU citizens, when taken collectively throughout the Union, would tally up to a sizeable amount – therefore undoubtedly deserving of protection and regulation – the PIF Directive being discussed in this paper establishes a narrower scope.

Article 2 of the PIF Directive defines the 'Union's financial interests' as meaning all "revenues, expenditure and assets covered by, acquired through, or due to" either the budget of the EU as a whole or, alternatively, the budgets of the EU institutions, bodies, offices and agencies.[27] The scope of the directive also extends to cover budgets "directly or indirectly managed or monitored [by such institutions, bodies, offices and agencies of the EU]".[28] The directive's focused scope on the EU's budget and that of its organs makes it more suitable to tackle criminal offences targeted against these bodies since a precise scope paves the way for precise measures to be taken in order to detect, investigate and prosecute such crimes. Special attention may, therefore, be given to specific cybercrimes which attempt to harm the above-mentioned financial interests of the EU. Consequently, the main offences to be tackled in the directive may be classified into four broad categories, mainly concerning fraud[29] but also including money laundering, corruption and misappropriation of funds.[30] Given this research paper's aim of examining cybercrime vis-à-vis the financial interests of the EU, the central themes to be hereunder discussed will be limited to those offences which may be executed with the

---

26 Jill Treanor, 'UK Fraud Hits Record £1.1bn as Cybercrime Aoars', *The Guardian*, 24 January 2017, https://www.theguardian.com/uk-news/2017/jan/24/uk-fraud-record-cybercrime-kpmg, accessed 8 July 2018.

27 *Op. cit.* Directive 2017/1371 Art. 2(1) (a).

28 *Ibid.*, Art. 2 (1) (a) (ii).

29 *Ibid.*, Art. 3.

30 *Ibid.*, Art. 4.

help of a 'cyber' element. Over and above this class of offences, particular focus will be given to those cybercrimes affecting the EU's financial interests.

Therefore, in the context of cybercrime, online fraud will be central to this discussion, with specific 'computer as a target' offences also being analysed insofar as such offences may cause harm to the EU's financial interests. In light of this, the offence of corruption will not be analysed in this paper since such crime appertains neither to the category of computer fraud nor does it satisfy the definition of 'computer as a target' crimes. With regard to money laundering, while the commission of this offence may certainly be aided with the use of ICT equipment, the PIF Directive makes it clear that the ruling legal instrument on this offence is the Fourth Anti-Money Laundering Directive,[31, 32] therefore making said crime go beyond the purpose of this research paper.

5.3   'CYBER-ENABLED' FRAUD

Cybercrime entails a multitude of offences and is often split up in various categories of specific criminal acts. These categories range from 'high-tech crime', defined by the International Criminal Police Organization (Interpol) as "sophisticated attacks against computer hardware and software"[33] all through to 'cyber-enabled crime' which may be described as traditional offences which have taken on a new dimension with the advent of the Internet.[34] While the former type of offences necessarily requires the existence of modern computer equipment for their perpetration, the latter category merely sees traditional crimes being consummated through the employment of more novel methods – in this case, with the aid of computer systems.

This section of the paper treats the subject of computer fraud under the PIF Directive as one type of the overarching offence of fraud, an offence which clearly pre-dates the existence of computers and the Internet. In light of this, this type of crime belongs to the category of 'cyber-enabled crime' as defined above. Article 8 of the Convention on Cybercrime caters for computer-related fraud as follows:

> Each Party shall adopt such legislative and other measures as may be necessary
> to establish as criminal offences under its domestic law, when committed

---

31   Directive (EU) 2015/849 of the European Parliament and of the Council of 20 May 2015 on the prevention of the use of the financial system for the purposes of money laundering or terrorist financing, amending Regulation (EU) No 648/2012 of the European Parliament and of the Council, and repealing Directive 2005/60/EC of the European Parliament and of the Council and Commission Directive 2006/70/EC [2015] OJ L141/73.

32   *Op. cit.* Directive 2017/1371 Art. 4(1).

33   Interpol, 'Cybercrime', *Interpol*, https://www.interpol.int/Crime-areas/Cybercrime/Cybercrime, accessed 9 July 2018.

34   *Ibid.*

intentionally and without right, the causing of a loss of property to another person by:

a. any input, alteration, deletion or suppression of computer data;

b. any interference with the functioning of a computer system, with fraudulent or dishonest intent of procuring, without right, an economic benefit for oneself or for another person.[35]

In accordance with the definition of computer-related fraud outlined above, and as with traditional fraud, computer fraud necessarily requires an element of deception for its perpetration. Indeed, it is this element of deception – forming the 'fraudulent or dishonest intent' – that distinguishes fraud from the more overt crime of theft. This intent to deceive may be directed either towards the end user as a natural person or, more abstractly, towards the end user's computer system. The possibility of a machine or computer as the target of the deception was entertained by the UK Law Commission, which concluded, "that it should be criminal to obtain a service without the permission of the person providing it, albeit without the deception of a human mind".[36] Reference is then made to Article 72(6) of the UK Value-Added Tax Act of 1994, wherein it is provided that:

Furnishing, sending or otherwise making use of a document which is false in a material particular, with intent to deceive, includes a reference to furnishing, sending or otherwise making use of such a document with intent to secure that a machine will respond to the document as if it were a true document.[37]

Having established the possibility of 'machine deception', the plethora of ways in which computer fraud can be carried out should be better appreciated. Whether the target of the deception is the end user or the computer, a common modus operandi remains the deliberate misrepresentation of the truth by the perpetrator. Consequently, the broad range of methods through which computer fraud may be committed adds significant risk to the EU's financial interests. Making matters worse is the rapidly changing nature of cybercrime, meaning that newer ways in which to perpetuate these older, 'traditional' crimes are envisaged to remain a constant threat going forward as they always have been in the past.[38] It is also interesting to note that, other than Articles 3 and 4 of Council Framework Decision 2001/413/JHA combating fraud and counterfeiting of non-cash means of payment,[39] there currently exists no dedicated EU legislation focusing

---

35 *Op. cit.* Council of Europe Convention on Cybercrime Art. 8.

36 Law Commission, *Legislating the Criminal Code – Fraud and Deception* (Law Com No 155, 1999) 123 para. 8.58.

37 Value Added Tax Act 1994, s 72(6).

38 Refer to Section 5.6 below.

39 Council Framework Decision 2001/413/JHA on combating fraud and counterfeiting of non-cash means of payment [2001] OJ L149 Art. 3 'Offences related to computers', Art. 4 'Offences related to specifically adapted devices'.

specifically on computer fraud. Overall, however, the most common types of computer fraud are covered by this Framework Decision. Further EU legislative action in this area could potentially provide guidance and direct action to be taken against computer fraud.

The financial interests of the EU, as defined within the PIF Directive, may be harmed by computer fraud. This vulnerability should prompt the EU to take the appropriate steps not only to prevent such crimes from taking place but also to detect, investigate and prosecute the commission of such acts after the fact.

5.4   DEFINING 'COMPUTER AS A TARGET' OFFENCES

In addition to the employment of acts from which the perpetrator derives a direct pecuniary benefit, as in the case of computer fraud, there also exist offences which do not provide the perpetrator with such a direct benefit. The offences falling under the latter category may still have an impact on the financial interests of the EU despite the fact that the perpetrator may not have made a direct monetary gain. One such class of offences includes 'computer as a target' offences. These crimes are relevant to this research paper in that the considerable harm caused through the perpetration of such offences may have an adverse effect on the financial interests of the EU, in spite of the fact that such offences are not explicitly catered for under the PIF Directive. Instead, these crimes are provided for under Directive 2013/40/EU. Secondly, these offences merit inclusion in this paper on the basis that the damage caused to the victim of a crime need not necessarily be accompanied by a respective profit being made by the perpetrator, meaning that the financial harm suffered by the victim does not always go hand in hand with an economic gain for the criminal.

Jonathan Clough equates 'computer as a target' offences with 'hacking'.[40] Clough uses the term 'hacking' in a broad sense and expands on its meaning by stating that "[hacking] and its variants [are] used to describe unauthorised access to computers and computer systems".[41] Moreover, Clough defines 'computer as a target' offences as those acts which involve the following three main types of conduct:
1. The gaining of unauthorized access to a computer or computer system;
2. Causing unauthorized damage or impairment to computer data or the operation of a computer or computer system; or
3. The unauthorized interception of computer data.[42]

The common thread shared by all three types of acts is the element of a lack of authorization. Thus, according to Clough, 'computer as a target' offences are necessarily

---

40   Jonathan Clough, *Principles of Cybercrime*, Cambridge University Press, 2nd ed, 2015, p. 31.
41   *Ibid.*, 31 footnote 1.
42   *Ibid.*, 31.

characterized by unauthorized access to the computer, impairment of systems or interception of data. Furthermore, what sets this category of cybercrime apart from computer fraud is the fact that no particular pecuniary benefit needs to be derived by the perpetrator. Hence, the researcher argues that while the PIF Directive does not include 'computer as a target' offences within its scope, the effects that such acts have on the victim of the crime are such as to cause considerable financial harm, a substantial portion of which is attributed to the repairing and recovery of computer systems and data after the fact.[43]

Clough's above-mentioned three types of conduct constituting 'computer as a target' offences are elsewhere categorized more exhaustively. Specifically, the corresponding Convention on Cybercrime section is titled 'Offences against the confidentiality, integrity and availability of computer data and systems'.[44] This section of the Cybercrime Convention is comprised of the following offences: the crimes of illegal access to a computer system, illegal interception of data, data interference, system interference and misuse of devices.[45] It should be noted that while none of these crimes is specifically related to financial gain for the perpetrator, they may nonetheless cause financial harm. In this regard, it is important for the EU to consider the potential damage which may be caused to its financial interests by 'computer as a target' offences.

5.5 THE SALIENT 'COMPUTER AS A TARGET' OFFENCES

The different types of 'computer as a target' offences, both as categorized by Jonathan Clough as well as in the manner classified under the Cybercrime Convention, may be perpetrated through various methods. The dynamic characteristic of these offences means that the perpetrator is not limited to the employment of one singular modus operandi. Consequently, the manner in which such crimes are carried out is in a constant state of flux, changing in step with technological developments and seldom being static. This feature of 'computer as a target' offences encapsulates one of the challenges which law enforcement authorities may face in tracking down and prosecuting such offences. This section of the paper focuses on two of the most prominent 'computer as a target' crimes: the offences of hacking and DoS attacks.

The financial interests of the EU may be jeopardized by the above-mentioned two crimes in different manners and to varying degrees. Hacking involves the illegal access to a computer system – an act which is clearly established as a 'computer as a target' offence under the Cybercrime Convention. DoS attacks, either in their original form or

---

43 Ponemon Institute and Accenture, *2017 Cost of Cyber Crime Study – Insights on the Security Investments that make a Difference* (2017) 30 'Cyber crime detection and recovery activities account for 55 percent of total internal activity cost'.

44 *Op. cit.* Council of Europe Convention on Cybercrime Chapter II, Section I, Title 1.

45 *Ibid.*, Arts. 2-6.

in the more complex DDoS version, seek to disrupt the use of one or more systems, thus constituting 'system interference' as per the Cybercrime Convention. These attacks may have an effect on the EU's financial interests since considerable expenses could be incurred in repairing and regaining control of targeted systems. While the direct financial loss caused by a DDoS attack is not the primary expense incurred by the targets of such attacks, the loss of trust in security systems and the risk of intellectual property theft are cited as constituting the bulk of the expenses brought about by this type of cybercrime.[46] Since DDoS attacks may disrupt or destroy information systems and/or networks which form part of the critical infrastructure of Member States and of the Union,[47] losses and/or damages directly attributable to or resulting from such disruption, as well as costs for infrastructure repair and maintenance after the attack, should also be factored in as part of the harm caused by such attacks. To this end, the indirect impact on the EU's financial interests caused by 'computer as a target' offences merits further examination.

The offence of hacking is sometimes also taken to encompass DoS and DDoS attacks, with a top anti-malware company stating that "hacking refers to manipulating the normal behaviour of a computer [and that] hacking techniques include using viruses, worms, Trojan horses, ransomware, browser hijacks, rootkits and denial of service attacks".[48] For the purposes of this section, the classification adopted by the Cybercrime Convention – which distinguishes between hacking, or illegal access,[49] and DoS attacks, or system interference[50] – shall be adopted. The researcher uses this latter connection between the two crimes and their respective Convention articles as a way of establishing a distinction between the two offences. It should be noted that the Convention uses technology-neutral terms and, consequently, offences are rarely pigeon-holed into only one particular article. On the contrary, the different acts constituting one specific cybercrime are often cited as being in breach of various articles of the Convention simultaneously. Therefore, any computer crime involving hacking or DoS may substantively violate multiple articles of the Convention due to the widely interpreted articles contained therein. In spite of their commonality under the Convention, the researcher has opted to distinguish between the two substantive cybercrimes owing to the different ends achieved by the perpetrator. While in hacking,

---

46   Warwick Ashford, 'DDoS Attacks Cost Up to £35,000', *Computer Weekly*, 18 April 2018, https://www.computerweekly.com/news/252439254/DDoS-attacks-cost-up-to-35000, accessed 16 August 2018.

47   *Op. cit.* Directive 2013/40/EU Recital (4), "Critical infrastructure could be understood to be an asset, system or part thereof located in Member States, which is essential for the maintenance of vital societal functions, health, safety, security, economic or social well-being of people, such as power plants, transport networks or government networks, and the disruption or destruction of which would have a significant impact in a Member State as a result of the failure to maintain those functions."

48   Avast Software Inc., 'What Is Hacking', *Avast Software Inc*, https://www.avast.com/c-hacker, accessed 20 August 2018.

49   *Op. cit.* Council of Europe Convention on Cybercrime Art. 2.

50   *Ibid.*, Art. 5.

computer usage is 'hijacked' illicitly in favour of the hacker, in DoS or DDoS attacks, the usage of the targeted system is merely taken away from the lawful user, but control of such is never obtained by the perpetrator.

5.5.1   Hacking as a Threat to the EU's Financial Interests

In computer networking, hacking is any technical effort to manipulate the normal behaviour of network connections and connected systems. A hacker is a person engaged in hacking. The term hacking historically referred to as constructive, clever technical work that was not necessarily related to computer systems. Today, however, hacking and hackers are most commonly associated with malicious programming attacks on networks and computers over the Internet.[51]

Hacking in today's culture is largely associated with criminal activity and thus carries with it a negative connotation.[52] According to the Cybercrime Convention, hacking is categorized under Article 2 as 'illegal access', and is taken to constitute "the [intentional] access to the whole or any part of a computer system without right".[53] Over and above this basic requirement for an act to be considered as constituting 'illegal access' under the Cybercrime Convention, the same Article 2 supplements this by stating that such access to a system may be required to be accompanied by further malicious conduct. This ranges from infringement of security measures to the intent of obtaining data or other dishonest intent.[54] These malicious acts or culpable intent may be required to accompany the principal act of hacking in order for such to be considered as a criminal act under the Cybercrime Convention. The discretion of whether to require such malicious acts or intent within the domestic criminal law definition is left entirely in the hands of the Parties to the Convention.[55]

In a study titled 'Legal Frameworks for Hacking by Law Enforcement'[56] conducted for the EU Committee for Civil Liberties in 2017, it is stated that the primary risk posed by hacking relates to the fundamental right to privacy and freedom of expression.[57] While this study assesses hacking in relation to its use as a law enforcement tool, the threats posed to fundamental rights by malicious hacking remain the same, regardless of whether hacking is being carried out for noble purposes or less. Admittedly, human rights grievances may only be redressed by legal action against the State, of which the

---

51 Bradley Mitchell, 'What Is Hacking?', *Lifewire*, 16 August 2018, https://www.lifewire.com/definition-of-hacking-817991, accessed 20 August 2018.
52 *Ibid.*
53 *Op. cit.* Council of Europe Convention on Cybercrime Art. 2.
54 *Ibid.*
55 *Ibid.*
56 European Parliament Directorate-General for Internal Policies, *Legal Frameworks for Hacking by Law Enforcement: Identification, Evaluation and Comparison of Practices,* Brussels, March 2017.
57 *Ibid.,* 9 para. 2.

executive law enforcement branch forms a party. Breaches to one's privacy and freedom of expression may also be brought about by other legal or natural persons, as in the case of a malicious hacking attempt. While the chief threats posed by hacking relate to the above-mentioned fundamental rights, an element of financial harm may also be created. Through illegal access, the integrity of the target system becomes compromised, and the legitimate user would no longer be able to use his system in a secure manner with respect to his privacy. Over and above this facet of the offence, the legitimate user may also have to face a ransomware attack as part of the hacking, which may be described as a type of malware attack that blocks user access to files or systems until the victim pays a ransom in exchange for regaining access.[58]

Ransomware attacks have seen considerable development in the recent past, with the recently coined 'RansomWeb' attacks being one prominent derivative.[59] These attacks combine elements of hacking and ransomware together and involve the use of hacking to gain illegal access to a system or website – this being the 'hacking' branch of the crime – with the second limb being the employment of ransomware in order to lock the system or website behind an illicit paywall.[60] This multifaceted crime enables the hacker to 'extort' monies from his target through the use of ransomware, thus creating a clear nexus of causality to financial damage. Applied on a larger scale, the websites, systems and online infrastructure of EU organs and institutions may fall prey to such RansomWeb attacks, thereby causing potential harm and adversely affecting the financial interests of the EU. Further compounding matters is the fact that these attacks are "difficult to prevent, due to the complexity of most web apps and their constant changing state".[61] Ilia Kolochenko, founder of High-Tech Bridge, a global provider of web and mobile security services,[62] had stated in 2015 that "the days when hackers were attacking websites for glory or fun are over, now financial profit drives them. The era of web blackmailing, racket and change are about to start".[63] This speculation has, over time, proven to be resoundingly accurate, with the reported number of types of ransomware increasing by a staggering 752 per cent from 2015 to 2016,[64] lending credence to Kolochenko's statement.

The link between hacking and the EU's financial interests may not be as readily visible as, for instance, the perceived impact that fraud may have on the same. Notwithstanding

---

58   Nate Lord, 'A History of Ransomware Attacks: The Biggest and Worst Ransomware Attacks of All Time', *Digital Guardian*, 6 April 2018, https://digitalguardian.com/blog/history-ransomware-attacks-biggest-and-worst-ransomware-attacks-all-time#1, accessed 12 September 2018.

59   Samuel Gibbs, 'Hackers Holding Websites to Ransom by Switching Their Encryption Keys', *The Guardian*, 3 February 2015, https://www.theguardian.com/technology/2015/feb/03/hackers-websites-ransom-switching-encryption-keys, accessed 21 August 2018.

60   *Ibid.*, para. 1, accessed 21 August 2018.

61   *Ibid.*, para. 9, accessed 21 August 2018.

62   High-Tech Bridge Web Security Company, https://www.htbridge.com/company/, accessed 21 August 2018.

63   Samuel Gibbs, *op. cit.* at para. 8.

64   Trend Micro, *Trendlabs 2016 Security Roundup: A Record Year for Enterprise Threats* (2017) 4.

this, the significant and steady rise of cybercrime – among which one may count hacking as a tool to cause financial harm – should be taken into consideration as a serious threat to the financial integrity of the EU. Coupled with the use of ransomware, hacking may create complex challenges for EU law enforcement authorities in the form of RansomWeb attacks. Lastly, one also has to take into account the ever-changing nature of malware, meaning that the detection and investigation of such offences are liable to never settle into a common method of execution. This is further compounded by developments in the way such crimes are perpetrated, in turn creating further obstacles to law enforcement authorities.

5.5.2 The Financial Risks Posed by Denial-of-Service Attacks

DoS attacks are the second type of 'computer as a target' offences, which will be examined in light of the harm that these attacks may cause to the EU's financial interests. Similar to the offence of hacking, DoS or DDoS attacks are not directly catered for under the PIF Directive. However, insofar as the potential for financial damage caused by DoS attacks is concerned, one may cite Europol's IOCTA report for the year 2017, which concludes with certainty that there exists a very real and significant threat in this regard.[65]

While DoS and DDoS attacks achieve the same outcome, the different method employed sets them apart. DoS attacks see the target system being overloaded by requests sent from the perpetrator's system, which has the effect of bringing the targeted system to a standstill. Once the request capacity supported by the bandwidth of the targeted system's server is exceeded, this server ceases to function correctly and consequently 'freezes' the targeted system, thereby resulting in the lawful user losing the use of – or, more accurately, being denied from using – his own system.[66] Anecdotally, and perhaps rather simplistically, the execution of a DoS attack is likened to "15 fat men trying to get through a revolving door at the same time – nothing can move".[67] DDoS attacks achieve the same goal, albeit through a different course of action. Succinctly, DDoS is the execution of DoS attacks *en masse*:

> The essential difference between a DoS and a DDoS attack is that a DDoS attack is a DoS attack launched from a multitude ... of computer systems simultaneously. DDoS attacks are used because at times a DoS attack may not

---

65   Europol, *op. cit.* at 10 para. 2.

66   Katia Schembri, *Legal Aspects of Distributed Denial of Service Attacks* (2012) 15 para. 4.

67   Graham Cluley, 'Twitter, Facebook and LiveJournal Hit by Massive Denial-of-service Attack', *Naked Security*, 6 August 2009, https://nakedsecurity.sophos.com/2009/08/06/twitter-hit-massive-denialof service-attack/, accessed 27 August 2018 para. 4.

have enough 'power' to overcome the security measures in place and bring down a large Target System and thus a DDoS attack would be more efficient.[68]

Having established the prominence of DoS and DDoS attacks vis-à-vis financially motivated attacks as evidenced in the IOCTA 2017 report, and the core feature which sets them apart, a definition of these crimes according to the Cybercrime Convention should follow. Article 5 of the Convention provides the following:

> Each Party shall adopt such legislative and other measures as may be necessary to establish as criminal offences under its domestic law when committed intentionally, the serious hindering without right of the functioning of a computer system by inputting, transmitting, damaging, deleting, deteriorating, altering or suppressing computer data.[69]

From the outset, it is apparent that the Cybercrime Convention, which is well over a decade into its operative term, makes use of technology-neutral wording in order to cater for technological developments as they occur going forward. Through the use of general terminology, a broad interpretation of the conduct constituting 'system interference' under the Convention may be made, thus never unduly restricting the application of Article 5. As one might expect, such a broad provision has led to both DoS and DDoS attacks to be categorized as 'system interference' under Article 5. This proves the adaptability of the Convention in the face of evolving crimes, which allows an aged legal instrument to still anticipate and cater to emerging crimes over 15 years after its inception. On the other hand, a disadvantage is also created by widely interpreted 'umbrella provisions' such as the above-mentioned article, namely that more specific guidance on any particular issue would have to be provided once certain conduct is deemed as falling under the broad category set by the article. With regard to DDoS attacks, this *ad hoc* guidance was offered by the Cybercrime Convention Committee in 2013.

The Cybercrime Convention Committee Guidance Note 5 on DDoS attacks[70] (Guidance Note) provides a more updated understanding of Article 5 of the Convention, in order to allow for a better application of the said article in relation to DDoS attacks. This Guidance Note was issued with the aim of "facilitating the effective use and implementation of the Budapest Convention on Cybercrime, also in the light of legal, policy and technological developments".[71] Furthermore, while the Guidance Note

---

68   Katia Schembri, *op. cit.* at 16 para. 2.
69   *Op. cit.* Council of Europe Convention on Cybercrime Art. 5.
70   Council of Europe, *Cybercrime Convention Committee (T-CY) T-CY Guidance Note #5 DDOS Attacks* (2013).
71   *Ibid.*, 3 para. 1.

refers solely to DDoS attacks in its official title, it is made clear that both DoS and DDoS attacks are addressed in it.[72] While the main article dealing with DoS and DDoS attacks under the Convention is undoubtedly Article 5 concerning 'system interference', in the Guidance Note, it is explained that such interference may be accompanied by several other offences under the Convention. For instance, it is established that DoS and DDoS attacks may be availed of "to attempt or to aid or abet several crimes ... such as Computer-related forgery, Article 7 [and] Computer-related fraud, Article 8".[73] Accordingly, the Cybercrime Convention Committee crystallizes the impact that DoS attacks may have in relation to financial integrity by stating that these attacks could potentially be used to aid or abet the perpetration of fraud. Over and above the connection between DoS attacks and computer-related fraud, financial damage may also be caused to the lawful user in the form of expenses incurred to repair and regain usage of the system, as is also the case with hacking.

While "the earliest DoS attacks, as with much early hacking, may have been carried out simply to demonstrate prowess in hacking, or out of sheer malice or spite",[74] the more recent examples of these attacks show an increasing correlation between this particular 'computer as a target' offence and financial harm.[75] The attractiveness of DoS attacks for criminals largely stems from two main reasons: the easy and inexpensive costs associated with launching a DoS attack,[76] and their effectiveness at causing damage to their victim, among which one finds financial harm.[77]

5.6   INCREASED CHALLENGES FOR LAW ENFORCEMENT: CROSS-BORDER COOPERATION AND MUTUAL LEGAL ASSISTANCE

Article 325 TFEU carves out an obligation of the EU and its Member States to cooperate in the combating of fraud and other illegal activities which affect the Union's financial interests.[78] To this end, Member States are obliged to combat any fraud affecting the EU's financial interests with the same vigour as that fraud which affects them domestically.[79] Thirdly, Article 325(3) TFEU provides that the Member States are bound to coordinate

---

72   *Ibid.*, 3 para. 3.
73   *Ibid.*, 4 para. 4.
74   Lillian Edwards, 'Dawn of the Death of Distributed Denial of Service: How to Kill Zombies' (2006) 24(23) *Cardozo Arts and Entertainment Law Journal* 32 para. 2.
75   Maria Korolov, 'DDoS Costs, Damages on the Rise', *CSO from IDG*, 5 May 2016, https://www.csoonline. com/article/3065999/security/ddos-costs-damages-on-the-rise.html, accessed 27 August 2018.
76   Denis Makrushin, 'The Cost of Launching a DDoS Attack', *Secure List*, 23 March 2017, https://securelist. com/the-cost-of-launching-a-ddos-attack/77784/, accessed 27 August 2018, para. 22.
77   *Ibid.*, para. 24.
78   *Op cit.* Consolidated Version of the Treaty on the Functioning of the European Union Art. 325(1).
79   *Ibid.*, 325(2).

their actions against fraud, and calls for "close and regular cooperation between the competent authorities".[80]

The obligations outlined in Article 325 TFEU are put into practice thanks in part to the role played by the European Anti-Fraud Office (OLAF), which has, as one of its objectives, the investigation of fraud against the EU budget.[81] In line with the executive summary of the Impact Assessment for the proposal of Directive 1371/2017,[82] OLAF is one of several key players who are expected to provide qualitative data on legislative and practical compliance once the directive becomes applicable.[83] The data gathered by OLAF should provide the EU with ample information upon which the EU and its Member States could draw conclusions on the effectiveness of the PIF Directive. An ex-post assessment of the PIF Directive's success (or otherwise) in protecting the Union's financial interests – especially insofar as fraud is concerned – should mean that the EU would be in a better position to protect its financial interests going forward. As pertains to 'computer as a target' offences, the role of Europol – specifically the European Cybercrime Centre – is expected to be a central one, and is anticipated to gain further prominence with the passage of time. It is evident that a strong law enforcement framework is vital for the success of the PIF Directive since without an effective policing force, there would be little to deter criminals from engaging in computer fraud and 'computer as a target' offences affecting the EU's financial interests.

As observed by Michael Edmund O'Neill in his article 'Old Crimes in New Bottles: Sanctioning Cybercrime',[84] "cybercrime is poised to become the most serious challenge facing international law enforcement".[85] O'Neill further expands by stating that "cybercrime is not only a growing threat, but its potential for mischief may be far greater than in traditional criminal enterprises",[86] speculation which, as demonstrated by the 2017 IOCTA, was proven to be true. To offset the momentum with which cybercrime continues to grow, an international response is more suited to combat such crimes. Article 15 of the PIF Directive provides for such cooperation between the Member States and OLAF, albeit in relation to the offences specifically outlined in the Directive. The researcher submits that such a pan-European approach to tackling fraud

---

80   *Ibid.*, 325(3).
81   European Commission, 'OLAF European Anti-Fraud Office', *EC Europa*, 12 September 2018, https://ec. europa.eu/anti-fraud/home_en, accessed 14 September 2018.
82   European Commission, *Commission Staff Working Document – Executive Summary of the Impact Assessment – Accompanying the Document – Proposal for a Directive of the European Parliament and of the Council on the Protection of the Financial Interests of the European Union by Criminal Law*, COM (2012) 363.
83   *Ibid.*, 9 para. 4.
84   Michael Edmund O'Neill, 'Old Crimes in New Bottles: Sanctioning Cybercrime' (2000) 9 *George Mason Law Review* 237.
85   *Ibid.*, 1 para. 3.
86   *Ibid.*

should also be mirrored in the fight against 'computer as a target' offences which impact the EU's financial interests.

5.7 CONCLUSION

The EU and its Member States have an obligation to combat fraud and any other similar illegal activity affecting the financial interests of the Union. This obligation arises from Article 310(6) of the TFEU[87] and is expanded upon by Article 325 of the same Treaty.[88] Among other provisions, Article 325 holds that the measures to be taken in order to counter fraud should act as a deterrent and must be such as to afford effective protection to the Member States individually, as well as to the EU's institutions and organs collectively.[89] Deterrence against fraud is then specifically catered for under the PIF Directive, which has two primary goals in this regard. Firstly, the directive seeks to create a "stronger and more harmonised system, with minimum common rules, to fight crime affecting the EU budget".[90] This objective is to be achieved by the transposition of the PIF Directive into Member State legislation by 6 July 2019. Secondly, the directive aims to "better protect the EU's financial interests and taxpayers' money across the EU".[91] In order for this second purpose of the PIF Directive to be fulfilled, a thorough understanding of the current climate of the relevant threats to these financial interests is required. In this regard, the major cybercrimes singled out throughout the course of this paper were three, namely computer fraud, hacking and DoS attacks.

These offences were analysed primarily in view of the economic impact that they may have on the EU and its Member States. While acknowledging that the PIF Directive does not directly mention cybercrime in its scope, justification still exists for the inclusion of the above-mentioned three major offences. Firstly, the link between fraud and computer fraud is readily apparent since computer fraud corresponds to the perpetration of traditional fraud albeit through newer means, and is therefore directly relevant to the scope of the PIF Directive. The remaining 'computer as a target' offences possesses a less direct connection to the PIF Directive since neither hacking nor DoS is exclusively related to economic harm. Notwithstanding this, an argument is made highlighting the rising costs associated with both crimes, especially in the form of expenses created in the aftermath of an attack, be it hacking or DoS. The potential for causing financial damage

---

87 *Op. cit.* Consolidated Version of the Treaty on the Functioning of the European Union Art. 310(6), "The Union and the Member States, in accordance with Article 325, shall counter fraud and any other illegal activities affecting the financial interests of the Union."

88 Refer to Section 6 above.

89 *Ibid.*, Art. 325(1).

90 'Fight against Fraud to the EU's Financial Interests by Means of Criminal Law', *EUR-lex*, 6 December 2017, https://eur-lex.europa.eu/legal-content/EN/TXT/HTML/?uri=LEGISSUM:4309224&from=EN, accessed 29 August 2018.

91 *Ibid.*

of both these 'computer as a target' offences is acknowledged by Europol in their IOCTA 2017 report and is reasonably expected to keep rising as was the case in the past. To this end, one may argue in favour of a more cybercrime-centric directive, which would also take more direct cognizance of cybercrime and the impact that this pervasive category of crimes may have on the EU's financial interests.

6   SELECTED CASE STUDIES: THE CASE STUDY OF GERMANY

Marc Engelhart

6.1   IMPLEMENTATION OF EU CRIMINAL LAW IN GERMANY

6.1.1   Overview

European law has had a powerful impact on the shaping of German criminal law, more so than any other supranational law. These developments took place rather late compared to other, especially economically oriented, areas of the law, as most competencies of the EU for criminal matters were introduced in the last 25 years. Because the regulation of criminal law is perceived as one of the core elements of German statehood,[1] European influences have been met with strong criticism and resistance by scholars and politicians.[2]

The degree of European influence on German criminal law varies from case to case. The impact on substantive law, in shaping the offences in the Special Part of the Criminal Code, the Strafgesetzbuch (StGB), has been significant. By contrast, the influence on the General Part of the StGB has been very limited, except for the rules on confiscation, as one example.[3] This is not only due to the lack of general principles at the European level (e.g., regarding attribution, participation or attempt) and of a European theory of criminalization but also because of long-standing (dating from the mid-nineteenth century), well-grounded, and highly developed criminal law concepts in Germany. These concepts are often open to integrating new aspects merely by an interpretation by the courts. At the same time, these concepts are also highly resistant to fundamental changes from outside the system.

The influence of European law on procedural law has so far been rather limited. The standards of the Code of Criminal Procedure, well established since they came into force

---

1   *See* BVerfG, BVerfGE 123, 267, para. 252 "Particularly sensitive for the ability of a constitutional state to democratically shape itself are decisions on substantive and formal criminal law" [Lisbon Decision].

2   Critical Dieter Krimphove, 'Fragwürdige Europäisierung' (2018) KritV 56; Bernd Schünemann and Benjamin Roger, 'Die Karawane zur Europäisierung des Strafrechts zieht weiter' (2010) ZIS 515-523; but also *see* Frank Meyer, 'Europäisches Wirtschaftsstrafrecht' (2017) wistra 209, 249; Ulrich Sieber, 'Die Zukunft des Europäischen Strafrechts' (2009) 121 ZStW 1.

3   The last major reform took place in 2017, *see* Gesetz zur Reform der strafrechtlichen Vermögensabschöpfung of 13 March 2017, BGBl. I 872; for details *see* Gerson Trüg, 'Die Reform der strafrechtlichen Vermögensabschöpfung' (2017) NJW 1913; Markus Köhler, 'Die Reform der strafrechtlichen Vermögensabschöpfung' (2017) NStZ 497, 665.

in 1879, govern the procedure to this day. In recent years, European influence has grown mainly because of the Commission's activities in regulating victims' rights and the rights of the accused, introducing several (limited) adjustments to procedural law.[4] The strongest impact on German law has been in the area of transnational cooperation. Instruments such as the European Arrest Warrant and the recognition and enforcement of foreign decisions on sanctions have significantly changed the traditional procedures of cooperation between German and foreign authorities in criminal (and also police) matters.

The following sections will present a more detailed analysis of the way in which European legislation has been implemented and led to adjustments in German legislation in terms of the impact of EU terrorism law, the Framework Decision 2002/475/JHA and the Framework Decision 2008/919/JHA, the impact of the criminalization of attacks against information systems and the impact of the criminalization of participation in a criminal group.

6.1.2   Impact of EU Law on the Criminalization of Terrorism

Experiences with terrorism and terrorism legislation are not new to Germany: the Red Army Faction (*Rote Armee Fraktion* (RAF)) triggered a first wave of legislation in the 1970s, introducing many changes in substantive and procedural criminal law.[5] The most recent wave of terrorism legislation began after 9/11, entailing a large number of changes in the German legal landscape,[6] many of them triggered by European legislation. Major changes were produced by Framework Decisions 2002/475/JHA and 2008/919/JHA.

6.1.2.1   Framework Decision 2002/475/JHA
For the implementation of Framework Decision 2002/475/JHA into German law, parliament drafted a separate bill introducing major changes to the then chief terrorist offence of forming a terrorist group (s 129a StGB).[7] Following the Framework Decision, s 129a StGB was restructured and can now be separated into three different acts considered to be terrorist acts if the aims or activities of an organization are directed at:
–   committing particularly serious offences (sub-s 1),

---

4   *See* Marc Engelhart, 'Europäisches Strafrecht', in Christian Müller-Gugenberger (ed.), *Wirtschaftsstrafrecht*, Otto Schmidt, 6th ed, 2015, § 6 paras 189-196.
5   *See* H.-J. Vogel, 'Strafverfahrensrecht und Terrorismus, eine Bilanz' (1978) NJW 1217, 1219ff; H.-J. Rudolphi, 'Die Gesetzgebung zur Bekämpfung des Terrorismus' (1979) JA 1ff. On terrorism legislation in Germany *see* Marc Engelhart, 'Countering Terrorism at the Limits of Criminal Liability in Germany', in Matthew Dyson and Benjamin Vogel (eds.), *The Limits of Criminal Law*, Intersentia, 2018, p. 435.
6   *See* Liane Wörner, 'Expanding Criminal Laws by Predating Criminal Responsibility' (2012) *German Law Journal* 1037.
7   Gesetz zur Umsetzung des Rahmenbeschlusses des Rates vom 13. Juni 2002 zur Terrorismusbekämpfung und zur Änderung anderer Gesetze vom 22. Dezember 2003.

- committing offences involving minor wrongdoings but requiring a particular terrorist intent (*Bestimmungsklausel*) and objective suitability for causing harm (*Eignungsklausel*) (sub-s 2),
- threatening to commit one of the aforementioned offences (sub-s 3).

In particular, the German lawmaker expanded the number of offences involving minor wrongdoings by adopting the terrorism definition used in the Framework Decision. The list now includes:
- causing serious physical or mental harm to another person,
- committing various offences related to criminal damage and offences causing a common danger,
- committing offences against the environment,
- committing various offences under the provisions of the Weapons of War (Control) Act,
- committing offences against s 51 of the Weapons Act.

Minimum and maximum sanctions in s 129a StGB were also adjusted on account of the Framework Decision and vary by type of contribution (e.g., sanctions for ringleaders were increased and are higher than for ordinary members of the group).

By following an organizational approach, the definition of terrorist organizations in 129a sub-s 1 StGB is based solely on objective elements; hence, a criminal organization is committing serious offences. But the definition lacks a subjective element, unlike the approach by the Framework Decision, and to this extent the transposition is incomplete,[8] a fact the commission pointed out several times.[9]

The scope of the offence was highly disputed in the law-making process, especially in terms of the appropriateness of the restriction to require '*serious* physical or mental harm to another person' and the limitation of the recruitment offence (s 129a sub-s 5 sentence 2 StGB) to the recruitment of only members or supporters (criticized as either too narrow or too broad depending on the point of view).[10] The controversial question of whether Article 2 of the Framework Decision calls for a modification of the term 'organization' has been debated for a long time:[11] the traditional German notion of an organization as a more formal structure establishes a higher threshold than the Framework Decision, which includes more flexible organizations with less formal structures. The courts have

---

8   Mark A. Zöller, 'Zehn Jahre 11. September – Zehn Jahre Gesetzgebung zum materiellen Terrorismusstrafrecht in Deutschland' (2012) StV 364, 367-368.
9   COM(2004)409 final, 6; *see also* COM(2014)554 final, 6.
10 Jürgen Schäfer, '§ 129a', in Klaus Miebach and Wolfgang Joecks (eds.), *Münchener Kommentar zum Strafgesetzbuch*, C.H.Beck, 3rd ed., 2017, para. 19.
11 *See* Kai Lohse, '§ 129a StGB', in Helmut Satzger, Wilhelm Schluckebier and Gunter Widmaier (eds.), *Strafgesetzbuch: Kommentar*, Wolters Kluwer Deutschland/Carl Heymanns Verlag, 3rd ed., 2017, para. 14.

not taken a clear position regarding s 129a StGB,[12] but the Federal Court decided that the term 'organization' in the context of forming a criminal organization (s 129 StGB) shall not be interpreted in the light of the broader European notion.[13]

Hence, the lawmaker reformed s 129 StGB in 2017 (see infra 6.1.4), adapted the European definition of organization and also applied it to s 129a StGB. As a result, German law now fully conforms to the Framework Decision. As such, the provision of s 129a StGB is subject to the same criticism as before – its complexity and the broad and exaggerated criminalization of predicate offences (*Vorfeldstrafbarkeit*) are considered the most worrisome details of the statutory offence.[14] But there is also an example to the contrary – offences related to criminal damage and offences causing a common danger were moved from sub-s 1 to sub-s 2 so that they now require (in accordance with the definition of the Framework Decision) a subjective element and take the consequences of the offences into account. This specific aspect was abridged compared to previous legislation.[15]

Particularly the extensive use of vague/indeterminate legal concepts makes it somewhat unfeasible.[16] Above all, the offence of s 129a StGB allows for extremely sensitive measures during the preliminary proceedings.[17] Besides, the interpretation of s 129a StGB is more complicated because the legislative materials refer to the Framework Decision without virtually any details or basis of interpretation for unfamiliar offence elements.[18]

6.1.2.2   Framework Decision 2008/919/JHA

Unlike the implementation of Framework Decision 2002/475/JHA, the Framework Decision 2008/919/JHA was not transposed into German law by specific legislation but much more indirectly by a major and general reform of terrorist legislation addressing, *inter alia*, the Council of Europe Convention on the Prevention of Terrorism (CETS no. 196).[19] This 2009 legislation introduced new terrorism offences (see s 89a et seq. StGB) punishing the preparation of serious violent offences endangering the state. It criminalizes a number of acts in the context of preparing terrorist attacks considered to be particularly dangerous. As this legislation does not directly implement Framework Decision 2008/919/JHA, it is in several respects different from it:

---

12   *See* BGHSt 54, 69 (110f).

13   BGH NJW 2008, 1012, para. 16ff.

14   Martin Helm, 'Die Bildung terroristischer Vereinigungen' (2006) StV 719.

15   Still, there is much criticism especially regarding sub-s 2, which is considered to be close to unconstitutional in light of the principle of certainty (*Bestimmtheitsgebot*), *see* Jürgen Schäfer, *op. cit.* at para. 21.

16   *Ibid.*

17   *Ibid.*

18   *Ibid.*

19   Gesetz zur Verfolgung der Vorbereitung von schweren staatsgefährdenden Gewalttaten (Act criminalizing the preparation of serious violent offences endangering the State) of 30 July 2009, BGBl. I 2437.

- The serious violent offences endangering the state are limited to offences against life under s 211 or s 212 StGB or against personal freedom under s 239a or s 239b StGB.
- It is considered sufficient to supply another person with written material (oral incitement is liable under the more general provision of s 111 StGB) capable of serving as an instruction to the commission of a serious violent offence endangering the state; accessibility to the public is not required.
- According to s 89a sub-s 2 no. 1 StGB (in its 2009 version) the rather passive act of receiving instruction and skills that can be of use for the commission of a serious violent offence endangering the state is also included.
- Moreover, the offence of establishing contacts for the purpose of committing a serious violent offence endangering the state (s 89b) can be seen as a supererogatory transposition of the Framework Decision.
- The recruitment for terrorist purposes is broadly covered by s 129a sub-s 5 StGB, also in combination with the general rule of attempted participation (s 30 StGB).[20]
- The German legislature also criminalized the act of obtaining or possessing material intended for terrorist propaganda purposes.
- Arguably, the term 'recruit', which is part of the German transposition, requires the existence of "some sort of plan or minimum institutional framework to which the recruited person is supposed to adhere to",[21] making it difficult to determine whether encouraging a 'lone actor' to commit terrorist acts is covered.
- The attempt of ss 89a et seq. StGB is not punishable.[22]

The German legislature accepted many aspects of the Framework Decision but neither in the structure of the framework nor with a clear reference to it. As the anti-terrorist legislation was reformed and expanded in 2015,[23] German criminal law now provides for a far-reaching criminalization of preparatory acts. This expansion has led to severe criticism for the excessive use of indeterminate/vague legal concepts, raising questions about the constitutionality and legitimacy of predicate offences (*Vorfeldstrafbarkeit*) such as these.[24] Also, s 89a sub-s 3 and s 89b sub-s 3 are alleged to be in contempt of international criminal law in terms of the expanded application of national criminal law

---

20 Anna Oehmichen and Astrid Klukkert, 'Evaluation des Gesetzes zur Verfolgung der Vorbereitung von schweren staatsgefährdenden Gewalttaten (GVVG)' 27-28, https://www.krimz.de/fileadmin/dateiablage/E-Publikationen/Endbericht_GVVG_Evaluierung.pdf.

21 European Commission, 'Report from the Commission to the European Parliament and the Council on the implementation of Council Framework Decision 2008/919/JHA of 28 November 2008 amending Framework Decision 2002/475/JHA on combating terrorism: COM(2014) 554 final', 5 September 2014, 7.

22 *Ibid.*, 9.

23 *See* 'Gesetz zur Änderung der Verfolgung der Vorbereitung von schweren staatsgefährdenden Gewalttaten' of 12 June 2015, BGBl I 926.

24 Henning Radtke and Mark Steinsiek, 'Bekämpfung des internationalen Terrorismus durch Kriminalisierung von Vorbereitungshandlungen?' (2008) ZIS, 383, 388-389; Ulrich Sieber, 'Legitimation und Grenzen von Gefährdungsdelikten im Vorfeld von terroristischer Gewalt' (2009) NStZ 353.

to all EU Member States.[25] This criticism is partly reflected in court decisions. For instance, the Federal Court of Justice held that with regard to fundamental principles of criminal law such as *nulla poena sine lege certa*, the principle of proportionality, the prohibition of excessiveness (*Übermaßverbot*) and of an attitude-based criminal law (*Verbot des Gesinnungsstrafrecht*), the forward displacement of culpability and the extensive reach of the *actus reus* (also containing rather neutral actions) demand an abbreviated interpretation of the *mens rea* requirement.[26] This means that the offender must have double intent (with regard to both the preparatory act and the serious crime intended) in the sense that he must be absolutely determined (*fest entschlossen*) to commit a serious violent offence endangering the state during the preparatory phase. Lesser forms of intent such as *dolus eventualis*[27] do not suffice. Nevertheless, the Court declared the relevant statutory offence (s 89a StGB) constitutional.[28]

6.1.3 Impact of EU Law on the Criminalization of Attacks Against Information Systems

The Framework Decision 2005/222/JHA was implemented into German law by the 4th Criminal Law Amendment Act (*Strafrechtsänderungsgesetz*), creating the new offences of s 202b StGB (phishing) and s 202c StGB (acts preparatory to data espionage and phishing) as well as expanding the main cybercrime offences in s 202a StGB (data espionage), s 303a StGB (data tampering) and s 303b StGB (computer sabotage).[29] Although this legislation made explicit reference to the Framework Decision, the German Act primarily incorporated aspects of the Council of Europe Cybercrime Convention of 2001 (also implemented by the Act).[30] This area needed regulation, as the modern threats to information systems required a more and more extensive interpretation of existing German offences (set forth in the Second Act on Fighting Economic Crime of 1986[31]).[32] To this extent, the transposition of the Framework

---

25 Mark A. Zöller, *op. cit.* at 369-370. *See also* Ulrich Sieber (above n 24), 356f; Kathrin Gierharke, 'Zur geplanten Einführung neuer Straftatbestände wegen der Vorbereitung terroristischer Straftaten' (2008) ZIS 397, 402 and Bernd Hecker, *Europäisches Strafrecht*, Springer, 5th ed., 2015, pp. 380-381.

26 *See* the decisions BGHSt 62, 102; 61, 36, 38; 59, 218, 234.

27 *Dolus eventualis* can be defined as conditional intent where the offender was aware of a risk and did not care that it might materialize.

28 *See* BGHSt 62, 102; 61, 36, 38; 59, 218, 234.

29 'Einundvierzigstes Strafrechtsänderungsgesetz zur Bekämpfung der Computerkriminalität (41. StrÄndG)' of 7 August 2007, BGBl. I 1786.

30 *See* BT-Drs 16/3656.

31 'Zweites Gesetz zur Bekämpfung der Wirtschaftskriminalität (2. WiKG)' of 15 May 1986, BGBl. I 721.

32 Alexander Schultz, 'Neue Strafbarkeiten und Probleme: Der Entwurf des Strafrechtsänderungsgesetzes (StrafÄndG) zur Bekämpfung der Computerkriminalität vom 20.09.2006' (2006) 30 DuD 778, 784.

Decision by the legislature was satisfactory,[33] but it failed to follow the structure of the Framework and to incorporate every detail.

Nor did the lawmaker make much use of its discretion in drafting clear and precise regulations. Mainly due to difficulties in identifying perpetrators and getting a conviction in the area of information technology, the legislature opted to create predicate offences with a far-reaching criminalization of preparatory acts (*Vorfeldstrafbarkeit*).[34] But even though the scope of criminalization was expanded, s 202a StGB does not cover all relevant forms of 'illegal access to information systems';[35] for instance, someone who intentionally gains access to an information system without having the right to do so (Article 2 s 1 Framework Decision) but fails to obtain access to data (s 202a sub-s 1 StGB) would not be punishable under German law.[36] Hence, there are scholars who claim that Article 2 has not been transposed at all.[37] Yet, limiting the data protected by s 202a StGB to data especially protected against unauthorized access can still be considered compatible with the Framework Decision, as it allows exceptions in minor cases (Article 2 s 1 Framework Decision).[38] Illegal system interference (Article 3) is covered by ss 263a, 269, 270 and 274 sub-s 2 no. 2 StGB and for the most part by s 303b StGB as amended.[39] But as the Framework Decision was not directly implemented, some still criticize that not all acts are covered by amended s 303b StGB.[40] The transposition of Article 4 in s 303a StGB turned out to be satisfactory,[41] even though the legislature refrained from further concretization despite constant requests by legal practitioners and scholars.[42] Thus Germany has a working system for regulating cybercrime, although the specifications are in several respects different from those of the EU and the Council of Europe frameworks.[43]

---

33 Concerning the draft of 2006, *see* Alexander Schultz (above n) 784.

34 Specifically concerning s 203c StGB.

35 But also *see* Bernd Hecker, *op. cit.* at p. 408.

36 Ulrich Sieber, '§ 24', in Ulrich Sieber, Helmut Satzger and Bernd von Heintschel-Heinegg (eds.), *Europäisches Strafrecht*, Nomos, 2nd ed., 2014, p. 88; Marco Gercke, 'Die Harmonisierung des europäischen Strafrechts am Beispiel des Internetstrafrechts' (2016) StV 391, 394.

37 Marco Gercke, 'Die Entwicklung des Internetstrafrechts 2013/2014' (2014) ZUM 641, 648.

38 On the discussion *see* Nadine Groveling and Frank M. Holinger, 'Hacking und Computerspionage' (2007) MMR 549, 553.

39 Bernd Hecker, *op. cit.* at p. 408.

40 *See* for details Nadine Gröseling and Frank M. Höfinger, 'Computersabotage und Vorfeldkriminalisierung' (2007) MMR 626, 627-628.

41 Ulrich Sieber, *op. cit.* at p. 88; Marco Gercke, *op. cit.* at 391, 92.

42 Nadine Gröseling and Frank M. Höfinger, *op. cit.* at 626.

43 Marco Gercke, 'Die Entwicklung des Internetstrafrechts 2016/2017' (2017) ZUM 915.

6.1.4 Impact of EU Law on the Criminalization of Participation in a Criminal Organization

The offence of participation in a criminal organization has been incorporated into German criminal law since 1951.[44] The first major reform[45] of the offence occurred in the context of implementing Framework Decision 2008/841/JHA, which took the legislature until 2017.[46] The reform was mainly triggered by a decision of the Federal Court, in which the Court decided not to interpret the term organization in s 129 StGB in light of the Framework Decision 2008/841/JHA, as this would be more than an interpretation and thus violate the constitutional *lex scripta* requirement.[47] Also, German criminal law distinguishes between joint principals, a gang and criminal organizations. Adopting the definition of the Framework Decision would blur the differences between gang and criminal organizations. The act of being a member of a gang is not punishable (only a qualification), whereas membership in a criminal organization is punishable. The court pointed out that it was the prerogative of the legislature to expand the definitional scope of organizations.[48] The legislature addressed the topic and introduced the implementing bill in 2017.[49] The reform also introduced different maximum sentences for different types of participation (distinguishing between founding members, supporting members, advertisers and recruiters).

6.1.5 Assessment

The aforementioned examples of implementation demonstrate that the German legislature does not apply a standard strategy, although a red line has become visible – German law adjusts to European legislation principally only in minor aspects (e.g., regarding a definition or a catalogue offence) but does not take European rules as a model law or model offence. The legislature tries to keep existing structures in the criminal code intact, and even if new offences need to be implemented, attempts are made to create a new offence in line with the German structure. To this extent, the approach attempts to maintain a coherent structure of criminal law. Other reasons for this approach are constitutional concerns that the vaguer and more general wording of

---

44 *See* '1. Strafrechtsänderungsgesetz' of 30 August 1995, BGBl. I 739.
45 On other reforms *see* Thomas Fischer, *Strafgesetzbuch*, Beck, 65th ed., 2018, § 129 para. 1.
46 'Gesetz zur Änderung des Strafgesetzbuches – Umsetzung des Rahmenbeschlusses 2008/841/JI des Rates vom 24. Oktober 2008 zur Bekämpfung der organisierten Kriminalität' of 17 July 2017, BGBl. I 2440.
47 BGHSt 54, 216; Christoph Safferling, *Internationales Strafrecht*, Springer, 2011, p. 468.
48 BGHSt 54, 216; Burkhard Jähnke and Edward Schramm, *Europäisches Strafrecht*, De Gruyter, 2017, pp. 197-198.
49 *See* BT-Drs. 18/11275. *See also* Mark A. Zöller, 'Strafrechtliche Verfolgung von Terrorismus und politischem Extremismus unter dem Einfluss des Rechts der Europäischen Union' (2017) KriPoZ 30-34.

European legislation might not be compatible with the principles of certainty or guilt, which require a very precise definition of the act.

6.2   Crimes Against the Financial Interest of the EU

6.2.1   General Development

The protection of the financial interests of the EU has played a vital role in the process of Europeanization of German criminal law not only by adjusting German law to European standards but also by triggering a vigorous debate on the creation of general European criminal law standards.[50]

In regard to the protection of the financial interests of the EU, the German legislature has so far (for the latest development see infra 6.3) refrained from creating a separate criminal code for EU-related offences but has integrated the European aspects into the German Criminal Code (StGB). Many aspects are already covered by traditional offences under German law (such as fraud, s 263 StGB; embezzlement and abuse of trust, s 266 StGB and money laundering, s 261 StGB). These offences do not explicitly include the EU's financial interests as protected interests but are generally open to such (judicial) interpretation. Other offences do in fact specifically mention European interests: subsidy fraud under s 264 sub-s 7 sentences 1 no. 2 StGB includes benefits from public funds under the law of the European Communities as protected subsidies, and tax evasion under s 370 sub-s 6 Fiscal Code explicitly protects import/export taxes and duties on goods administered by another EU Member State.

Corruption offences are important for the protection of public funds and the integrity of public institutions (see also infra 6.3.2.c). The pertinent statutes under German criminal law are as follows: ss 331, 332, 333, 334, 335, 335a, 336, 337 StGB criminalize the classic acts of bribery in connection with public (European) officials and civil servants; ss 299, 300 StGB cover bribery in the private economic sector; ss 108b, e StGB criminalize bribing voters and delegates; Article 2 s 2 IntBestG[51] covers the bribery of foreign parliamentarians. S 298 StGB criminalizes restricting competition through agreements in the context of public bids. There are additional special provisions.[52]

So far, Germany has fully supported the creation of (legal) instruments and institutions such as OLAF, Europol or Eurojust entrusted to fight crimes against the financial interests of the EU and supports and encourages the close cooperation of all

---

50   *See* Marc Engelhart, *op. cit.* at § 6 paras 43-44; Gerhard Dannecker and Jens Bülte, 'Die Entwicklung des Wirtschaftsstrafrechts unter dem Einfluss des Europarechts', in Heinz-Bernd Wabnitz and Thomas Janovsky (eds.), *Handbuch des Wirtschafts- und Steuerstrafrechts*, Beck, 4th ed., 2014, ch 2.
51   'Gesetz zur Bekämpfung internationaler Bestechung' of 10 September 1998, BGBl. II 2327.
52   S 119 sub-s 1 BetrVG; s 405 sub-s 3 nos. 6, 7 AktG; s 152 sub-s 1 no. 1, 2 GenG; s 23 sub-s 1 SchuldVG.

German authorities with these institutions. The German federal structure does not make it easy to put this into practice; depending on the subject matter, the responsibility may lie with a large number of different state or federal authorities. Let's take the topic of EU subsidies or funding relevant for EU funds – there are more than 100 Public Prosecutor's Offices responsible for the prosecution of subsidy fraud (fraudulent obtaining of subsidies) under s 264 StGB in accordance with general criminal procedural law. In certain cases, the main customs offices (*Hauptzollämter*) or the customs investigation offices (*Zollfahndungsämter*) are responsible for the investigations.[53] In case of a trial at the provincial court, the commercial crime chamber (*Wirtschaftsstrafkammer am Landgericht*) may be responsible for the court proceedings pursuant to s 74c sub-s 1 no. 5 German Judicature Act.[54] For the effective prosecution of subsidy fraud, the prosecuting criminal authorities rely on the assistance provided by the offices dealing with subsidy procedures. Thus, S 6 SubVG requires the courts and authorities of the federal government, federal states and municipal authorities of the public administration to notify the prosecution authorities of suspected subsidy fraud.[55] Therefore, a substantial number of authorities are involved in the protection of the financial interests of the EU, in the sense that each acting authority has to keep in mind when and how to cooperate with the European institutions. Initiatives such as those launched by the Federal Ministry for Economic Affairs and Energy in developing guidelines and a compliance strategy for subsidies (implementing the State Aid Modernisation (SAM) initiative of the European Commission)[56] help to provide information and standardize procedures.[57]

In the past decades, cooperation with other Member States in order to fight crimes against the financial interests of the EU as well as transnational crime has constantly intensified, particularly regarding police and criminal justice cooperation. The Prüm Convention regime, Europol and (still) ICPO-Interpol provide the context for the exchange of important information and for coordination. In addition, numerous bi-/multilateral Police Agreements between Germany and its neighbouring states enable cross-border police measures such as surveillance and controlled supplies and joint police operations (in particular joint patrols, mutual exchange of information and cross-border personnel support).[58] Joint centres such as those in Kehl (with France),

---

53 Gerhard Dannecker and Jens Bülte (above n) ch 2 para. 316.
54 Gerichtsverfassungsgesetz (GVG).
55 Uwe Hellmann, '§ 264', in Urs Kindhäuser, Ulfrid Neumann and H.-U. Paeffgen (eds.), *Strafgesetzbuch*, Nomos, 5th ed., 2017, para. 183.
56 *See* http://ec.europa.eu/competition/state_aid/modernisation/index_en.html [as of 15 November 2018].
57 *See* https://www.bmwi.de/Redaktion/DE/Artikel/Europa/beihilfenkontrollpolitik.html [as of 15 November 2018].
58 *See* the Overview of Relevant Acts of the Ministry of the Interior: BMI, Referat ÖSI4, Übersicht bilateraler Polizei- (und Zoll)verträge, Stand: 29. Mai 2017, https://www.bmi.bund.de/SharedDocs/downloads/DE/veroeffentlichungen/themen/sicherheit/uebersicht-polizeiabkommen.pdf?__blob=publicationFile&v=2 [as of 15 November 2018].

Luxembourg (with Luxembourg, Belgium and France), Padborg (with Denmark), Swiecko (with Poland) or Petrovice and Schwandorf (with the Czech Republic) provide and ensure the necessary infrastructure.

6.2.2   EPPO

For years, Germany has also backed the project of the European Public Prosecutor's Office (EPPO), despite some criticism on individual points. Germany supported the establishment of the EPPO by participating in enhanced cooperation pursuant to Article 86 sub-s 1 TFEU. In July 2017, the German ministers voted to submit the draft regulation to the European Parliament.[59] The final regulation was welcomed by the German government,[60] the federal parliament[61] and the majority of the legal community.[62]

Criticism of Council Regulation (EU) 2017/1939 addressed several more general issues on how to approach the subject matter and various aspects in detail.[63] Some of the issues are the following: the regulation fails to explicitly regulate the use of evidence and especially the extent of an exclusionary rule (fruit of the poisonous tree doctrine).[64] Article 37 Regulation (EU) 2017/1939 is not very precise in that it only states that evidence may not be refused merely based on the fact that it was gathered in another Member State. If Article 5(3) Regulation (EU) 2017/1939 is applied, the question of admissibility of evidence is left to national law. Yet, the preamble (paragraph 80) reiterates Article 37 Regulation (EU) 2017/1939 by adding that evidence should be allowed provided the fairness of the procedure and the rights of the suspect under the Charter are respected. Does this create a different standard of review in such procedures if the evidence is brought by the EPPO (compared to other evidence collected abroad)? Or does this mean that national systems are still free to apply their own (often long-established) rules? Many questions remain for the judiciary to decide.

---

59   Council Decision 11324/17 (3356) of 17 July 2017, 23.
60   Speech by the Minister of Justice, Heiko Maas, 25 October 2017, https://www.bundesregierung.de/breg-de/aktuelles/kampf-der-wirtschaftskriminalitaet-466706 [as of 15 November 2018].
61   BT-Drs. no. 18/1658, 3.
62   *See* for details Martin Böse, 'Die Europäische Staatsanwaltschaft "als" nationale Strafverfolgungsbehörde?' (2017) JZ, 82; Dorothea Magnus, 'Die endgültige EU-Verordnung zur Europäischen Staatsanwaltschaft' (2018) HRRS, 155; Peter Schneiderhan, 'Das Ende des nationalen Anklagemonopols naht' (2017) DRiZ 360.
63   *See* (besides the aforementioned literature) also Kai Ambos, *Internationales Strafrecht*, Beck, 5th ed., 2018, d§ 13 para. 24 for further references. On the principle of mutual recognition also Christoph Safferling, *op. cit.* at § 12 Rn. 40.
64   Dorothea Magnus, *op. cit.* at 145-146.

The aspect of admissibility of evidence is an illustration of the more comprehensive criticism on the lack of a European Code of Procedure in the concept of the EPPO.[65] Although the regulation provides some basic rules, much is left to the national systems and, therefore, to varying standards in criminal procedures. This is not problematic as such; however, as the area of criminal procedure has not been harmonized much, the differences (and, therefore, potential conflicts) are greater than in other areas of the law.

The issue of judicial control exemplifies the lack of a European Code of Procedure. Judicial control over the EPPO is transferred to the national courts (following national rules) rather than to an EU court. It remains to be seen whether national courts will be in a position to effectively control a supranational institution, as it will be difficult for the national court to review all enforcement and investigative measures, particularly the legality of the evidence that may cover the several Member States.[66] Any 'help' from the EU judiciary is likely to be limited because Article 42 states that the CJEU supervises only the interpretation and compliance with the regulation (and not the vast amount of applicable national rules).

Germany is particularly concerned about an effective guarantee of the 'Richtervorbehalt', the requirement of a court order in case of measures seriously interfering with the individual rights of the accused, but also of witnesses and other persons affected by investigations. Article 30 Regulation (EU) 2017/1939 regulates the EPPO's investigation measures and allows under Article 30(3) a higher threshold for investigative measures subject to certain restrictions in national law. Still, the regulation allows different standards to exist, and therefore, especially in cases where national systems do not require a court decision, the danger of very different levels of protection of individual rights and an inconsistent legal approach within the EU is real.[67] Although consideration no. 66 Regulation (EU) 2017/1939 makes express reference to the principle of legality, the regulation does not provide possibilities for sanctions when the principle of legality is violated (e.g., through the obstruction of criminal justice). Thus it remains to be seen how courts will attempt to guarantee the accused a sufficient level of protection.

The lack of a more comprehensive approach can also be seen in with regard to the protection of suspects in general. Article 41(3) Regulation (EU) 2017/1939 provides only that suspects, accused persons and all parties to the EPPO procedure enjoy all the procedural rights accorded to them by applicable national law. However, as the due process standards for the accused in the national legal systems still vary considerably, the treatment of persons accused (in cases where the same accusation applies) may

---

65 *See, e.g.,* the Joint Statement of the *German Federal Bar Association* (BRAK) and *German Bar Association* (DAV) on the EPPO: Bundesrechtsanwaltskammer und Deutscher Anwaltverein, Stellungnahme Nr. 13/2015 bzw. Stellungnahme Nr. 19/2015 (April 2015), Gemeinsame Stellungnahme zum Vorschlag der Europäischen Kommission für eine Verordnung des Rates über die Errichtung der Europäischen Staatsanwaltschaft, 2.

66 Dorothea Magnus, *op. cit.* at 154.

67 *Ibid.,* 145.

differ substantially because of nationally varying procedural rights. There is also the problem of a lack of further rules for the accused and for the defence (or for legal aid). For example, there is still no counterpart to public institutions such as a 'Eurodefensor' or European Public Defender, a request some scholars have voiced for a long time.[68] And indeed, the lopsided approach raises the question of whether there is not too much emphasis on a strict criminal law enforcement policy that puts civil rights in second place.

Other criticism addresses further details, e.g., concerning instructions. Article 13(2) Regulation (EU) 2017/1939 includes the European Delegated Prosecutor's duty to comply with the EPPO's instructions. Yet, the regulation fails to provide a detailed right to the EPPO to give instructions (as in 147 German Judicature Act[69]) to the European Delegated Prosecutors.[70] Furthermore, the distribution of tasks within the office might disguise the responsibilities of individual participants.[71]

6.2.3   VAT Fraud

Fighting fraud and especially VAT fraud has been a constant topic on the agenda of the German lawmaker and the German authorities in recent years.[72] Several measures were taken in the recent past to improve federal-state cooperation and nationwide information exchange. Because the German states are responsible for the collection and control of VAT (see Article 108 of the Basic Law), a successful fight against VAT fraud requires the effective coordination and control of the authorities involved. The Federal Central Tax Office (*Bundeszentralamt für Steuern* – BZSt) founded in 2006, plays a vital part in this. For example, it assists in the cross-border coordination of audit measures (VAT special audits and tax investigations), which is particularly effective in reducing the number of loopholes when persons move from one state to another with a corresponding transition to a different tax office. In 2016, the lawmaker created a sound legal basis for cross-border retrieval and use of data among the German states to

---

68   Bernd Schünemann, 'Grundzüge eines Alternativ-Entwurfs zur europäischen Strafverfolgung' (2004) 116 ZStW 376; Joachim Vogel, 'Licht und Schatten im Alternativ-Entwurf Europäische Strafverfolgung' (2004) 116 ZStW 400, 414. For the suggestion of a 'Eurodefensor' *see* Bernd Schünemann, 'Mindestnormen oder sektorales Europastrafrecht?' in Bernd Schünemann (ed.), *Alternativentwurf Europäische Strafverfolgung*, Heymann, 2004, p. 75 (*see* especially arts 111-174a).

69   Gerichtsverfassungsgesetz (GVG).

70   Dorothea Magnus, *op. cit.* at 151.

71   *See* the statement by the German Association of Judges: *Deutscher Richterbund* 'Stellungnahme # 8/17 zum Vorschlag für eine Verordnung zur Errichtung einer Europäischen Staatsanwaltschaft' of 3 February 2017, 6.

72   *See* the monthly reports of the German Federal Ministry of Finance of 21 July 2014 ('Bekämpfung des Umsatzsteuerbetrugs'; https://www.bundesfinanzministerium.de/Content/DE/Monatsberichte/2014/07/Inhalte/Kapitel-3-Analysen/3-2-bekaempfung-umsatzsteuerbetrug.html) and of 22 October 2018 ('Bekämpfung des Umsatzsteuerbetrugs'; https://www.bundesfinanzministerium.de/Monatsberichte/2018/10/Inhalte/Kapitel-3-Analysen/3-3-Bekaempfung-des-Umsatzsteuerbetrugs.html).

prevent, investigate and prosecute tax reductions.[73] The aim is to reduce implementation deficits in the taxation procedure.

The BZSt has also been assigned crucial tasks in the fight against national and international VAT fraud. In 2014, a nationwide database was established at the BZSt. This database records all national VAT fraud cases, evaluates them and creates risk profiles.[74] It can be accessed online by all VAT-related staff in the German states. In addition, nationwide online access was provided to basic data on companies registered in Germany for tax purposes.[75] Also, the national and international mutual support between the German Federal Central Tax Office and other administrative agencies was strengthened by the exchange of information in the areas of value-added tax and income tax in recent years. Cooperation between the tax authorities and the customs administration has also intensified. By coordinating information exchange and hence case management, the role of the BZSt in international cases is particularly crucial (comparable to the Federal Police office).

In the last decade, the automation in administrative networking and tax/case assessment has increased. The introduction of the electronic balance sheet a decade ago was one of the first steps in this direction. Electronic systems are also used for the detection of tax-relevant facts with respect to sales tax evasion, etc., for example, to identify tax-relevant activities of entrepreneurs on sales platforms on the Internet.

In order to stay current with technical developments, the German government proposed in September 2018 new legislation to prevent VAT fraud on the Internet ('Law on the prevention of sales tax losses on trade-in goods on the Internet and amending further tax regulations').[76] It aims at tackling VAT fraud when trading goods in electronic marketplaces. Operators of electronic marketplaces must record certain seller-related data for review by the tax authorities and, under certain conditions, may become liable even if no sales tax has been paid for deliveries via their marketplace.

---

73 *See* s 88b Fiscal Code introduced by 'Gesetz zur Modernisierung des Besteuerungsverfahrens' of 18 July 2016, BGBl. I S. 1679.

74 So-called 'Datenbank ZAUBER', Zentrale Datenbank zur Speicherung und Auswertung von Umsatzsteuer-Betrugsfällen und Entwicklung von Risikoprofilen (Central database for the storage and evaluation of VAT fraud cases and development of risk profiles).

75 There are several databases for the storage of VAT-relevant information. *See* the brief overviews in PStR 2018, 139 and BT-Drs. 18/568.

76 BT-Drs. 19/4455.

6.3 THE IMPLEMENTATION OF DIRECTIVE (EU) 2017/1371

6.3.1 Overview

Unlike the project of the European public prosecutor, the reform of the substantive law on the protection of the financial interests of the EU drew less attention. The statements by the Federal Council of Lawyers are quite illustrative of this debate in that they commented extensively on the EPPO[77] (as did the scientific community),[78] and much less so on the PIF Directive,[79] even though this is the only somewhat extensive statement on the directive at all.

There was some uneasiness on the part of the German government concerning the scope of the directive. It was considered to be too far-reaching, especially when taking into account the rather vague wording of the provisions and the application of the directive to VAT issues.[80] As the German criticism was not reflected in the final draft of the directive, the German government voted in the Council (along with five other Member States) against the directive.[81]

So far, the legislature has not implemented the directive.[82] On 11 October 2018, the Federal Ministry of Justice and Consumer Protection published the first draft for the implementation of the directive.[83] The draft proposes to implement the directive by amending the existing provisions on subsidy fraud and corruption and by introducing a new 'Law on Strengthening the Protection of the Financial Interests of the EU'.[84] This new law will comprise two new offences for the protection against fraud affecting the Union's financial interests and a special provision on corruption.

---

77 See the Joint Statement of the *German Federal Bar Association* (BRAK) and *German Bar Association* (DAV): Bundesrechtsanwaltskammer und Deutscher Anwaltverein, Stellungnahme Nr. 22/2013 bzw. Stellungnahme Nr. 48/2013 (October 2013), Gemeinsame Stellungnahme zum Vorschlag der Europäischen Kommission für eine Verordnung des Rates über die Errichtung der Europäischen Staatsanwaltschaft. *See also* the Joint Statement of the German Federal Bar Association (BRAK) and German Bar Association (DAV) on the EPPO (above n 62) 1 *et seq.*

78 See *supra* n 63 and n 64.

79 Bundesrechtsanwaltskammer (BRAK), Stellungnahme Nr. 36/2017 (November 2017), Umsetzung der Richtlinie (EU) 2017/1371 des Europäischen Parlaments und des Rates vom 5. Juli 2017 über die strafrechtliche Bekämpfung von gegen die finanziellen Interessen der Union gerichtetem Betrug.

80 BRAK (above n 77), 3.

81 Besides Germany Cyprus, Hungary, Ireland, Malta and Poland were against the Directive, *see* Council Doc. 5478/17 of 1 February 2017, 2.

82 As of mid-November 2018.

83 Referentenentwurf des Bundesministeriums der Justiz und für Verbraucherschutz, Entwurf eines Gesetzes zur Umsetzung der Richtlinie (EU) 2017/1371 des Europäischen Parlaments und des Rates vom 5. Juli 2017 über die strafrechtliche Bekämpfung von gegen die finanziellen Interessen der Union gerichtetem Betrug, 11 October 2018 (available on the Ministry website: https://www.bmjv.de/).

84 'Gesetz zur Stärkung des Schutzes der finanziellen Interessen der Europäischen Union (EU-Finanzschutzstärkungsgesetz – EUFinSchStG)', *see* Referentenentwurf (n 83), p. 3.

6.3.2 The Requirements of the Directive in Detail

6.3.2.1 Article 3 (fraud affecting the Union's financial interests)

Germany had adjusted its legislation on fraud affecting the EU's financial interests in 1998 by changing s 264 StGB (subsidy fraud) in order to implement Article 1 paragraph 1 of the 1995 PIF Convention.[85] Apart from that, the EU fraud offence is secured by several other offences such as fraud (s 263 StGB), embezzlement and abuse of trust (s 266 StGB), restricting competition through agreements in the context of public bids (s 298 StGB) and tax evasion (s. 370 AO), each also in connection with s 13 StGB (liability for omission). These provisions typically also cover the new distinction in Article 3 Directive (EU) 2017/1371 between procurement-related and non-procurement-related expenditures. The commission confirmed in 2004 that Germany had met all the PIF Convention requirements regarding revenues.[86] There was some criticism as to the implementation with regard to expenditures[87] because the definition of the German [offence of] 'Betrug' requires elements such as deception, mistake, disposal of property or intent of unjust enrichment (Täuschung, Irrtum, Vermögensverfügung, Bereicherungsabsicht) not explicitly provided for by the convention.[88] Yet, to the extent that at least the basic features of these elements are inherent in a 'fraud concept', this legislation can be considered in compliance with the approach of the directive (especially in view of a lack of a more detailed European concept of fraudulent behaviour).

And s 264 StGB (subsidy fraud) as a special form of fraud does not have the same features as s 263 StGB so the criticism does not apply in this regard. Also, by requiring specific intent ('to make an unlawful gain'), the directive itself recognizes in Article 3 s 2 letters a that some limitations might apply. The creation of a general offence without a detailed concept of fraud would be in conflict with the principles of guilt and proportionality and raise questions of constitutionality under German law.

As the PIF Directive now distinguishes more clearly between procurement-related and non-procurement-related expenditures and specifically addresses revenue aspects,[89] German legislation does not fully cover the constellations of Article 3 Directive (EU) 2017/1371 (regarding attempt see infra 6.3.2.e).[90] This applies to expenditures

---

85 Gesetz zu dem Übereinkommen vom 26. Juli 1995 über den Schutz der finanziellen Interessen der Europäischen Gemeinschaften (EG-Finanzschutzgesetz – EGFinSchG), BGBl. 1998 II, p. 2322; for the draft and explanations see BT-Drs. 13/10425, 11 et seq.

86 COM(2004) 709 final of 25 October 2004, 5. Revenues are now covered by Art. 3 para. 1, para. 2 c and d of the Directive (EU) 2017/1371.

87 Now covered by Art. 3 para. 1, para. 2 a and b of the Directive (EU) 2017/1371.

88 COM(2004) 709 final of 25 October 2004, 4.

89 See Lukas Staffler, 'Schutz der finanziellen Interessen der Union mittels Strafrecht' (2018) ZfRV, 52 (57).

90 See Referentenentwurf (n 83), 6-12. But see Bundesrechtsanwaltskammer (BRAK), Stellungnahme Nr. 36/2017 (November 2017), Umsetzung der Richtlinie (EU) 2017/1371 des Europäischen Parlaments und des Rates vom 5. Juli 2017 über die strafrechtliche Bekämpfung von gegen die finanziellen Interessen der Union gerichtetem Betrug, 5, that does not see any need for legislative action.

according to Article 3 s 2 sub-s b letter iii that are not subsidies and therefore not covered by s 264 StGB. The Ministry draft, therefore, proposes to introduce a separate offence for the misapplication of European Union benefits (s 1 of the proposed 'Law on Strengthening the Protection of the Financial Interests of the EU'):[91]

> § 1 Misapplication of European Union benefits
> Anyone who damages the assets of the European Union by using benefits granted by public resources of the European Union, the use of which is restricted by law or contract, contrary to this restriction on use, intending to obtain an unlawful financial advantage to himself or a third party, is punished with imprisonment up to five years or a fine. Sentence 1 does not apply to subsidies within the meaning of s 264 sub-s 8 no. 2 of the Criminal Code.[92]

The other aspect not completely covered by present law is the unlawful reduction of revenues as the PIF Directive covers several different kinds of revenues in Article 3 s 2 sub-s c (and d regarding VAT fraud). Hence the Ministry draft proposes to introduce a separate offence for the unlawful reduction of European Union revenue (s 1 of the proposed 'Law on Strengthening the Protection of the Financial Interests of the EU'):[93]

> § 2 Unlawful reductions of European Union revenue
> Liable to imprisonment not exceeding five years or a fine is whoever unlawfully reduces the revenue of the European Union by causing or maintaining an error by:
> 1.   Providing inaccurate or incomplete information to a body responsible for the management of revenue of the European Union, or

---

91   *See* Referentenentwurf (n 83), 3, 9-10.
92   Translation by the author. Original in German: "§ 1 Missbräuchliche Verwendung von Leistungen der Europäischen Union: Wer in der Absicht, sich oder einem Dritten einen rechtswidrigen Vermögensvorteil zu verschaffen, dem Vermögen der Europäischen Union dadurch einen Nachteil zufügt, dass er ihm aus öffentlichen Mitteln der Europäischen Union gewährte Leistungen, deren Verwendung durch Rechtsvorschrift oder Vertrag beschränkt ist, entgegen dieser Verwendungsbeschränkung verwendet, wird mit Freiheitsstrafe bis zu fünf Jahren oder mit Geldstrafe bestraft. Satz 1 gilt nicht für Subventionen im Sinne des § 264 Absatz 8 Nummer 2 des Strafgesetzbuches."
93   *See* Referentenentwurf (n 83), 3, 10-11.

2. Ignoring, for the purposes of the management of revenue of the European Union, any activities that are unlawful.[94]

Thus, the German approach keeps the general framework of its fraud offences intact and amends the provisions specifically by additional legislation.

6.3.2.2   Article 4 section 1 (money laundering)

The catalogue of predicate offences for money laundering in s 261 subs 1 sentence 2 StGB fails to be clear in covering all the required offences relating to acts contrary to the financial interests of the EU, which the commission pointed out before.[95] This is why it needs to be supplemented by a new number adding offences with special reference to harm done contrary to the financial interests of the European Union.[96] Yet, as the necessary scope of criminalization is not entirely clear and as the Fifth Money Laundering Directive still has to be implemented by the end of 2020, the Ministry draft refrains from reforming the German money laundering offence.[97]

6.3.2.3   Article 4 section 2 (passive/active corruption)

German criminal law has an elaborate system of addressing corruption.[98] Ss 331-335 StGB covers both active and passive bribery of public officials. Since the end of 2015, not only German public officials but also European and foreign public officials as well as other officials of international organizations have been covered.[99] In addition, s 299 StGB prohibits both active and passive bribery in the private sector involving employees or agents of a company as recipients of an undue advantage in competitive situations both in Germany and abroad. Since 2016, the specific offences of ss 299a and 299b StGB have covered active and passive bribery in the health sector.[100]

---

94 Translation by the author. Original in German: "§ 2 Rechtswidrige Verminderung von Einnahmen der Europäischen Union: Mit Freiheitsstrafe bis zu fünf Jahren oder mit Geldstrafe wird bestraft, wer die Einnahmen der Europäischen Union dadurch rechtswidrig vermindert, dass er einen Irrtum erregt oder unterhält, indem er
  1. einer für die Verwaltung von Einnahmen der Europäischen Union zuständigen Stelle über einnahmeerhebliche Tatsachen unrichtige oder unvollständige Angaben macht oder
  2. eine für die Verwaltung von Einnahmen der Europäischen Union zuständige Stellepflichtwidrig über einnahmeerhebliche Tatsachen in Unkenntnis lässt."
95 COM(2008) 77 final of 14 February 2008, 3.
96 *See also* Bundesrechtsanwaltskammer (BRAK), Stellungnahme Nr. 36/2017 (November 2017), Umsetzung der Richtlinie (EU) 2017/1371 des Europäischen Parlaments und des Rates vom 5. Juli 2017 über die strafrechtliche Bekämpfung von gegen die finanziellen Interessen der Union gerichtetem Betrug, 8 with a proposal for legislative implementation.
97 *See* Referentenentwurf (n 83), 17.
98 *See* Till Zimmermann, 'Das Unrecht der Korruption' (Nomos 2018) 551.
99 'Gesetz zur Bekämpfung der Korruption' of 20 November 2015, BGBl. I 2025. S 11 sub-s 1 no 2a StGB defines the European Official ('Europäischer Amtsträger') that covers Art. 4 s 4 of the Directive, *see* Referentenentwurf (n 83), 18-19.
100 'Gesetz zur Bekämpfung von Korruption im Gesundheitswesen' of 30 May 2016, BGBl. 2016 I 1254.

The corruption offences (s 332 and s 334 StGB) are in almost complete compliance with the requirements of Article 4 s 3 Directive (EU) 2017/1371. Yet, as the commission has criticized,[101] ss 332, 334 StGB fails to be clear in covering bribery for licit deeds, as the offences require the violation of official duties (beyond merely accepting the bribe etc.).[102] A bribe for licit deeds frequently falls under s 266 StGB (embezzlement and abuse of trust) as there is at least an endangerment of EU funds and to this extent meets the Article 4 s 2 Directive (EU) 2017/1371 requirement that the relevant behaviour shall damage or is likely to damage the Union's financial interests.[103] But s 266 StGB neither reflects the typical corrupt practice[104] nor does it provide for an extension to foreign nationals, which means that the normal rules apply and the act must take place in Germany or must be committed by a German national. Thus it appears that the StGB does not cover all the scenarios provided for by the directive. It seems more advisable to create a specific EU corruption offence that does not include the violation of official duties requirement.[105] The draft by the Ministry takes the middle way by creating a specific provision (s 3 of the proposed 'Law on Strengthening the Protection of the Financial Interests of the EU') stating that damaging or endangering assets of the EU is equivalent to the violation of official duties.[106]

6.3.2.4   Article 4 section 3 (misappropriation)

Subsidy fraud (s 264 sub-s 1 no. 2 StGB), as well as the offence of embezzlement and abuse of trust (s 266 sub-s 1 StGB), already comply with the requirements of Article 4 s 3. There is no need for further implementation.[107]

6.3.2.5   Article 5 (Incitement, aiding and abetting, and attempt)

There is no need for further implementation. Incitement and aiding and abetting are already punishable under German law as elements of participation in a criminal offence, independent of the nature of the offence (ss 26, 27 StGB).

This also applies to the attempt of the relevant offences, with one exception. Offences are either punishable because they qualify as 'Verbrechen'[108] (see s 23 sub-s 1 StGB criminalizing the attempt of all 'Verbrechen') or because the offences specifically provide so (attempted fraud is punishable under s 263 sub-s 2 StGB; attempted tax evasion is punishable under s 370 sub-s 2 AO).

---

101 COM(2008) 77 final of 14 February 2008, 3.
102 See, e.g. Thomas Fischer, op. cit. at § 332 paras 7-10.
103 So the position of the BRAK (above n) 7.
104 See Till Zimmermann, op. cit. at 553.
105 See also COM(2012) 363 final of 11 July 2012, 9.
106 See Referentenentwurf (n 83), 4, 11-12, 18.
107 See Referentenentwurf (n 83), 18.
108 These are crimes with a minimum sentence of one year of imprisonment (s 12 sub-s 1 StGB).

There are three offences covering behaviour addressed by the directive where the attempt is not explicitly punished: ss 264, 266 and 298 StGB. However, in the cases of ss 264 and 298 StGB, an extension is not necessary as the description of the relevant conduct covers a wide range of preparatory acts.[109] One exception is s 264 sub-s 2 no. 2 StGB (covering Article 3 s 2 sub-s a no. 3 of the directive) where the description of the conduct does not cover the attempt. Therefore the draft for implementing the directive provides an amendment of s 264 StGB explicitly criminalizing the attempt in this case.[110]

In the case of s 266 StGB (embezzlement and abuse of trust) the damage requirement is interpreted to cover serious risks to assets ('*schadensgleiche Vermögensgefährdung*'), which means that attempts to cause damage are to some extent covered so that a separate legal provision appears to be dispensable (and is generally declined for reasons of overcriminalization[111]).

6.3.2.6 Article 6 (liability of legal persons), Article 9 (sanctions with regard to legal persons)

German criminal law does not provide for corporate criminal liability in the criminal code. Yet, legal entities can be subject to criminal confiscation orders under s 73b StGB (e.g., if the company obtained some gain from a bribe committed by its staff).

Also, the Administrative Sanction Act (OWiG) provides for a corporate fine in case of violations of criminal and administrative offences provisions by senior staff of the legal entity (s 30 OWiG). In these cases, fines up to €10 million for intentional crimes or up to €5 million in negligence cases are possible. As the illegal gain can be added to this, confiscation can be part of an overall fine. In the Volkswagen (VW) emission case, VW was fined €1 billion, consisting of €5 million for the punitive part and €995 million for the confiscation part. Apart from monetary sanctions, the Administrative Sanction Act under s 29a OWiG specifies only confiscation (in case no fine is ordered under s 30 OWiG) and thus fails to make use of the other options provided in Article 9. Yet, German law allows for such other options (such as winding up the company) under administrative law for which a conviction is a relevant factor in determining taking up action.[112]

In view of these legal options, there is no need for further implementation.[113] The criticism voiced by the commission in 2008 to the effect that German practice raises questions about effective, proportionate and dissuasive sanctions in corporate

---

109 *See also* BRAK (n 77) 6.

110 *See also* Referentenentwurf (n 83), 12, 19-20.

111 *See* BT-Drs. 13/9064, 20; Thomas Fischer, *op. cit.* at, § 266 para. 187; Kristian Kühl, 'Versuchsstrafbarkeit und Versuchsbeginn', in Michael Hettinger and Thomas Hillenkamp (eds.), 'Festschrift für Wilfried Küper zum 70. Geburtstag', Müller, 2007, pp. 289, 293.

112 For details *see e.g.* Marc Engelhart, *Sanktionierung von Unternehmen und Compliance*, Duncker & Humblot, 2nd ed., 2012, pp. 423-429.

113 *See also* Referentenentwurf (n 83), 20.

misconduct cases[114] is no longer an issue as corporate entities today (due to changing prosecution patterns) are regularly the focus of prosecution services in such cases. Nonetheless, the introduction of a system of corporate criminal liability is the subject of vigorous debate, not only to be in line with the majority of (European) countries but also to modernize the system and increase the pressure on companies. Scholars,[115] as well as the state of Northrhine-Westfalia,[116] have proposed respective bills in the last decade. The federal government is currently working on a proposal that includes increased sanctions and new rules for internal investigations, cooperation with authorities and compliance. The reform is likely to be presented in 2019.

6.3.2.7 Article 7 (penalties for natural persons), Article 8 (aggravating circumstance)

All relevant German offences (e.g., ss 263, 264, 266, 298 StGB, s 370 AO) provide the criminal sanction of imprisonment. The maximum sentence for the aforementioned offences is a minimum of five years' imprisonment, in serious cases even more. As this approach fulfils the requirement under Article 7 s 3 of a maximum sentence of at least four years, there is no need for further implementation.

Regarding the obligation in Article 8 to consider the commission of a crime in a criminal organization as an aggravating circumstance, the approach of German law is to criminalize participation in a criminal organization as a separate offence (s 129 StGB, see supra I.4.),[117] resulting in a higher total sentence than the sentence for the single fraud offence etc.

6.3.2.8 Article 10 (freezing and confiscation)

Germany reformed its provisions on freezing and confiscation in 2017,[118] *inter alia* to implement Directive 2014/42/EU.[119] The new rules in the General Part (ss 73-76b StGB) provide conviction-based as well as (in some cases) non-conviction-based confiscation for all criminal offences.[120] The rules of procedure were adjusted as well (see especially ss 111b-111q StPO) to facilitate the freezing and the arrest of assets for the purpose of confiscation. These rules facilitate the confiscation of assets used for or as proceeds of

---

114 COM(2008) 77 final of 14 February 2008, 4.

115 *See* Marc Engelhart, *op. cit.* at pp. 720-729; Martin Henssler et al., 'Kölner Entwurf eines Verbandssanktionengesetzes' (2017).

116 Land Nordrhein-Westfalen, 'Entwurf eines Gesetzes zur Einführung der strafrechtlichen Verantwortlichkeit von Unternehmen und sonstigen Verbänden' (2013), https://www.landtag.nrw.de/portal/WWW/dokument enarchiv/Dokument/MMI16-127.pdf [as of 15 November 2018]. *See* Frank Zieschang, 'Das Verbandsstraf-gesetzbuch' (2014) GA 91; Julien Schlagowski, 'Originäre Verbandsstrafbarkeit' (Nomos 2018).

117 Referentenentwurf (n 83), 21.

118 'Gesetz zur Reform der strafrechtlichen Vermögensabschöpfung' of 13 March 2017, BGBl. I 872.

119 *See* BGBl. I 872 of 21 March 2017.

120 *See* Frank Saliger, 'Grundfragen der Vermögensabschöpfung' (2017) 129 ZStW 995; Frank Meyer, 'Abschöpfung von Vermögen unklarer Herkunft' (2017) NZWiSt 246.

crime, e.g., for purposes of victim restitution. These new rules comply with Article 10 Directive (EU) 2017/1371 as well as with the requirements of Directive 2014/42/EU.

6.3.2.9   Article 11 (jurisdiction)

German jurisdiction extends to all acts committed in whole or in part on German territory (ss 3, 9 StGB). As Germany follows the 'effects principle', even acts committed outside the EU are covered, provided the effect of the act occurs in Germany or – for offences protecting EU interests – in the EU.[121] As such, the territoriality principle is broadly construed.

S 7 StGB supplements the principle of territoriality by providing jurisdiction for acts committed by German nationals abroad provided the act is equally criminalized abroad or in the absence of criminal jurisdiction abroad, thus implementing the active personality principle. The preconditions for jurisdiction in Article 11 s 1 Directive (EU) 2017/1371 do not apply in these cases so that authorizations by the victim or a foreign authority are not required. In addition, following the protective principle, s 5 no. 15, 16 StGB specifically provides jurisdiction for certain corruption cases irrespective of any criminalization of the offence abroad.[122] Following the principle of universal jurisdiction, s 6 no. 8 StGB provides general jurisdiction over subsidy fraud (s 264 StGB). Thus, German law complies with Article 11 Directive (EU) 2017/1371.

6.3.2.10   Article 12 (limitation periods)

The limitation period in Germany begins as soon as the offence is completed (s 78a StGB). According to s 78 StGB, the limitation period for offences with a maximum sentence of five years' imprisonment is five years. As the maximum sentence for the offences in this context is at least five years' imprisonment (see supra under g.), the limitation period is also at least five years. The period may be suspended (s 78b StGB) or interrupted (s 78c StGB), e.g., by the interrogation of the accused. This is more than the minimum period of three years the directive requires.

After a final decision on the sentence, the limitation period for enforcing the sentence is ten years for a term of imprisonment of more than one but not more than five years, and five years for a term of imprisonment not exceeding one year and for criminal fines of more than 30 daily units (s 79 StGB). Therefore, convictions in crimes against the financial interests of the EU are routinely subject to a limitation period of at least five years, which is more than the minimum three-year period required by the directive. Thus, the German rules fully comply with Article 12 Directive (EU) 2017/1371.

---

121 For details *see* Referentenentwurf (n 83), 21-23.

122 According to Art. 11 s 2 Directive (EU) 2017/1371 the commission has to be notified that German criminal law extends to acts abroad if Union officials have their office in Germany, *see* Referentenentwurf (n 83), 23.

6.4   CONCLUSION

The strategy for implementing the rules on the protection of the financial interests of the EU follows the line of implementing other strategies – the lawmaker attempts to preserve as many of the existing structures of the criminal code as possible by merely amending or changing offences. Additional rules and, in rare cases, a separate legislative act is created only if this is not possible. Against this background, setting up a new 'Law on Strengthening the Protection of the Financial Interests of the EU' would be a big step towards the development of separate protection under criminal law for this area of the law.

The development also shows that even though Germany supports the aim of the directive and the harmonization of substantive criminal law, implementing European legislation is by no way an easy task. Too strong is the fear that the rights of persons affected at present are not sufficiently guaranteed and should, therefore, be more comprehensively protected. Also, European rules frequently do not meet the degree of precision necessary to meet the requirements of Article 103 II GG, which means that the national legislature must further define and clarify the rules. This, in turn, keeps raising the issue of whether the European rules have actually been fully implemented. Thus, the development of a European concept of criminal law continues to be indispensable not only regarding general aspects such as participation or attempt but also regarding specific offences such as fraud or corruption. The creation of a European rationale for criminalizing certain acts would very much foster a stringent national implementation strategy and an adjustment (which in many cases also means modernization) of national concepts.

7   SELECTED CASE STUDIES: THE CASE STUDY OF GREECE

Helen Xanthaki & Efstatios Vournos

7.1   THE IMPLEMENTATION OF EU CRIMINAL LAW IN THE HELLENIC REPUBLIC

The transposition of EU legislation has gone through distinct phases in the Hellenic legal history. The start of EU criminal law presented an obvious challenge for the Hellenic legislators. Until then, all of the criminal law was neatly placed within the Criminal Code. The notion that criminal law could live outside of the Code was simply outside the ethos of Hellenic legal theory and practice. International agreements within the sphere of criminal law existed but were implemented, to the extent dictated by domestic diplomacy, mainly by means of one-provision laws declaring that the annexed agreement or treaty was now part of the Hellenic legal order. These laws remained foreign to the judiciary that applied them with varied intensity and mainly when prompted by the litigant parties.

When EU criminal law started to form, Hellenic legislators attempted to transpose it in the way they knew best – via the incorporation of the new EU instruments to the Criminal Code, to which the EU reacted negatively. From the Commission's point of view, this was not enough. EU criminal law instruments tend to include non-criminal provisions, which requires incorporation of the criminal offence in the national legal order plus the introduction of administrative implementing measures guaranteeing the effectiveness of the substantive criminal provision. The classic example of this negative reaction was the Commission's poisonous response to the introduction of money laundering as a criminal offence in the Hellenic Criminal Code. Although the Hellenic legislator was transposing in a manner that was familiar to the judiciary, and this probably much more effective for the use of the provision by the judges, the Commission was right to point out that the administrative part of the first Money Laundering Directive was completely ignored by the Hellenic legislator. Was this a conscious effort of the Hellenic Parliament and government to ignore EU criminal law and simply introduce a toothless criminal provision? The answer to the Commission's question seems to be no, quite the opposite. The introduction of the offence in the Criminal Code was indeed an attempt to transpose fully and effectively. The accuracy of this perception is strengthened by the lack of any prosecutions and convictions for money laundering in the first few years of the introduction of the special criminal law on money laundering; the law was left on the shelf by our judges who were accustomed to searching through the Criminal Code for criminal offences.

The maturity of EU criminal law, which brings us to the current state of affairs, sees a maturity in the legislative approaches for its transposition in the Hellenic Republic. The tale of implementation of the new PIF Directive shows great effort to actually implement, not just transpose, the new instrument in the Hellenic legal order via a holistic review of the current state of EU criminal law provisions within the variety of national legal texts found both in the Criminal Code and in the now-familiar special criminal laws.

It would be unfair to present the Hellenic implementation of the new PIF as anything other than a concerted effort to implement it fully and effectively, but it would be untrue to state that there is no room for further improvement.

7.2   Generic Frictions Arising from the Transposition of EU Law on the Financial Interests of the EU

7.2.1   Prescription (Limitation) Periods

The Hellenic Penal Code sets generic offence prescription periods starting from the date when the offence was committed. For felonies, the prescription period is 20 years, where the law foresees life imprisonment and 15 years in any other case of felony. Misdemeanours carry a five-year prescription period. For summary offences, the prescription period is one year after the date when the offence was committed. Prescription periods are suspended for the duration of the criminal trial until a final conviction for a maximum period of five years for felonies, three years for misdemeanours and one year for minor offences. Prescription periods stop on the date of a final conviction.

The Code also introduces sanction prescription periods. Sanctions are prescribed after 30 years for life sentences, after 20 years for imprisonment between five and 20 years, after 10 years from imprisonment and financial penalties and after two years for lower penalties of temporary imprisonment or fines.

The periods of prescription, or limitation, imposed in the Hellenic legal order are far stricter than those introduced by EU criminal law. The friction between the two legal orders caused considerable concern after the CJEU's judgment in *Taricco I* (C-105/14), where the court applied the principle of supremacy of EU law to give precedence to the periods of limitation introduced by EU law against those imposed by Italian law. Thankfully, the matter is resolved by *Taricco II* (C-42/17, MAS and MB), which revokes the obligation of Italian courts to ignore the Italian statutes of limitation in VAT cases as a means of giving full effect to Article 325 TFEU. And so, although the discrepancies between periods of limitation caused implementation issues in the Hellenic

Republic, *Taricco II* finally opened the way for the unhindered application of the generic prescription periods of the Criminal Code.

The relative uncertainty of this position, in view of the fluid nature of CJEU judgments, is further resolved by Directive (EU) 2017/1371, the new PIF Directive, which in Article 12 offers further leeway to Member States in introducing their own prescription periods as part of the 'necessary measures' to be taken for the effective investigation and conviction of the offences that affect the financial interests of the European Union. Even in Article 12(3), prescription periods range within those prescribed in the Hellenic Code.

The combination of *Taricco II* and the new PIF Directive pacify concerns on prescription periods and smoothen the coexistence of the generic provisions of the Hellenic Criminal Code and EU criminal law.

7.2.2   *Monitoring: A Multitude of National Agencies*

Unfortunately, as is frequently the case with the transposition of EU law into the Hellenic legal order, the real issues arise in the administrative processes foreseen within the actual application of the legal provisions in practice.

A classic example of this position is the multitude of national agencies assigned with the task of monitoring the implementation of the protection of the EU's financial interests. Article 6 of Law 4557/2018, which implements the new PIF Directive and brings together all relevant EU criminal laws, splits this monitoring into no less than nine umbrellas. Eleven types of banking, insurance and exchange service providers are subject to the supervision of the Bank of Greece. Seven types of mainly investment service providers fall under the supervision of the Hellenic Capital Market Commission. Pawn agencies fall under the supervisory umbrella of the Department of Financial Police and Combat of Cybercrime. The Commission for Accounting Standards and Controls monitors chartered accountancy service providers. The Independent Authority for Public Income monitors non-chartered accountancy service providers, estate agents and traders and auctioneers of valuable goods (there is no definition of 'valuable' in the law). The Commission for Gaming Supervision and Control monitors casinos and gaming agencies. The Ministry of Justice, Transparency and Human Rights monitors notaries and lawyers. The Ministry of Finance and Development and the respective authority of financing monitor the rest.

Just reading through the many categories and subcategories of persons falling under the supervision of these nine different bodies creates an impression of chaos. One wonders who can classify these entities with an adequate degree of certainty to allow them to become aware of the respective monitoring body. The confusion for both the monitoring and the monitored is inevitable.

Perhaps what is even more worrying is that monitoring of obligations related to the protection of the financial interests of the EU is both a vague (general and dynamic) but also a highly specialized task. Where this is piled on top of the already heavy menu of prioritized tasks for each of these entities, monitoring cannot be undertaken with due diligence or due expertise. The excess fragmentation of monitoring duties among so many generic bodies is a recipe for incomplete and erroneous implementation of the monitoring obligations, as the bodies' main tasks take precedence over this secondary monitoring task, which is expected to be completed by non-specialized staff.

To make matters worse, the law's attempt to rationalize this chaos seems rather futile. Indeed the law introduces a Central Supervisory Body, which is the Ministry of Finance. There are two issues of concern here. One, the Ministry of Finance has limited access to and less competence over the Ministry of Justice and the Police. Although one can see how the Ministry of Finance could extend its supervision to the rest of the monitoring bodies that undertake finance-related tasks in the widest sense, its competence over another Ministry or indeed the Police is simply not existent. Being under the delusion that this provision can work effectively in practice, is simply naïve or indeed ill-informed. Two, the relevant department of the Ministry of Finance, mentioned in the same article of the law, is the General Directorate of Financial Policy. But, by definition, this General Directorate deals with strategy and policy, not investigation, monitoring or implementation. The lack of authority and expertise is evident. It is therefore highly doubtful that, even for these bodies that accept to be subject to the monitoring of the Ministry of Finance, monitoring can be effective in practice. A *male fide* commentator could argue that the assignment of that Directorate to the monitoring duty is either a bad attempt to quickly drop the bombshell on someone within the Ministry or, worse, a devious attempt to undermine monitoring altogether.

Further concerns arise from the express continuation of the Strategy Commission for the combat of money laundering, the financing of terrorism and the financing of weapons of mass destruction, which was established at the same Ministry of Finance under Article 9 of Law 3691/2008 (A'166). Similarly, the Mediation Service of the private sector for the combat of money laundering and the financing of terrorism, which was established by Article 11 of Law 3691/2008, remains in action. Moreover, the now renamed Authority for the Combat of Money Laundering established under Article 7 of Law 3691/2008 remains in action. The parallel existence of no less than four authorities tasked with the same monitoring duties on similar areas can only accentuate the complexity of the monitoring bodies, which in turn may lead either to a duplication of efforts or, worse, to ineffective monitoring from agents who expects another body to pick up the issue.

7.2.3   *Investigations and Prosecutions: The Chasm after Monitoring*

The assignment of monitoring tasks to the Ministry of Finance as a supervisory body creates concerns about the effectiveness of investigations and prosecutions. This arises from the independence of the judiciary, as introduced by Article 85 of the Constitution and its supplementing provisions on the functioning of the courts and the prosecution service. In the application of the principle of the independent judiciary, none of the monitoring bodies introduced by the law can in any way influence the decision of the prosecution service to initiate an investigation or to prosecute a monitored person for breaches of criminal law, Hellenic and EU. Therefore, supervision ends with the Ministry of Finance.

Even worse, at the immediately lower level of monitoring, none of the monitoring bodies has any competence to influence the investigation or prosecution of suspected offences against the financial interests of the EU or other EU law offences. And so, monitoring ends with a possible report that a breach of the person's obligation to protect the financial interests of the EU seems to have been committed. This is a rather ineffective end to an already flawed monitoring process.

Thus, the question is what happens after monitoring has been completed, and breaches have come to light. The law foresees an obligation of the monitoring bodies to alert the Ministry of Finance and Development as the supervisory body. The law also foresees the obligation of the prosecuting authorities to alert the monitoring bodies of any prosecutions and convictions, so that administrative penalties can also be imposed. However, there is no obligation of the monitoring bodies to report any alleged breaches to the prosecution authorities, thus allowing the burden of reports to the prosecuting authorities to an inexperienced supervisory body whose main task is policy formulation.

7.2.4   *Ne Bis In Idem*

However, the lack of communication from the monitoring bodies to the prosecuting authorities works both ways. The prosecuting authorities have no obligation to inform the monitoring bodies of any investigations or even prosecutions that have already begun. This may prove detrimental for any investigations on the administrative side. The monitoring bodies have limited powers of investigation and limited access to documentation and information, compared to prosecutors. An administrative investigation would greatly benefit from information from the prosecution. Unfortunately, this exchange of information is not encouraged or secured by the law.

Although the administrative and criminal investigation processes may remain independent, they do have an effect on each other under the *ne bis in idem* principle. The latter forms part of the Hellenic legal system under Article 5(2)(b) of the Code of

Administrative Procedure, as interpreted and applied by the Council of State judgment 951/2018. However, the principle has its limitations. One, the judgment confirms that the principle applies in the case of an administrative trial after a convicting criminal trial. It is not yet tested whether the principle applies to administrative investigations of the monitoring type undertaken by the monitoring bodies for the protection of the financial interests of the EU. It remains to be seen whether a monitoring body is obliged to comply with a criminal judgment. Two, the criminal judgment must be final. Criminal trials in Greece may take a number of years, especially if an appeal and then a cassation is sought by the accused. It is quite possible that the administrative process will be completed before the judgment of the criminal courts become final. Moreover, an application to revoke the administrative penalty imposed by the monitoring body after the end of the final criminal trial will be successful in the case of non-conviction. As this may come years after the imposition of the administrative trial, the administrative process seems to be further undermined by the law. This position is strengthened by Article 94(1) of the Constitution, as interpreted by the judgment. Although judgment on administrative matters is assigned exclusively to the administrative judge, and consequently *ne bis in idem* do not apply to the imposition of taxes and levies, penalties or fines for administrative breaches are indeed covered by the principle. This position reflects the content of Article 4(1) of the 7th Protocol of the ECHR and Articles 50 and 52 (1) of the Charter of Fundamental Rights. Nevertheless, it clearly allows the criminal judge to have the final say on any penalty imposed by the monitoring bodies, whose competence and power is undermined even further by virtue of an independent process to which the monitoring bodies have no access. In addition, it poses serious obstacles to the implementation of Article 7(1) of the PIF Directive.

7.3 FRICTIONS FROM THE TRANSPOSITION OF THE NEW PIF

7.3.1 *The Drafting Instructions: What Changes in EU Criminal Law?*

The task of the Hellenic legislators lies with the complete and full implementation of the new PIF Directive. The question is what changes in EU criminal law warrant a change in national legislation. Let us briefly focus on the points of reform, as a means of enabling the assessment of their implementation by the Hellenic legislator.

The Council adopted the PIF Directive on 25 April 2017, and the European Parliament approved the Council position in its first reading on 22 June 2017:
- The directive defines the Union's financial interests quite broadly including infringements of the common VAT systems, to the extent that they are linked to more than two Member States and the losses incurred exceed €10,000. This introduces a broad substantive basis for the offence and a rather light threshold of

losses, probably in anticipation of the notorious difficulties in pinpointing the exact
level of losses in these cases.

– The directive provides a number of definitions of offences including active and
passive fraud, corruption, the misappropriation of funds, money laundering and
related offences. The breadth of the offences is extensive, and it is questionable
whether the list is exclusive or not.

– The minimum penalties introduced are now complemented by generous periods of
limitation, allowing for sufficient time to investigate, prosecute and prepare for trial.
This is crucial in cases such as the ones envisaged by the directive, where the volume
of the activity in question is large, and the trans-border nature of the relevant actions
and therefore the evidence for the prosecution is probable.

– The directive requires that the Member States, the Commission, the criminal law
agencies, and the Court of Auditors cooperate. The directive must be read in
conjunction with EU criminal law provisions on the European Public Prosecutor,
whose decentralized office is awarded exclusive jurisdiction for investigating,
prosecuting and bringing to judgment crimes against the EU budget.

The directive is quite ambitious. The breadth of offences, the depth of involvement within
national legal orders and the new EPP are balanced by the high threshold of losses
required. Let us now assess how the Hellenic legislator copes with this bombardment of
reforms.

7.3.2   *A Hellenic Holistic Review of EU Criminal Law and the Resulting Consolidation*

At the time of writing, the Hellenic legislator is in the process of passing the
implementing law through Parliament. It is draft law titled 'Preventing and Suppressing
Money Laundering and Terrorist Financing (Transposition of Directive 2015/849/EU)
and other provisions' has been presented in Parliament. In its Introductory Report, the
law is described in some detail. The draft law transposes Regulation (EC) 2015/849 of
20 May 2015 on the prevention of the use of the financial system for the purpose of
money laundering and terrorist financing, amending Regulation (EU) 648/2012 and
repealing Directive 2005/60/EC and the Council, as well as Commission Directive
2006/70/EC, as transposed in the Hellenic Republic by means of Law 3691/2008, now
under repeal.

The draft law consolidates the currently fragmented provisions on the protection of
the financial interests of the EU. In doing so, it amends the current regime on the
following points. First, it introduces two new offences, namely intermediary trade and
bribery, and bribery in the private sector. Second, it enhances the competence of the

Ministry of Justice, as the Central Coordinating Body, for the implementation of the provisions of the enacted law, and sets up a Strategy Committee to tackle money laundering and terrorist financing. Third, it amends, in compliance with the new PIF Directive, the grounds for liability, the measures for due diligence and the cases in which the persons liable apply simplified or increased custody of the client. Fourth, it adds leasing companies, third-party asset factoring companies, portfolio investment companies, investment intermediation companies and e-money institutions to the list of third parties that may apply due diligence measures. Fifth, it introduces the obligation to abstain from engaging in transactions that bodies within the field of application of the draft law know or suspect to be linked to products of criminal activity or to the financing of terrorism. Sixth, the draft law introduces a requirement to keep a record of earnings per player payouts for persons providing gambling services. Seventh, the draft law prohibits the processing of personal data for purposes that fall outside those in the draft law.

In addition to the constituting elements of offences, the draft law amends the financial penalties imposed on convicted persons. First, the minimum amount of fines imposed is abolished. The maximum fine foreseen by the draft law is €1,000,000 evidenced as twice the benefit of the offender, and €5,000,000 if the person liable is a credit institution or a financial institution (currently these fines range from €10,000 to €1,000). Second, a fine of up to €1,000,000 may be imposed on the members of the board of directors, the executive director and other employees of the legal person or entity (currently ranging from €5,000 to €50,000). Third, the draft law waives the penalty of imprisonment and replaces it with a fine for cases of breach of the prohibition of data disclosure to affected customers or third parties.

In addition to these substantive law reforms, the draft law enhances the administrative framework for the actual implementation of the new substantive provisions. First, the draft law introduces a Special Registry of Real Beneficiaries from corporate and other entities based in the Hellenic Republic. Failure to comply with this register will result in administrative sanctions such as the suspension of tax evasion of the legal entities and the imposition by the competent authority of a fine of €10,000 with a deadline for their compliance. In the event of non-compliance or recurrence, the fine is doubled. This fine is revenue from the state budget. Second, the draft law introduces a Registry of Real Beneficiaries, to the General Secretariat of Information Systems (GSIS), which is linked electronically to the VAT number of each legal entity. This Registry may be linked to the General Commercial Registry (GEMI) of the Ministry of Economy and Development, in which the legal entity is registered, as well as to the Securities Depositories. Third, the draft law introduces a Special Register of Trustholders Received by Trustees. Fourth, it enhances the framework for cooperation on the exchange of confidential data between the authority and other competent authorities. Fifth, it introduces an independent audit service operated by the persons responsible for verifying the implementation of the internal policies, controls and procedures applied by them. And sixth, it introduces an internal procedure for complaints by employees on violations of provisions of the law.

The administrative framework for implementation of the new PIF Directive is detailed in the second part of the draft law. This establishes a new Anti-Money Laundering Authority within the Ministry of Finance and organizes the processes for international cooperation as introduced in the new PIF Directive. The draft law appoints the Third Unit for the Control of Asset Statements as a participant to European and international organizations, and contact point for exchanges of information between relevant authorities. In fact, for exchange of information with other entities in the Hellenic Republic or abroad, the units use communication channels that fully safeguard the protection of personal data and, where feasible, state-of-the-art technologies that allow anonymous data comparison. For the fulfilment of their purpose, the units may conclude memoranda of understanding with authorities and bodies of the public and private sector in the country or abroad.

The scope and overview of the draft law are clearly expressed in its Reasoned Report. The law regulating the combat of money laundering and the financing of terrorism has been amended numerous times. For example, via Law 3691/2008, which replaced Law 2331/1995 and transposed Directives 2005/60/EC and 2006/70/EC and a list of Recommendations of Financial Action Task Force (FATF); its amending Law 3875/2010, which also ratified the UN Palermo Convention against International Organised Crime; Law 3932/2011, which established the current authority against money laundering and financing of terrorism as an independent authority; and Law 4478/2017, which ratified the 2005 Warsaw Recommendation of the Council of Europe on the same topic. The further lighter amendment includes Article 116 of Law 4099/2012, Article 68 of Law 4174/2013 and Article 182 of Law 4389/2016. The picture painted by the high number of these amendments is that of a fragmented regime, with multiple legislative texts applying in parallel, all combining ratifications with transposition and implementing measures of national eccentricities.

This evidences the need for a holistic review of the existing provisions. The opportunity to do so was ideal, as the new PIF Directive also takes into account revised FATF Recommendations and the new models from the UN, the Council of Europe and the Egmont Group. The new EU framework is balanced against the Union's regulatory agenda, which promotes a reduction of bureaucracy and administrative burdens in new legislative proposals. The Hellenic legislator expresses great trust in the new directive as a measure of rationalization of a legislative labyrinth, and of effective regulation without financial or administrative costs. This enthusiasm is evident in the verbatim copying of most provisions by the draft law, and the mirroring of the provisions of the directive within the draft law, as showcased in the transposition correlation table annexed here. Unfortunately, as is common in the country, the deadline for the implementation of the directive passed on 22 June 2017, a date acknowledged by the draft law that has yet to come into effect, let alone be implemented.

7.3.3 Implementation of the New PIF

However, it is worth stating that the approach of consolidation chosen by the Hellenic legislator for the transposition of the PIF Directive is a rather bold one. This is a unique opportunity for the jurisdiction to assess what worked in the past and what needed to be revised. And to promote the interrelation between the great number of legislative texts in the field of the protection of the financial interests of the Union, which in the past led to a user-unfriendly, dysfunctional framework with clashing provisions, duplication of regulation and gaps. This approach, as described in the Reasoned Opinion of the draft law, is evidenced by the addition of mechanisms that are not foreseen in the directive but enhance the achievement of its objectives, such as the Strategic Commission and the Agency of Mediation of the Private Sector.

However, one wonders whether the opportunity was indeed seized to its fullest. There are a number of new committees overseeing a great number of aspects of transactions, all contributing to the objectives of the directive. But these committees lack concrete tasks, and perhaps, more importantly, lack coordination. One wonders if there is indeed need for so many new bodies, all looking after fragmented aspects of a puzzle, which is notoriously difficult to put together anyway. How these numerous fragmented bodies will combine their fragmented data with working with the already fragmented EU agencies and bodies from other Member States remains to be seen. But, in view of the plague of fragmentation within the country and the equally destructive plague of fragmentation at the EU level, one wonders whether compartmentalization is indeed the approach needed for trans-border crimes.

An additional point of criticism lies with close adherence to the text of the directive within the draft law. One understands that it feels safer to stick with what the EU has decided to place in the directive. But surely provisions of the directive inviting Member States or Commissions to take the necessary measures to achieve the directive's aims cannot remain unaltered in the implementing of national measures. These are the places where these national measures will be introduced, listed and foreseen in a manner that is exhaustive, detailed and administratively supported. And the draft law fails to do that. What remains is a list of requests to national bodies to do whatever is necessary. But on the basis of which criteria? And in consultation with whom? Or will this remain yet another transposition without full implementation, as has been the case with laws of the Republic in the history of its EU membership?

In addition, the draft law misses the golden opportunity to insert the European Public Prosecutor's Office (EPPO) in the web of national criminal law. In reviewing the whole system of processes for the protection of the financial interests of the EU and the financing of terrorism, the Hellenic legislator has missed the unique chance to weave into it the forthcoming EPPO and its tasks. Although it would be premature to do this with immediate effect, a transitional provision to how the law will bring the EPPO into the national legal order would have worked well.

7.4   CONCLUSION

Timely, complete and effective implementation is a generically weak point in Hellenic legislation. This also applies to the transposition of EU legislation. EU criminal laws, with their inherent ineffectiveness,[1] struggle for timely, complete and effective implementation even further. The transposition pattern observed in the parliamentary process of transposition of EU criminal laws in the Hellenic Republic is as follows. The Hellenic Republic rushes to transpose EU criminal law directives. This usually takes places after the expiry of the transposition deadline. Implementing measures are taken, nonetheless. However, they tend to copy the provisions of the instruments in a manner that renders full implementation rather debatable.

Transposition of EU criminal laws takes place at the last possible minute before infringement proceedings begin. This prevents the drafters of the Hellenic Republic from the opportunity to fully comprehend the content of EU criminal law measures as supplementing existing EU criminal law; to compare them in-depth with the existing provisions of Hellenic legislation as interpreted and applied by the courts; to conclude what elements of the EU measure need to be added in Hellenic legislation; and to ensure the smooth incorporation of the new law to the legal order by identifying and curing, where needed, the effect of the new law on previous laws and provisions. Putting the administrative measures for a timely, complete and effective implementation after transposition is also missed.[2]

Instead, what one observes is a rushed transposition by a quick passing of a copy-pasted text. This has a detrimental effect on the effectiveness of the Hellenic transposing measure; this cannot be a good criminal law. In its concrete, rather than abstract, conceptual sense, effectiveness requires a legislative text that can (i) foresee the main projected outcomes and use them in the drafting and formulation process; (ii) state clearly its objectives and purpose; (iii) provide for necessary and appropriate means and enforcement measures; (iv) assess and evaluate real-life effectiveness in a consistent and

---

1   Helen Xanthaki, 'Improving the Quality of EU Legislation: Limits and Opportunities?', in Sasha Garben and Inge Govaere (eds.), *The Better Regulation Agenda: A Critical Assessment*, Hart, Oxford, 2018, pp. 28-47.

2   Helen Xanthaki, 'Good Criminal Laws and How to Draft Them', in C. D. Spinellis, N. Theodorakis, E. Billis, and G. Papadimitrakopoulos (eds.), *Europe in Crisis: Crime, Criminal Justice, and the Way Forward – Festschrift für Nestor Kourakis*, Ant. N. Sakkoulas, Athens, 2017, pp. 273-287, http://en.crime-in-crisis.com/.

timely manner.[3] Within this context, criminal regulation is the process of putting criminal policies into effect to the degree and extent intended by the government.[4] Criminal legislation, as one of the many regulatory tools available to the regulators,[5] is the means by which the production of the desired regulatory results is pursued. In the application of Stefanou's scheme on the policy, legislative and drafting processes, legislative quality is a partial but crucial contribution to regulatory quality.

There is no doubt that such legislative quality cannot be achieved by means of copy-pasting a generic – and consequently already ineffective for the purposes of national legal orders[6] – EU criminal law. And before being accused of purely academic analysis on this point, it is worth showcasing the issues in practice. One, the Hellenic transposing texts repeat verbatim the EU provisions on the obligation of national authorities to take all necessary measures to achieve the objectives of the EU text! But the provision is simply an invitation of the EU legislator to its Hellenic counterparts to identify these necessary measures and to list them in the transposing text. The generic EU provision has no place whatsoever in the national measure. Two, the Hellenic measures annexe to the law the correspondence table between the EU and national criminal provisions! But this is an internal affair between the Hellenic Republic and the Commission. It has no place in the Hellenic text. Even if one supported the view that it is included so that the user can read the EU and Hellenic text together, it fails to serve its purpose without an annexe of the EU text, to which the user is allegedly referred. Perhaps more importantly, what is the value of referring the user to provisions that are identical? Three, recent Hellenic transposing texts, including the new PIF Directive, attempt to holistically transpose a number of EU criminal laws that have remained on the shelves of the Parliament for a number of years. Although it is commendable to finally see Hellenic drafters taking the interrelation of different EU laws into account for the purposes of transposing them, the use of the copy-paste transposition method results in a mosaic of legal provisions that lack coherence and therefore effectiveness. Four, the selective treatment of older EU provision in the process of creating this omnibus Hellenic transposition laws leads to a partial transposition. For example, in the omnibus new

---

3   *See* M. Mousmouti, 'Operationalising Quality of Legislation Through the Effectiveness Test' (2012) 6 *Legisprudence* 191, 202; also, W. Voermans, 'Concern about the Quality of EU Legislation: What Kind of Problem, by What Kind of Standards?' (2009) 2 *Erasmus Law Review* 59, 223 and 225; and R. Baldwin and M. Cave, *Understanding Regulation: Theory, Strategy and Practice*, Oxford University Press, Oxford, 1999.

4   *See* National Audit Office, Department for Business, Innovations and Skills, 'Delivering regulatory reform', 10 February 2011, para. 1.

5   Tools for regulation vary from flexible forms of traditional regulation (such as performance-based and incentive approaches), to co-regulation and self-regulation schemes, incentive and market based instruments (such as tax breaks and tradable permits) and information approaches. *See* Better Regulation Task Force.

6   *See* Helen Xanthaki, 'Quality of Legislation: Focus on Smart EU and post-Smart Transposition' (2015) 2 *TPLeg* 329-342.

law transposing the new PIF Directive, there is no mention of the European Public Prosecutor, an issue that is completely ignored despite its express mention in the EU text.

To conclude this analysis, it would be fair to state that the transposition of EU criminal laws in the Hellenic Republic is far from perfect. The combination of a superficial approach to legislative drafting and the consequently unsurprising use of the copy-paste method of transposition results in ineffective national texts with prominent gaps and equally obvious frictions. This picture, which is not at all unique among the EU Member States, reflects a focus on formal transposition as opposed to effective implementation. It seems like the focus of the Hellenic legislator is to simply tick the boxes put forward by the Commission and waive any liability for non-compliance. There is, unfortunately, little focus on actual implementation for the purposes of yielding the regulatory results pursued by the EU by means of EU criminal laws.

It would be unfair to find fault with solely the national legislators. There is an element of fear of infringement proceedings in the use of the copy-paste method, which is often seen as safer than creative transposition. This perception seems to be finding fertile ground in the Commission's formalistic approach to post-legislative monitoring, which seems to be stopping at corresponding tables rather than conducting an in-depth analysis of the predicted regulatory results at the national level. An example of this is the stern opposition of the Commission to the Hellenic Republic's choice of the Criminal Code as the host of the first Money Laundering Directive, as opposed to a fully inclusive special criminal law. Here full correspondence was prioritized against effectiveness. The result was complete ignorance of the special criminal law by the Hellenic judges and prosecutors, resulting in a lack of prosecutions and convictions for money laundering over a period of a few years. The Commission failed to acknowledge that criminal lawyers would look at the Criminal Code for any offence at a time when special criminal laws were an unknown beast in the Hellenic criminal order.

If anything, this analysis demonstrates the need for a change in the transposition mentality both of the Hellenic legislator and of the EU monitoring agency, the Commission. A new focus on the effective implementation by both sides would ensure minimization of the current ineffectiveness in the transposition of the criminal laws for the protection of the financial interests of the EU both in the Hellenic Republic and beyond.

8   Selected Case Studies: The Case Study of Spain

Pablo Martín Rodríguez

8.1   Introduction: European Union Criminal Law and the Spanish Legal System

In Spain, as in any other Member State of the European Union (EU), the impact of the Area of Freedom, Security and Justice (AFSJ) on the domestic legal system has been ever-growing as successive AFSJ Programmes (Tampere, The Hague and Stockholm) have been established and implemented. No one would doubt its importance nowadays.

However, despite the outward unity of the AFSJ, its different components deserve quite specific analyses because of their very uneven legal connotations. This is particularly illustrated with regard to EU criminal law and EU judicial cooperation in criminal matters. The constitutional significance thereof demands careful and stringent scrutiny by judiciary and academia in terms of respect of fundamental rights and constitutional guarantees. Hence, the generally acknowledged conclusion is the extraordinary impact of this EU law on the Spanish legal system, even in the absence of a legislative volume of other EU policies such as the Internal Market or the Common Agricultural Policy. Hence too, one can see the hard criticisms often raised by legal literature.[1]

With regard to this branch of EU law, Spain has played, in my opinion, a somewhat paradoxical role – while offering robust political support to the development of this area, I do not believe that Spain has taken its implementing tasks diligently enough.[2]

---

1   *See* this evolution across the entire Spanish criminal legal system in F. Javier Álvarez García (dir), *La adecuación del Derecho penal español al ordenamiento de la Unión Europea,* Tirant lo blanch, Valencia, 2009 and José Luis de la Cuesta Arzamendi (dir), *Adaptación del Derecho Penal español a la política criminal de la Unión Europea,* Thomson Reuters, Cizur Menor, 2017. Concerning Spanish procedural law, *see* Fernando Jiménez Conde (dir), *Adaptación del Derecho procesal española a la normativa europea y a su interpretación por los tribunals,* Tirant lo blanch, Valencia, 2018.

2   Noelia Corral Maraver, 'La irracionalidad de la política criminal de la Unión Europea' (2016) 4 *InDret,* www.indret.com/es/derecho_penal/8/, accessed 31 January 2019.

8.1.1   A Positive Attitude Towards the Adoption of EU Criminal Law

The most salient trait is the welcoming attitude of Spanish authorities towards EU substantive and procedural criminal law. This positive attitude can be found not only within the executive but also in the Spanish judiciary.

From the beginning, the Spanish Government wholeheartedly supported cooperation in criminal matters since any advance was in Spain's national interest for a smoother, quicker international collaboration to fight terrorism. This has not changed since then. Spain has been an active Member State promoting the development of European judicial cooperation (e.g., the European Protection Order) as well as regarding approximation of substantive criminal laws. When negotiating in Brussels, the Spanish government has neither delayed the adoption of old, third pillar instruments (requiring unanimity within the Council) nor remained outside enhanced cooperation initiatives such as the European Public Prosecutor's Office (EPPO).[3] This participation has occurred even when these instruments might be manifestly strange or even contrary to the Spanish legal tradition.[4] The renowned *Melloni* case is probably the most conspicuous example. In this case, the government managed to trump, through European third pillar channels, a clear line of the case law of the *Tribunal Constitucional* (Spanish Constitutional Court) regarding fundamental rights.[5]

The Spanish Parliament shares this welcoming attitude towards the adoption of EU criminal law, either substantive or procedural. In fact, it has not opposed any single legislative proposal in these matters within the framework of the subsidiarity control procedure created by the Treaty of Lisbon.[6] Truly the central government exerts a

---

3   David Vilas Álvarez, 'The EPPO Implementation. A Perspective from Spain' (2018) 3 Eucrim 124.

4   Criminal liability of legal persons is frequently mentioned to illustrate the impact of EU law and the introduction of legal categories that do not easily fit (José Luis De la Cuesta Arzamendi, *Nuevas fronteras del Derecho Penal*, Ed. Olejnik, 2018, p. 93). Actually, 9 years later the legal characterization thereof is still controversial between the *Tribunal Supremo* and the *Fiscalía General del Estado* (State Prosecutor Office) (Alejandro Ayala González, 'Responsabilidad penal de las personas jurídicas: interpretaciones cruzadas en los más altos niveles' (2019) 1 *InDret*, www.indret.com/pdf/1437.pdf, accessed 31 January 2019).

5   See Aida Torres Pérez, 'Melloni in Three Acts: From Dialogue to Monologue' (2014) 10 *European Constitutional Law Review* 308; Leonard F. M. Besselink, 'The Parameters of Constitutional Conflict after *Melloni*' (2014) 39 *European Law Review* 531; Pablo Martín Rodríguez, 'Crónica de una muerte anunciada: Comentario a la Sentencia del Tribunal de Justicia (Gran Sala) de 26 de febrero de 2013, Stefano Melloni, C-399/11' (2013) 30 *Revista General de Derecho Europeo* 1.

6   Both procedural and substantive limbs of EU criminal law are usually understood by the Spanish legislature not only as compliant with subsidiarity but to be positive and opportune. *See, e.g.*, Report 13/2017 approving the use of a regulation instead of a directive for establishing the mutual recognition of freezing and confiscating orders and Report 25/2017 regarding the proposal for a directive on combating fraud and counterfeiting of non-cash means of payment. As to the protection of EU financial interests, see also the positive report concerning the 2013 EPPO proposal (Report 66/2013) or the more recent one regarding the amendment of the OLAF Regulation (Report 46/2018).

distinct influence in this parliamentary control procedure, but this does not obscure the general support that Spanish major political parties have awarded to this EU policy.[7]

Moreover, the judiciary in Spain has been quite favourably predisposed to apply this EU law to the full extent. Spanish ordinary courts have strongly assumed the principles of mutual trust and mutual recognition in a consistent way, as the praxis of the *Audiencia Nacional* (National High Court) proves when it comes to the execution of a European Arrest Warrant (EAW).[8] No preliminary reference has been made by Spanish judges in order to contest the validity of EU substantive criminal law either. Even the Spanish *Tribunal Constitucional*, whose position towards EU law is ambivalent, has shown a certain deference in this field overruling its caselaw in order to align it to the *Melloni* Judgment of the European Court of Justice or recognizing the direct effect of Article 7 of the Directive 2012/13/EU on the right to information in criminal proceedings pertaining to the Stockholm package.[9] By no means do we find in Spain any sort of judicial constitutional reservation or caveats with regard to EU criminal law such as those stated by the *Bundesverfassungsgericht* in the Lisbon Treaty Judgment.[10] Neither does the case law of the *Tribunal Supremo* (Spanish Supreme Court) seem to be wary vis-à-vis the incriminating mandates encapsulated in international or, in this case, European law.[11]

However, the continuance of this positive attitude cannot be taken for granted. We should wait to see whether the currently prevailing atmosphere questioning the principle of mutual trust in Europe[12] and particularly the refusal by German and Belgian judicial authorities to execute the EAWs issued by the *Tribunal Supremo* in the pending criminal proceedings against Catalan secessionist leaders might inaugurate a less cooperative

---

7   Pablo Martín Rodríguez, 'National Report. Spain', in Jenö Czuczai et al. (eds.), *Division of Competences and Regulatory Powers Between the EU and the Member States*. XXVII FIDE Congress, Wolters Kluwer, Budapest, 2016, pp. 707, 711-713.

8   Pablo Martín Rodríguez, 'The Area of Freedom, Security and Justice and the Information Society. Spanish Report', in Julia Laffranque (ed.), *The Area of Freedom, Security and Justice Including Information Society Issues* – XXV FIDE Congress, Tartu University Press, 2012, p. 575.

9   *See Tribunal Constitucional*, Ruling 26/2014, of 13 February 2014, ECLI:ES:TC:2014:26, paras. 5-6 and Judgment 13/2017, of 30 January 2017, ECLI:ES:TC:2017:13, paras. 5-7.

10   Kai Ambos, *Derecho Penal Europeo*, Thomson Reuters, Cizur Menor, 2017, pp. 364-367.

11   On the Spanish approach to the principle of legality in criminal matters, see *in extenso* the chapters of Enric Fossas Espadaler, Ignacio Villaverde Menéndez and Juan Antonio Lascuraín Sánchez in Mercedes Pérez Manzano and Juan Antonio Lascuraín Sánchez (dirs), *La tutela multinivel del principio de legalidad penal*, Marcial Pons, Madrid, 2016, pp. 29-148 (There is a 2018 English version of this book published in Springer).

12   *See* Case C-404/14 *Pál Aranyosi and Robert Căldăraru v. Generalstaatsanwaltschaft Bremen* [2016] EU:C:2016:198; Case C-220/18 PPU *Generalstaatsanwaltschaft (ML)* [2018] EU:C:2018:589; Case C-216/18 PPU *Minister for Justice and Equality v. LM* [2018] EU:C:2018:586. Scientific literature has contributed to this atmosphere prone to limit the principle of mutual trust, *see* Ermioni Xanthopoulou, 'Mutual Trust and Rights in EU Criminal and Asylum Law: Three Phases of Evolution and The Uncharted Territory Beyond Blind Trust' (2018) 55 *CML Rev* 489; Pablo Martín Rodríguez, 'Confianza mutua y derechos fundamentales en el Espacio de Libertad, Seguridad y Justicia', in Ana Salinas de Frías and Enrique Martínez Pérez (dirs), *La Unión Europea y la protección de los derechos fundamentales*, Tirant lo blanch, Valencia, 2018, p. 247.

attitude by the Spanish judiciary.[13] This possible after-effect would concur with a less welcoming political landscape because of the rise of extreme political parties in Spain.

Not even legal doctrine in Spain seems to be frontally opposed to EU criminal law, although it has evolved towards a greater criticism, perhaps partly provoked by the poor transposition carried out in Spain. Procedural law literature has not been so critical as criminal law scholars who proved a distinct German resonance, dating back to the Manifesto on European Criminal Policy.[14] Naturally, scholars have shown strong doubts regarding some EU legislative choices because of their imprisonment penalty bias, unreasonably pre-emptive approach or vague over-broadly worded terms,[15] but frontal opposition to EU criminal law or the rejection of conferred competences in this field is rare, if not totally absent.[16]

8.1.2   The Technically Poor Performance of EU Law Implementation

As stated, the positive attitude described above has not been accompanied by a diligent implementation of these norms into the Spanish legal system. So Spain is no exception to the defective transposition of third pillar acts common to most Member States. Unfortunately, nor has communitarization in this field meant a substantially better performance under the new rules set forth in the Treaty of Lisbon.

Procrastination is a first distinct trait. On-time transpositions, even including last-minute ones, are the exception and not the rule. For example, the implementation of most of the mutual recognition instruments that were adopted during The Hague Programme (i.e., before the entry into force of the Treaty of Lisbon in December 2009) was not accomplished till December 2014 when Act 23/2014 on the mutual recognition of

---

13   See two contrasting views in Daniel Sarmiento, 'The Strange (German) Case of Mr. Puigdemont's European Arrest Warrant', VerfBlog, 11 April 2018, https://dx.doi.org/10.17176/20180411-14113, accessed 1 November 2018 and Florentino G. Ruiz Yamuza, 'La doble incriminación en el sistema de la Euroorden o de la necesidad de una exégesis realista del principio de reconocimiento mutuo. Apuntes en relación con el asunto Puigdemont' (2018) 61 *Revista de Derecho Comunitario Europeo* 1059.

14   See the conspicuous Manifesto on European Criminal Policy, first published in (2009) Zeitschrift für Internationale Strafrechtsdogmatik, 697-747, signed by Prof. Adán Nieto Martín who is probably the Spanish reference in *European Criminal Law*.

15   For instance, with regard to organized crime, see Cristina Méndez Rodríguez, 'La lucha contra la delincuencia organizada: Comentario a la Decisión marco 2008/841' (2008) 18 *Revista General de Derecho Europeo* 1, 21 (www.iustel.com); Lucas J. Ruiz Díaz, 'Diez años de la adopción de la Decisión Marco 2008/841/JAI del Consejo relativa a la lucha contra la delincuencia organizada. Luces y sombras de un legado más que dudoso' (2018) 61 *Revista de Derecho Comunitario Europeo* 1091.

16   See Marta Muñoz de Morales Romero, *El legislador penal europeo: legitimidad y racionalidad*, Thomson Reuters, Cizur Menor, 2011 and Clara Mappeli Marchena, *El modelo penal de la Unión Europea*, Aranzadi, Cizur Menor, 2014.

judicial decisions within the European Union was enacted.[17] Act 23/2014 also transposed Directive 2011/99/EU on the European protection order *in extremis* but its amendment in order to introduce the European Investigation Order in criminal matters (EIO) was again overdue by more than a year.[18] Delayed transposition has also been frequent with regard to substantive criminal law, as the two major amendments of Organic Act 10/1995 on the Criminal Code show.[19] Once again, the adaptation of Spanish law to Directive (EU) 2017/541 on combating terrorism is already tardy. Better performance may only be found with regard to the Stockholm package strengthening the rights of individuals in criminal procedure or the rights of victims of crime.[20]

Although there is a lack of a clear uniform legal guidelines, the second characteristic of Spanish implementation is the trend to carry out literal transposition, often thoughtlessly or uncritically. So the implementing law sometimes uses the domestic legal concepts that match those of EU law and sometimes it does not (i.e., it uses EU law notions although they are strange to Spanish legal jargon). This is quite visible regarding mutual recognition instruments, and it creates unnecessary interpretive complications.[21]

However, the most disturbing consequence of this tendency to transpose EU law to the letter concerns EU criminal law because it amplifies the flaws already mentioned of excessive punishment and loosely defined felonies.[22] This is somehow incentivized by the Commission. In its assessment procedure and evaluation reports, the Commission has, in my opinion, wrongly reproduced the standard requiring literal transposition that is

---

17   Act 23/2014, of 20 November, on the mutual recognition of criminal judicial decisions within the European Union [BOE 2014/282, p. 95437], entered into force on 11 December, transposed up to nine old third pillar Council framework decisions.

18   Act 3/2018, of 11 June [BOE 2018/142, p. 60161].

19   Organic Act (also named 'institutional Act' in EU documents) 5/2010, of 22 June, amending Organic Act 10/1995, on the Criminal Code [BOE 2010/152, p. 54811] implemented two Directives and eight Council Framework Decisions. Organic Act 1/2015, of 30 March, amending Organic Act 10/1995, on the Criminal Code [BOE 2015/77, p. 27061] transposed six Directives and yet another Council Framework Decision. All transpositions were overdue except for five of them, which were done at the very last moment.

20   Valentina Faggiani, *Los derechos procesales en el espacio europeo de justicia penal. Técnicas de armonización*, Thomson Reuters, Cizur Menor, 2017.

21   Spanish procedural law literature has become more and more aware about the impact that piecemeal EU legislation may have on the integrity of domestic approach to judicial procedures and, therefore, criticisms are now more frequently raised (*e.g.*, Federico Adán Doménech, 'Deconstrucción del ordenamiento jurídico español').

22   For example, the 2008 framework decision on terrorism (Council Framework Decision 2008/919/JHA of 28 November 2008 amending Framework Decision 2002/475/JHA on combating terrorism, [2008] OJ L330/21) broadened the definition to an extent that Spanish criminal law already covered. However, an amendment was enacted in order to introduce a verb that was a synonym of one already there [Pablo Martín Rodríguez, 'The Area of Freedom, Security and Justice and the Information Society. Spanish Report', *op. cit.*]. Exactly the same conclusion can be argued with respect to the new terrorism directive (Directive (EU) 2017/541 of the European Parliament and of the Council of 15 March 2017 on combating terrorism [2017] L88/6) as legal doctrine has explained (Elena Núñez Castaño, 'Algunas consideraciones sobre la trasposición al Derecho penal español de la Directiva 2017/541/UE del Parlamento europeo y del Consejo, en materia de terrorismo: ¿una tarea necesaria?', in María Isabel González Cano (coord), *Integración Europea y Justicia Penal*, Tirant lo blanch, Valencia, 2018).

usually used in Internal Market matters. Nonetheless, in the criminal law field, this insistence on vague incriminations may certainly encroach upon the EU general principle of legality in criminal matters (*lex certa, lex stricta*).[23]

Moreover, scholars have rightly criticized that the Spanish legislature often uses EU law as an excuse for incriminating vaguer and further conduct or for setting longer penalties than required in EU law.[24]

8.2 THE PROTECTION OF EU'S FINANCIAL INTERESTS IN SPAIN

Spain as a Member State does not stand out, either positively or negatively, with regard to the protection of financial interests of the EU (PIF). Although sound doubts have been raised as to the accuracy of fraud calculations, particularly tax fraud, in Spain,[25] usual reports on EU fraud do not really single out Spain positively or negatively in any regard.[26] In order to understand how Spain protects the EU's financial interests by means of criminal law, two different aspects will be examined: the actual scope of criminalization, including two recently controversial topics in EU law – the statute of limitations and the respect of the *ne bis in idem* principle – and how the criminal justice system deals with these crimes.

8.2.1 The Scope of Criminalization: Compliance with the PIF Acquis

The introduction of criminal offences protecting Community financial interests dates back to 1995, especially after an entire new Criminal Code was enacted in Spain. This EU-inspired regulation did not only ease the application of the assimilation principle set

---

23   *See* Fernando G. Sánchez Lázaro, 'Evaluation and European Criminal Law: The Evaluation Model of the Commission', in Adán Nieto Martín and Marta Muñoz de Morales Romero (eds.), *Towards a Rational Legislative Evaluation in Criminal Law,* Springer International Publishing, Switzerland, 2016, pp. 201, 203-209.

24   Norberto de la Mata Barranco, 'La influencia del Derecho penal de la Unión Europea en el Derecho penal de sus Estados miembros', in José Luis de la Cuesta Arzamendi (dir), *Adaptación del Derecho Penal español a la política criminal de la Unión Europea,* Thomson Reuters, Cizur Menor, 2017, pp. 105, 131-132.

25   *See* Enrique Giménez-Reyna and Salvador Ruiz Gallud (coords), *El fraude fiscal en España,* Thomson Reuters, Cizur Menor, 2018, in particular chapters 13 ('Una valoración del sistema fiscal español desde la perspectiva del fraude', by José Manuel Domínguez Martínez) and 16 ('El fraude fiscal en el IVA', by Carlos Gómez Barrero), claiming that in Spain these calculations are even less reliable than in other MSs.

26   *See* European Commission, 29th Annual Report on the Protection of the EU's financial interests – Fight against fraud – 2017, COM(2018) 553 (Brussels, 3 September 2018) and the accompanying Commission Staff Working Paper, Follow-up on recommendations to the Commission report on the protection of the EU's financial interests – Fight against fraud – 2016, SWD(2018) 383 final.

out by the Court of Justice in the *Greek Maize* case but came way ahead of Spain's ratification of the conventional PIF *acquis* that occurred in 2000.[27]

This regulation has been modified several times since, particularly in 2010, 2012 and 2015,[28] but the main legislative choices remain the same, that is, the provision of specific criminal offences protecting EU's financial interests against fraud in respect of expenditure or revenue. The maintenance of this option and regulation seems reasonable since Spain has usually scored well in the Commission's assessments of compliance following Article 10 PIF Convention.

The 2004 Report already stated that Spain was completely compliant from the point of view of the definition of the criminal offences of expenditure and revenue-related fraud or the intentional preparation of false documents or statements. Only some doubts were suggested about corruption offences covering EU officials, the scope of confiscation rules or the effect of the Spanish reservation criminalizing money laundering only in serious cases.[29] The Second Report of 2008 appeared even more positive, and it only raised the topic of the liability of legal persons provided for in the (at the time still not in force) second protocol, whose introduction was then being considered in Spain.[30]

However, perhaps the situation is not so positive as these evaluations may suggest. Let us review the extant offences briefly:

(a) Article 305(3) Criminal Code lays down the basic fraud offence from the perspective of EU revenues.[31] It takes the definition of fraudulent conduct used in domestic revenue frauds, i.e., any action or omission defrauding the treasury of the European Union by means of avoiding the payment of any tax, withholding tax, instalment or payment on account or by unduly obtaining any refund, reimbursement

---

27 Spain notified the adoption of the whole PIF *package* (the 1995 Convention and its three Protocols) on 20 January 2000. Thus, the Convention, the first protocol and the ECJ protocol entered into force for Spain on 17 October 2002 [BOE 2003/180, p. 29301]. The second protocol to which Spain had formulated a reservation entered into force on 19 May 2009 [BOE 2009/286, p. 100506].

28 Modifications have related to (a) imposing larger penalties (pecuniary and imprisonment); (b) the admission of regularization; (c) a better concretization of civil liability and (d) the introduction of criminal liability of legal persons (Norberto de la Mata Barranco, 'Delitos contra la Hacienda Pública y la Seguridad Social', in *Derecho Penal Económico y de la Empresa*, Dykinson, Madrid, 2018, pp. 529, 531).

29 European Commission, Report on the Implementation by Member States of the Convention on the Protection of the European Communities' financial interests and its protocols, COM(2004) 709 final (Brussels 25 January 2004). *See also* the Annex embodying the corresponding Commission Staff Working Paper, SEC(2004) 1299 (Brussels, 25 October 2004) [hereinafter CSWP (2004)].

30 European Commission, Second Report on the Implementation by Member States of the Convention on the Protection of the European Communities' financial interests and its protocols, COM(2008) 77 final (Brussels 14 February 2008). *See* Table 'Overview of transposition' in the Second Report's Annex encapsulating the corresponding Commission Staff Working Paper, SEC(2008) 188 (Brussels, 14 February 2008) 71 [hereinafter CSWP (2008)].

31 Smuggling and illicit trade is regulated in the specific Organic Act 12/1995, of 12 December, repressing smuggling [BOE 1995/297, p. 35701]. Art. 2 of this Act provides for several offences depending on the conduct carried out and the kind of goods affected. It uses three different thresholds (€150,000, 50,000 and 15,000) and incriminates not only intentional conduct but also gross negligence.

or tax benefit. It also foresees the same penalty: a prison sentence between one and five years and a fine of up to six times the defrauded amount. With regard to sanctions, tax and EU fraud also end for the person responsible in losing the possibility of obtaining public grants, subsidies and aids or enjoying tax benefits or fiscal incentives during three to six years.

There is an aggravated offence of serious fraud in Article 305 bis, when any of these three circumstances are met: (1) the amount exceeds €600,000; (2) the fraud is committed within a criminal organization or criminal group or (3) some methods are used in order to hide or hinder identifying the taxpayer or determining the tax debt, such as using natural persons, legal persons or entities without legal personality as proxies, tax havens, business or trust instruments. This aggravated offence is punishable by between two and six years of imprisonment (the fine stands between two and six times the amount and the barring from subsidies or fiscal benefits or incentives runs from four to eight years). According to legal doctrine, this aggravated offence would apply to EU fraud as well.[32]

There are, however, some differences. In domestic tax fraud offences, the threshold is €120,000, but with regard to EU revenue, the €50,000 threshold of the PIF Convention applies.[33] On the other hand, with regards to VAT fraud, except where organized crime or the simulation of real economic activity is involved, the threshold amount ought to be determined per natural year.

Spanish courts apply this offence, for example, in relation to customs duties,[34] but they are sentencing based on the domestic tax offence in cases of VAT fraud (including carrousel type), thereby requiring an amount of €120,000 instead of €50,000.[35]

---

32   *See* Norberto de la Mata Barranco, 'Delitos contra la Hacienda Pública y la Seguridad Social', in *op. cit.* at p. 550.

33   The 2015 reform eliminated the category of '*faltas*' (misdemeanours) but assumed the existence of '*delitos leves*' (minor felonies). When the amount defrauded is between €4,000 and €50,000, the penalty to impose is either a prison sentence from three months to one year or a fine of up to three times the said amount.

34   *Audiencia Provincial de Valencia* (provincial criminal court), Ruling 464/2013 of 27 June, *Aranzadi* ARP 2013\1110, ECLI:ES:APV:2013:3035.

35   *See*, recently, *e.g. Audiencia Provincial de Barcelona*, Ruling 113/2018 of 11 February, *Aranzadi* ARP 2018 \534, ECLI:ES:APB:2018:3605; *Audiencia Nacional* (national high court), Ruling 6/2015, of 6 March, *Aranzadi* ARP 2015\244 and Ruling 8/2017 of 13 March, *Aranzadi* JUR 2017\61682, ECLI:ES: AN:2017:499; *Tribunal Supremo*, Ruling 632/2018, of 12 December, *Aranzadi* RJ 2018\5422, ECLI:ES: TS:2018:4176 and Ruling 407/2018 of 18 September, *Aranzadi* RJ 2018\4154, ECLI:ES:TS:2018:3159.

(b) Concerning expenditure-related fraud, the basic offence is now foreseen in Article 306 whereby any action or omission defrauding (*ergo* intentionally) the general budget of the EU – or any other budget managed by it or on its behalf – is punishable.[36] This fraud may consist of (1) any non-payment other than revenues; (2) using funds for other purposes than intended or (3) wrongfully obtaining funds falsifying the conditions required to get them or hiding any condition that would have prevented them from being granted. The same penalties and the same amount thresholds as those foreseen in revenue-related fraud apply. Due to its wording, the offence in Article 306 would only cover funds managed by the EU, but not EU funds managed by Member State administrations to which courts anyway apply the domestic fraud offence provided in Article 308 with the relevant consequence of requiring a fraud of €120,000 instead of €50,000.[37]

(c) Concerning other EU fraud-connected offences,[38] corruption has been controversial because of the definition of a public official in Spanish law. Article 24 only mentions Members of the European Parliament as 'public authority'.[39] In fact, Article 427, introduced in 2010, gives a broader definition of public official as far as corruption offences are concerned and, after being amended in 2015, it now encompasses

'any person holding an office, either elected or appointed, in the legislative, judicial or administrative branch in any EU Member State or third country'; 'any person exerting public functions including public agencies or companies on behalf of another EU MS or third country or on behalf of the EU or any international organisation' and 'any civil servant or agent of the EU or any international organisation'.

---

36   Former regulations (composed of two different offences and a more detailed wording) provoked some technical problems of overlapping offences and ironically legal gaps as well (*see in extenso* Javier Prieto Valls, *El fraude de subvenciones de la Unión Europea*, Dykinson, Madrid, 2005). This was solved by the 2012 amendment of the Criminal Code. There remained, however, differences with regard to the penalties compared to domestic budget fraud that could be considered incompatible with the assimilation and equivalence principles [Norberto de la Mata Barranco (n 24) 58]. This was corrected by the 2015 reform, which also modified expenditure fraud in the sense mentioned in (n 33) (*i.e.*, the suppression of a misdemeanour and the introduction of a minor felony covering fraud between €4,000 and €50,000).

37   *See, e.g., Tribunal Supremo*, Ruling 890/2016, of 25 November, *Aranzadi* RJ 2016\6095 or *Juzgado de lo Penal* núm. 4 de Valladolid (criminal court), Ruling 217/2018, of 5 September, *Aranzadi* ARP 2018\947. It should be noted that, concerning non-procurement-related expenditure domestic fraud, the amount is calculated combining all grants or aids coming from all public administrations.

38   Criminalizing preparatory acts such as intentionally providing or offering false documents in order to commit EU fraud (Art. 1(3) PIF Convention) is achieved in Spanish law through the general rules on inchoate offences (Arts. 15-18) and participation (Arts. 27-29) and particularly because of the autonomous offence of forgery of documents in Arts. 390-396 either committed by a public official or by a private individual and covering public, commercial and/or private documents. *See* CSWP (2008), 29-30.

39   *See* CSWP (2004), 42-43.

With regard to the definition of these offences, passive and active corruption is provided for with a larger scope than in the PIF *acquis*.[40] Whereas the basic behaviour described in Articles 2 and 3 of the protocol are foreseen with slight literal differences in Articles 419 and 424(1) *ab initio* respectively, the Spanish Criminal Code completes those with additional criminalized conduct such as improper, previous or ulterior passive corruption not requiring the breach of any official duty or even the realization of any action (Articles 420-422) and it also covers their reflection in active corruption (Article 424(1) *in fine*). All those offences lead to different imprisonment sentences and other penalties (fines, barring, suspension of duties without pay, temporary deprivation of the right to stand for elected office, etc.) The common sanctions of both basic corruption offences are imprisonment between two and six years and a fine of 12 to 24 months.

(d) Finally, the liability of legal persons has been a recurring issue in EU criminal law in general and PIF in particular. The responsibility of the head of businesses was undisputedly foreseen in Article 31[41] and subsidiary civil liability of legal persons was put in force. However, in 2010, the Criminal Code was amended and criminal liability of legal persons *stricto sensu* was adopted overcoming the traditional assumption of *societas delinquere non potest*.[42] This liability can be characterized by these features:[43] (1) it is not a general system but a '*numerus clausus*' one, i.e., it only applies when explicitly stated (which is the case for most offences protecting the EU's financial interests);[44] (2) a legal person may be rendered liable because of any action of their CEOs, heads and any other representatives or because of the actions of an employee or a person under their command if they fail in their duty of diligence, control, vigilance or supervision; (3) therefore compliance programmes within the company (or the lack thereof) are key in establishing and/or mitigating this liability; (4) liability of legal persons coexists with the criminal liability of the concrete individuals committing the actions and (5) the penalties provided for in the law always include a fine. The law may optionally compel or entitle the judge to impose other penalties such as suspension of activities or prohibition to carry them out, closure of premises, barring from public procurement bidding or from obtaining public subsidies or aids or benefitting from fiscal incentives and even the dissolution of the legal person (Article 33).

---

40 Norberto de la Mata Barranco and Leyre Hernández Díaz, 'Delitos contra la corrupción en el sector público', in José Luis de la Cuesta Arzamendi (dir), *Adaptación del Derecho Penal español a la política criminal de la Unión Europea*, Thomson Reuters, Cizur Menor, 2017, pp. 385, 389-390.

41 CSWP (2004) 49-53.

42 Arts. 31 bis-31 quinquies Criminal Code. As to the still controversial legal nature of this liability see above (n. 5).

43 Jacobo Dopico Gómez-Aller, 'Responsabilidad penal de las personas jurídicas', in *Derecho Penal Económico y de la Empresa*, Dykinson, Madrid, 2018, pp. 129, 130-132.

44 *See* as regards to fraud (Art. 310 bis), money laundering (Art. 302), corruption (Art. 427 bis) and smuggling (Arts. 2-3 of Organic Act 12/1995). Nevertheless liability of legal persons is not foreseen in case of document forgery or misappropriation (*malversation*).

8.2.2   Statute of Limitations and the Principle of Legality in Criminal Matters in Spanish Law

Concerning the protection of EU's financial interests, the *Taricco* saga has posed the problematic issue of time periods and the interpretation of the principle of legality in criminal matters in national and EU laws. As is known, the Court of Justice held that the statute of limitation periods laid down in the Italian penal code might be deemed incompatible with the principles of assimilation and equivalence of EU law, thereby infringing the unconditional mandate to protect the financial interests of the EU incumbent upon the Member States in Article 325 TFEU. This leaves the national judge obliged to disapply those national rules by virtue of EU law primacy. The Court of Justice also affirmed in the *Taricco* ruling that limitation periods are procedural rules and consequently disapplying them does not encroach upon the principle that offences and penalties must be defined by law.[45] This consideration drastically differs from Italian constitutional law where those rules are considered to be part and parcel of the principle of legality of criminal offences and penalties. Thus the Italian *Corte costituzionale* referred a preliminary question to the Court of Justice whose answer in the *MAS* case lacked, in my view, the clarity and straightforwardness required by the importance of the rights involved.[46]

This topic is relevant because, in Spanish law, the interpretation of the principle that offences and penalties must be defined by law is similar to the Italian approach. The Spanish *Tribunal Constitucional* might not have stated explicitly that prescription rules form part of the core of the principle of legality in criminal matters, but it has done it implicitly because it has totally and clearly rejected that limitation periods have a purely procedural nature. Being thus connected to the conditions for exercising the State *ius puniendi*, the rules of limitation periods demand the same strict interpretation criteria as substantive criminal law.[47] With regards to limitation periods that means (1) that the *tempus regit actum* principle applies, i.e., the judge must apply the prescription rules in force when the crime was committed unless subsequent rules are more lenient; and (2) that those prescription rules cannot be interpreted broadly or to the detriment of the

---

45   Case C-105/14, *Ivo Taricco and others* [2015] ECLI:EU:C:2015:555.

46   Case C-42/17, *M.A.S. and M.B.* [2017] ECLI:EU:C:2017:936. As is known, without reversing the *Taricco* case law, the Court of Justice admitted an exception to it based on two somewhat mixed arguments: (1) PIF being a shared competence that the EU has not exercised, Italy could at the time set forth rules on limitation periods and considering them part of substantive criminal law and thereby subject to the principle that criminal offences must be defined by law; and (2) the latter principle demands foreseeability, precision and non-retroactivity regarding criminal offences and penalties which, according to the first conclusion, Italy could apply to prescription rules. This would prevent the application of the *Taricco* case law in case those requirements are not met in the national court's view.

47   *Tribunal Constitucional*, Ruling 63/2001 of 17 March, ECLI:ES:TC:2001:63, paras 6-8; Ruling 63/2005 of 14 March, ECLI:ES:TC:2005:63, para. 6.

accused rendering analogy *in malam partem* prohibited.[48] For its part, the Spanish Supreme Court, the *Tribunal Supremo*, has explicitly and traditionally considered that the statute of limitations is part of the fundamental right of *nullum crimen sine lege*.[49] Spanish legal literature has done so as well.[50]

While on the level of legal principles Spain and Italy are commensurate, the concrete problem does not occur in Spain because our prescription rules are different and compatible with the *Taricco* requirements. Following Articles 131 to 135 of the Criminal Code, crimes may be time-barred in Spain depending on the maximum penalty. Thus money laundering, corruption and misappropriation (*malversation*) will be prescribed after 10 years; frauds will do so after five years.[51] However, if criminal proceedings are brought against someone deemed to be responsible, the limitation period is interrupted, leaving the time elapsed without effect. Both Spanish higher courts disputed some time ago over which concrete judicial acts could amount to interrupting the limitation,[52] so current Article 132(2) sets forth more detailed rules now.[53]

Penalties also are time-barred in Spanish law, according to Article 133. Whenever a person is sentenced to imprisonment up to five years, that penalty will prescribe after five years, dating from the day of the final sentencing or conviction breaking. If sentenced imprisonment exceeds five years (up to 10), a prescription will obtain after 15 years.[54] The *Tribunal Constitucional* also applied the relevantly *pro reo* interpretative criteria mentioned above to penalty prescription,[55] encouraging the adoption of some new

---

48 *See* especially *Tribunal Constitucional*, Ruling 25/2018, of 5 March, ECLI:ES:TC:2018:25, para. 2.

49 *Tribunal Supremo*, Ruling 101/2012, of 27 February, *Aranzadi* RJ 2012\3659, para. 3.; Ruling 9/2018, of 15 January, *Aranzadi* JUR 2018\15885, para. 4.

50 Antoni Gili Pascual, 'La interrupción de la prescripción penal, diez años después de la STC 63/2005' (2015) 35 *Estudios Penales y Criminológicos* 291, *passim* 306.

51 There is an exception since 2012: the aggravated offence of 'serious tax fraud', as provided for in Art. 305 bis Criminal Code, is punishable by up to six years of imprisonment and therefore shall not be time-barred until 10 years have elapsed since the fraud was committed.

52 Contrariwise to the *Tribunal Supremo*'s case law, the *Tribunal Constitucional* considered that a simple complaint was not enough, an act of the investigative judge being necessary. This position notably affected fiscal crimes, with regard to which public prosecutors tended to wait as much as possible to filing the lawsuit (Ramón Ragués i Vallès, 'La guerra de la prescripción. Crónica y crítica del conflicto entre el Tribunal Constitucional y el Tribunal Supremo a propósito del artículo 132.2 del Código Penal' (2011) 91 *Revista Española de Derecho Constitucional* 381, 384.

53 Basically a reasoned judicial resolution is required where that person is presumed to have participated in a criminal act. The person must be sufficiently determined in that resolution even if it not directly identified. Finally, merely pressing charges or filing a suit would suspend the limitation period up to six months, giving the judge time to adopt the said reasoned judicial resolution.

54 Prescription of the sanction of barring, also applicable in these felonies, follows different rules, but in essence if the barring sentenced exceeds five years, it will not be proscribed until 10 years have elapsed.

55 *See Tribunal Constitucional*, Ruling 81/2014, of 28 May, ECLI:ES:TC:2014:81, para. 3; Ruling 97/2010, of 15 November, ECLI:ES:TC:2010:97, para. 4.

rules from 2015 onwards concerning the interruption and the suspension of this limitation period.[56]

Closely connected with prescription is the issue of 'regularization' in cases of revenue fraud or *mutatis mutandis* reimbursement in cases of expenditure fraud,[57] which are admitted in Spanish law with powerful consequences, especially since the 2012 amendment of the Criminal Code. This amendment has generated a complex debate as to the legal nature of this operation.[58] Article 305(4) Criminal Code (and tax law now concurs) defines regularization as the taxpayer acknowledging the tax debt and paying it in full (i.e., including interest and any other due surcharges such as late fees). This regularization has to be done before any formal investigative proceeding by the tax administration, or the judicial authority has been initiated. This regulation raises three different questions from the point of view of EU law:

1. Neither in the PIF Convention nor in the PIF Directive is there such an excuse. So the question of its compatibility could be posed, particularly because the regularization is established with broad effects indeed since it explicitly prevents prosecution for any "possible accounting irregularities or other documentary misrepresentations" that may have been committed exclusively in relation to that concrete tax liability.

2. This regulation facilitates a larger recovery of VAT debts since regularization would offer the faulting taxpayer an escape from criminal responsibility by regularizing old tax debts that would have been rendered time-barred in administrative tax law.[59]

3. In the distinct direction of promoting cashing in, according to Article 305(6) Criminal Code, paying the debt early – within two months after the criminal

---

56 Criticizing its ambiguity, *see* Sergi Cardenal Montraveta, *La prescripción de la pena tras la reforma del Código Penal de 2015*, Tirant lo blanch, Valencia, 2015.

57 With regards to domestic expenditure fraud, the reimbursement of funds (*i.e.,* amount granted plus interest) as an exculpatory or a mitigating circumstance is provided for in Art. 308. Rules on this grant refund are parallel to those applied in regularization in respect of revenue-related fraud.

58 Some authors maintain that regularization currently equates to the complete removal of the illegal behaviour (*i.e.,* there never was a felony) while others claim that this is a matter of non-punishment but it does not affect the illegal condition of the fraud committed. This theoretical discussion is relevant in order to decide whether regularization benefits all participants and whether the possibility of a subsequent money laundering infraction disappears (*See* Fernando Bertrán Girón, 'La regularización en el delito contra la Hacienda Pública: luces y sombras de las reformas legales', in Carmen Almagro Martín (dir), *Estudios sobre Control del Fraude Fiscal y Prevención del Blanqueo de Capitales*, Thomson Reuters, Cizur Menor, 2016, p. 339).

59 Tax debts, including VAT, are proscribed after four years. Thus the tax administration cannot pursue recovery of older tax debts. However, serious VAT fraud (exceeding €10 million damage) by definition qualifies as a serious tax offence (Art. 305 bis only requires exceeding €600,000), therefore it is punishable with up to six years of imprisonment, which means that it is only proscribed after ten years. This gap between tax law and criminal law limitation periods would promote larger recoveries (*Ibid.,* 351).

proceeding has started – may be considered by the judge as a mitigating circumstance. The same mitigation applies to participants other than the author if they cooperate decisively with the prosecution.[60]

Some authors deny that this regularization applies to EU fraud.[61] However, as mentioned before, Spanish courts apply the domestic fraud offences to VAT or EU funds managed by Spanish administrations, regularization/reimbursement thus being applicable to those cases at least.

8.2.3   The Ne Bis In Idem Principle

In fighting fraud concerning public funds or revenues, Member States may resort to both administrative sanctions and criminal penalties. To a certain extent, this is inevitable or is a desired result of EU law. On the one hand, even in the absence of EU secondary law, the Court of Justice has ruled that Article 325 TFEU requires Member States to protect the financial interests of the EU with effective, dissuasive and proportionate sanctions that at least in most serious cases have to be of a criminal nature.[62] This is further specified as involving deprivation of liberty by Article 2(1) PIF Convention. However, basic classic principles in criminal law stemming from the Enlightenment compel the Member States and the EU to leave menial infractions damaging the EU's financial interests out of the criminal domain and keep them in the administrative field (so-called *ultima ratio* or minimum intervention principle). In fact, Council Regulation 2988/95 sets forth a general framework for this administrative protection of the EU's financial interests, including administrative measures and penalties.

This poses the thorny question of the coexistence and/or concurrence of criminal and administrative penalties in light of the respect for the principle *ne bis in idem* which has lately become a controversial issue in EU law. After setting a relatively high standard of protection in the *Åkerberg Fransson* case,[63] the Court of Justice, following in the footsteps

---

60   Some authors doubt the compatibility of this regulation with EU law, since it might contradict the obligation (incumbent upon Member States *ex* Art. 325 TFEU) to protect the EU's financial interests by means of effective, proportionate and dissuasive penalties. It should be borne in mind that in judicial praxis this mitigation means a sanction of around 40 per cent of the minimum [Norberto de la Mata Barranco, 'Delitos contra la Hacienda Pública y la Seguridad Social', in *op. cit.* at p. 556].

61   Norberto de la Mata Barranco and Leyre Hernández Díaz, 'Delitos contra el patrimonio y el orden socioeconómico, contra la Hacienda Pública y de contrabando', in José Luis de la Cuesta Arzamendi (dir), *Adaptación del Derecho Penal español a la política criminal de la Unión Europea*, Thomson Reuters, Cizur Menor, 2017, pp. 290-291. This conclusion seems more solid concerning EU expenditure-related fraud, because it is provided for in a different article of the Criminal Code. However, as we will see later in Section 3.1, the amendment transposing the new PIF Directive precisely aims in the opposite direction.

62   Case C-105/14, *Ivo Taricco and others* [2015] ECLI:EU:C:2015:555, para. 39.

63   Case C-617/10, *Åkerberg Fransson* [2013] ECLI:EU:C:2013:105 para. 32-37. Administrative and criminal sanctions can only be applied cumulatively if administrative sanctions are not criminal in nature.

of the European Court of Human Rights, has lowered these exigencies in the recent judgment in *Luca Menci* where it has admitted that a Member State may impose both a criminal penalty and a formally administrative sanction (that according to the Engel criteria has the nature of a criminal penalty) if some conditions are met.[64]

This is an interesting development even for Spain, which is a country whose courts adhere to a strong version of the *ne bis in idem* principle.[65] In Spain, both administrative and criminal penalties cannot be imposed cumulatively in a single case (i.e., when there is identity in facts, subjects and legal ground[66]). Here criminal law prevails and has the priority.[67]

Thus, when the tax administration in its ordinary verification and inspection activities comes across a situation that could amount to a fiscal offence, it is obliged to pass it on to the judicial authorities (either a judge or a prosecutor).[68] This has traditionally meant that any proceedings in motion by the tax administration were suspended until the criminal proceedings ended in conviction or acquittal. Only in the latter would the tax administration resume all administrative proceedings with the proviso of abiding by the facts as declared in the judicial resolution.

---

64 Case C-524/15, *Criminal proceedings against Luca Menci* [2018] ECLI:EU:C:2018:197 para. 63.

65 Although this fundamental right is not mentioned by name in the Constitution, *ne bis in idem* is linked to Art. 9(3) (legal certainty and interdiction of arbitrariness) and, in the *Tribunal Constitutional*'s view, it is contained in Art. 25 on *nullum crimen nulla poena sine lege*, which makes it protectable with the Spanish constitutional appeal *recurso de amparo* (*Tribunal Constitucional*, Ruling 177/1999 of 11 October, ECLI:ES: TC:1999:177 para. 4).
    However, the *Menci* case law would be very difficult to apply in Spain in substantive terms since, as stated before, the penalties in EU fraud offences consist not only in the deprivation of liberty but also in a criminal fine (up to six times the amount defrauded). So it may hardly be argued that proportionality or even complementary aims are met. See V. Alberto García Moreno, 'El Tribunal de Justicia de la Unión Europea y la posibilidad de sancionar dos veces'. Recientes aportaciones sobre el contenido del principio *non bis in idem*, Diario La Ley, No 9198, 16 May 2018.

66 Miguel Ángel Sánchez Huete, 'La prohibición de acumulación de sanciones fiscales y penales. Sentencia del Tribunal de Justicia de 20 de marzo de 2018 asunto C-524/15: Menci', La Ley Unión Europea, No 64 (November 2018); Miren Ocriozola Gurrutxaga, 'Duplicidad de sanciones administrativas y penales en la Unión Europea y en España. Comparación de la jurisprudencia europea y española desde la perspectiva del principio ne bis in idem', in José Luis de la Cuesta Arzamendi (dir), *Adaptación del Derecho Penal español a la política criminal de la Unión Europea*, Thomson Reuters, Cizur Menor, 2017, p. 143.

67 Until 2015 Art. 180(1) of Act 58/2003, of 17 December (General Taxation Act) [BOE 2003/302, p. 44987] expressly stated that "the conviction sentence would prevent imposing a fiscal penalty". This provision is now in Art. 250(2). The general provision in administrative law protecting *ne bis in idem* is Art. 31(1) Act 40/2015, of 1 October [BOE 2015/236, p. 89411].

68 Act 58/2003, of 17 December (General Taxation Act) [BOE 2003/302, p. 44987], Art. 95(3).

However, and using EU law as a pretext,[69] the Spanish legislature has drastically changed the situation from 2015 on.[70] Currently, after giving the judge the *notitia criminis*, the tax administration shall split the case into two files, one for the tax debt relating to the presumed crime and another for the remaining tax debt. Of course, the latter is not affected at all. With regard to the former, unless the investigative judge decides otherwise, the tax administration will continue verifying and determining the tax debt and enforcing it, even if that decision is provisional and dependent on the final judicial ruling.[71] The aim of this legal reform is undoubtedly to privilege tax collection, i.e., the tax debt, without including any administrative penalty; but legal literature has pointed out the extremely delicate situation that this *de facto* administrative preliminary procedure creates from the point of view of the respect for fundamental rights.[72]

Thus, the *Menci* case law might not be pertinent in Spain from the point of view of the penalties (substantive *ne bis in idem*), but it might be from a procedural point of view (instrumental *ne bis in idem*) legalizing this anomalous tax procedure parallel to the criminal proceedings. In both respects, the real issue is whether or not there might arise a new *Melloni* situation where the level of protection in Spanish law is higher than in EU law.[73]

8.2.4   The Practice of Criminal Investigation and Prosecution of PIF Offences

Nieto and González López have called the Spanish approach to the investigation of economic crimes chaotic not only because of the many actors involved but also because of the existing gap between the letter of the law and the practical investigation.[74] There is, of course, much truth in that statement. Spain still maintains its traditional model of an

---

69   Juan López Martínez, 'Naturaleza y alcance del procedimiento de inspección tributaria y sus repercusiones con el delito y el proceso penal', in Carmen Almagro Martín (dir), *Estudios sobre Control del Fraude Fiscal y Prevención del Blanqueo de Capitales,* Thomson Reuters, Cizur Menor, 2016, pp. 367, 373.

70   This possibility was introduced in Art. 305(5) of the Criminal Code in 2012, but its application could not take place till 2015 when the General Taxation Act was amended in order to regulate the administrative procedure regarding the offence-related tax debt (Act 34/2015, of 21 September 2012, partially amending the General Taxation Act [BOE 2015/227, p. 83633]).

71   Arts. 250-259 General Taxation Act.

72   Individual guarantees are quite disparate (if not diametrically opposed) in tax inspecting/collecting procedures and in criminal proceedings. So legitimate doubts have been raised as to evidence gathering, non self-incrimination, *excès de pouvoir* of the tax administration by being able to regularize time-barred fiscal years instead of passing the *notitia criminis* on to the judicial authorities, not to mention the very peculiar features of the enforcement of a provisional tax determination by the administration while a judicial proceeding is still pending. See López Martínez (n 69 above) 382-406; Jordi de Juan Casadevall, 'Actuaciones y procedimientos tributarios en supuestos de delito contra la Hacienda Pública: crónica de una reforma anunciada', (2015) 5/6 Carta Tributaria.

73   *See* above (n 6).

74   Adán Nieto Martín and Juan José González López, 'Investigating Economic Crimes in Spain: An Attempt to Find Order in Chaos', in Alessandro Bernandi and Daniele Negri (eds.), *Investigating European Fraud in the EU Member States,* Hart Publishing, Oxford, 2017, p. 31.

investigative judge or *juge d'instruction* (*Juzgado de Instrucción*),[75] but he or she timidly shares that competence with the public prosecutor's office (*Fiscalía* or *Ministerio fiscal*).[76] Anyway, judges and prosecutors both rely upon the law enforcement agencies (LEAs) (*policía judicial*) for carrying out investigative activities,[77] as well as on the cooperation duties borne by every public agency, including the Court of Auditors (*Tribunal de Cuentas*) or the tax administration.

The model provided for in the *Ley de Enjuiciamiento Criminal* (Act on Criminal Procedure[78]) is not very complicated, granting the investigative judge a prominent leading role, particularly once formal proceedings are open. Public prosecutors may open a preliminary investigation, but they can only perform investigative tasks that do not affect fundamental rights; otherwise, they must pass it on to the judge whom they continue to assist subsequently. The investigative room for the police without any judicial involvement is very small, at least in theory.

However, investigative practices and professional routines of specialized bodies and units have naturally evolved adapting the law into different investigative models where the leading role is actually played by the prosecutor's office, the police or even the tax administration. This trend is all the more understandable because, formally complying with the law, these models take advantage of the specialization of these professionals and overcome the excessive burden borne by investigative judges, notably in the *Audiencia Nacional*. Nevertheless, these models pose different questions as to the respect for fundamental rights or the uncertainty stemming from this convoluted picture, particularly in the light of the impending European Public Prosecutor's Office (EPPO).[79]

---

75   The investigative judge is determined by the place where the crime is presumably committed or by the office that the accused holds. Thus, due to its usual characteristics, most important economic crimes have a broad territorial scope and therefore they are investigated on a national scale by a *Juzgado Central de Instrucción* (within the *Audiencia Nacional*) whose territorial competence covers the whole country.

76   The Public Prosecutor's Office is also organized geographically. However, there is a section specialized in corruption and organized crime (commonly called *Fiscalía anticorrupción*) based in Madrid with delegated prosecutors in most important provinces.

77   The *policía judicial* (judicial police) designs those duties that all Spanish LEAs have in assisting judges and prosecutors in their criminal investigations (Art. 547 Organic Act 6/1984, on the Judiciary [BOE 1985/157, p. 20632]. However, two specialized units have been created in both national LEAs dealing with complex economic crimes. On the one hand, within the *Policía Nacional* (national police) there is in Madrid the *Unidad Central de Delicuencia Económica y Fiscal* (central unit of economic and fiscal crime) responsible for the investigation of tax crimes and crimes against EU's financial interests. On the other hand, there is a unit belonging to the *Guardia Civil* (civil guard) dedicated to the investigation of organized crime and economic and international offences. There are some special units within the Spanish Tax Agency (*Agencia Española de Administración Tributaria*) that may act also as judicial police assisting judges and prosecutors, such as the *Unidad de Apoyo a la Fiscalía Especial (Delitos económicos)* or *Servicio de Vigilancia Aduanera* (custom and revenue surveillance service).

78   Royal Decree approving the Act on the Criminal Procedure [*Gaceta de Madrid*, 1882/260, p. 1882]. Its last amendment has been introduced by Act 41/2015, of 5 October, amending the Criminal Procedure Act in order to speed up criminal justice and strengthen procedural guarantees [BOE 2015/239, p. 90220].

79   *See* Adán Nieto Martín and Juan José González López, *op. cit.* at pp. 52-53.

8.3   The Adaptation of Spain to the New Legal Framework Protecting EU's
       Financial Interests

The new legal framework protecting the EU's financial interests has three main limbs: the new PIF Directive, the EPPO Regulation and the amendment of the European Anti-Fraud Office (OLAF) Regulation.

As is well known, the latter is planned in the long run, whereas a more limited proposal focusing on clarifying OLAF's legal framework and defining its relationship with the EPPO is now ongoing.[80] Although we will not expand on this proposal,[81] it should be borne in mind that beyond the obvious implications because it is embedded with the future EPPO work, this amendment includes relevant clarifications with regard to OLAF external investigations (including VAT fraud) and its cooperation with the national Anti-Fraud Coordination Services (AFCOS).[82]

8.3.1   The Transposition of Directive (EU) 2017/1371

Directive (EU) 2017/1371 has finally replaced the former conventional framework for protecting EU's financial interests by means of criminal law.[83] Despite being the result of a long legislative procedure, it largely builds on the conventional PIF *acquis*.[84] So it does not entail an outstanding legal change, at least for those States already fully applying the former legal regime, such as Spain.

---

80 European Commission, Proposal for a Regulation amending Regulation (EU, Euratom) No 883/2013 concerning investigations conducted by the European Anti-Fraud Office (OLAF) as regards cooperation with the European Public Prosecutor's Office and the effectiveness of OLAF investigations, COM(2018) 338 final (Brussels, 23 May 2018).

81 Koen Bovend'Eerdt, 'The Commission Proposal Amending the OLAF Regulation' (2018) 1 Eucrim 73, 75.

82 With regard to this complex coordination between the OLAF and MS administrations *see* Manuel López Escudero, 'Autonomie procédurale des États membres et lutte contre la fraude aux intérêts financiers de l'Union européenne', in Dominique Berlin, Francesco Martucci and Fabrice Picod (dirs), *La fraude et le droit de l'Union européenne*, Bruylant, Brussels, 2017, p. 105. In Spain, besides the units belonging to the Spanish Tax Agency mentioned above (above n 78), there was created in 2012 the *Servicio Nacional de Coordinación Antifraude* as the Spanish AFCOS set forth in Art. 3(4) OLAF Regulation (Act 38/2003, of 17 November, on Subsidies and Grants [BOE 2003/276, p. 40505], 25th additional provision). Concerning the Spanish AFCOS, *see* José Antonio Fernández Ajenjo, 'El Papel del Servicio Nacional de Coordinación Antifraude en el proceso de lucha contra la corrupción' (2017) 5 *Revista Internacional Transparencia e Integridad*.

83 Directive (EU) 2017/1371, on the fight against fraud to the Union's financial interests by means of criminal law [2017] OJ L198/29 (PIF Directive).

84 The long process was due to the reticence of Member States to include VAT within the PIF regime and to the interinstitutional legal basis dispute. The Commission initially argued for Art. 325 TFEU, but the European Parliament and the Council later agreed on using Art. 83 (2) TFEU. The consequence has been the full application of the opt-outs granted to Ireland, Denmark and the UK. As is known, only Ireland took part in its adoption and is bound by the PIF Directive.

The most remarkable innovations in the directive are the introduction of the new criminal offence of misappropriation, the explicit inclusion of VAT fraud and some clarifications regarding limitation periods or the definition of public officials.[85] Bearing in mind the previous considerations on the implementation of PIF *acquis*, the task of adapting domestic law to the PIF Directive does not seem to be really daunting.[86] However, as mentioned above, Spain has the regrettable habit of fulfilling directives after the transposition period has expired. Luckily and surprisingly, this tendency has been reversed in this case since the adoption of the law implementing PIF Directive has materialized despite the highly volatile Spanish political landscape of late.

An Organic Act proposition modifying the Criminal Code was introduced at the end of 2017. The parliamentary procedure required both chambers of Parliament to examine and approve it. Throughout 2018, the Congress of Deputies debated and approved a text that the Senate has endorsed in February 2019. The proposition intended to adapt Spanish law to some international commitments and several EU directives that comprise, besides the PIF Directive, the 2017 Terrorism Directive and the 2014 Market Abuse Directive. The two latter have attracted more parliamentary attention, unlike the modifications relating to the PIF Directive that has been considered almost technical.[87] Finally, the Organic Act 1/2019 amending the Criminal Code has been published and will enter into force on 13 March 2019.[88]

In this regard, the Spanish legislator has evaluated that in order to abide by the new PIF Directive the following changes are needed: (1) raising the damage thresholds; (2) enlarging the concept of public official; (3) extending legal person liability to misappropriation and (4) a more coherent regulation of expenditure fraud that puts an

---

85   There are of course some other minor changes, such as raising the criminalization thresholds, better concretizing procurement-related fraud or aligning the definition of passive/active corruption with the United Nations Convention. *See* Adam Juszczak and Elisa Sason, 'The Directive on the Fight against Fraud to the Union's Financial Interests by Means of Criminal Law' (2017) 2 *Eucrim* 80.

86   With regard to procurement-related expenditure, the situation in Spain is compliant with the incrimination mandate of Art. 3 (2) (b) PIF Directive. The conduct thereunder is covered by the corruption offences and the instrumental felonies of document forgery already mentioned, but also by the criminal offences of misappropriation (Arts. 432-433) and some complementary offences specifically aimed at preserving the integrity of public servants (Art 404 incriminates the conduct of a public servant that adopts an illegitimate decision knowing full well that it is illegitimate) and the public procurement procedure (Art 436 criminalizes all types of collusion, arrangements or schemes between any interested party and a public official acting at any stage of a public procurement procedure if they defraud any public institution or administration).

87   *See* the text approval by the full chamber of the Congress of Deputies in *Boletín Oficial de las Cortes Generales, Congreso de los Diputados*, Serie B, No 228-7, 28 December 2018, 1. *See* both the debate and its approval by the Senate in *Boletín Oficial de las Cortes Generales*, Senado, No 331, 29 January 2019, 274 and No 340, 12 February 2019, 3, respectively. Since it had been approved by the Senate, only the royal proclamation of the organic law remained, which was not affected by the dissolution of the Parliament on the call for a new election announced by the President Sánchez on February 15.

88   Organic Act 1/2019 of 20 February, amending Organic Act 10/1995, of 23 November, in order to transpose EU directives in the financial field and fighting terrorism and to address some international issues [BOE 2019/45, p. 16698].

end to some overlapping issues.[89] As we see, the intended amendment was quite modest. So in the view of the Spanish legislator, domestic law was already almost fully compliant with EU law on this matter. Most authors agree with this diagnosis.[90]

Nevertheless, as insignificant and simple as the transposition job may have appeared, some more attention was necessary, since serious technical mistakes have been made.

(1) One obvious objective of Organic Act 1/2019 was to increase the damage thresholds, as the PIF Directive does compare to the PIF Convention. The PIF Directive sets out three different thresholds with regard to EU fraud. An amount above €100,000 should be deemed considerable damage unleashing penalties of deprivation of liberty of a minimum-maximum of four years. With regard to VAT fraud, considerable damage requires at least €10,000,000 (and the involvement of two or more Member States). Fraud above €10,000 should attract effective, proportionate and dissuasive criminal sanctions (but not necessarily imprisonment). Below €10,000 Member States retain the option of not imposing penalties.

As mentioned earlier, the Spanish Criminal Code until this amendment, stuck to the PIF Convention amounts (€50,000 and €4,000) but it already foresaw higher penalties (up to five years, a fine and barred from future public subsidies or aids) in Articles 305(3) and 306. Let us remember that whereas the same penalties are applied to domestic fraud offences, the latter has a different threshold of €120,000 in Articles 305(1) and 308. An aggravated tax fraud offence in Article 305 bis adopts a €600,000 threshold. In updating the damage figures, the most prominent mistake has been that the legislator has forgotten to abrogate Article 306 (old EU expenditure fraud offence) while the reform, I believe, was supposed to include its content in Article 308 along with expenditure-related domestic fraud (i.e., using the assimilation technique instead of keeping the specific offence technique). So, after Organic Act 1/2019, there are two provisions incriminating EU expenditure fraud to the same extent but requiring different amounts, one in Article 306 using the PIF Convention thresholds and another in Article 308 applying to both domestic and EU fraud that uses the PIF Directive amounts. This is a phenomenal legal blunder that will probably soon be corrected by abrogating the old specific EU fraud offence of Article 306.[91] In the meantime, I think that courts will practically reach the

---

89 *See* Organic Act 1/2019, recital IV.
90 Norberto de la Mata Barranco and Leyre Hernández Díaz, 'Delitos contra el patrimonio y el orden socioeconómico, contra la Hacienda Pública y de contrabando', *op. cit.* at pp. 290-292.
91 Some Tables are annexed for better understanding.

same result (i.e., not applying Article 306) since classic criminal law principles compel applying more lenient law and interpreting it *pro reo*.[92]

Nonetheless, it is important to recall that the reform implies a change in the legal technique of fighting this EU non-procurement-related expenditure fraud since, instead of a specific offence, EU funds are equated to domestic funds. This change should most certainly be irrelevant from the point of view of the description of the offence because Article 308(1) and (2) essentially covers the conduct depicted in Article 3(2) (a) of the PIF Directive.[93] This means that all public funds, including the EU's, are combined in calculating the damage threshold of €100,000, which offers better protection of EU funds and puts an end to the question of under which provision subsuming fraud when national and European funds are involved. It also means that in a non-disputable way, the reimbursement/regularization mentioned above now applies to EU fraud as well.

In addition, in order to describe EU revenue fraud in a more PIF Directive-like manner, the wording of this offence has been changed in a very confused way, i.e., by plainly adding to the criminalized conduct "avoiding payment of any amount that he/she ought to pay or unduly to enjoy a benefit legally obtained". This open-ended expression will require courts to use the *Pupino* case law and interpret it according to the directive (i.e., requiring the misapplication of the benefit legally obtained to have the effect of illegally reducing the EU's resources).

(2) Concerning the rest of the modifications, Organic Act 1/2019 seems to have done a better job. No major changes were needed for misappropriation. Misappropriation is already a punishable offence in Spain whose definition in both Articles 432 and 433 Criminal Code does need to be amended; it comprises (in my opinion) the directive definition in Article 4(3), including the minimum-maximum of four years' imprisonment.[94] Interestingly, the offence of misappropriation keeps the old threshold of €50,000 (and €4,000) without any increase. However, to comply with the directive's

---

92 These principles obviously solve the question of EU fraud between €50,000 and €100,000: it should be considered a minor felony according to new Art. 308 (4). The only remaining doubt is what will happen to frauds between €4,000 and €10,000. The amendment most certainly intended to depenalize them, but they are still seen in the outdated Art. 306.
   Another conceivable interpretation for this coexistence would confine Art. 306 to exclusively EU funds, that is applying a €50,000 threshold when only EU funds are involved and a €100,000 when the amount defrauded involves other public funds as well. I do not think that this interpretation is correct or that Spanish courts will maintain it.

93 Art. 308 clearly addresses EU expenditure focusing on wrongfully obtained grants and aids falsifying the conditions required to get them or hiding any condition that would have prevented them from being granted (para. 1) or in using them for other purposes than intended (para. 2). As mentioned above in Section 2.1, Art. 306 still in force covers that conduct, but also any non-payment other than revenues defrauding the EU budget. It is to be known whether Art. 306 will still be used for procurement-related fraud.

94 Art. 432 defines misappropriation as a public official legally entitled to administer or manage public property and/or funds breaking his/her duties and thereby causing loss to the public administration.

criminal liability of legal persons, a new Article 435(5) has been introduced for misappropriation.

Connected to misappropriation, but also covering passive/active corruption, the wider definition of a 'public official' in Article 4(4) (b) PIF Directive needs to have been included. As explained, despite its enlargement in 2015, the notion embodied in Article 427 was insufficient. After Organic Act 1/2019, the Spanish Criminal Code literally takes the definition of the directive adding that public official will encompass "a person assigned and exercising a public service function involving the management of or decisions concerning the Union's financial interests in the Member States or third countries".

8.3.2 The EPPO Regulation and Its Application in Spain: A Legal Reform Still Awaited

Unlike the PIF Directive, the adaptation of the Spanish criminal justice system to the EPPO is not technical. As mentioned, Spain still adheres to the leading investigative judge. Prosecutors may initiate a preliminary investigation where they can execute or order investigative measures except personal or patrimonial precautionary measures or other measures affecting fundamental rights.[95] In this vein, the *Tribunal Supremo* has even affirmed that investigative measures conducted by the prosecutor are intended as to whether or not to bring an accusation, but these measures do not possess evidentiary value as such and have to be reproduced before the judge. Thus there appears to be a fundamental or structural problem for applying the EPPO in Spain – prosecutors do not possess full investigative powers, and investigative judges cannot see their independence affected (i.e., they cannot receive instructions if they were to act as European delegated prosecutors). In addition, in order to be fully operational, the EPPO Regulation requires Member States to decide on several issues.[96]

However, with the exception of minor details such as initiating the procedure to name the candidates for European Prosecutor and Delegated European Prosecutor in Spain,[97] no other legislative initiative has been tabled (and this will be impossible until the next term begins after the April general elections). This actually leaves not much time for embarking on a comprehensive reform of the Spanish criminal justice system giving prosecutors the investigation powers before the EPPO Regulation enters into force, which is a topic that is being long continuously debated in Spain. For this reason, even if it implies a burdensome legislative procedure, a tailor-made solution for PIF investigations seems more probable. Since large VAT frauds (i.e., missing trader and

---

95 *Tribunal Supremo*, Ruling 980/2016, of 11 January, *Aranzadi* RJ 2017/6.
96 *See* David Vilas Álvarez, *op. cit.*
97 Royal Decree 37/2019, of 1 February [BOE 2019/29, p. 9403].

carousel schemes) are few in Spain, the EPPO rules on the exercise of competences (especially in Article 25(2) and (3) will make EPPO concentrate on EU non-procurement expenditure fraud cases.[98] Let us just hope that by the time the EPPO becomes active, at least all technical mistakes mentioned earlier will be solved.

---

98 David Vilas Álvarez, 'La competencia material de la Fiscalía Europea', in Lorena Bachmaier Winter (coord), *La Fiscalía Europea*, Marcial Pons, 2018, pp. 52, 75-76.

8.4   ANNEX TO CHAPTER 8

Table 8.1   Revenue fraud offence (*)

* Excluding smuggling
** Regularization (payment of due tax debt) is admitted as an exculpatory or mitigating circumstance

	Prior to Organic Act 1/2019		After Organic Act 1/2019	
	Domestic revenue	EU revenue	Domestic revenue	EU revenue
Criminal Code Provision	Article 305(1)	Article 305(3)	Article 305(1)	Article 305(3)
Conduct described	The same description of incriminating conduct: any action or omission defrauding the Treasury by avoiding any kind of due payment, unduly obtaining any refund or benefitting of fiscal incentives		No change	[an addition] Whoever avoids the payment of any amount he/she must pay or unduly enjoys a benefit legally obtained
Penalties provided for	Same penalties		Same penalties	
	Imprisonment (1-5 years)		Imprisonment (1-5 years)	
	Fine (up to six times the amount defrauded)		Fine (up to six times the amount defrauded)	
	Barred from obtaining public grants/ aids or enjoying tax benefits/incentives (3-6 years)		Barred from obtaining public grants/ aids or enjoying tax benefits/incentives (3-6 years)	
Damage threshold	€120,000	€50,000	€120,000	€100,000
Regularization (**)	Yes	Yes/No (debatable)	Yes	Yes (debatable)
Minor offence	No	> €4,000	No	> €10,000
Aggravated offence	(Article 305 bis) amount > €600,000		(Article 305 bis) amount > €600,000	
	Within criminal organization or group		Within criminal organization or group	
	Resort to proxies/tax havens or other methods blurring the taxpayer's identity or the tax debt		Resort to proxies/tax havens or other methods blurring the taxpayer's identity or the tax debt	

Table 8.2   Non-procurement-related expenditure fraud

* Excluding Social Security fraud
** Regularization (reimbursement) is admitted as an exculpatory or mitigating circumstance

	Prior to Organic Act 1/2019		After Organic Act 1/2019	
	Domestic fraud (*)	EU fraud	Fraud of funds (including EU's)	EU funds
Criminal Code Provision	Article 308	Article 306	Article 308	Article 306
Description of incriminating conduct	Obtaining grants and aids:	Action/omission defrauding the EU budget by:	No change obtaining grants and aids:	No change action/ omission defrauding the EU budget by:
	Falsifying the required conditions	Non-payment of any due amount other than revenues	Falsifying the required conditions	Non-payment of any due amount other than revenues
	Hiding any preventing condition	Using funds for other purposes than intended	Hiding any preventing condition	Using funds for other purposes than intended
	Using them for other purposes than intended	Wrongfully obtaining funds falsifying the required conditions or hiding any preventing condition	Using them for other purposes than intended	Wrongfully obtaining funds falsifying the required conditions or hiding any preventing condition
Penalties provided for	Same penalties		Same penalties	
	Imprisonment (1-5 years)		Imprisonment (1-5 years)	
	Fine (up to six times the amount defrauded)		Fine (up to six times the amount defrauded)	
	Barred from obtaining public grants/ aids or enjoying tax benefits/incentives (3-6 years)		Barred from obtaining public grants/ aids or enjoying tax benefits/incentives (3-6 years)	
Damage threshold	€120,000	€50,000	€100,000	€50,000
Regularization (**)	Yes	No (debatable)	Yes	Yes (debatable)
Minor offence	No	> €4,000	Yes > €10,000	> €4,000

9 SELECTED CASE STUDIES: THE CASE STUDY OF ESTONIA

Jaan Ginter

9.1 IMPLEMENTATION OF EU CRIMINAL LAW IN ESTONIA

9.1.1 The First Stages of Implementation

The impact of the European criminal law on the Estonian criminal law can be seen since drafting the Estonian Penal Code[1] (hereinafter EPC) which was adopted in 2001 and entered into force on 1 September 2002. At the time Estonia was not a member of the European Union. But according to Article 68 of the Europe Agreement establishing an association between the European Communities and their Member States, on the one side, and the Republic of Estonia, of the other side (OJ L 068, 9 March 1998) it was agreed that Estonia shall endeavour to ensure that its legislation will be gradually made compatible with that of the Community.

The drafters of the EPC took into account the conventions and joint actions developed in the third pillar of the European Union as follows:
- The chapter on offences against the person and the chapter on offences against family and minors of the EPC takes into account the Joint Action of 24 February 1997 concerning action to combat trafficking in human beings and sexual exploitation of children, (OJ L 63/2, 24 February 1997).
- The offence fraud was drafted taking into account Article 209a of the Maastricht Treaty and the Convention on the Protection of the European Communities' Financial Interests (OJ C 316 27 November 1995).
- The offences like granting, arranging and accepting of gratuities and giving, arranging and accepting of bribes were drafted taking into account the Convention on the Fight Against Corruption Involving Officials of the EC or Officials of Member States of the EU (OJ C 195, 25 June 1997).

The drafting commission followed Council of Europe recommendations for the criminalization of the offences committed by a legal person (Recommendations No.

---

1 Estonian Penal Code, (RT I 2001, 61, 364, RT I, 07.07.2017, 5) Karistusseadustik, KarS, available at: https://www.riigiteataja.ee/akt/129062018066?leiaKehtiv, English translation available at: https://www.riigiteataja.ee/en/eli/509072018004/consolide.

R 81(12) and 88(18) of the Committee of Ministers of the Council of Europe) and for introducing a new penalty – community service (Recommendations No. R (92)16 and (2000)22).

Still, the drafters were not able to introduce all offences that were necessary for full compliance with the European Law. For example, an act making an illegal offence receipt of information society services and media service that was necessary for compliance with the Directive 98/84/EC of the European Parliament and of the Council of 20 November 1998 on the legal protection of services based on, or consisting of, conditional access (OJ L 320, 28 November 1998) was adopted only on 19 April 2006. And an act making unlawful alteration or removal of technical protective measures preventing the infringement of copyright or related rights from implementing the Information Society Directive 2001/29/EC (OJ L 167, 22 June 2001) an offence was adopted on 24 January 2007.

The impact of the EU procedural criminal law on the Estonian Code of Criminal Procedure can be seen since drafting the Estonian Code of Criminal Procedure, which was adopted in 2003 and entered into force on 1 July 2004. At the time Estonia was already a member of the European Union, and the drafter's aim was to draft the Code in full compliance with the European law, the Council of Europe conventions on cooperation in criminal procedure, the ECHR, its additional protocols and the requirements of the case law of the Strasbourg Court. But actually, the compliance with the European Arrest Warrant Directive (2002/584/JHA – OJ L 190, 18 July 2002) was achieved only after an amendment adopted on 28 June 2004, i.e., after the Code was adopted but before it entered into force.

9.1.2 Impact of the Framework Decisions 2002/475/JHA and 2008/919/JHA on the Criminalization of Terrorism in Estonia

Although Member States should have taken the necessary measures to comply with the Framework Decision 2002/475/JHA (OJ L164/3, 22 June 2002) by 31 December 2002, the EPC was redesigned to comply with the framework decision (FD) only in 2007. The amendment to the EPC was passed on 24 January 2007 and entered into force on 15 March 2007. The legislator did not attempt to employ language rigidly aligned to the wording of the FD. For example, it nowhere refers directly to "drawing up false administrative documents with a view to committing" a terrorist act.[2] And these activities are criminalized under the general term "knowing supporting in another manner of commission" of a terrorist criminal offence.[3]

---

2   FD 2002, Article 3 (c).
3   EPC § 237³ (1).

Still, there seems to be one lacuna as the EPC describes as a terrorist offence only as "manufacture, distribution or use of prohibited weapons". But the FD 2002 requires that the list of activities that may be considered terrorist activities include "manufacture, possession, acquisition, transport, supply or use of weapons, explosives or of nuclear, biological or chemical weapons, as well as research into, and development of, biological and chemical weapons".[4] Under the EPC manufacture, distribution and use of non-prohibited weapons for the terrorist purposes is criminalized as "knowing supporting in another manner of commission" of a terrorist criminal offence.[5] Yes, the activities are criminalized, but the difference is that as the manufacture of non-prohibited weapons is not a terrorist activity, the training for the manufacture of non-prohibited weapons is not criminalized, and this kind of training can be punished only as "knowing supporting in another manner of commission" of a terrorist criminal offence.

Framework Decision 2008/919/JHA (OJ L330/21, 9 December 2008) established three new offences linked to terrorism, i.e., 'public provocation to commit a terrorist offence', 'recruitment to terrorism' and 'training for terrorism'. Report from the Commission to the European Parliament and the Council on the implementation of Council Framework Decision 2008/919/JHA of 28 November 2008 amending Framework Decision 2002/475/JHA on combating terrorism erroneously asserts that Estonia chose to rely on provisions criminalizing the dissemination of messages to the public with a view to inciting terrorist offences in general terms and therefore it is possible that in Estonia direct provocation of terrorist acts is criminalized and indirect provocation merely causing a danger that one or more offences be committed is not criminalized.[6] The EPC employs in this respect not the EPC General Part term, employed to refer to acts aimed to encourage a concrete person to commit a crime (the term in Estonian is 'kihutamine' and usually translated as 'instigation') but a term employed only in the Special Part of the EPC 'avalik üleskutse' (usually translated as 'public incitement') and in all instances it criminalizes public activities that are addressed to not specified persons and may, as a result, produce a crime committed by a person unknown to the person who committed the public incitement.

Estonia did not need to take any new legislation to comply with the Framework Decision as Estonia was one of the Member States which, subsequent to the adoption of the 2005 Council of Europe Convention on the Prevention of Terrorism, had already adopted measures to criminalize the three new offences. The Commission Report asserts erroneously as well that in Estonia "only recruitment to carry out terrorist offences

---

4   FD 2002. Article 1(1) (f).
5   EPC § 237³ (1).
6   Report from the Commission to the European Parliament and the Council on the implementation of Council Framework Decision 2008/919/JHA of 28 November 2008 amending Framework Decision 2002/475/JHA on combating terrorism, pp. 5-6. Available at: https://ec.europa.eu/home-affairs/sites/homeaffairs/files/e-library/documents/policies/crisis-and-terrorism/general/docs/report_on_the_implementation_of_cfd_2008-919-jha_and_cfd_2002-475-jha_on_combating_terrorism_en.pdf.

appears to be punishable, and not recruitment to take part in the activities of terrorist groups as defined in Article 2(2) of FD 2002".[7] But both types of recruitment are criminalized separately in the EPS – § 273[2] and §273[1] respectively.

9.1.3 Impact of the Framework Decision 2005/222/JHA [2005] on the Criminalization of Attacks Against Information Systems in Estonia

As Estonia is, since 1 April 2004, a member of the Council of Europe Convention on Cybercrime[8] the EPC criminalized illegal data, and system interference and illegal access to computer systems already before the Framework Decision 2005/222/JHA (OJ L69/67, 16 March 2005, pp. 67-71) was introduced.

There were some discrepancies between the FD and the EPC regarding penalties. The EPC § 207 offered only pecuniary punishment for system interference although the FD Article 6 required at least one year imprisonment. And the EPC § 217 did not criminalize the action if it was taken by a legal person. Estonia reported to the Commission that rules on civil liability covered all the cases described in the FD Article 8(1), but it is difficult to imagine how the civil liability could comply with the FD requirement to provide 'effective, proportionate and dissuasive penalties' for legal persons as Estonia does not employ punitive damages system for these cases.

The amendment to the EPC adopted on 21 February 2008 (entered into force on 24 March 2008) got rid of these discrepancies and introduced language closer to the FD.[9] Still there remained one discrepancy between the EPC and the FD. The EPC § 217 does not consider the fact that illegal access was committed within the framework of a criminal organization to be an aggravating circumstance as required by the FD Article 7 as the EPC has taken the position that as membership in a criminal organization is a separately punishable offence, it cannot be an aggravating circumstance.

The European Commission produced a report on compliance of the Member States legislation with the FD on attacks against information systems.[10] The report asserts that Estonian law made criminal responsibility for illegal system interference and illegal data interference conditional on the criterion that "significant damage is ... caused".[11] The EPC § 207 (illegal system interference) did not have this condition. Before 24 March 2008, in this Section, the only thing in compliance with the FD was that it did not

---

7   *Ibid.*, p. 6.
8   http://conventions.coe.int/Treaty/en/Treaties/Html/185.htm.
9   https://www.riigiteataja.ee/akt/12937096.
10 Report from the Commission to the Council based on Article 12 of the Council Framework Decision of 24 February 2005 on attacks against information systems. Available at: https://eur-lex.europa.eu/legal-content/EN/TXT/?uri=COM:2008:0448:FIN.
11 *Ibid.*

allow the use of imprisonment as a punishment. But the EPC § 206 (illegal data interference) did have this conditional criterion until 24 March 2008.

9.1.4   *Commission Proposal for a New Directive on Cybercrime (COM (2010) 517*
            Final) and Subsequent Legislation such as Directive 2013/40/EU of the
            European Parliament and of the Council of 12 August 2013 on Attacks
            against Information Systems and Replacing Council Framework Decision
            2005/222/JHA

Estonia has not criminalized producing, selling, procuring for use, importing, distributing or otherwise making available a tool with the intention that it be used to commit illegal interception of non-public transmissions of computer data.

With regard to the aggravating circumstance, the Directive Article 9(3) requires illegal system or data interference to be punishable by a maximum term of imprisonment of at least three years where a significant number of information systems *have been affected* through the use of a tool, referred to in Article 7 of the Directive. But the EPC §§ 206 and 207 wordings are respectively "committed *against* data in numerous computer systems" (emphasis added) and "committed *against* numerous computer systems" (emphasis added). As it is mentioned in the Report from the Commission to the European Parliament and the Council assessing the extent to which the Member States have taken the necessary measures in order to comply with Directive 2013/40/EU on attacks against information systems and replacing Council Framework Decision 2005/222/JHA, the aggravating circumstance was generally designed to refer to botnet offences. But at least the EPC § 206 wording (and most likely the EPC § 207 wording as well) does not cover the situations where a botnet is involved in committing a crime *against* a single computer system.

The directive does not require the fact that illegal access was committed within the framework of a criminal organization to be an aggravating circumstance as it was required by the FD Article 7. Report from the Commission to the European Parliament and the Council assessing the extent to which the Member States have taken the necessary measures in order to comply with Directive 2013/40/EU on attacks against information systems and replacing Council Framework Decision 2005/222/JHA asserts that discrepancies between Article 7 and the Estonian national measures are found in the lack of transposition of all the possible acts listed.[12] The report seems to have overlooked EPC § 216[1] that covers all the directive offences: 'supply' covers 'procurement for use' and

---

12   Report from the Commission to the European Parliament and the Council assessing the extent to which the
     Member States have taken the necessary measures in order to comply with Directive 2013/40/EU on attacks
     against information systems and replacing Council Framework Decision 2005/222/JHA. Available at:
     https://eur-lex.europa.eu/legal-content/EN/TXT/?uri=COM:2017:474:FIN.

'import', 'production' covers 'production', 'distribution' covers 'sale' and 'distribution', 'making otherwise available' covers 'otherwise making available'. EPC § 216[1] has introduced an extra offence – possession of the mentioned tools.

9.1.5 The Impact of the Framework Decision 2008/841/JHA on the Criminalization of Participation in a Criminal Organization in Estonia

The Commission report on the implementation of the FD 2008/841/JHA indicated that Estonian legislation had narrowed the scope of the definition of 'criminal organization' by adding the attribute "division of tasks or functions in the criminal organisation".[13] The Estonian legislator has decided that the wording employed in the EPC § 255 'distribution of tasks' does not require any closer cooperation between the members of a criminal organization than wording 'acting in concert' employed in the FD Article 1(1). The position is reasonable because it is impossible to act in concert without any distribution of tasks. The FD Article 1(2) declares that there is no requirement for 'formally defined roles for its members', but the necessity for acting in concert with minimal distribution of tasks does not in any sense mean formal definition of roles.

The Report asserts that the EPC § 255 term 'permanent' "restricts the scope of application of [the FD] by excluding non-permanent criminal organisations".[14] Here the problem is most likely in the English translation of the EPC 255. In Estonian, the term is 'püsiv', meaning not functioning only for a certain period and this is the same criterion as "established over a period of time"[15] and "not randomly formed for the immediate commission of an offence".[16]

9.1.6 Limits of Mutual Trust in the Execution of European Arrest Warrants (EAW)

The major concern in respect of mutual recognition matters has been a deficiency in trust in other Member States' diligence in employing coercive measures.

The mutual trust in the execution of European Arrest Warrants (EAW) was acutely questioned in a case of an EAW issued by Italy. It concerned a man who was in some database connected to a phone number employed during a jewellery store heist in Italy. In Estonia, there was no difficulty in finding out that the person had not left Estonia

---

13 Report from the Commission to the European Parliament and the Council based on Article 10 of Council Framework Decision 2008/841/JHA of 24 October 2008 on the fight against organized crime. Available at: https://eur-lex.europa.eu/legal-content/en/ALL/?uri=CELEX:52016DC0448.

14 Ibid.

15 FD 2008/841/JHA, Article 1(1).

16 FD 2008/841/JHA, Article 1(2).

during the heist, and the phone number did not belong to the man any more. Still, the Office of the Prosecutor General agreed that there are no grounds for refusing the request and the man had to be surrendered even if there is every ground to be certain that the man is innocent. Luckily, there was a possibility to contact the Italian police officers face to face to offer them the new information and three days after the person was arrested, the EAW was revoked by the Italian court.[17] In one case, the court decided that as according to the evidence the requested person could not have committed the crime, it would be in conflict with the basic principles of the Estonian criminal procedure to surrender the person and the surrender was refused by the court.[18]

According to some reviews, there have been several EAWs issued by Spain that do not match even the most elementary content requirements – the circumstances are described very superficially, and the whole text sometimes arises doubts.[19] There have been a few cases involving issuing EAWs in cases involving trivial offences not punishable as crimes in Estonia and not included in the FD 2002/584/JHA Article 2 list of crimes that give rise to surrender pursuant to an EAW without verification of the double criminality of the act (e.g., minor traffic offences, arrest for not paying debt etc.).[20] These cases have given grounds to question whether there are sufficient grounds to believe that in these Member States, the EAW is always employed only as *ultima ratio,* and the coercive measure is proportional to the situation.[21]

9.1.7 The Impact of EU Measures Facilitating the Exchange of Personal Data Between National Police and Judicial Authorities on the Legal Orders of EU Member States

Council Framework Decision 2008/977/JHA of 27 November 2008 on the protection of personal data processed in the framework of police and judicial cooperation in criminal matters (EJ L 350, 30 December 2008, pp. 60-71)[22] has been implemented in Estonia and in the majority of other Member States. The implementation facilitated an increase in trust in fellow Member States' ability and ambition to protect personal data processed in the framework of police and judicial cooperation in criminal matters.

---

17 Eesti Ekspress, 26 April 2007, Italy requested the surrender of an innocent Estonian man (in Estonian). Available at: http://ekspress.delfi.ee/kuum/itaalia-noudis-eestist-valja-suutu-mehe?id=69107847.

18 Harju County Court decision in the case No 1-07-3718. Marje Allikmets, Loovutatava isiku õigused loovutamismenetluses – kohtupraktika analüüs (in Estonian), Tartu 2013. Available at: https://www.advokatuur.ee/action/advokatuur/downloadFile?hash=151b3fa64600e59b36226d50db38ab3a2699d661.

19 Joanna Paabumets, Refusal to consent to surrender as a legal problem (in Estonian), Tartu, 2013, p. 56, http://dspace.ut.ee/bitstream/handle/10062/31880/paabumets_joanna.pdf?sequence=1.

20 *Ibid.,* p. 57.

21 *Ibid.*

22 https://eur-lex.europa.eu/legal-content/EN/TXT/?uri=CELEX%3A32008F0977.

Further on, the Directive (EU) 2016/680 of the European Parliament and of the Council of 27 April 2016 on the protection of natural persons with regard to the processing of personal data by competent authorities for the purposes of the prevention, investigation, detection or prosecution of criminal offences or the execution of criminal penalties, and on the free movement of such data, and repealing Council Framework Decision 2008/977/JHA (OJ L 119, 4 May 2016, pp. 89-131)[23] was adopted. The directive should have been implemented by 6 May 2018. In Estonia, the government drafted the new Personal Data Protection Act,[24] but the first version of the bill faced serious criticism in the *Riigikogu* (the Parliament), and the government ordered the bill back from the *Riigikogu* and introduced two months later a new slightly changed bill which has passed only the first reading now. Hence, the directive has still not had any influence on the exchange of personal data between national police and judicial authorities with the other Member States.

9.1.8 Use of General Principles of EU Law (In Particular Indirect Effect in the Light of Pupino) in Interpreting National Legislation/Implementing EU Criminal Law Domestic Courts

Estonian Supreme Court *en banc* decided on 19 April 2005 that primacy of European Union law means that European Union law prevails over Estonian law, according to the practice of the Court of Justice of the European Union (CJEU); when conflicting EU and national acts have to be applied, EU law prevails (see also Joined Cases C-10/97 and C-22/97, *Ministero delle Finanze vs IN.CO.GE.'90*, [1998] ECR I-6307). But the primacy of European Union law does not mean that the Estonian Supreme Court can repeal an Estonian legislative act if the Court considers it to be in conflict with European Union legal act.[25]

The Administrative Chamber of the Supreme Court decided on 25 April 2006 that as the Constitution of the Republic of Estonia Amendment Act – adopted by the referendum on 14 September 2003 to supplement the Constitution of the Republic of Estonia – rules that "[w]hen Estonia has acceded to the European Union, the Constitution of the Republic of Estonia is applied without prejudice to the rights and obligations arising from the Accession Treaty" the Estonian Constitution has to be

---

23 https://eur-lex.europa.eu/legal-content/EN/TXT/?uri=CELEX:32016L0680.

24 https://www.riigikogu.ee/tegevus/eelnoud/eelnou/e14c5e2f-b684-4aa4-a7dd-ffb76f63f395/Isikuandmete%20kaitse%20seadus.

25 Supreme Court judgment in the case No 3-4-1-1-05, Chancellor of Justice application for the partial repeal of § 70¹ of the Municipal Council Election Act and § 1(1), § 5(1), first sentence and § 6(2) of the Political Parties Act. Available at: https://rikos.rik.ee/LahendiOtsingEriVaade?asjaNr=3-4-1-1-05, p. 49.

always interpreted in compliance with the Accession Treaty and other primary European Union law[26] except if EU law is in conflict with the fundamental principles of the Constitution of the Republic of Estonia.[27] EU secondary legislation (regulations, directives and decisions) issued by the EU institutions under the EC Treaty must be in line with the EC Treaty. Disputes concerning the legality of secondary European Union law are settled by the Court of Justice or by the Court of First Instance of the European Communities. Hence, Estonian courts do not have the jurisdiction to declare any secondary European Union legal act to be in conflict with the EU primary law.[28]

The *Pupino* case has been referred to in two Supreme Court cases, but in both, the Supreme Court decided that it is impossible to apply the *Pupino* case because it does not offer a basis for a *contra legem* interpretation.[29]

9.2   CRIMES AGAINST THE FINANCIAL INTERESTS OF THE EU

9.2.1   *Estonian Substantive and Procedural Criminal Law – Protecting the Financial Interests of the EU*

Estonia ratified the PIF Convention[30] and its additional protocols[31] on 23 November 2004.[32] And the EPC offers the European Union's financial interests the same protection as to the financial interests of the Republic of Estonia. As every year there are new legal acts introduced to enhance the protection of national financial interests,

---

26 The Constitution of the Republic of Estonia Amendment Act, RT I 2003, 64, 429, Article 2, available at: https://www.riigiteataja.ee/en/eli/530102013005/consolide.

27 *Ibid.*, Article 1.

28 Supreme Court judgment in case No 3-3-1-74-05, *OÜ XXXXXXX complaint to cancel the Minister of Agriculture decree No. 394 of 30 October 2004, Item 1, Paragraph 1, and the Taxation and Customs Board's tax notice No. 16.2.2-9 / 45 of 10 December 2004 and OÜ XXXXXX application for suspension of proceedings*, pp. 12-14. Available at: https://www.riigikohus.ee/et/lahendid?asjaNr=3-3-1-74-05.

29 Supreme Court judgments in criminal cases No 3-1-1-45-07, *against Meelis Hansar*, available at: https://www.riigikohus.ee/et/lahendid?asjaNr=3-1-1-45-07 and 3-1-1-125-06 *against Jüri Rosin*, available at: https://www.riigikohus.ee/et/lahendid?asjaNr=3-1-1-125-06.

30 Council Act of 26 July 1995 drawing up the Convention on the protection of the European Communities' financial interests, OJ C 316, 27.11.1995, pp. 48-57, available at: https://eur-lex.europa.eu/legal-content/EN/TXT/PDF/?uri=CELEX:31995F1127(03)&from=EN.

31 Protocol drawn up on the basis of Article K.3 of the Treaty on European Union to the Convention on the protection of the European Communities' financial interests – Statements made by Member States on the adoption of the Act drawing up the Protocol – OJ C 313, 23 October 1996, pp. 2-10. Available at: https://eur-lex.europa.eu/legal-content/EN/TXT/?qid=1537877274276&uri=CELEX:41996A1023(01). Second Protocol, drawn up on the basis of Article K.3 of the treaty on European Union, to the Convention on the protection of the European Communities' financial interests – Joint Declaration on Article 13(2) – Commission Declaration on Article 7 OJ C 221, 19 July 1997, pp. 12-22. Available at: https://eur-lex.europa.eu/legal-content/EN/TXT/?qid=1537877414814&uri=CELEX:41997A0719(02).

32 Act of Accession to the Convention on the protection of the European Communities' financial interests and its additional protocols, RT II 2005, 1, 1. Available at: https://www.riigiteataja.ee/akt/827807.

the protection of the EU's financial interests is improving as well. Last year, the new Public Procurement Act[33] was adopted (entered into force 1 September 2017).

9.2.2 Estonian Participation in the Institutions and Bodies Entrusted in the Fight Against Crimes Against the Financial Interest of the EU

Estonia is represented in Eurojust. Raivo Sepp is the National Member and Eve Olesk is Deputy National Member for Estonia. Estonia is active in the European Judicial Network – the Estonian partners to the EJN are the Office of General Prosecutor, the Ministry of Justice and the Police and Border Guard Board. The Prosecutor's Office is also cooperating with the European Anti-Fraud Office of the European Commission (OLAF), participates in the work of the Camden Asset Recovery Inter-Agency Network (CARIN) and in the unofficial cooperation network connecting police officers and other crime fighters in the field of environmental crime (ENVICRIMENET).[34] For many years the Estonian Government had a pretty hesitant view on introducing a European public prosecutor until on 26 September 2013 the government reached the conclusion to fully support the conception of the European Public Prosecutor's Office (EPPO).[35] Meanwhile, some doubts arose concerning the effectiveness of the criminal procedure involving EPPO, but eventually, the idea to follow the Swedish model was abandoned, and Estonia is supporting the EPPO project. The implementing legislation is currently being drafted, but it is not public yet.

There are no other major constitutional or legal issues that make it difficult to cooperate with EU bodies and other Member states in the field of protection of the financial interests of the EU. According to the Estonian Constitution Article 36,

> [n]o citizen of Estonia may be extradited to a foreign state, except under conditions prescribed by an international treaty and pursuant to a procedure provided by such treaty and by law. Extraditions are decided by the Government of the Republic. Any person who is subject to an extradition order has the right to challenge this order in an Estonian court.[36]

---

33 Public Procurement Act, RT I, 01.07.2017, 1... RT I, 29.06.2018, 4. Available at: https://www.riigiteataja.ee/akt/129062018079?leiaKehtiv. English translation available at: https://www.riigiteataja.ee/en/eli/504072018004/consolide.

34 Prosecutor's Office, International cooperation. Available at: www.prokuratuur.ee/en/prosecutors-office/international-cooperation.

35 Ministry of Justice, The Government supports the creation of the European Public Prosecutor's Office (in Estonian). Available at: https://www.just.ee/et/uudised/valitsus-toetab-euroopa-prokuratuuri-loomist.

36 Estonian Constitution, RT 1992, 26, 349... RT I, 15.05.2015, 1. Available at: https://www.riigiteataja.ee/akt/115052015002?leiaKehtiv. English translation available at: https://www.riigiteataja.ee/en/eli/521052015001/consolide.

But this has not impeded the execution of EAWs. If "an arrest warrant has been issued with regard to an Estonian citizen for the execution of imprisonment and the person applies for enforcement of the punishment in Estonia" surrender of a person to a foreign state is not allowed.[37] And

> Estonia surrenders its citizens who reside permanently in Estonia on the basis of a European arrest warrant for the period of criminal proceedings provided that the punishment imposed on a person in a Member State is enforced in the Republic of Estonia.[38]

But nevertheless, it has not caused difficulties in the surrender process because as a rule, the Estonian citizens whom the other Member States have requested to surrender have agreed to the surrender.[39]

9.2.3   Legal Actions Taken in Estonia to Fight Corruption and Fraud

The Estonian government adopted on 03 October 2013 the 'Strategic plan for fighting corruption 2013-2020'.[40] The strategic plan focuses on three areas: a) increasing awareness concerning corruption; b) raising transparency in the functioning of public institutions and c) improving capabilities of law enforcement to fight corruption. Last year, a new Public Procurement Act[41] was adopted (entered into force on 1 September 2017) introducing a fully electronic procurement process guaranteeing maximum transparency. The Estonian Ministry of Justice and Ministry of Internal Affairs introduced in 2015 'Priorities in fighting criminality', and one of the priorities is "serious corruption, in particular, the corruption threatening national security and honest business".[42]

In 2014 the *Riigikogu* (the Parliament) introduced an amendment to the Value-Added Tax Act requiring that the value-added tax return has to be supplemented with an appendix reflecting all the invoices in which the transferor of the goods or provider of services has marked the supply taxable at the 20 per cent and 9 per cent value-added tax rate if the invoice or the total amount of invoices without value-added tax makes up at

---

37   ECCP § 492 (1) (4).
38   ECCP § 492 (3).
39   Joanna Paabumets, *op. cit.* at p. 57.
40   Strategic plan for fighting corruption 2017-2020 (in Estonian). Available at: www.korruptsioon.ee/sites/ www.korruptsioon.ee/files/elfinder/dokumendid/korruptsioonivastane_strateegia_2013-2020_1.pdf.
41   Public Procurement Act, RT I, 01.07.2017, 1. RT I, 29.06.2018, 4. Available at: https://www.riigiteataja.ee/ akt/129062018079?leiaKehtiv. English translation available at: https://www.riigiteataja.ee/en/eli/ 504072018004/consolide.
42   Ministry of Justice, Priorities in fighting criminality. Available at: https://www.just.ee/et/eesmargid-tegevused/kriminaalpoliitika/kuritegevusvastased-prioriteedid.

least 1,000 euros for one transaction partner during the taxation period.[43] The data from the appendixes to the VAT return helps the tax authority to detect various deceptive schemes before the shell buffer companies manage to dissolve or disappear, as well as helps to reduce the proportion of fictitious bills and increased the obligation to pay VAT.[44]

9.2.4 Estonian Steps Vis-à-Vis the European Commission Report on the Protection of the EU's Financial Interests, COM (2017) 383 Final

Estonia has fully transposed Directives 2014/23/EU, 2014/24/EU and 2014/25/EU by adopting a new Public Procurement Act in 2017.[45] From 18 October 2018, all communication and information exchange related to public procurement between the contracting authority or entity and the economic operator, including making procurement documents available and submitting tenders, requests to participate and clarifications, will be carried out by electronic means, *id est* everything will be done via an e-procurement system.[46]

The new Customs Act[47] was adopted in 2017 and entered into force on 1 July 2017 bringing the Estonian law into accordance with the EU Customs Code. The new Customs Act introduced some new customs databases – the x-ray images database will collect all images made during customs check and the collected information will be used for preventing smuggling and tax fraud. For the same purposes, the database for the carriage of passengers was added, which will collect information regarding international bus and train passengers.[48] In case reasonable doubts are not dispelled, and the transaction value method is not applicable, Estonian customs use customs valuation methodology provided by customs law. Estonia has included EU-wide risk profiles based on 'clean average prices' in its risk management system. Potentially undervalued goods are systematically checked by means of risk profiles, but non-release of potentially undervalued goods has not been applied.

---

43 Value-Added Tax Act, RT I 2003, 82, 554. RT I, 24.04.2018, 2, § 27 (1²). Available at: https://www. riigiteataja.ee/akt/124042018004?leiaKehtiv. English translation available at: https://www.riigiteataja.ee/en/ eli/526042018002/consolide.

44 M. Aasmäe, MTA: käibedeklaratsiooni lisa on vähendanud fiktiivsete arvete osakaalu. Available at: https:// www.emta.ee/et/uudised/mta-kaibedeklaratsiooni-lisa-vahendanud-fiktiivsete-arvete-osakaalu.

45 Public Procurement Act, RT I, 01.07.2017, 1. RT I, 29.06.2018, 4. Available at: https://www.riigiteataja.ee/ akt/129062018079?leiaKehtiv. English translation available at: https://www.riigiteataja.ee/en/eli/ 504072018004/consolide.

46 *Ibid.*, § 23(9), § 45(1) and § 238(3).

47 Customs Act, RT I, 16.06.2017, 1... RT I, 11.01.2018, 1. Available at: https://www.riigiteataja.ee/ akt/111012018014?leiaKehtiv. English translation available at: https://www.riigiteataja.ee/en/eli/ 504062018001/consolide.

48 *Ibid.*, § 15 and 16.

Estonia has enhanced the quality of reporting irregularities to OLAF and includes information about the location and, if applicable, the priority area of the measures/projects affected. Concerning low detection rate in ETC programmes and the increasing threat of transnational fraud, Estonia has increased attention and enhanced cooperation with the other Member States.

9.3   The Implementation of Directive (EU) 2017/1371 of the European Parliament and of the Council of 5 July 2017 on the Fight Against Fraud to the Union's Financial Interests by Means of Criminal Law

9.3.1   *Reactions to the PIF Directive and Its Transposition*

As Estonia had fully implemented the PIF Convention, there was no major discussion concerning the PIF Directive. The implementing legislation is being drafted. No drafts are public yet.

9.3.2   *Estonian Supreme Court Case Law Touching the PIF Directive Legal Domain*

There have been very few cases concerning the PIF Directive legal domain in the Supreme Court. The two cases involve benefit fraud. In one case the Supreme Court decided that although according to the wording of the EPC § 210 only a 'person engaging in economic activities' can be convicted for benefit fraud, a local government may be considered to be a person engaging in economic activities.[49] In the second case it was decided that although it is possible that without providing the fraudulent information the accused would have been awarded some benefit, the whole awarded benefit is considered to be an asset acquired through offence and therefore subject to confiscation.[50]

9.3.3   *Issues to Be Solved in Legislation Implementing the PIF Directive*

There are two important issues to be solved in legislation implementing the PIF Directive.

---

49   The Estonian Supreme Court case No 3-1-1-96-16. Available in Estonian: https://www.riigikohus.ee/et/lahendid?asjaNr=3-1-1-96-16.
50   The Estonian Supreme Court case No 3-1-1-54-15. Available in Estonian: https://rikos.rik.ee/?asjaNr=3-1-1-54-15.

a)   *Ne bis in idem*

The most difficult issue is compliance of the directive provisions with the *ne bis in idem* principle. The first sentence of the Article 14 of the directive provides that

> [t]he application of administrative measures, penalties and fines as laid down in Union law, in particular those within the meaning of Articles 4 and 5 of Regulation (EC, Euratom) No 2988/95, or in national law adopted in compliance with a specific obligation under Union law, shall be without prejudice to this Directive.

The sentence makes no reference to the character of the possibly applied administrative measures, penalties and fines. Therefore, literal interpretation of the sentence would consider mandatory criminal prosecution even after an administrative penalty of criminal nature has been already applied for the offence. Articles 5 of Regulation (EC, Euratom) No 2988/95 foresees the possibility of applying administrative fines. And the CJEU has so long interpreted administrative fines (at least in certain cases) to be of criminal nature and to arise the *ne bis in idem* issues.[51] The European Court of Human Rights has taken a similar position.[52]

The second sentence of Article 14 of the directive applies to the connection between two possible procedures in another direction. It stipulates that

> Member States shall ensure that any criminal proceedings initiated on the basis of national provisions implementing this Directive do not unduly affect the proper and effective application of administrative measures, penalties and fines that cannot be equated to criminal proceedings, laid down in Union law or national implementing provisions.

This sentence explicitly excludes the situations concerning the application of administrative measures, penalties and fines that can be equated to criminal proceedings.

The aspect that the second sentence explicitly excludes administrative fines of a criminal nature makes it very difficult to interpret the first sentence that does not make a similar exclusion to include nevertheless the exclusion. The same issue arises regarding Article 7(5) providing that paragraph 1 of the Article "shall be without prejudice to the exercise of disciplinary powers by the competent authorities against public officials". The text of the article does not make a distinction between the disciplinary measures of criminal nature. Fortunately, the Recital 17 of the directive can help to interpret the

---

51 ECJ 20 March 2018, Case 537/16, *Garlsson Real Estate and Others*, ECLI:EU:C:2018:193, paras. 53-57.
52 *See, e.g.*, Grande Stevens and Others v. Italy (App No. 18640/10, 18647/10, 18663/10, 18668/10) (2014) ECHR 4 March, para. 222.

article to exclude the cases of disciplinary penalties of a criminal nature. The first sentence of Recital 17 states that "this Directive does not affect the proper and effective application of disciplinary measures or penalties **other than of a criminal nature**" (emphases added).

b)   *The limitation period for the execution of judgment*
Article 12(4) of the directive requires that

> Member States shall take the necessary measures to enable the enforcement of:
> a. a penalty of more than one year of imprisonment; or alternatively,
> b. a penalty of imprisonment in the case of a criminal offence which is punishable by a maximum sanction of at least four years of imprisonment, imposed following a final conviction for a criminal offence referred to in Article 3, 4 or 5, for **at least five years** from the date of the final conviction. That period may include extensions of the limitation period arising from interruption or suspension (emphases added).

The EPC § 82 foresees a long limitation period (five years) only for the execution of judgments in case of criminal offences in the first degree (i.e., punishable by over five years' imprisonment). The limitation period for the execution of judgments in case of criminal offences punishable from four to five years' imprisonment is three years. In the EPC § 82 there are several situations in which the limitation period for the execution of a judgment is suspended:
1. the period during which the person evades service or payment of the punishment;
2. a period of probation imposed on the basis of the provisions of § 73 or 74 of the EPC;
3. the period during which enforcement of the punishment imposed on the person is postponed or by which the term of the punishment has been extended;
4. the period during which the person is in a foreign state and is not or cannot be extradited.

The final sentence of Article 12(4) states that "[t]hat period may include extensions of the limitation period arising from interruption or suspension". But it does not mention that the limitation period could be shorter under the condition that the period may be suspended in the event of specified acts (as it is foreseen for the limitation period that enables the investigation, prosecution, trial and judicial decision of criminal offences in the Article 12 (3)). Therefore, most likely the last sentence of Article 12(4) cannot be interpreted to allow shorter limitation periods than mentioned in Article 12(4). Consequently, the implementing legislation has to reconsider the whole mechanism of limitation periods for the execution of judgments.

10 SELECTED CASE STUDIES: THE CASE STUDY OF FRANCE

Arceli Turmo

10.1 GENERAL IMPACT AND IMPLEMENTATION OF EU CRIMINAL LAW IN FRANCE

France, notably through its successive governments, has generally presented itself as favourable to the development of European Union criminal law. It has taken a leadership role in negotiations concerning the adoption of new instruments and tried to influence the choices made, generally considering them to be broadly compatible with French criminal law. This presentation must nevertheless be contrasted with the less enthusiastic points of view of a number of criminal lawyers warning that certain aspects of EU criminal law could prove more difficult to implement in France, or could lead to calling into question key principles of French substantive or procedural criminal law. This contrast is visible in the French attitude to the European Public Prosecutor's Office (EPPO)[1] and the PIF Directive.[2] After a brief overview of the general attitude of France towards EU criminal law (Section 10.1 of this chapter), this paper will examine the specific issues related to the fight against fraud affecting the EU's financial interests in France (Section 10.2 of this chapter) and, more specifically, with the implementation of the EPPO Regulation and the PIF Directive in this Member State (Section 10.3 of this chapter).

In general, France takes a rather favourable view towards European criminal law, although the reality of implementation is sometimes more complex. European Union law, especially as the efficiency of the available has improved, is seen as a welcome addition to the tools at the disposal of police and judicial powers where it concerns operational cooperation, and as a rather inoffensive confirmation of European human rights standards in other cases. Special attention will be given to the use of European Arrest Warrants (EAWs) and to the standard of protection of *ne bis in idem*, of particular interest in this regard.

---

1   Council Regulation 2017/1939 of 12 October 2017 implementing enhanced cooperation on the establishment of the European Public Prosecutor's Office ('the EPPO'), OJ L 283, 31 October 2017, p. 1.
2   Directive 2017/1371 of the European Parliament and of the Council of 5 July 2017 on the fight against fraud to the Union's financial interests by means of criminal law, OJ L 198, 28 July 2017, p. 29.

10.1.1   The General Impact of EU Criminal Law

Advances such as the establishment of Eurojust have been welcomed, and France has seized on the opportunities to make this body more efficient, as evidenced by two decisions to add personnel to its French office in 2002 and 2007.[3] Recourse to Common Investigation Teams[4] has been high, and France was the first Member State to request an opinion on a conflict of competence from the Eurojust College and to comply with[5] the political statements made by the French Ministry of Justice on the progress made in EU criminal law, and more generally France's support for European institutions in this area confirms this positive attitude and the State's attempt to position itself as a leader in this field.[6]

Although France is happy to push for the introduction of new EU instruments, it does not always appear to be favourable to very centralized options or to significant harmonization. Moreover, in the area of procedural criminal law, a 2018 Report commissioned by the European Parliament found that France had not seemed particularly ready to introduce significant changes to its own legal system through the implementation of EU instruments.[7] This is generally explained away by an assumption that EU instruments are compatible with the main aspects of French procedural law. In a number of cases where the EU introduced new instruments aimed at guaranteeing respect for fundamental rights, such as in the case of the directives on procedural criminal law, French institutions generally held the view that it was already in compliance because those instruments were based on the standards established by the European Court of Human Rights (ECtHR). Previous efforts to comply with those standards could, therefore, be considered sufficient to comply with the requirements of EU law.[8]

However, in the case of older directives, where we already have some evidence on the interpretation of the EU instruments by French courts and the appropriateness of the implementation, there are some indications that the situation is not ideal and some

---

3   Jean-Marie Huet, 'L'expérience française', in Cour de cassation (dir.), *Quelles perspectives pour le ministère public européen ? Protéger les intérêts financiers et fondamentaux de l'Union,* Dalloz, 2010, p. 142.

4   Under Council Resolution on a Model Agreement for Setting Up a Joint Investigation Team (JIT) [2017] OJ C 18/1.

5   Jean-Marie Huet, *ibid.*, 139-140.

6   *See* the Press Releases published by the Ministry of Justice on 14 November 2016, confirming its support for the European Court of Human Rights ('Cour européenne des droits de l'Homme et Conseil de l'Europe', Jean-Jacques Urvoas, Garde des Sceaux, Minister of Justice), and on 8 December 2016, 28 March 2017, 12 October 2017 All confirming support for the EPPO ('Création du parquet européen', 'Vers un Parquet européen', 'Le règlement instituant le Parquet européen adopté').

7   Perrine Simon, Report on France, in Elodie Sellier and Anne Weyembergh, Criminal Procedural Laws across the Union – A Comparative Analysis of Selected Main Differences and the Impact they Have over the Development of EU Legislation, Study requested by the European Parliament's Committee on Civil Liberties, Justice and Home Affairs (European Parliament 2018), 15.

8   For further details on this issue, *see* Perrine Simon, *ibid.*, 7.

problems do exist. General statements expressing a favourable attitude towards European cooperation in the field of criminal law must not mask the fact that legislative intervention to implement new secondary law is sometimes insufficient, and the supreme courts are not always as enthusiastic. The implementation of Directive 2010/64 on the right to interpretation and translation[9] provides a good illustration of this type of issue. The directive was implemented through new legislation on 5 August 2013.[10] The new provisions introduced in the French Criminal Procedure Code did not, however, bring about significant changes, and they required case law to establish the details and truly ensure compliance with the directive. The Cour de Cassation's first rulings concerning the French provisions implementing the directive are disappointing in this respect,[11] but this appears to be a failure of legislative implementation rather than a failure strictly attributable to the supreme court.

In general, however, French courts have been willing to comply with ECtHR case law as well as European Court of Justice (ECJ) case law for a number of years, without any significant resistance except in very specific cases. In cases where European law allows them to find better human rights protection, or where there is clear ECtHR case law establishing the insufficiency of the current French legal framework, judges have been willing to refer to European law and comply with ECHR or EU law standards.[12]

10.1.2   Specific Issues Related to the Implementation of EU Criminal Law

10.1.2.1   European Arrest Warrant

The European Arrest Warrant (EAW)[13] is now well established among the instruments at the disposal of the French police and judiciary institutions.[14] In 2014, France was among the Member States which gave full statistical data on the execution of EAWs and was third out of 26 over 2005 to 2013 in terms of issued EAWs (10,000) and fourth in the number of EAWs that resulted in effective surrender (2600).[15] Thus as issuing

---

9   Directive 2010/64/EU of the European Parliament and of the Council on the right to interpretation and translation in criminal proceedings [2010] OJ L 280/01.

10   Loi n° 2013-711 du 5 août 2013 portant diverses dispositions d'adaptation dans le domaine de la justice en application du droit de l'Union européenne et des engagements internationaux de la France, JO n°181, 6 August 2013, 1338.

11   Rodolphe Mésa, 'La sanction de la transgression du droit à la traduction des pièces essentielles à l'exercice des droits de la défense', [2016] 12 Gazette du Palais 23.

12   *See*, for instance, the general study by Olivier Dutheillet de Lamothe, 'L'influence de la Cour européenne des droits de l'homme sur le conseil constitutionnel' (2009), Speech made on a visit of a delegation from the European Court of Human Rights to the Conseil constitutionnel.

13   Council Framework Decision 2002/584/JHA on the European arrest warrant and the surrender procedures between Member States [2002] OJ L 190/1.

14   Jean-Marie Huet, 'L'expérience française', in *op. cit.* at p. 136 *et seq.*

15   Giulio Sabbati, European Parliament, European Arrest Warrant – At a Glance Infographic (2014).

authorities, French courts and judges have used the EAW increasingly and in a way that is consistent with most comparable EU Member States.

In recent years, cooperation with other Member States' judicial authorities in order to implement EAWs has generally been smooth and French courts seldom try to challenge mutual recognition. In the cases where additional information was requested on fundamental rights protection, such information was generally provided to the satisfaction of French authorities. *Ne bis in idem* and *in absentia* rulings were two of the main grounds for concern expressed in the French Report in the 2018 Study commissioned by the European Parliament.[16] However, in practice, much of the problem appears to be based not strictly on the standards for fundamental rights protection being enforced in the Member States, but on insufficient streamlining and difficulties in accessing similar documents and translations across the EU. Indeed, one of the major obstacles to judicial cooperation in criminal matters in France seems to be that communicating with the other Member States' judicial authorities remains difficult, especially where there are specific issues or concerns that require further correspondence. More streamlined, digital documents based on common models, which could be automatically translated, would help solve such problems.[17]

Up to 2018, no cases were found where differences between national criminal procedures were directly perceived as an obstacle to the implementation of the instrument or to mutual recognition.[18] However, French authorities as executing judges do control respect for the rights of the defence in both the French proceedings and in the issuing Member State, both before and after the person is surrendered. This is now consistent with ECtHR and CJEU case law, especially after *Aranyosi*,[19] under which the executing State must take into account the probable status and treatment of the person in the issuing State.[20] France itself is not exempt from human rights-related concerns, especially related to the state of its prisons.[21]

Another issue mentioned in the 2018 Study was that the 'proportionality test' practised by French public prosecutors in deciding which EAWs to transfer to the investigating chamber can also be construed as the result of a similar lack of trust for the other Member States' standards in issuing EAWs. French public prosecutors generally seem to consider the EAW as an instrument to be used (only) in the case of serious offences, which excludes a number of cases for which such warrants are issued by the

---

16 Perrine Simon, *op. cit.* at p. 15.
17 Interview with Thomas Cassuto, Conseiller, Cour d'appel de Lyon (27 September 2018).
18 Perrine Simon (above n 16), 6.
19 ECJ *Aranyosi and Caldararu* (2016) C-404/15 and C-659/15.
20 The Cour de cassation seems to apply the *Aranyosi* case law in a strict manner: Crim 20 mai 2014 n° 14-83.138, Crim 12 juillet 2016 n° 16-84.000; Crim 12 juillet 2016, n° 16-84-000; 19 août 2016 n° 16-84.725.
21 *See*, for example, ECtHR *Canali v. France* (2013) app. No 40119/09; *Yengo v. France* (2015) app. no 50494/12; *F.R. v. France* (2016) app. no 12791/05; and the pending applications in cases *J.M.B. v. France* and others, app. nos 9671/15 et al.

other Member States, especially Poland whose use of the EAW is determined by the requirement that all offences be prosecuted.[22] If this type of test is considered contrary to the aims of the EAW, European standards, or better guidelines concerning the use of this instrument, appear to be the best solution to prevent French or other national authorities from, in a sense, taking matters into their own hands.

10.1.2.2   Ne Bis in Idem

One significant difficulty remains *ne bis in idem*, and its implementation in cases of double-track enforcement involving both an administrative and a criminal sanction. French courts and the Conseil constitutionnel resisted ECtHR's case law before *A & B v. Norway*[23] on the basis of France's reservations to Article 4 of Protocol 7 to the Convention. They maintained exceptions where *ne bis in idem* were not considered incompatible with double-track enforcement, especially in the field of tax law.[24] The ECtHR's new position, excluding certain types of double-track enforcement from the scope of *ne bis in idem*, seems more compatible with the French position. However, the ECJ partly rejected the ECtHR's new position in three rulings made on 20 March 2018.[25] In these judgments, the CJEU held that such cases of double-track enforcement are, in principle, incompatible with *ne bis in idem* but may be justified under Article 52§1 of the European Charter of Fundamental Rights by reference to objectives in the general interest of the European Union such as the protection of the Union's financial interests.[26] Such objectives may justify limited violations of *ne bis in idem*, but only under a strict proportionality review. The compatibility of both European Courts' new case laws remains to be determined,[27] but more specifically, there are also uncertainties as to French courts' willingness to adopt the CJEU's new position within the scope of EU law and the compatibility of the strands of case law concerning VAT fraud, under the influence of CJEU case law, and purely domestic tax cases.[28]

---

22   Perrine Simon, *op. cit.* at p. 7 – similar findings of a 'proportionality' test in appraising EAWs appear concerning other States such as Germany or Estonia: Micaela del Monte, 'Revising the European Arrest Warrant. European Added Value Assessment accompanying the European Parliament's Legislative Own-Initiative Report', EAVA 6/2013, p. 20.

23   ECtHR *A & B v. Norway* (2016) app. nos 24130/11, 29758/11.

24   Cour de cassation, Crim. 13 January 2010, no 09-84.977; Crim. 13 Sseptember 2017, no 15-84.823; Conseil constitutionnel *M. Alec W. e.a.* (2016) no 2016-545 QPC. Concerning the compatibility of French case law with *A & B v. Norway, see* Olivier Décima, 'Unum in idem: cumul des sanctions pénales et fiscales' (2017) 7-8 JCP G. 183.

25   ECJ *Menci* (2018) C-524/15; *Garlsson Real Estate e.a.* (2018) C-537/16; CJEU *Di Puma & Zecca* (2018) Joined Cases C-596 & C-597/16.

26   *See* §18-19 of *Menci.*

27   *See* Araceli Turmo, 'L'art du compromis: la Cour de justice opte pour une résistance modérée à l'arrêt *A et B / Norvège*' [2018] RAE 149; Olivier Décima, *op. cit.*

28   Nicolas Guilland and Arsene Taxand, 'Cumul de sanctions de la fraude fiscale: pas de requiem pour *ne bis in idem*' (2018) 21 Droit fiscal comm. 285.

The standard of protection for *ne bis in idem* in double-track enforcement is a very specific issue, but it is particularly relevant in relation to tax regimes. Considering the scope of new instruments such as the PIF Directive, the ECJ could be called upon to clarify the new limitations on *ne bis in idem* and their implementation in the Member States rather soon. It is difficult to predict whether French courts will make significant efforts to comply with the ECJ's new approach, whether they will favour the ECtHR's approach or whether the standard of protection of this fundamental right in French law will become ever more fragmented as certain lines of case law follow the position of the ECJ while others do not.

Overall, EU criminal law is rather well received in France, and there are few implementation issues. Where these exist, the roots of the problem may vary from incompatibilities with key aspects of French criminal law to the sometimes uneasy relationship between the national supreme courts and EU law, or in the limitations of the EU instruments themselves.

10.2   The Fight Against Fraud Affecting the EU's Financial Interests

France was rather late in developing a modern legal framework to fight against corruption and fraud. However, significant progress has been made in recent years. This has also had a significant impact on the protection of the European Union's financial interests since, for the most part, national rules apply, and there are no general provisions dealing with fraud affecting the EU specifically.

10.2.1   Recent Legal Developments in the Fight Against Fraud

France ranked 23rd in Transparency International's Corruption Perceptions Index in 2017,[29] equal to Uruguay and far below the northern European states such as Denmark, Finland or the Netherlands. This perception must be understood as related to a lack of willingness to take firm actions to fight corruption and fraud, especially when the acts were committed by high-ranking officials or politicians, or took place on an international scale. There has been a gradual change, however, especially after the 1990s during which a number of high-profile corruption scandals triggered legislative and institutional reforms. France started developing an 'extensive anti-corruption framework'[30] in line with the major international conventions such as the UN

---

29   Transparency International Corruption Perceptions Index 2017 (2018).
30   Piotr Bąkowski and Sofija Voronova, 'Corruption in the European Union. Prevalence of Corruption, and Anti-Corruption Efforts in Selected EU Member States' (2017) European Parliamentary Research Service Study 47.

Convention Against Corruption (UNCAC) of 2005.[31] The current president Emmanuel Macron and his first government had included in their platforms a plan to take major initiatives to fight against corruption, making a number of Transparency International France's recommendations their own. A report by Transparency International France published in 2018 indicated that the current government's reforms were somewhat satisfactory but remained insufficient.[32]

A number of provisions of the Criminal Code now establish criminal offences covering different types of corruption including conflicts of interest, and a new section on breaches of the duty of probity including types of embezzlement and breaches of public procurement rules.[33] Sanctions and fines for corruption offences have been increased, and anti-corruption organizations have the right to file civil party claims. NGOs such as Anticor or Sherpa have seized upon this opportunity to participate in judicial proceedings concerning ill-acquired gains involving foreign public officials.[34] These efforts go hand in hand with a number of reforms aimed at improving the transparency of public institutions and the exemplarity of public officials, including an organic statute and an ordinary statute of 15 September 2017.[35] The fight against fraud and corruption has also benefited from the extension of the statute of limitation from three to six years for all *délits*.[36]

One of the most important statutory instruments introduced in recent years is the 'Loi Sapin II' (Sapin II Act)[37] which aimed to introduce new mechanisms enabling efficient detection, prevention and sanction of corruption. This statute was presented as answering UNCAC requirements. It introduces a better approach to prevention in the fight against corruption, for instance, by requiring companies above a certain size as well as public agents to have prevention plans with internal channels for reporting misconduct. This

---

31   United Nations Convention against Corruption, 31 October 2003. France ratified the Convention on 11 July 2005.

32   Transparency International France, 'Un an après l'élection présidentielle: l'éthique et la transparence de la vie publique doivent redevenir des priorités' (2018).

33   Articles 432-10 etc. Criminal Code.

34   Most recently, Sherpa filed a claim on 16 October 2018 against members of the entourage of Djibouti President Ismaïl Omar Guelleh, alleging abuse of corporate assets, embezzlement of public funds, breach of trust and bribery of foreign public officials (Press Release, 30 November 2018, https://www.asso-sherpa.org/biens-mal-acquis-plainte-contre-lentourage-president-de-djibouti).

35   Loi organique n° 2017-1338 du 15 septembre 2017 pour la confiance dans la vie politique, JO 217, 16 septembre 2017, and Loi n° 2017-1339 du 15 septembre 2017 pour la confiance dans la vie politique, JO n° 217, 16 septembre 2017. These acts aim in particular to help elected officials avoiding conflicts of interest, including for example employing family members, but also to improve transparency of their assets, and to establish rules on political party funding, and to this end give significant powers to the Haute autorité pour la transparence de la vie publique (the High authority for transparency of public life).

36   Loi n° 2017-242 du 27 février 2017 portant réforme de la prescription en matière pénale, JO n°50, 28 février 2017. *Délits* are the intermediary category of criminal offences, punishable by a short prison sentence or a fine, between *crimes*, the most serious, and *contraventions*, the least serious offences.

37   Loi n° 2016-1691 du 9 décembre 2016 relative à la transparence, à la lutte contre la corruption et à la modernisation de la vie économique, JO n° 297, 10 décembre 2016.

statute increases sanctions, protection for whistle-blowers and extends the offence of influence peddling to cases concerning foreign public officials, an issue that had long been a cause of concern. It introduces a public registry of lobbies intervening in Parliament's work on legislative proposals, managed by the *Haute Autorité pour la transparence de la vie publique*, although this register is not fully operational at present.[38] The same statute also established the *Agence française anticorruption* (French Anticorruption Agency (AFA)), inaugurated in March 2017. The Agency is subordinated to the Ministry of Justice and the Ministry of Finance, a choice which was harshly criticized by organizations such as the *Syndicat National de la Magistrature* (a left-leaning union of magistrates).[39] However, it does have relatively broad advisory and investigation powers, including the prevention and detection of corruption, influence trading, conflicts of interest, abuse of public funds and favouritism.[40]

A recent statute passed on 23 October 2018[41] introduces significant improvements in the fight against tax fraud, although they have been considered insufficiently ambitious by NGOs such as Anticor and Sherpa.[42] The new statute introduces a type of *'name and shame'* rule in French tax law,[43] similar to those established by a number of other Member States in recent years.[44] Under Article 18 of the statute, tax authorities will be able to publish on a government website the taxes and fines imposed on legal persons for cases involving fraudulent manoeuvres concerning amounts of at least 50,000 euros.[45] Moreover, criminal judges finding a person guilty of an offence in the field of tax law will now have an obligation to order this decision to be displayed and published.[46]

---

38 *See*, in particular, the criticism of the implementation regulation which, according to the Haute Autorité's 2017 Report, severely restricts the potential of the register: Haute Autorité pour la transparence de la vie publique, 'Rapport d'activité 2017, p. 88 *et seq*.

39 Syndicat de la magistrature, 'Observations du Syndicat de la magistrature sur le projet de loi relatif à la trasnsparence, à la lutte contre la corruption et à la modernisation de la vie économique' (2016), 2.

40 Its first Annual Report indicates broad regulatory and advisory competences as well as a competence in developing international cooperation and domestic administrative cooperation: Agence Française Anticorruption, Rapport annuel d'activité 2017.

41 Loi n° 2018-898 du 23 octobre 2018 relative à la lutte contre la fraude, JO n° 246, 24 octobre 2018.

42 Common Press Release of Anticor, ATTAC, CCFD-Terre Solidaire, Oxfam, Sherpa, Syndicat de la Magistrature, 'Fin de l'examen du projet de loi contre la fraude fiscale à l'Assemblée nationale', 19 September 2018.

43 For greater details on this aspect of the reform, *see* Daniel Gutmann, 'La pratique du *'name and shame'* (2018) Dalloz 2224.

44 *See, e.g.* the publication of the details of deliberate tax defaulters by HM Revenue & Customs in the United Kingdom under Section 94 of the Finance Act 2009: https://www.gov.uk/Government/publications/publishing-details-of-deliberate-tax-defaulters-pddd.

45 *'Les amendes ou majorations appliquées à l'encontre de personnes morales à raison de manquements graves caractérisés par un montant de droits fraudés d'un minimum de 50 000 € et le recours à une manœuvre frauduleuse, au sens des b et c de l'article 1729, peuvent faire l'objet d'une publication, sauf si ces manquements ont fait l'objet d'un dépôt de plainte pour fraude fiscale par l'administration'.*

46 Article 16, Loi n° 2018-898 du 23 octobre 2018 relative à la lutte contre la fraude, JO n° 246, 24 octobre 2018.

Some progress has also been made in limiting the reach of the *'verrou de Bercy'* (the 'Bercy-lock'), a rule dating back to 1920[47] under which fraud cases may only be prosecuted if the Ministry of Finance files a complaint. This rule has come under very harsh criticism in recent years[48] as it meant public prosecutors could not bring charges without the Ministry's intervention, which allows a number of perpetrators of fraud to avoid criminal trials and convictions. Under Article 36 of the October 2018 statute, the most serious cases of fraud (amounting to over 100,000 euros[49] and indicating an intention to avoid tax) will be put directly in the hands of public prosecutors and investigating judges by forcing tax authorities to inform the public prosecutor of their findings. This reform is expected to allow magistrates to directly prosecute about 2000 cases per year, double the current numbers, but still a small minority – most tax offences remain under the previous system of the *verrou de Bercy*.[50] Another limitation of the scope of these harsher measures comes from the extension, in Article 25 of the same statute, of the scope of the *convention judiciaire d'intérêt public* to these offences. Under this mechanism,[51] judges can approve settlements between the guilty party and the prosecution, allowing them to avoid publicity or criminal records in exchange for a fine. Although this is meant to allow shorter trials and greater efficiency, this does seem to contradict the simultaneous introduction of a *'name and shame'* system.[52]

Although all of these recent reforms are presented as primarily aimed at the domestic context and as reforms of domestic law, they have significant impacts on the protection of the EU's financial interests to the extent that the general legal framework protecting public finances applies to measures safeguarding both the State's and the Union's interests. For instance, the reform of the *'verrou de Bercy'* can be construed as an attempt to bring French law into compliance with the requirements of the EPPO and the PIF Directive.

---

47   Article 112, Loi du 25 juin 1920 portant création de nouvelles ressources fiscales, codified in Article 1741 of the Code Général des Impôts (*General Tax Code*).

48   Béatrice Guillemont, 'Le nouveau 'verrou de Bercy'' (2018) AJ Pénal 502. *See* also Olivier Cahn, 'Criminal Investigations in Financial-Economic Matters in France', in Alessandro Bernardi and Daniele Negri (eds.), *Investigating European Fraud in the EU Member States,* Hart, 2017, pp. 57, 80 *et seq.*

49   50,000 euros for elected officials and high public officials.

50   Béatrice Guillemont, *op. cit. See* also Olivier Cahn, *op. cit.* at p. 503.

51   Article 41-1-2 Code de Procédure pénale.

52   Béatrice Guillemont (above n 48), 503.

10.2.2 Specific Measures Concerning the Protection of the Union's Financial Interests

There is no specific set of rules in the French legal order aiming to protect the EU's financial interests. Moreover, fraud is not in itself an offence, but should rather be considered a 'structural notion' in French private law.[53] However, issues affecting the EU's financial interests, such as VAT fraud, are gaining more importance in the public sphere. As stated above, the French Penal Code includes an updated list of offences related to fraud and corruption. Articles 435-1 et seq. establish offences of passive and active corruption and influence-peddling affecting public administration and the action of justice in the European Union and other public international organizations as well as in other States, be they the EU Member States or third countries. These provisions are presented as implementing the PIF Convention.[54]

Recent reforms have also specifically sought to reduce the impact of VAT fraud, which amounts to 10 to 12 billion euros a year, 17 billion in 2012 according to a confidential study by the Ministry of Finance.[55] The 2016 Loi de Finances introduced a new Article 286, I, 3° bis in the Tax Code, which complies businesses that pay VAT to use a secure and certified computer programme or cash registers, on pain of a fine of up to 7500 euros and a possibility of unscheduled checks by the tax authorities.[56] Moreover, the 2016/2018 National Plan for the Fight against Fraud[57] endorsed by the Comité National de Lutte Contre la Fraude (CNLF) contains, for the first time, actions that are specific to the fight against fraud affecting the EU's financial interests, thus recognizing this as part of a national strategy.

The Délégation Nationale à la Lutte contre la Fraude[58] (DNLF)'s Annual Report for 2016 states that notifications to OLAF from France had significantly risen, with more notifications of cases concerning expenditures, be it regarding supposed fraudulent or non-fraudulent irregularities,[59] although there was a small drop in the number of reported cases concerning revenues. As compared with the average across the Member

---

53 Pascal Beauvais, 'Chronique Droit pénal de l'Union européenne – Le renforcement de la protection pénale des intérêts financiers de l'Union européenne' (2017) RTDeur 875, 877.

54 Convention on the Protection of the European Communities' Financial Interests. This was signed by the members of the Council on 26 July 1995: Council Act 95/C Drawing Up the Convention on the Protection of the European Communities' Financial Interests [1995] OJ C 316/48.

55 '17 milliards d'euros de fraudes à la TVA par an: la note secrète de Bercy', Le Parisien (Paris, 22 December 2015).

56 Article 88 of the Loi n° 2015-1785 du 29 décembre 2015 de finances pour 2016, JO n° 302, 30 décembre 2015.

57 Plan national pluriannuel de lutte contre la fraude 2016-2018. See the Press release of the Ministry of the Economy, 'Le Comité national de Lutte contre la Fraude adopte son plan triennal', 14 September 2016, https://www.economie.gouv.fr/le-comite-national-de-lutte-contre-la-fraude-2016-adopte-son-plan-triennal.

58 National Delegation for the Fight against Fraud. For further details on the DNLF.

59 DNLF, 'Lutte contre la fraude aux finances publiques. Bilan 2016', p. 18.

States, France seemed to have made good progress in detecting irregularities both in the agricultural sector and in cohesion funds.[60]

Overall, there is no real, separate set of measures to protect the Union's financial interests in French law, but the progress made in recent years should benefit the EU and has also led to better consideration being given to the specific challenges of transnational cases within the EU as well as beyond, as well as the need to avoid the misuse of EU funds.

10.2.3   Competent National Authorities

France takes part in European Union bodies specializing in the protection of the Union's financial interests, and EU-wide cooperation is presented as a priority. No major issues have arisen to prevent such cooperation beyond those already criticized by French authorities themselves, such as the *verrou de Bercy*, for instance. French authorities generally see themselves as willing to use European instruments to cooperate and to promote further progress. They take part in cooperation and in the exchange of best practices, through instruments such as the Open Government Partnership,[61] or the Open Data Charter.[62] Since there is no single authority specifically tasked with protecting the EU's financial interests or with cooperation with other EU or Member State bodies, those responsibilities are distributed among the institutions and authorities which are competent on a domestic level. France's institutional framework is characterized by significant complexity linked to a high degree of specialization.[63]

The fight against fraud affecting the EU's financial interests is led by the *Comité National de Lutte Contre la Fraude* (CNLF).[64] This body comprises all competent ministers and is chaired by the prime minister. It is responsible for steering the government's policy on fighting fraud which affects public finances, including those affecting the EU's interests. It adopts national plans setting out policy guidelines for the

---

60   *Ibid.*, p. 19.
61   The Open Government Partnership was launched in 2011 by eight founding governments including Brazil, Norway, the United Kingdom and the United States. France joined the Open Government Partnership in April 2014 and has made 51 commitments under its Action Plans presented to the OGP.
62   The Open Data Charter is a collaboration between governments and private parties set up in 2015 in order to promote transparency in public governance. France adopted the Charter in 2015 and presented a number of recent legislative and government initiatives as helping to implement the principles set out in the Charter.
63   For a more detailed overview, *see* Olivier Cahn, *op. cit.* at pp. 57, 80 *et seq.*
64   The Committee was set up by Article 5 of the Décret n° 2008-371 relatif à la coordination de la lutte contre les fraudes et créant une délégation nationale à la lutte contre la fraude, JORF n° 93, 19 April 2008.

country, including the first strategic plan introduced for the years 2016-2018. This policy-making body is complemented by operational bodies such as the DNLF.

The DNLF is the main body tasked with fighting fraud. It is part of the Ministry of the Economy and is France's Anti-Fraud Coordination Service (AFCOS) under Regulation 883/2013.[65] It is OLAF's main interlocutor in France and thus has to help OLAF carry out administrative investigations, and collect information by coordinating national administrations through administrative assistance and alert systems. The DNLF also takes part in the Advisory Committee for the Coordination of Fraud Prevention (COCOLAF). This Commission expert group led by OLAF was created by Decision 94/140/EC[66] to allow coordination and exchanges of views between the Member States and advise the Commission on matters related to preventing and prosecuting fraud affecting the financial interests of the EU. The DNF takes part in the COCOLAF's plenary meetings as well as some of its expert groups' meetings. It is also developing cooperation with other Member States' OLAF correspondents to share experiences and best practices[67] and to participate in training programmes through TAIEX and Twinning.[68] In practice, cooperation with OLAF and other national authorities has been welcomed as allowing better and more efficient investigation and prosecution of transnational offences.[69]

Customs officers also contribute to the fight against offences which affect the Union's financial interests. The *Direction Générale des Douanes et des Droits Indirects* (DGDDI) is in charge of customs duties and indirect taxes such as VAT and works in close cooperation with the *Direction Générale des Finances Publiques* (DGFiP), the body in charge of internal taxation. The fight against VAT fraud, in particular, requires close cooperation between the two. Both the DGDDI and the DGFiP jointly take part in EUROFISC,[70] the network created in 2010 to help identify and combat cross-border VAT fraud. Through this network, they both engage in dialogue with other Member

---

65 AFCOS are designated under Article 3(4) of Regulation 883/2013 of the European Parliament and of the Council of 11 September 2013 concerning investigations conducted by the European Anti-Fraud Office (OLAF) and repealing Regulation (EC) No 1073/1999 of the European Parliament and of the Council and Council Regulation (Euratom) No 1074/1999, OJ L 248 18 September 2013, p. 1.

66 Commission Decision of 23 February 1994 setting up an advisory committee for the coordination of fraud prevention, OJ L 61, 4 March 1994, as modified by Decision 2005/223/EC, OJ L 71, 17 March 2005.

67 The 2016 Report (DNLF, *op.cit.* at p. 19) mentions visits by delegations from Italy and Montenegro.

68 The Technical Assistance and Information Exchange instrument of the European Commission and the EU instrument for institutional cooperation between the public administrations of Member States and of beneficiary or partner countries, which provide assistance to Turkey and Balkan countries as well as other neighbouring countries. France notably took part in a Twinning mission concerning public finance management in Algeria in the years 2015-2017, and in TAIEX missions in the Ukraine and Serbia in 2016: TAIEX and Twinning 2017 and 2016 Activity Reports, European Commission; DNLF, *op. cit.* at p. 19.

69 Jean-Marie Huet, 'L'expérience française', in *op. cit.* at p. 141.

70 Eurofisc is a decentralized network of national public officials without legal personality, established by Article 33 *et seq.* of Council Regulation 904/2010 on administrative cooperation and combating fraud in the field of value-added tax [2010] OJ L 268/1.

States' tax and customs authorities. Both the DGDDI and the DGFiP also participate in multilateral controls.[71] Overall, here too, the protection of the financial interests of the European Union is gaining importance in the action of bodies also responsible for protecting national interests.

A number of other bodies contribute to specific aspects of cooperation in the fight against fraud affecting the financial interests of the European Union. Among them, two noteworthy examples are Tracfin and OCRGDF. Tracfin[72] is the French cell in the Ministry of Economy, which specializes in the fight against money laundering and terrorism financing. It takes part in the Financial Intelligence Units (FIUs) platform created by the European Commission. This informal platform provides advice to the European Commission on operational matters in issues related to the FIUs' activities and facilitates cooperation. It is also related to FIU.net,[73] a computer network which supports the FIUs in the fight against money laundering and the financing of terrorism. Tracfin is part of FIU net's board of the partners and also takes part in its training activities.[74]

The *Office Général pour la Répression de la Grande Délinquance Financière* (OCRGDF) is the Serious Financial Crime Office of the French Judicial Police, part of France's central police services. It was established on 9 May 1990, and its missions are to promote, lead and coordinate the actions of the police and gendarmerie within its remit; to study and take part in other institutions' studies of the appropriate measures to prevent and punish these crimes; to intervene wherever the law gives it the competence to do so; to lead or have foreign authorities lead investigations in cooperation with Interpol or through any other organization. The OCRGDF is particularly involved in national and international scams and the fight against money laundering and terrorism financing. It cooperates with Tracfin and also participates in the protection of the European Union's financial interests through its specialized central brigade for the repression of Community frauds (*Brigade Centrale de Répression des Fraudes Communautaires*) which works in close cooperation with OLAF.

Overall, the protection of the European Union's financial interests in France has benefited from the growing realization of the importance of fighting against corruption and fraud since the 1990s. The complexity of the institutional framework does not seem to have had a significant impact on French authorities' capacity to interact with their

---

71   In 2016 the DGDDI initiated three multilateral controls on movements of alcoholic goods involving several EU Member States and took part in 13 controls initiated by other Member States in the same field.

72   Traitement du Renseignement et Action contre les Circuits FINanciers clandestins (Unit for Processing Intelligence and Action Against Illicit Financial Networks).

73   Council Decision 2000/642 concerning arrangements for cooperation between financial intelligence units of the Member States in respect of exchanging information [2000] OJ L 271/4. FIU.net has since been incorporated into Europol.

74   *See* Tracfin's 2017 Activity Report: Rapport d'activité Tracfin 2017, Ministère de l'action et des comptes publics, 2018.

counterparts in the other Member States and to contribute to the current efforts being undertaken on a European level. However, a number of specific features of the French criminal justice system will probably need to evolve in response to the establishment of a European Public Prosecutor's Office and the PIF Directive.

10.3 Reception of the EPPO and the PIF Directive

As with other aspects of European Union criminal law, France's recent attitude has been rather favourable towards the project of a European Public Prosecutor's Office (EPPO) and of a Directive on the Protection of the Union's Financial Interests (PIF Directive) giving it relatively broad competences. However, as the French government prepares to present the legislative and regulatory instruments necessary to implement those instruments in the French legal order, a number of doubts remain as to the scope of the reforms that will be necessary.

10.3.1   Favourable Attitude Towards the New Instruments

France positioned itself early on, with Germany, as one of the leaders in the negotiations on the EPPO and the PIF Directive. France and Germany published a joint declaration on the EPPO during the 18th French-German Council of Ministers that took place in Metz on 7 April 2018.[75] Following the Council's decision to proceed on the path of enhanced cooperation, the French and German Ministers for Justice issued a joint press release following a meeting of the Justice and Home Affairs Council on 8 December 2016,[76] calling for quick action for the establishment of the EPPO and welcoming progress on the PIF Directive. France worked at the European level in favour of the EPPO, albeit on a more decentralized model than that initially proposed by the European Commission. The French government defended a collegiate structure, rejecting the more integrated structure suggested by the Commission on the basis that the EPPO would be more efficient if it was established within existing national structures.[77] Concerning the PIF Directive and the EPPO's competence, initially France was not favourable to the inclusion of VAT, but later it changed its negotiating position and became one of the

---

75 French-German Councils of Ministers were established in 2003, on the 40th anniversary of the Treaty of the Elysée; they take place once or twice a year and bring together all or some of the members of both Member States' cabinets as well as the President of the French Republic and the German Federal Chancellor.

76 Declaration of France and Germany on the European Public Prosecutor, 8 December 2016, co-signed by Mr Jean-Jacques Urvoas, French Minister for Justice and *Garde des Sceaux*, and Mr Heiko Maas, German Federal Minister for Justice and the Protection of Consumer.

77 Charlotte Huet, 'Lectures appliquées comparées. Les autorités françaises et le parquet européen' (2018) *Revue des sciences criminelles* 653, 654.

major proponents for a wider range of competences.[78] This policy orientation did not change after the 2017 presidential and legislative elections.

When the final EPPO Regulation was presented, an interesting disagreement became apparent between the French National Assembly and the French Senate.[79] The National Assembly was very favourable to a centralized, European body and would have wished its competences to include grave cross-border criminal offences.[80] To the contrary, the French Senate issued a yellow card under the subsidiarity control mechanism,[81] on the basis that the Commission's initial proposal was too centralized and prescriptive and went beyond what was necessary to attain the treaty's objectives. The Senate stated in its resolution that it would be favourable to a step-by-step approach, initially focusing on the protection of the EU's financial interests. The French government's negotiating position was much closer to the Senate's views, and the final Regulation is definitely closer to them than to those expressed by the National Assembly.

High-ranking French magistrates have expressed favourable views despite some concerns among magistrates and other lawyers, related to the preservation of sovereignty and of significant aspects of French criminal law. Mr Jean-Claude Marin, General Prosecutor before the Cour de cassation, has stated that despite such concerns that this was an extremely important reform, he called upon other lawyers not to create obstacles to its implementation and he welcomed the significant progress it would allow.[82] Mr François Falletti, General Prosecutor before the Court of Appeal in Aix-en-Provence, also thought these new instruments would be beneficial and would help improve efficiency, notably by introducing faster cooperation and decision making but also through the complementary nature of actions undertaken in different states and the ability to apprehend complex cross-border offences.[83] Similarly, favourable reactions can be found in a special issue of one of the most influential criminal law journals, *Actualité juridique pénal*, in June 2018,[84] which notably included an interview of the president of the National Conference of General Public Prosecutors, Jean-Marc Thony, who also expressed a favourable opinion.[85]

---

78   *Ibid.*, 656.
79   Marc Segonds, 'Le périmètre d'intervention du parquet européen. A propos de la compétence *ratione delicti commissi* du parquet européen' (2018) AJ Pénal 287.
80   European Resolution, 31 January 2014, French National Assembly, n° 285.
81   European Resolution, 15 January 2013, French Senate, n° 70.
82   Jean-Claude Marin, Statement at the Conference on the 10th Anniversary of the EU Network of General Public Prosecutors, 17 May 2018.
83   François Falletti, 'Introduction', in Cour de cassation by Jean-Marie Huet, 'L'expérience française', in *op. cit.* at pp. 142., 67, 68-69.
84   Special issue of the journal AJ Pénal, titled 'Parquet européen: c'est parti !' (2018) AJ Pénal 275.
85   Jean-François Thony, 'Genèse du Parquet européen. Interview de Jean-Marc Thony' (2018) AJ Pénal 276.

10.3.2   Possible Issues in the Implementation of the EPPO

The measures necessary to introduce the European Public Prosecutor in the French judicial system are currently being prepared by the government. Unfortunately, at the time of the publication, no measures have been published, and there are no precise indications as to the choices made. The integration of the EPPO framework within the French judicial system should not, in principle, raise many issues requiring changes in the structure of the judicial system and the competences of French public prosecutors. In particular, the compatibility of the powers of the delegated European public prosecutors with the inquisitorial system and the powers of the *juges d'instruction* is not expected to cause any significant problems.[86]

However, there are significant concerns regarding three significant aspects of French criminal law. The first is the compatibility of the status of French public prosecutors with the independence of the European Public Prosecutor required in the Regulation. Although certain authors do not believe there will be an incompatibility, especially since the 2013 reform of public prosecutors,[87] other scholars express doubts due to long-term concerns that French public prosecutors do not comply with ECHR standards of independence.[88] French public prosecutors indeed remain hierarchically subordinate to the Ministry for Justice, which could create difficulties, be it only in setting up recruitment procedures for the members of the EPPO.[89]

Those lawyers who already believed France would have to modify its judicial system to comply with European human rights standards appear to hold the view that the EPPO will finally be the instrument to force France to carry out this reform.[90] Until recently, there had been very little political will to bring about such changes. The current government had included the issue in a plan for constitutional reform,[91] but this was delayed over the Summer 2018, and parliamentary debates will likely not resume before January 2019. According to Thomas Cassuto,[92] if France does not choose to implement this change before the establishment of the EPPO, it will likely be forced to do so later on as concerns are raised within the EPPO framework. For instance, the persisting

---

86   Thomas Cassuto, 'La collaboration entre le procureur européen et les parquets nationaux' (2018) AJ Pénal 279, 281.

87   Jean-François Thony, *op. cit.* at 278.

88   ECtHR *Moulin v. France*, app. no 37104/06 (2010), §§ 58-59; *Medvedyev et al. v. France* app. no 3394/03 (2011), §124; *Vassis et al. v. France*, app. no 62736/09 (2013), § 52; *Hassan et al. v. France*, app. no 46695/10 (2014), §§ 101-104.

89   Mireille Delmas-Marty, 'Propos introductifs. Le double contexte du règlement instituant le parquet européen' (2018) *Revue de science criminelle* 619, 620.

90   Thomas Cassuto, 'La collaboration entre le procureur européen et les parquets nationaux', *op. cit.* at 279; Guillemine Taupiac-Nouvel and Antoine Botton, 'Coopération renforcée pour la création du Parquet européen' (2018) JCP G. ét. 122, 204.

91   Projet de loi constitutionnelle pour une démocratie plus representative, responsible et efficace, n° 911, depose le 9 mai 2018.

92   Interview with Thomas Cassuto, Conseiller, Cour d'appel de Lyon (27 September 2018).

hierarchical links with the Ministry of Justice are generally considered justified by referring to the need to ensure that prosecutors act in the general national interest. However, the EPPO and the delegated prosecutors will have to act in the EU's public interest, which may prove to be incompatible with active pursuit of the French government's views of the national public interest.[93] At the time of writing, the French government cannot provide any indication of any plans for reform in the immediate future.

The second issue is the so-called *verrou de Bercy*. As noted above, the establishment of the EPPO and the PIF Directive have provided France with an opportunity to reduce the scope of the exception to the powers of magistrates to investigate and prosecute tax-related offences. The Report published by the Common Information Commission on the draft bill on the prosecution of tax-related offences confirmed that the current state of French law was likely incompatible with the EPPO Regulation.[94] Outside the limited scope of the new provisions, the *verrou* remains intact, and only the Ministry of Finance can file a complaint against persons suspected of tax fraud, which means that public prosecutors or investigative judges cannot initiate prosecutions. This rule does not apply to offences such as VAT scams but does apply to VAT fraud. However, the EPPO will be competent in certain cases of VAT fraud and Article 5§1 of the EPPO Regulation explicitly states that the EPPO's intervention cannot be conditioned to authorizations or instructions from any national institution. The reform of the *verrou* system does provide for more systematic competence of prosecutors and investigating judges in serious tax offences, which should be compatible with the thresholds set in the European Union instruments.[95] The October 2018 reform, therefore, solves a major issue of incompatibility and constitutes significant progress in the prosecution of tax offences in France, although specific issues may arise with implementation.

Lastly, one significant uncertainty remains the impact of the principle of the *opportunité des poursuites* ('opportunity of prosecution')[96] on the ability to fully cooperate within the structure of the EPPO. Under this principle, set out in Article 40 of the *Code de Procédure Pénale* (Criminal Procedure Code), the public prosecutor can decide what action to undertake after receiving a complaint or accusation.[97] Although public prosecutors have an obligation to prosecute where an offence has been committed, they also have to evaluate the advisability of such prosecution, for example, in cases that do not seem serious enough. This has already raised some issues concerning the EAW since similar principles do not exist across the Member States, which can create

---

93   Thomas Cassuto, 'La collaboration entre le procureur européen et les parquets nationaux', *op. cit.* at 280.
94   Mission d'information commune sur les procédures de poursuite des infractions fiscales, Rapport d'information n° 982 déposé le 23 mai 2018, p. 41 *et seq.*
95   Article 22 of the EPPO Regulation and Articles 2(2) and 3 of the PIF Directive.
96   Pascal Beauvais, *op. cit.* at 875, 879.
97   'Le procureur de la République reçoit les plaintes et les dénonciations et apprécie la suite à leur donner conformément aux dispositions de l'article 40-1.'

significant disparities in the actual prosecution of offences and the frequency of use of European instruments. This could, in principle, mean that some offences which affect the financial interests of the European Union are not in fact prosecuted. It could also create difficulties in pursuing common strategies or policies within the EPPO.

10.3.3   Possible Issues in the Implementation of the PIF Directive

The PIF Directive appeared in the French Official Journal in July 2017,[98] but no implementation measures have been taken at the time of writing. Although it is clear that its implementation will require new legislation, it is as yet unclear whether the government will choose to introduce an autonomous statutory bill in Parliament, which would require an opinion from the Conseil d'État, or whether it will introduce the necessary reforms by means of amendments and other provisions within other bills. However, the government did not indicate that it expected major reforms to be necessary in order to ensure implementation.

Scholars have expressed a different view, raising concerns as to the compatibility of a number of aspects of French criminal law with the directive. One major issue was the *verrou de Bercy*, which has hopefully been solved, at least to the extent that it was explicitly incompatible with the EPPO's competences as defined in the EPPO Regulation and the PIF Directive. However, other issues have been raised, which could require legislative reforms during the implementation process or could create compatibility issues later. Among such issues, Marc Segonds underlines[99] the restriction of the provision on embezzlement to national public agents, thus excluding European public agents; or the lack of inclusion of organized crime as an aggravating factor, or of a possible link with the offence of criminal conspiracies, in the use of forgeries. More generally, the compatibility of the French understanding of the criminal liability of legal persons with European law has already been questioned. In particular, the general requirement in French law is that the offence must have been committed on behalf of the legal person, whereas the criteria in the PIF Directive are for the offence to have been committed for its benefit.[100] The extent to which the directive's implementation will require substantive changes in French legislation remains to be determined, but some adjustments will likely be necessary if France is to avoid conflicts of laws.

---

98 French OJ n° 198, 28 July 2017, p. 29.
99 Marc Segonds, *op. cit.* 289.
100 *Ibid.*

10.4   CONCLUSION

It is too early to tell whether the implementation of the PIF Directive and adaptation to the requirements of the European Public Prosecutor's Office will require major reforms. The government seems quite confident that there will be no major issues for the PIF Directive after the reform of the *verrou de Bercy* in October 2018. Recent progress in operational cooperation on the basis of European Union instruments and in training lawyers, in particular magistrates, in EU law means adequate implementation can be expected, and no major problems should arise. However, some concerns common to the other Member States, such as the lack of sufficient mutual trust in relation to human rights standards or difficulty in communicating with interlocutors in other States could remain obstacles for the efficient operation of the EPPO. Moreover, certain aspects of French law remain problematic in view of European standards or of the requirements of certain EU instruments. However, these issues are not significant enough to prevent French authorities from ensuring compliance in general or from adhering, in a general sense, to the standards and requirements set out in these instruments.

11   SELECTED CASE STUDIES: THE CASE STUDY OF IRELAND

Ruairi O'Neil

11.1   IMPLEMENTATION OF EU CRIMINAL LAW IN IRELAND

This report on Ireland analyses, where applicable, the implementation of EU procedural instruments in the field of criminal law. It attempts to consider the effect of EU law on substantive criminal law, particularly in the area of cross-border terrorism and cybercrime, as well as substantive offences concerning the financial interests of the EU.

11.1.1   EU Law in Ireland

The legal basis for the application of EU law in Ireland is Article 29 of the Constitution of Ireland, which deals with international relations and authorized the State to become a member of the EU, as well as guarantees the supremacy of EU law in Ireland so as to ensure that nothing invalidates laws enacted, acts passed or measures adopted by the State which are required by members of the European Union. The European Communities Act 1972 (as amended) was adopted to give both domestic effects to EU law[1] and to permit the government to implement EU law in the form of secondary regulations.[2]

As a result of the judgment of the Supreme Court of Ireland in *Crotty v. An Taoiseach* (1987),[3] any substantive changes or additions to an EU Treaty require an amendment to the Constitution, which can only be made by a referendum before being ratified, and as such, all amending EU Treaties since the Single European Act have been subject to public referenda. The Supreme Court held that, under Article 29 of the Constitution, the government could ratify treaty amendments without need for a referendum "so long as such amendments do not alter the essential scope or objectives of the Community".[4]

---

1   European Communities Act (as amended), s. 2(1).
2   *Ibid.*, s.3.
3   *Crotty v. An Taoiseach* [1987] IESC 4.
4   [1987] I.R. 713, 767, as per Finlay J.

11.1.2   EU Criminal Law in Ireland

There are two aspects to the post-Lisbon Treaty legal framework that is worth noting with regard to Ireland. The first is that Section 3(3) of the European Communities Act 1972, prior to being amended by the European Communities Act 2007, stated that regulations could not be adopted that create an indictable offence; as such, laws could not be adopted to implement serious crimes established explicitly by EU law. The 2007 Act altered Section 3(3) so that it now reads:

> Regulations under this section may –
> a. make provision for offences under the regulations to be prosecuted on indictment, where the Minister of the Government making the regulations considers it necessary for the purpose of giving full effect to –
>   i. a provision of the treaties governing the European Union, or
>   ii. an act, or provision of an act, adopted by an institution of the European Union, an institution of the European Communities or a body competent under those treaties, and
> b. make such provision as that Minister of the Government considers necessary for the purpose of ensuring that penalties in respect of an offence prosecuted in that manner are effective and proportionate, and have a deterrent effect, having regard to the acts or omissions of which the offence consists, provided that the maximum fine (if any) shall not be greater than €500,000 and the maximum term of imprisonment (if any) shall not be greater than 3 years.

The participation of – and implementation by – Ireland in EU legislative measures in the field of Freedom, Security and Justice (hereafter 'FSJ') is regulated by Protocol 19 (the Schengen Protocol) and Protocol 21 (the Area of Freedom, Security and Justice Protocol) to the Lisbon Treaty. Protocol 21 constitutes an opt-out from the entire Area of Freedom, Security and Justice and excludes the applicability of any decision of the CJEU interpreting any provision of the Area of Freedom, Security and Justice. It has been described as the epitome of multi-speed integration.[5] Articles 3 and 4 of the protocol outline the procedure for the practical operation of opting-in to FSJ measures.

One novelty of the protocol as it applied to Ireland (and not the UK and Denmark) is that Article 8 provided the State with the option to notify the Council within three years that it no longer wishes to be covered by the terms of the Protocol, meaning that the normal treaty provisions applicable to the Area of Freedom, Security and Justice would

---

5   Elaine Fahey, 'A Jagged-Edged Jigsaw: The Boundaries of Constitutional Differentiation and Irish-British-Euro Relations After the Treaty of Lisbon', in Martin Trybus and Luca Rubini (eds.), *The Treaty of Lisbon and the Future of European Law and Policy*, Edward Elgar Publishing, 2012.

apply to Ireland without the need for future referenda in this area. However significant Article 8 may have potentially been at the time, the notification was not availed of, and Ireland continues to be bound by the protocol.

Irrespective of the constitutional restraints imposed by the protocols, Ireland has opted into many of the legislative measures adopted by the EU legislature in this area and its institutions fully participate in their application, especially where there is a clear need for cross-border coordination, such as with terrorism or white-collar crime. It is apparent, however, that Protocol 21 has been used to avoid opting into other 'vertical' measures, such as the European Public Prosecutor's Office (EPPO); this, however, does not present a simple picture, since Ireland, unlike the UK, did agree from the beginning to participate in Regulation 2016/794 on Europol.[6]

11.1.3   Implementation of EU Laws on Terrorism

Council Framework Decision 2002/475/JHA on Combating Terrorism, as amended by Framework Decision 2008/919/JHA ('FD on Terrorism'), sets out the legal framework for the harmonization of criminal legislation on terrorist and related offences in the EU Member States. The original FD on Terrorism was implemented into Irish law by the Criminal Justice (Terrorist Offences) Act 2005, with the amended FD on Terrorism[7] given effect by the Criminal Justice (Terrorist Offences) (Amendment) Act 2015.[8] According to the government, the provisions of the latest Directive 2017/541/EU of 15 March 2017 on combating terrorism are mostly in force already in the Criminal Justice (Terrorist Offences) Acts, but because Ireland did not notify the European Commission in time under Article 3 of Protocol 21, it has not officially opted into the directive.

In Ireland, the criminalization of terrorism was provided for in the Offences Against the State Acts 1939-1998. The Acts made provisions for the criminalization of actions and conduct calculated to undermine the public authority and the authority of the State[9] and were enacted primarily to deal with the threat posed by the Irish Republican Army (IRA) and its various manifestations at the domestic level. The Criminal Justice (Terrorist Offences) Act 2005 was enacted to amend Irish terrorism laws and to give effect to both

---

6   Regulation 2016/794, available at: https://eur-lex.europa.eu/legal-content/EN/TXT/?uri=CELEX%3A32016R0794.

7   Council Framework Decision 2008/919/JHA of 28 November 2008 amending Framework Decision 2002/475/JHA on Combating Terrorism.

8   Criminal Justice (Terrorist Offences) (Amendment) Act 2015, www.irishstatutebook.ie/eli/2015/act/17/enacted/en/html.

9   Irish Government Report to the United Nations Counter Terrorism Committee on the Implementation of Security Council resolution 1373 (Report S/2001/1252), available at: https://www.un.org/sc/ctc/resources/assessments/, accessed 7 August 2018.

the original FD on Terrorism and related international obligations developed as a response to international terrorism.

The revised law on terrorism, the Criminal Justice (Terrorist Offences) (Amendment) Act 2015, created three new substantive terrorist offences:[10] the offence of public provocation to commit a terrorist offence, the offence of recruitment for terrorism and the offence of training for terrorism. All three are indictable offences which carry a maximum of 10 years' imprisonment. Introducing the bill in the Dáil (lower house of Parliament), the Minister for Justice and Equality, Frances Fitzgerald, T.D., said at the time

> The publication of this Bill is an important milestone towards the enactment of this legislation and the transposition of the EU Framework Decision on combating terrorism. It also lays the groundwork for Ireland's ratification of the Council of Europe Convention on the Prevention of Terrorism in due course.[11]

The government has also exercised its discretion under Article 4 of Protocol 21 to notify the Commission of its intention to participate in Directive 2015/849 on the prevention of the use of the financial system for the purpose of money laundering or terrorist financing ('MLD4'). The Criminal Justice (Money Laundering and Terrorist Financing) (Amendment) Bill 2018,[12] currently at the final legislative stage in the Irish Seanad (Senate, upper legislative chamber), will implement the MLD4, and must be in force before the European Commission can confirm Ireland's participation in the measure, pursuant to Article 4 of the Protocol.

11.1.4   Implementation of EU Laws on Cybercrime

Cybercrime is a policy area where EU law has led to several substantive offences being created in Ireland. While the deadline for implementing Framework Decision 2005/222/ JHA [2005] OJ L69/67) on the criminalization of attacks against information systems was 16 March 2007, the Criminal Justice (Offences Relating to Information Systems) Act 2017, which implemented Directive 2013/40/EU on attacks against information systems and replacing the Framework Decision,[13] only came into force on 12 June 2017.[14]

---

10   Criminal Justice (Terrorist Offences) (Amendment) Act 2015 Sections 4-6.
11   Available at: www.inis.gov.ie/en/JELR/Pages/PR14000219.
12   Criminal Justice (Money Laundering and Terrorist Financing) (Amendment) Bill 2018, available at: https:// www.oireachtas.ie/en/bills/bill/2018/40/.
13   Which itself needed to be implemented by August 2015.
14   Criminal Justice (Offences Relating to Information Systems) Act 2017, available at: www.irishstatutebook. ie/eli/2017/act/11/enacted/en/html.

Prior to the entry into force of the new Act, cybercrime, which incorporated computer fraud, theft and forgery, was dealt with as a subdivision of dishonesty offences in the Criminal Damage Act 1991. The first major attempt at updating the law to take account of the transnational nature of cybercrime was the Criminal Justice (Theft and Fraud Offences) Act 2001. Section 9 of the Act created a new offence, where a person

> dishonestly, whether within or outside the State, operates or causes to be operated a computer within the State with the intention of making a gain for himself or herself or another, or of causing loss to another.[15]

Whereby the 2001 Act established several new substantive offences relating to cybercrime, the Criminal Justice Act 2011 was introduced to update procedural matters and facilitate investigations by the national police force of Ireland, the Garda Síochána, with Part 3 of the Act permitting access to information and documentation in the course of an investigation, pursuant to an application by a member of the police force to the District Court.[16]

The Criminal Justice (Offences Relating to Information Systems) Act 2017 has significantly updated and consolidated the substantive law and procedures relating to cybercrime in Ireland. The 2017 Act implemented the 2013 Directive as well as provisions of the Council of Europe Convention on Cybercrime (the Budapest Convention), to which Ireland is a signatory, but which, at the date of writing, has not ratified.[17] Among the changes brought about by the Act, Section 13 amends the Criminal Damage Act 1991 to remove all reference to data and cybercrime, thus ensuring that the 2017 Act is the only necessary reference point for these types of offences. Further, it adopts the definition of data provided by the directive. Section 1(1) of the Act defines data as

> any representation of facts, information or concepts in a form capable of being processed in an information system and includes a programme capable of causing an information system to perform a function.

Also taken verbatim from the directive, an information system is defined in Section 1(1) as

---

15 For discussion of the ineffectuality of the law, *see* Pierce Ryan and Andy Harbison, 'The Law on Computer Fraud in Ireland – Development of the Law of Dishonesty', www.scl.org, 2009.
16 Criminal Justice Act 2011, available at: www.irishstatutebook.ie/eli/2011/act/22/enacted/en/html.
17 Council of Europe Convention on Cybercrime (ETS No.185), which Ireland signed on the 28th of February 2002.

a. a device or group of interconnected or related devices, one or more than one of which performs automatic processing of data pursuant to a programme, and

b. data stored, processed, retrieved or transmitted by such a device or group of devices for the purposes of the operation, use, protection or maintenance of the device or group of devices, as the case may be.

A number of new substantive offences have been created by the Act, which are listed in Sections 2 to 6. Section 2 of the Act repeats the repealed Section 5 of the 1991 Act to make it an offence to intentionally access an information system without lawful authority. Section 3 creates an offence of interference without lawful authority, by way of hindering or interruption, with an information system. This section legislates for a denial of service attack for the first time in Irish law.[18] Section 4 makes it an offence to unlawfully interfere with data, replacing Section 2 of the 1991 Act, which is repealed. As such, it would be a criminal offence under Section 4 to intentionally destroy data, whereas it would be an offence under Section 2 if the data was copied but not followed by an element of destruction. Section 5 introduced a new offence of intentionally intercepting any transmission of data without lawful authority, and Section 6 makes it an offence to produce, sell, procure for use, import, distribute or otherwise make available the tools that can be used to commit the primary offences contained in the Act, which, in accordance with the directive, would include malicious software.[19] Section 9 of the Act provides the mechanisms of attributing liability for an offence to a body corporate: Section 9(1) implements the vicarious liability of a body corporate, giving effect to Article 10(2) of the Cybercrime Directive. The Act also enables the Garda Síochána to apply to the District Court to obtain wide-ranging and technology-specific investigatory and evidence gathering powers.

Given the need for a coordinated, cross-border approach to cybercrime, the provisions of the Act are given extraterritorial effect, in the sense that they can be applied to a person carrying out such activities in Ireland, but also to a person outside Ireland who is carrying out the prohibited acts within Ireland.[20] While the Act is indeed considered to be a necessary update for Irish law in the field of internet-related crime, and provides the tools deemed necessary by the directive for investigation and coordinated international action in the field of cybercrimes within the State, time will tell if the Act proves effective, or results in more effective prosecution of cybercrime in Ireland. As of September 2018, no prosecutions have been made pursuant to the Act.

---

18 P. Ryan, T. Browne, and S. Mc Dermott, 'Cybercrime Legislative Developments in Irish Law' (8 March 2016), www.arthurcox.com/wp-content/uploads/2016/03/Cybercrime-Legislative-Developments-In-Ireland-March-2016.pdf, accessed 30 August 2018.

19 *Ibid.*

20 Criminal Justice (Offences Relating to Information Systems) Act 2017 s.10.

11.1.5   European Arrest Warrant (EAW)

The European Arrest Warrant Act 2003 (as amended) gave effect to the EAW procedure in Irish law. According to Ryan and Hamilton, the approach of Irish courts to the problems inherent in the EAW system are difficult to characterize, with examples of courts reading down human rights' guarantees in the implementing legislation and the adoption of a high threshold for the denial of surrender where breaches of fundamental rights are alleged as well as examples of unwillingness to blindly trust the criminal justice systems of other EU Member States.[21]

As an adversarial legal system, it is both sensible and normal that defendants would utilize any possible exceptions to the principles of mutual recognition and mutual trust whenever the facts render it a possibly successful defence. For example, the principle of mutual recognition in criminal law and its limits were considered in 2018 in a number of decisions of the Irish High Court, and the CJEU concerning the execution of a Polish EAW against a Polish national suspected of drug trafficking, Artur Celmer, currently residing in Ireland. In March 2017, the High Court suspended Celmer's EAW due to concerns about the judicial reforms being enacted in Poland and their effect on the independence of the courts of Poland and the ability of the respondent to receive a fair trial if the EAW was executed.[22] The Court instead submitted an Article 267 TFEU reference under the PPU procedure to the CJEU asking whether the double test for suspending EAWs on human rights grounds, established in *Aranyosi and Căldăraru* (requiring an assessment by the executing authority, firstly, of general deficiencies in the issuing State, and, secondly, and individual assessment for the person concerned),[23] applied where there was evidence of systemic breaches of the rule of law. The decision had the potential to greatly impact the system of mutual trust and recognition in both criminal law and civil cooperation, as well as judicialization of what had until that point been a political dispute between the European Commission and an EU Member State under Article 7 TEU.

In its judgment, delivered on 28 July 2018,[24] the CJEU started by stating that an EAW may only be suspended in accordance with Recital 10 of the Framework Decision[25] if the European Council has already determined that a Member State has persistently and seriously breached the principles set out in Article 2 TEU, including the rule of law, and applied the sanctions provided by Article 7(2) (3) TEU.[26] Since the sanctions

---

21   Andrea Ryan and Claire Hamilton, 'Criminal Justice Policy and the European Union', in Deirdre Healy, Claire Hamilton et al. (eds.), *The Routledge Handbook of Irish Criminology*, Routledge, 2015, p. 470.

22   *Minister for Justice and Equality v. Artur Celmer* [2017] EXT 291.

23   Joined Cases C-404/15 and C-659/15 PPU *Pál Aranyosi and Robert Căldăraru* ECLI:EU:C:2016:198.

24   Case C-216/18 PPU *LM* ECLI:EU:C:2018:586.

25   Council Framework Decision of 13 June 2002 on the European arrest warrant and the surrender procedures between Member States 2002/584/JHA.

26   *LM* (n24), [70].

regime envisaged by Article 7(2) TEU requires unanimous voting in the Council, it is likely that the CJEU was aware that it would never be used, especially in relation to the case at hand, since Hungary and the UK have repeatedly stated that they would veto any attempt to sanction Poland; it is clear that the Court sees the task of suspending mutual trust for systemic breaches of Article 2 TEU as belonging exclusively to the European Council.[27] The Court then moved to consider that the two-stage test from *Aranyosi and Căldăraru* must be applied by an executing authority that is considering suspending an EAW.[28] Once the issue had returned to the High Court, the presiding judge explained what was required to be proved in the present case in her judgment of 8 August 2018.[29]

Under the first limb of the test, which required that the executing authority must assess specific, reliable and current material regarding the operation of the justice system in the issuing state,[30] the Court relied on the materials disclosed during the first stage of the litigation to find that there was a real risk of a fundamental right to a fair trial being breached, connected with a lack of independence of the courts of Poland on account of systemic or generalized deficiencies there.[31] Under the second limb, which required an assessment of the extent to which those deficiencies are liable to have an impact on the ability of the affected person to receive a fair trial, the Judge referred to the obligations of Poland regarding the presumption of innocence under Article 6 ECHR[32] and Directive 2016/343 on the strengthening of certain aspects of the presumption of innocence and of the right to be present at the trial in criminal proceedings, which applies to Poland but not Ireland,[33] which were at odds with statements made by members of the Polish government regarding the person to whom the EAW was directed. Ultimately, however, the judge concluded that it was necessary, in light of the answers given by the CJEU, to obtain further information from the issuing authority in Poland in order to fully assess the existence of a substantial risk of breach of the defendant's right to a fair trial if the EAW is executed.[34] The outcome thus guarantees the continuance of the system of mutual recognition by particularizing the case exclusively to the respondent; a situation that is likely to be followed by other executing

---

27 For more, *see* van Ballegooij, Wouter; Bárd, Petra, 'The CJEU in the Celmer Case: One Step Forward, Two Steps Back for Upholding the Rule of Law Within the EU', VerfBlog, 29 July 2018, https://verfassungsblog. de/the-cjeu-in-the-celmer-case-one-step-forward-two-steps-back-for-upholding-the-rule-of-law-within-the-eu/, DOI: https://doi.org/10.17176/20180730-095503-0, accessed 30 July 2018.

28 *LM* (n24), [73].

29 *Minister for Justice and Equality v. Artur Celmer (No.4)* [2018] IEHC 484.

30 *LM* (n11), [61].

31 *Celmer (No 4)*, (n16), [25].

32 *Ibid.*, [40].

33 *Ibid.*, [39].

34 The information that was received from two senior Polish judges openly contradicted each other, and as such, the issue has not been resolved, available at: https://www.irishtimes.com/news/crime-and-law/courts/high-court/polish-judges-disagree-with-each-other-in-letters-to-high-court-1.3686259.

authorities in the EU that are called upon to suspend EAWs issued by Polish authorities.[35]

The interaction between the application of the EAW Framework Decision and fundamental rights was also discussed relatively recently in the case *of Minister for Justice and Equality v. Francis Lanigan.*[36] Lanigan was arrested in January 2013 in Dublin pursuant to an EAW issued in Northern Ireland (UK) in connection with a 1998 murder believed to be drug-related. The defendant remained in custody until December 2014, having refused consent to his surrender to UK authorities, firstly on the grounds that surrender could endanger his life, as he was a former member of a Republican paramilitary organization, and latterly, on the grounds that the time limits stipulated in the Framework Decision had not been complied with.[37] While the CJEU ultimately rejected the arguments of the defendant on time limits,[38] it affirmed that continuing detention of the defendant had to be consistent with the right to liberty as protected by Article 5 ECHR and Article 6 of the EU Charter of Fundamental Freedoms.[39] In doing so, the Court effectively ruled that time limits in the Framework Decision did not have the effect of invalidating the EAW – an interpretation compliant with the authority given by the Supreme Court of Ireland in *Dundon*[40] – but it also did not impose an obligation on the Irish authorities to release the defendant from prison,[41] other than to confirm that detention conditions must comply with the rules set out in Article 5 ECHR, as interpreted by the European Court of Human Rights.[42] Applying these interpretations, the High Court relied on the test established by the Supreme Court in *Rettinger*, namely that the executing Irish court must have "substantial grounds for believing that the person would be exposed to a real risk of ill-treatment",[43] to conclude that execution of the EAW would not endanger the life of the defendant.[44]

While there are many Brexit-related issues that are affecting and will affect, Ireland, unfortunately, the pre-Brexit EAW system is one of them. To date, Irish courts have dealt with three Brexit-related arguments as to why a UK-issued EAW should not be executed. In the first, *Minister for Justice and Equality v. A.M.*,[45] the challenge arose at a time when

---

35   As has already happened in England and Wales, *see Lis, Lange and Chmielewski v. Regional Court in Warsaw and Radom* [2018] EWHC 2848 (Admin).

36   Case C-237/15 PPU *Minister for Justice and Equality v. Francis Lanigan* ECLI:EU:C:2015:474.

37   Art. 17 or the Framework Decision requires that a final decision on executing an EAW be made at the latest within 90 days.

38   *Lanigan* (n36), [37].

39   *Ibid.*, [53-62].

40   *Dundon v. The Governor of Cloverhill Prison* [2005] IESC 83.

41   Steve Peers, 'Free at Last? Detention, the European Arrest Warrant and Julian Assange', 5 February 2016, http://eulawanalysis.blogspot.com/2016/02/free-at-last-detention-european-arrest.html, accessed 28 July 2018.

42   *Lanigan* (n36), [55-56].

43   *Minister of Justice, Equality and Law Reform v. Rettinger* [2010] IESC 45.

44   *Minister for Justice and Equality v. Lanigan* [2015] IEHC 677, [23].

45   *Minister for Justice and Equality v. A.M.* [2016] IEHC 568.

the majority of the UK population had voted to leave the EU but the Article 50 TEU notifications had not yet been made. Rejecting the defendant's arguments, the Irish High Court held that:

> 53. Despite the existence of the risk of the U.K. leaving the E.U., the court is required to make a decision on this otherwise valid EAW in accordance with the provisions of the Act of 2003. The court would not be acting in accordance with law if it was to adjourn, or postpone, or otherwise refuse this surrender application on the basis of an event which may take place in the future, the parameters of which have not been delineated. At present, the U.K. is bound by its commitments under E.U. law and under the 2002 Framework Decision in particular. The court is bound to act upon the presumption set out in the Act of 2003 and the 2002 Framework Decision that the U.K. will comply with its obligations under the 2002 Framework Decision in so far as this surrender is concerned.
>
> 54. Moreover, the Court is quite clear that there is nothing to support the submission that there is a real risk that the U.K. would, even supposing it leaves the E.U., renege on any commitments as to speciality, fundamental rights or otherwise, given while it was a party to surrenders carried out under the EAW process. In short, there is no evidence giving rise to any reason to believe that the U.K. would not respect and uphold the specific guarantees that are contained within the 2002 Framework Decision, or indeed to believe that there is even a risk that the U.K. will not respect those guarantees. There is no evidence to suggest that any single aspect of the guarantees that the U.K. gives in seeking surrender under an EAW with regard to how it will treat a person who has been surrendered will be at risk.
>
> 55. Not only is there a lack of evidence but common sense dictates that the U.K. will have a vested interest in ensuring that it does comply with any guarantees she has given with respect to surrenders completed under the EAW process. If the U.K. is to leave the EAW Framework Decision procedure, she will have to engage in extradition treaties with the other states if she is to ensure that those sought by her to face trial or punishment can forcibly be brought within the U.K.'s jurisdiction. A disregard of commitments made in respect of surrenders under the EAW procedure would make entering into any other extraditions treaties extremely difficult. Thus, it is in the self-interest of the U.K. to comply with her obligations.

In *Minister for Justice and Equality v. O'Connor*,[46] the UK had already made the Article 50 TEU notification by the time the Irish High Court was asked to execute an EAW issued by a UK court against the defendant, who had already been found guilty of tax fraud offences and sentenced, before absconding to Ireland. Nevertheless, the High Court held that, just because a country was leaving the European Union, it does not mean that it is simultaneously reneging on its commitments to the principles contained in Article 6 TEU and reflected in the EU Charter.[47] The issue was referred to the Irish Supreme Court on what was described as the 'Brexit point': the fact that the legal framework that will govern the majority of the time that the defendant will spend in prison in England if the EAW is executed is not yet known.[48] In a surprise decision, the Supreme Court, on 1 March 2018, decided to refer questions to the Court of Justice of the EU under the PPU Procedure, asking, among other things, under what circumstances the executing court of an EU Member State is required to decline to surrender a person to the United Kingdom. On 30 May 2018, however, the CJEU issued an order rejecting the request that the issue is heard under the expedited procedure, and as such it is still pending before the Court.[49]

The judgment that the Court will eventually deliver should it arrive before 'Brexit day', is likely to be shaped by another case referred to it by an Irish Court on the same legal point. On 19 September 2018, the CJEU delivered its judgment in *RO*, which dealt with the same issues as *KN*.[50] The Court began its judgment by restating the nature of the principle of mutual trust between the Member States,[51] and that limitation may be placed on the principle in "exceptional circumstances".[52] It then goes on to state that notification by a Member State of withdrawal from the EU under Article 50 TEU cannot be regarded as an exceptional circumstance. Repeating language used in the *Celmer* judgment concerning judicial independence in Poland, the Court left it up to the executing authority to conduct a specific and precise assessment of the particular case in order to determine if there are substantial grounds to believe that the person who is subject to the EAW was at risk of being deprived of his fundamental rights after Brexit.[53] On this point, however, the Court was of the opinion that it was unlikely that those rights could not be asserted in the UK after Brexit, on the grounds that the rights contained in the Framework Directive are protected by provisions of national law anyway,[54] and furthermore, that it should be remembered that the CJEU did not always enjoy

---

46   *Minister for Justice and Equality v. O'Connor & anor* [2017] IEHC 518.
47   *Ibid.*, [53].
48   [2018] IESC 19.
49   Case C-191/18 *KN v. Minister for Justice and Equality* ECLI:EU:C:2018:383.
50   Case C-327/18 PPU *RO* ECLI:EU:C:2018:733.
51   *Ibid.*, [35].
52   *Ibid.*, [39].
53   *Ibid.*, [49].
54   *Ibid.*, [59].

jurisdiction over the EAW system, and so the absence of recourse to the CJEU in the UK post-Brexit would not be an arguable ground to use before the executing court.[55] If anything, therefore, this CJEU judgment is confirmation that, from a legal point of view, nothing will change in the field of mutual trust and mutual recognition until the UK actually leaves the EU.[56]

11.1.6   Fundamental Rights and Personal Data

As an adversarial legal system, Ireland requires a characteristic high standard to the functioning of its judiciary. As a result, it is difficult to say if there are gaps in the protection of fundamental rights which are guaranteed by the Constitution, the EU Charter of Fundamental Rights and international agreements to which the State is party, including the European Convention of Human Rights, which has domestic effect at the sub-constitutional level through the European Convention of Human Rights Act 2003.[57]

With regards to the *Pupino* judgment of the CJEU and the principle of indirect effect and FSJ measures, Irish courts have fully incorporated the concept into their toolkit for the application of national law in conformity with EU law. The key authority that is frequently cited in Irish courts stems from the statement of Murray C.J. in *Minister for Justice, Equality and Law Reform v. Altaravicius*:[58]

> When applying and interpreting national provisions giving effect to a Framework Decision the courts "must do so as far as possible in the light of the wording and purpose of the Framework Decision in order to attain the result which it pursues" (see criminal proceedings against Pupino Case C-105/03 [2005] E.C.R. 1-05285).
>
> The principle of conforming interpretation is limited, as the Court of Justice has pointed out in Pupino and other cases, to the extent that it is possible to give such an interpretation. It does not require a national court to interpret national legislation contra legem. If national legislation, having been interpreted as far as possible in conformity with community legislation to which it purports to give effect, but still falls short of what is required by the latter, a national court must, as a general principle, apply that legislation as

---

55 *Ibid.*, [60].

56 Steve Peers, 'Brexit Means ... No Legal Changes Yet: The CJEU Rules on the Execution of European Arrest Warrants Issued by the UK Prior to Brexit Day', 19 September 2018, http://eulawanalysis.blogspot.com/2018/09/brexit-meansno-legal-changes-yet-cjeu.html1, accessed 22 September 2018.

57 European Convention of Human Rights Act 2003, available at: www.irishstatutebook.ie/eli/2003/act/20/enacted/en/html.

58 C.J. Murray in *Minister for Justice, Equality and Law Reform v. Altaravicius* [2006] 3 IR 148 at p. 156.

interpreted although there may be other consequences for a member state which has failed to fully implement a directive or framework decision.

This statement has been applied at all levels of the judiciary, including in the Supreme Court. For example, Justice Fennelly in his Supreme Court judgment in *Minister for Justice v. Bailey* stated:

> There does not seem to me to be any reason in principle to exclude the principle of conforming interpretation from a measure merely because it implements an "opt-out." On the contrary, logic demands that the principle be applied equally to such a situation. Indeed, it might well be that a correct interpretation would lead to the exclusion of an individual from the benefit of a national measure, once it was correctly interpreted as a matter of European Union law. Accordingly, I am satisfied that Section 44 must be interpreted in conformity with Article 4.7(b) and not merely with the general objectives of the Framework Decision.[59]

Ireland was also the forum for firing the starting gun on some of the great legal battles regarding data protection and fundamental rights in recent years: In *Digital Rights Ireland*, the Irish High Court accepted arguments from the claimant as to whether the Retention Directive[60] was compatible with the EU Treaties, as well as the Charter and ECHR, and submitted a preliminary reference under Article 267 TFEU.[61] The directive, which was originally presented in draft form by Ireland,[62] was ultimately invalidated by the CJEU.[63] Despite this, the implementing legislation, the Communications (Retention of Data) Act 2011, remains in force as of 25 May 2018.[64] The government has pledged to replace the legislation, and the Communications (Retention of Data) Bill 2017 is currently working its way through the Oircheachtas (Parliament), which will take account of the unconstitutional elements determined by the *Digital Rights Ireland* and

---

59 *Minister for Justice v. Bailey* [2012] IESC 16, [2012] 4 IR 1.
60 Directive 2006/24/EC.
61 *Digital Rights Ireland Ltd v. Minister for Communication & Ors* [2010] IEHC 221, [113].
62 The French Republic, Ireland, the Kingdom of Sweden and the U.K., "Draft Framework Decision on the retention of data processed and stored in connection with the provision of publicly available electronic communications services or data on public communications networks for the purpose of prevention, investigation, detection and prosecution of crime and criminal offences including terrorism" Council Document 8958/04 (Brussels, 28 April 2004).
63 Case C-293/12 *Digital Rights Ireland* ECLI:EU:C:2014:238.
64 http://revisedacts.lawreform.ie/eli/2011/act/3/revised/en/html.

Tele2 judgments,[65] which will include the requirement of prior judicial approval for metadata requests by the Garda Síochána and other investigation authorities.[66]

With regards to GDPR, while the regulation[67] was not required to be transposed, Ireland implemented the accompanying Law Enforcement Directive 2016/680[68] in the form of the Data Protection Act 2018.[69] Part 2 of the Act established a new body, the Data Protection Commission, as the State's data protection authority, thus replacing the existing Data Protection Commissioner. It transposed the other aspects of the directive and gave further effect to the areas of GDPR where the Member States have flexibility, such as the digital age of consent, which was designated as 16 years.[70]

11.1.7   Gaps in EU Criminal Law Implementation

Among the other measures adopted by the EU in the FSJ Area under the Stockholm Programme of the European Council to improve the laws relating to victims of crime, Ireland's contribution has been piecemeal. With regards to the Victims' Rights Directive,[71] Ireland chose to opt in,[72] as it did with the Regulation on Mutual Recognition of Protection Measures in Civil matters. Unlike the UK, however, Ireland did not opt into the Directive on the European Protection Order (EPO), and as such, the directive cannot be enforced in Ireland. The failure to implement the directive will theoretically have an adverse effect on EU migrants in Ireland, such as, for example, Polish nationals, who make up the second-largest population group in Ireland, since protection orders in Poland are imposed almost exclusively within criminal proceedings.[73]

---

65 Joined Cases C-203/15 and C-698/15 *Tele2 Sverige AB* ECLI:EU:C:2016:970.

66 www.justice.ie/en/JELR/General_Scheme_-_Communications_(Retention_of_Data)_Bill.pdf/Files/ General_Scheme_-_Communications_(Retention_of_Data)_Bill.pdf.

67 Regulation (EU) 2016/679.

68 Directive (EU) 2016/680 of the European Parliament and of the Council of 27 April 2016 on the protection of natural persons with regard to the processing of personal data by competent authorities for the purposes of the prevention, investigation, detection or prosecution of criminal offences or the execution of criminal penalties, and on the free movement of such data, and repealing Council Framework Decision 2008/977/ JHA.

69 https://www.oireachtas.ie/en/bills/bill/2018/10/.

70 Data Protection Act 2018 s. 31(1).

71 Directive 2012/29/EU of the European Parliament and of the Council of 25 October 2012 establishing minimum standards on the rights, support and protection of victims of crime, and replacing Council Framework Decision 2001/220/JHA.

72 Criminal Justice (Victims of Crime) Act 2017.

73 Dr Andrea Ryan, 'A Lot is Happening in European Criminal Justice … But Not in Ireland' (5 June 2016), https://criminaljusticeinireland.wordpress.com/2016/05/06/a-lot-is…1, accessed 10 July 2018.

11.2 CRIMES AGAINST THE FINANCIAL INTEREST OF THE EU

Generally speaking, Ireland is fully involved in the EU action to protect the financial interests of the EU and combat fraud. Ireland has already implemented parts of the directive on the fight against fraud to the Union's financial interests by means of criminal law ('The PIF Directive') in the Criminal Justice (Corruption Offences) Act 2018 and intends to implement the remaining parts of the directive by the transposition deadline of July 2019. The State has, however, decided not to participate in the EPPO Regulation. In Parliamentary debates on the topic of the EPPO in 2013, Minister of State Paul Kehoe explained that the government did not believe the proposed EPPO Regulation complied with the principles of subsidiarity,[74] and was likely concerned about the potential incursion into Ireland's criminal justice system.[75]

11.2.1 Corruption in Ireland

Corruption has been a persistent problem in Ireland, from as far back as the adoption of the Act of Union establishing the United Kingdom of Great Britain and Ireland to recent times, which have seen numerous public inquiries established over the past 30 years into state corruption; the latest being the Commission of Investigation to investigate the sale of a portfolio of Northern Ireland properties by the National Asset Management Agency.[76] In 2017, Ireland was also the subject of two reviews into anti-corruption law enforcement. The first originated in the Council of Europe Group of States Against Corruption Fourth Round Report on preventing corruption in respect of politicians, prosecutors and judges.[77] The report assessed that the level of compliance with previous recommendations on corruption by the State was 'globally unsatisfactory'. The second report, by the Financial Action Taskforce, concerned Ireland's anti-money laundering and terrorist financing legislative framework, which concluded that, while the legal instruments in place were adequate, further work could be done to effectively investigate and enforce them.[78]

11.2.1.1 Institutions Dealing with White-Collar Crime

Ireland does not have a specialized agency for investigating corruption, with the Garda Síochána having primary responsibility for investigations, and the Criminal Assets Bureau the authority to investigate bribery or corruption when exercising its powers to

---

74 Dáil Debates, 23 October 2013, https://www.oireachtas.ie/en/debates/debate/dail/2013-10-23/5/
75 Andrea Ryan and Claire Hamilton, *op. cit.* at p. 472.
76 https://www.taoiseach.gov.ie/DOT/eng/NAMA_Commission/Interim_Report_NAMA_Commission.html.
77 Report No. GrecoRC4(2017)7, last accessed 30 September 2018.
78 www.fatf-gafi.org/media/fatf/documents/reports/mer4/MER-Ireland-2017.pdf, last accessed 30 September 2018.

seize the proceeds of crime in civil law.[79] The Garda National Economic Crime Bureau is additionally responsible for investigating international allegations of bribery.[80] In terms of cross-border mutual assistance in criminal matters, generally, the Irish Central Authority For Mutual Assistance is stated in legislation as being the appropriate unit within the Ministry for Justice, Equality and Law Reform.[81] It is to the Central Authority also that applications for the recognition and enforcement of external freezing orders[82] and confiscation orders are communicated, which will then cause an application to the High Court to be made. As Ireland has agreed to participate in the European Account Preservation Order Regulation,[83] the Minister of Justice, Equality and Law Reform has also been designated as the 'information authority' for the purposes of the Regulation.[84]

11.2.1.2   Irish Anti-Corruption Laws

Corrupt practices have traditionally been outlawed by a combination of both common law and statutory offences in Ireland. The primary statutory offences were provided by the Prevention of Corruption Acts 1889-2010, and the Criminal Justice (Theft and Fraud Offences) Act 2001 criminalized bribery which damages the EU's financial interests. Section 42 of the Act states that:

> A person who –
> a. commits in whole or in part any fraud affecting the European Communities' financial interests,
> b. participates in, instigates or attempts any such fraud, or
> c. obtains the benefit of, or derives any pecuniary advantage from, any such fraud,
> d. is guilty of an offence and is liable on conviction on indictment to a fine or imprisonment for a term not exceeding 5 years or both.

---

79 https://www.garda.ie/en/about-us/specialist-units/criminal-assets-bureau/, last accessed 30 September 2018.

80 https://www.garda.ie/en/about-us/specialist-units/garda-national-economic-crime-bureau/, last accessed 30 September 2018.

81 As provided for in the Criminal Justice (Mutual Assistance) Act 2008.

82 Pursuant to Council Framework Decision 2003/577/JHA of 22 July 2003 on the execution in the European Union of orders freezing property or evidence.

83 Regulation (EU) No 655/2014 of the European Parliament and of the Council of 15 May 2014 establishing a European Account Preservation Order procedure to facilitate cross-border debt recovery in civil and commercial matters.

84 https://www.williamfry.com/newsandinsights/news-article/2017/01/25/eu-cross-border-asset-freezing-has-just-become-easier, accessed 10 November 2018.

With regards to VAT fraud specifically, the Finance Act 2014 introduced a new Section 108C in the Value-Added Tax Consolidation Act 2010,[85] which imposes joint and several liabilities on third parties who are involved in the VAT fraud supply chain, where those persons "know that, or are reckless as to whether or not that supply of goods or services or intra-Community acquisition is connected to the fraudulent evasion of tax".

It has been claimed that the knowledge threshold of 'recklessness' in Irish civil law required to impose liability on third parties is a less onerous burden placed on legitimate undertakings than that applied in other EU jurisdictions.[86]

Pursuant to an updated reform package announced by the government in 2017,[87] following a public consultation by the Law Commission – the statutory body responsible for proposing changes to the law[88] – a number of new laws have been adopted to deal with corruption and white-collar crime. The most recent measures to be adopted are in addition to other measures designed to enhance transparency in the workplace, such as the Protected Disclosures Act 2014 and the Regulation of Lobbying Act 2015, which provided a code of conduct relating to carrying out lobbying activities.[89]

The latest major piece of legislation, which repealed and replaced most of the laws in Ireland on corruption, is the Criminal Justice (Corruption Offences) Act 2018, which came into force on 31 July 2018. The Act applies to offences committed in Ireland, with Section 12 of the Act extending the personal scope of the substantive offences listed in the statute to Irish citizens and corporate bodies registered in Ireland who commit acts outside the State which would constitute offences under the Act if committed within the territory of the State. Furthermore, it extends white-collar crime offences to cover actions not only of public officials, as in previous Acts, but also of individuals, companies, voluntary bodies, foreign and Irish officials, directors and employees.

Among the actions that would now constitute a criminal offence under the Act, it is illegal to actively or passively engage in corruption[90] or trade-in influence (a new offence established by the Act),[91] for a public official to use confidential information to obtain an advantage[92] and to makes payments to a third party who intends to use that property as a bribe.[93]

---

85   http://revisedacts.lawreform.ie/eli/2010/act/31/revised/en/html#SEC108C.

86   Pascal Brennan and Conor Walsh, 'VAT – Whose Liability Is It Anyway?', Deloitte Insights, https://www2.deloitte.com/ie/en/pages/tax/articles/VAT-whose-liability-is-it.html#, accessed 18 September 2018.

87   https://merrionstreet.ie/en/News-Room/News/Government_Publishes_a_Package_of_Measures_aimed_at_Fighting_White_Collar_Crime.html, accessed 25 September 2018.

88   Law Commission of Ireland, 'Issue Paper: Regulatory Enforcement and Corporate Offences' (LRC IP 8-2016).

89   www.anticorruption.ie/en/abc/pages/legislation, accessed 30 September 2018.

90   Criminal Justice (Corruption Offences) Act 2018, s. 5.

91   *Ibid.*, s. 6.

92   *Ibid.*, s. 7(2).

93   *Ibid.*, s. 8.

11.2.2   Implementation of the PIF Directive

According to the Minister of Justice and Equality, Alan Shatter T.D., the purpose of the PIF Directive was to "move the basis for criminal laws to protect the financial interests of the EU from the 1995 PIF Convention to a basis under the provisions of the Lisbon Treaty".[94] This was during the parliamentary discussion on the decision of Ireland to exercise the Protocol 21 right to the participant and therefore implement the directive. The government has stated in the Dáil (the lower house of the Irish Parliament) that it intends to implement the directive in the third quarter of 2019.[95]

Ireland ratified and implemented the original Convention on the Protection of the Communities Financial Interests by enacting codified legislation. The provisions on criminal offences relating to the PIF instruments were implemented by Part 6 of Criminal Justice (Theft and Fraud Offences) Act 2001, with the exception of offences relating to money laundering.[96] The wording of Part 6 allowed for fraud against the Communities' financial interests to also be applied to existing fraud offences and all possible forms of fraud were criminalized. Section 31 of the Criminal Justice Act 1994 was amended to provide for compliance with the PIF instruments as regards money laundering.[97]

Since the adoption of the PIF Directive replacing the Convention, Ireland has only given effect to some of the changes required by the directive, which were made by the Criminal Justice (Corruption Offences) Act 2018. The first changes made to bring Irish law into line with the PIF Directive is with regard to the definition of active and passive corruption. Section 40 of the 2001 Act implemented into Irish law the precise definitions of active and passive corruption provided by Articles 3.1 and 2.1 of the First Protocol to the Convention, respectively. These definitions of active and passive corruption have been repealed and replaced by Section 5 of the 2018 Act, which now states:

(1) A person who, either directly or indirectly, by himself or herself or with another person –
a. corruptly offers, or
b. corruptly gives or agrees to give,
a gift, consideration or advantage to a person as an inducement to, or reward for, or otherwise on account of, any person doing an act in relation to his or her office, employment, position or business shall be guilty of an offence.

---

94 Speech by Minister for Justice, Equality and Defence, Alan Shatter TD, to the Oireachtas Joint Committee on Justice, Equality & Defence -Fraud Against EU, 17 July 2013, available at: www.justice.ie/en/JELR/Pages/SP13000304, accessed 10 November 2018.

95 Minister for Justice and Equality, Charles Flanagan (29 March 2018), available at: www.justice.ie/en/JELR/Pages/PQ-29-03-2018-209.

96 www.irishstatutebook.ie/eli/2001/act/50/section/40/enacted/en/html#part6, accessed 9 November 2018.

97 www.irishstatutebook.ie/eli/1994/act/15/section/31/enacted/en/html#partiv, accessed 9 November 2018.

(2) A person who, either directly or indirectly, by himself or herself or with another person –

a.   corruptly requests,

b.   corruptly accepts or obtains, or

c.   corruptly agrees to accept,

for himself or herself or for any other person, a gift, consideration or advantage as an inducement to, or reward for, or otherwise on account of, any person doing an act in relation to his or her office, employment, position or business shall be guilty of an offence.

The adoption of passive corruption in Section 5 of the Act is considered to be a partial implementation of the PIF Directive, specifically Article 4(2) of the Directive. Article 4(2) defines active and passive corruption as:

Member States shall take the necessary measures to ensure that passive and active corruption, when committed intentionally, constitute criminal offences.

a.   For the purposes of this Directive, 'passive corruption' means the action of a public official who, directly or through an intermediary, requests or receives advantages of any kind, for himself or for a third party, or accepts a promise of such an advantage, to act or to refrain from acting in accordance with his duty or in the exercise of his functions in a way which damages or is likely to damage the Union's financial interests.

b.   For the purposes of this Directive, 'active corruption' means the action of a person who promises, offers or gives, directly or through an intermediary, an advantage of any kind to a public official for himself or for a third party for him to act or to refrain from acting in accordance with his duty or in the exercise of his functions in a way which damages or is likely to damage the Union's financial interests.

In addition to adopting clear definitions of active and passive corruption, the 2018 Act creates a new criminal offence of active and passive trading in influence, which can be seen as incorporating the recommendations of Recital 8 to the PIF Directive, which advises that:

Since all public officials have a duty to exercise judgment or discretion impartially, the giving of bribes in order to influence a public official's judgment or discretion and the taking of such bribes should be included in the definition of corruption.

Section 6 of the 2018 Act states that:

1) A person who, either directly or indirectly, by himself or herself or with
another person –
a. corruptly offers, or
b. corruptly gives or agrees to give,
a gift, consideration or advantage in order to induce another person to exert an
improper influence over an act of an official in relation to the office,
employment, position or business of the official shall be guilty of an offence.
2) (2) A person who, either directly or indirectly, by himself or herself or with
another person
a. corruptly requests,
b. corruptly accepts or obtains, or
c. corruptly agrees to accept,
for himself or herself or for any other person, a gift, consideration or advantage
on account of a person promising or asserting the ability to improperly
influence an official to do an act in relation to the office, employment,
position or business of the official shall be guilty of an offence.

For the offences listed in Sections 5(1) and 6(1) of the 2018 Act, Sections 11 and 12
extend criminal conduct to include conduct that occurred outside the State.

11.2.2.1   Liability of Legal Persons
Additionally, changes envisaged by the PIF Directive were made regarding the question
of criminal liability for legal persons. Article 6(1) of the PIF Directive provides:

> Member States shall take the necessary measures to ensure that legal persons
> can be held liable for any of the criminal offences referred to in Articles 3, 4 and
> 5 committed for their benefit by any person, acting either individually or as
> part of an organ of the legal person, and having a leading position within the
> legal person, based on:
> a. a power of representation of the legal person;
> b. an authority to take decisions on behalf of the legal person; or
> c. an authority to exercise control within the legal person.

Section 18(1) of the Criminal Justice (Corruption Offences) Act 2018 implements this
provision, stating:

> A body corporate shall be guilty of an offence under this subsection if an
> offence under this Act is committed by –
> a. a director, manager, secretary or other officer of the body corporate,
> b. a person purporting to act in that capacity,

    c. a shadow director within the meaning of the Companies Act 2014 of the body corporate, or

    d. an employee, agent or subsidiary of the body corporate,

with the intention of obtaining or retaining –

    i. business for the body corporate, or

    ii. an advantage in the conduct of business for the body corporate.

Furthermore, where liability is directed towards a body corporate, Section 18(2) of the Act provides a defence to legal persons who can show "it took all reasonable steps and exercised all due diligence to avoid the commission of the offence".[98] This gives explicit reference in Ireland law to the requirement that offences covered by the PIF Directive, and implemented in the Act, must require intent, as affirmed in Recital 11 to the directive.[99] Furthermore, under Section 18(3) of the 2018 Act, in the event that an offence committed by a body corporate is proven to have been committed with the consent, connivance or wilful neglect of senior officers, those officers will be guilty of the same offence, thus giving effect to Article 6(3) of the directive. Despite this inclusion, however, it only covers actions of legal persons that amount to criminal conduct under the 2018 Statute, which does not cover all of the offences required to be implemented by the PIF Directive, specifically fraud affecting the Union's financial interests (Article 3) and money laundering (Article 4).

11.2.3 Other PIF Directive Related Issues

At the time of writing, effects were the only provisions of the PIF Directive that had been implemented in Ireland, though it does not appear to require a great deal of legislative change to align Irish law with the substantive offences covered by the PIF Directive. For example, the money laundering offences required by Article 4(1) of the PIF Directive refer to the Fourth Anti-Money Laundering Directive (EU) 2015/849, which Ireland is currently in the course of implementing through the Criminal Justice (Money Laundering and Terrorist Financing) (Amendment) Bill 2018, which is currently in the final legislative stage in the Seanad.[100] Among the provisions of the directive that will be implemented by the 2018 Bill once it comes into force, Sections 21 to 23 of the bill put the State Financial Intelligence Unit, part of Garda Síochána, on a statutory footing. They also give the FIU additional power to obtain information needed to tackle money

---

98 *Ibid.*, s. 18(2).

99 Recital 11 states that "with regard to the criminal offences provided for in this Directive, the notion of intention must apply to all the elements constituting those criminal offences. The intentional nature of an act or omission may be inferred from objective, factual circumstances. Criminal offences which do not require intention are not covered by this Directive".

100 Updated 11 October 2018, https://www.oireachtas.ie/en/bills/bill/2018/40/.

laundering and terrorist financing and allow the FIU to share information on request with certain bodies in Ireland and with FIUs in the other Member States. Given that the directive was due to be transposed by 26 June 2017, and following the Reasoned Opinion sent to Ireland by the European Commission as part of ongoing infringement proceedings for non-implementation on 8 March 2018, the time frame for completing the legislative process on the 2018 Bill is extremely tight. It should come into force before the end of the year.

Issues specific to Ireland include references in the PIF Directive to prescription periods that enables the investigation, prosecution, trial and judicial decision of criminal offences covered by the directive. These are required to be implemented pursuant to Article 12 of the PIF Directive. Recital 22, however, states that the requirements are without prejudice to the Member States which do not set limitation periods for investigation, prosecution and enforcement. As Ireland does not have prescription periods, it will not include them in the final implementation of the directive.[101]

As with other criminal offences that have been implemented pursuant to EU criminal law, offences established through the implementation of the PIF Directive give rise to the risk of double jeopardy for cross-border conduct. Recital 21 to the PIF Directive reiterates the importance of the principle as it relates to offences under the directive. The principle against double jeopardy is established in the common law of Ireland through the pleas in bar of *autrefois acquit*[102] and *autrefois convict*.[103] Furthermore, the Irish Supreme Court has held that where a heavy administrative penalty has been imposed, the Court will examine the process leading to the imposition of the penalty and may treat the administrative penalty as a criminal sanction in substance if it was excessive or disproportionate to the administrative objective to be achieved.[104] While Ireland is not bound by the Convention Implementing the Schengen Agreement, the State did request to be bound by Articles 54 to 56 CISA relating to the *ne bis in idem* principle,[105] which was accepted by the Council.[106] In addition, Ireland signed and ratified Protocol 7 to the European Convention of Human Rights on 1 November 2001,[107] Article 4 of which protects against double jeopardy.

---

101 Speech of Minister of Justice and Equality, above n 94.

102 *The People (Director of Public Prosecutions) v. O'Shea* [1982] IR 241.

103 *The State (Attorney General) v. Judge Deale* [1973] IR 180.

104 *Registrar of Companies v. Anderson* [2005] 1 IR 21.

105 Commission Staff Working Document: Annex to the Green Paper on 'Conflicts of Jurisdiction and the Principle of Ne Bis In Idem in Criminal Proceedings' SEC (2005) 1767, p. 45.

106 2002/192/EC: Council Decision of 28 February 2002 concerning Ireland's request to take part in some of the provisions of the Schengen acquis.

107 https://www.coe.int/en/web/conventions/search-on-treaties/-/conventions/treaty/117/signatures?p_auth=4DsJt24x, last accessed 30 September 2018.

11.3   CONCLUSION

Until now, Irish institutions have appeared willing to engage in the area of freedom, security and justice, despite the exclusionary options provided by Protocol 21. Despite being a relatively small EU Member State, the Irish Parliament has busily implemented a large number of AFSJ Directives in the last three years alone. Additionally, Irish courts have fully embraced the EAW regime, and are active both in executing EAWs and in accepting challenges based on fundamental rights. The Irish Supreme Court, theoretically the court of last instance only for matters of constitutional significance, has issued a large number of judgments regarding the EAW since 2004, dealing with interpretations of matters relating to human rights challenges on everything from the quality of prisons in Northern Ireland and Poland, the ability of the UK to protect the lives of members of paramilitary organizations and Brexit to the lawfulness of relying on evidence from civil law jurisdictions that had not been subject to challenge by cross-examination. Yet a number of issues will test this system in the future. The first is Brexit and all of the practical and legal implications that will result from it. Prominent among these issues is the potential for heightened terrorism-related activity on both sides of the physical land border in Ireland, as well as VAT- and other financial-related criminal activity should the UK leave the EU Customs Union. It will be essential that measures are put in place during a transition period that will allow for the continuation of an efficient extradition system as well as cross-border cooperation in the investigation of criminal activity and the sharing of evidence.

With regard to criminal offences related to the protection of the Union's financial interests, the Irish legislature is currently in the process of completely implementing the PIF Directive. Steps have already been taken to give effect to the parts of the directive that fall under the competence of the Ministry of Justice, with the aspects of the directive relating to financial crimes currently being processed by the Ministry of Finance, with the stated objective of the government being to bring Irish law fully into line with the directive by the transposition date.

As a small EU Member State, which is a member of the Eurozone and whose capital city is competing with several other EU cities to become the main European financial services centre post-Brexit, it is important for Ireland to be seen to have a modern, efficient legal system with up-to-date rules on the efficient investigation and enforcement of criminal activity in the field of financial and tax-related crimes, including where they affect the interests of the Union.

12 SELECTED CASE STUDIES: THE CASE STUDY OF CROATIA

Zlata Đurđević

12.1 INTRODUCTION[*]

This chapter is dedicated to the protection of the financial interests of the European Union by transposition of the Directive (EU) 2017/1371 of the European Parliament and of the Council of 5 July 2017 on the fight against fraud to the Union's financial interests by means of criminal law (PIF Directive) in national legal orders, with a particular focus on Croatia. The PIF Directive was adopted after five years of negotiation between the Union's institutions, Commission, Council and Parliament and it differs in some crucial aspects from the previous Commission's proposals for a directive on the fight against EU fraud[1] including the version from 11 July 2012 which served as a negotiation starting point. The PIF Directive is based on the Article 83(2)[2] of the Treaty on the Functioning of the European Union (TFEU) as the European Council and the European Parliament rejected the Commission's proposal of Article 325(4)[3] TFEU as a

---

[*] This paper is a product of work which has been supported in part by the Croatian Science Foundation under the project 8282 Croatian Judicial Cooperation in Criminal Matters in the EU and the Region: Heritage of the Past and Challenges of the Future (CoCoCrim).

1 The European Commission has already presented the proposal for a directive of the European Parliament and of the Council on the criminal law protection of the Community's financial interests (COM(2001)272 final) on May 23 2001 under Article 280 of the EC Treaty of Amsterdam.

2 Art. 83(2) TFEU: "If the approximation of criminal laws and regulations of the Member States proves essential to ensure the effective implementation of a Union policy in an area which has been subject to harmonisation measures, directives may establish minimum rules with regard to the definition of criminal offences and sanctions in the area concerned. Such directives shall be adopted by the same ordinary or special legislative procedure as was followed for the adoption of the harmonisation measures in question, without prejudice to Article 76."

3 Art. 325(4) TFEU: "The European Parliament and the Council, acting in accordance with the ordinary legislative procedure, after consulting the Court of Auditors, shall adopt the necessary measures in the fields of the prevention of and fight against fraud affecting the financial interests of the Union with a view to affording effective and equivalent protection in the Member States and in all the Union's institutions, bodies, offices and agencies."

basis for the directive.[4] The use of Article 83(2) TFEU prevented the European Union from adopting a regulation on the criminal law protection of the EU's financial interests as could have been suggested by the Article 86(2) TFEU on the establishment of the European Public Prosecutor and placed the offences against the Union's financial interests within the area of freedom, security and justice where the EU and Member States have shared competence and where the principles of subsidiarity and proportionality apply. Thus, if crime against the EU budget is a particularly serious crime with a cross-border dimension, it is an area where the European Union by means of directives may in accordance with the ordinary legislative procedure, establish minimum rules concerning the definition of criminal offences and sanctions (Article 83 (1) TFEU). Thus, Member States could have used the emergency brake procedure if the draft directive would have to affect fundamental aspects of their criminal justice systems (Article 83(3) TFEU) and they have freedom on how to achieve the goal set in the PIF Directive adapting it to its criminal law offences and principles. Regulations, contrary to directives, have to be transposed automatically and identically in all Member States without any changes that are contrary to the coherence of the national criminal justice systems.

The PIF Directive replaces the previous instruments for the protection of the EU's financial interests (PIF) by criminal law (Article 17): the Convention on the Protection of the European Communities' Financial Interests of 26 July 1995 (PIF Convention)[5] as well as its two protocols – the anti-corruption[6] Protocol of 27 September 1996 ('first Protocol') and the Protocol dealing with the liability of legal persons and money laundering of 19 June 1997 ('second Protocol').[7] They were international treaties that were adopted as third pillar instruments under the 1992 Maastricht Treaty of the European Union. The deadline to transpose the PIF Directive into national law of the Member States was 6 July 2019 (Article 16). Hence two years after the adoption of the directive and since then, the Convention on the protection of the Union's financial interests and its protocols should not be in force any more. The risk of a legal gap in the national criminal law protection of the EU's financial interests arises if a Member

---

4   On discussion on the legal basis of the Directive *see* in: Negotiations of the Commission Proposal for the Directive in Adam Juszczak and Elisa Sason, 'The Directive on the Fight against Fraud to the Union's Financial Interests by Means of Criminal Law (PIF Directive): Laying Down the Foundation for a Better Protection of the Union's Financial Interests?' (2017) Eucrim – The European Criminal Law Associations' Forum. 10.30709/eucrim-2017-009; Constanza Di Francesco Maesa, 'The Directive on the Fight against Fraud to the Union's Financial Interests by Means of Criminal Law: A Missed Goal?' (2018) Insight, European Forum, 22 October 2018, 1-15, 3-7.

5   OJ C 316 from 27 November 1995, 49-57.

6   Protocol drawn up on the basis of Art. K.3 of the Treaty on European Union to the Convention on the protection of the European Communities' financial interests (OJ C 313 from 23 October 1996, 2-10).

7   Second Protocol, drawn up on the basis of Art. K.3 of the treaty on European Union, to the Convention on the protection of the European Communities' financial interests (OJ C 221 from 19 July 1997, 12-22).

State fails to implement the PIF Directive or if the implementation of the PIF Directive is inadequate or incomplete.

If we assume that more than 20 years after the adoption of the PIF instruments the Member States have transposed them adequately in the national criminal law, the correct transposition of the PIF Directive presupposes the identification of the differences between the PIF Directive and the previous PIF instruments. Is the scope and content of the protection of the Union's financial interests in the Convention and its protocols the same as in the directive? Is the only reason for adopting the PIF Directive the abolishment of the third pillar instruments by the Lisbon Treaty and replacing them by directives or so-called 'Lisbonization' of the EU legal acts? If the answer to both questions is positive, we can conclude that the national criminal law protection of the Union's financial interests is adequate and transposition of the directive in the national law does not require any changes. From the Croatian implementation act and its explanation, it is plausible to conclude that this was the conclusion of the Croatian legislator. However, if the adoption of the directive is not only the question of legal basis and the type of EU legal instrument before and after the Lisbon Treaty but provides for some substantial changes in the protection of the Union's interests, if it broadens the scope of the criminal law provisions on the fight against fraud to the EU's financial interests comparing to the PIF Convention and its two Protocols,[8] the Member States are required to verify whether their national law corresponds to the changes in the protection of the Union's financial interests. The answer can be positive or negative, but it presupposes the identification of the differences between the previous PIF instruments and the directive and the explanation of why the national implementation act satisfies the requirements of the directive. Therefore, this paper shall be divided into four chapters. After the introduction, in the second section the novelties with regard to fraud against the Union's financial interests in the directive shall be presented; the third chapter shall deal with the transposition of the PIF Directive in Croatia and the fourth chapter shall be a conclusion on the Croatian transposition of the directive in national law.

The PIF Directive covers the content of the PIF Convention and its two protocols and includes, beside EU fraud, offences of passive and active bribery and money laundering, liability of legal persons, general concepts of substantive criminal law such as incitement, aiding and abetting, and attempt, sanctions with regard to natural and legal persons, aggravating circumstances, freezing and confiscation, jurisdiction, limitation periods and cooperation. Taking into account the comprehensive approach in regulating EU fraud in the PIF Directive, this paper will be limited to the analysis of offences of EU fraud, including a new offence of misappropriation in the PIF Directive.

---

8   Maria Kaiafa-Gbandi, 'The Protection of the EU's Financial Interests by Means of Criminal Law in the Context of the Lisbon Treaty and the 2017 Directive (EU 2017/1371) on the Fight Against Fraud to the Union's Financial Interests' (2018) 12 *Zeitschrift für Internationale Strafrechtsdogmatik* 581.

12.2 NOVELTIES WITH REGARD TO THE OFFENCES OF FRAUD AGAINST THE UNION'S FINANCIAL INTERESTS IN THE DIRECTIVE

12.2.1 *More Precise Definition of the Union's Financial Interests (Article 2(1)(a))*

The object of fraud in the PIF Directive is defined more precisely and extensively than in the PIF Convention. This relates to the definition of financial interests as well as to the budgets within the scope of the directive. The PIF Directive did not eliminate the traditional division of the Union budget fraud from the PIF Convention as revenue (resources) related fraud (Article 3 (2)(c)(d)) and expenditure (funds) related fraud (Article(2)(a)(b)), but has extended the notion of the 'Union's financial interests' to assets as a third element. The PIF Directive covers the fraudulent conduct with respect to revenues, expenditure and assets at the expense of the Union budget, including financial operations such as borrowing and lending activities (Recital 4).

Also, the notion of the Union budget is defined more accurately. The definition from the Article 1(1) of the PIF Convention: "the general budget of the European Communities or budgets managed by, or on behalf of, the European Communities", is replaced by the "(i) the Union budget and (ii) the budgets of the Union institutions, bodies, offices and agencies established pursuant to the Treaties or budgets directly or indirectly managed and monitored by them". The precision about the object of the fraud is crucial for the correct implementation in the national criminal law and the effective prosecution and adjudication of fraudulent behaviour by national judicial authorities.

12.2.2 *VAT Fraud*

The EU budget is funded from the EU's own resources.[9] There are three main types of EU budget own sources: a) customs duties and sugar levies on imports from outside the EU, b) the proportion of the value-added tax (VAT) collected by each Member State, c) a proportion of Member States' gross national income (GNI).[10] In 2017 the GNI participated with 65 per cent, customs duties with 16 per cent, VAT with 12 per cent and other revenue with 7 per cent in the EU budget.[11] Therefore, there is no doubt that VAT is a part of the EU's own resources, the revenue of the EU budget and present financial interests of the EU.

---

9   Art. 311 of the Treaty on the Functioning of the European Union. On EU budget law *see*: https://ec.europa. eu/info/about-european-commission/eu-budget/how-it-works/budget-law_en.

10   Council Regulation (EU, Euratom) No 609/2014 of 26 May 2014 on the methods and procedure for making available the traditional, VAT and GNI-based own resources and on the measures to meet cash requirements, OJ L 168, 7 June 2014, pp. 39-52.

11   The OLAF Report 2017, p. 11.

In the area of VAT, it is estimated that cross-border fraud, such as 'missing-trader' or 'carousel' fraud, generates budgetary losses of around €50 billion a year.[12] Also, the OLAF and Eurojust reports revealed numerous large-scale VAT fraud cases that they are dealing with. The majority of VAT fraud damage is borne by the Member States but also proportional to the part of the VAT paid to the EU, it affects the EU budget as well. The action and cooperation at the EU level are needed not only because the VAT fraud affects the financial interests of the Union but also because the perpetrators of the VAT fraud take advantage of the open system of trading within the single market.[13]

12.2.2.1   Member States' Opposition to EU VAT Fraud

However, one of the major issues with regard to the criminal law protection of the Union's financial interests was whether the value-added tax (VAT) could be considered Union revenue in the sense of the PIF instruments. The PIF Convention did not mention expressly that VAT is under its scope, and the Member States claimed that the VAT fraud is in national competence. The treatment of the VAT was also the biggest stumbling block in the negotiation on the 2012 Commission's proposal for the PIF Directive. During the negotiation, the Council insisted on excluding revenues arising from the VAT from the notion of the Union's financial interests in the directive.

There are several arguments that corroborate that position. The first one is related to the shifting of competences from the Member States to the European Union bypassing the division in the treaties. The taxation and the power to tax is the Member State competence, and the EU has only very limited EU tax competences related to the single EU market. Therefore, the Member States feared that the PIF instruments had the capacity to expand the EU's competence in the sphere of tax.[14] They claimed that the proposed directive could encroach on the Member States' responsibilities to control and operate the VAT system.[15] The second argument was that the Member States receive 97 per cent of VAT while only 3 per cent of the VAT is paid to the EU budget and therefore the Member States should address the VAT fraud and not the EU.[16] The third argument was related to the method of payment of VAT to the EU. The VAT is paid to the Member States which then allocate a certain percentage to the EU and therefore it was claimed that the VAT proceeds do not constitute EU revenue in and of themselves.[17]

---

12   Commission Anti-Fraud Strategy: enhanced action to protect the EU budget, European Commission, Brussels, 29 April 2019 COM (2019) 196 final, p. 10.
13   *See* The Fight Against Fraud on the EU's Finances, 12th Report of Session 2012-13, House of Lords, European Union Committee, p. 22.
14   *Ibid.*, p. 20.
15   *Ibid.*, p. 20.
16   *Ibid.*, p. 22.
17   Maria Kaiafa-Gbandi, *op. cit.* at p. 577.

Any perceived damage to the EU assets is *indirect*, i.e., it affects the ability of Member States to apportion a fraction of evaded earnings from their own assets.[18]

It is even claimed that the same logic should apply to the proportion of Member States' GDP allocated to the EU budget.[19] This is an invalid argument as the VAT is tax and the gross national income is not a tax but the value produced by a country's economy in a given year. It is irrelevant whether the percentage of the VAT is paid directly to the EU or a Member State pays a percentage of the VAT to the EU.

12.2.2.2   The CJEU Judgments

This issue was resolved by three judgments of the European Court of Justice (ECJ) that all stated that VAT fraud is affecting EU financial interests. In the judgment of 15 November 2011, C-539/09, *Commission v. Germany*, the Court stated that any lacuna in the collection of the VAT revenue in compliance with the applicable Union law potentially causes a reduction of the availability of the VAT resources to the Union budget.[20] In judgment *Åkerberg Fransson*, C-617/10 of 26 February 2013, the Court proclaimed that

> In order to ensure that all VAT revenue is collected and, in so doing, that the financial interests of the European Union are protected, the Member States have the freedom to choose the applicable penalties.[21]

So the Court clearly stated that VAT revenue is a financial interest of the EU and that VAT fraud diminishes the EU's budget.

The negotiations on the PIF Directive gave results only after the *Taricco* judgment of 8 September 2015[22] where the ECJ repeated that "the European Union's own resources include revenue from application of a uniform rate to the harmonized VAT assessment

---

18   *Ibid. See* reference 14.
19   "The problem inherent in this view can be grasped if conceived that – according to it – any fraudulent violation against a Member State's GDP should be considered an abuse against the financial interests of the Union." *Ibid. See* reference 16.
20   Para. 72: "There is thus a direct link between, on the one hand, the collection of VAT revenue in compliance with the Community law applicable and, on the other, the availability to the Community budget of the corresponding VAT resources, since any lacuna in the collection of the first potentially causes a reduction in the second." *See* Proposal for a Directive of the European Parliament and of the Council on the fight against fraud to the Union's financial interests by means of criminal law, Brussels, 11 July 2012, COM (2012) 363 final, p. 8.
21   Case C-617/10, judgment *Åkerberg Fransson* of 26 February 2013, § 34.
22   Adam Juszczak and Elisa Sason, *op. cit.* at p. 83; Constanza Di Francesco Maesa, *op. cit.* at p. 7.

bases determined according to EU rules",[23] that "the Member States must fight against tax evasion regarding the VAT"[24] and that

> in order to ensure that all VAT revenue is collected and, in so doing, that the financial interests of the European Union are protected criminal penalties may nevertheless be essential to combat certain serious cases of VAT evasion in an effective and dissuasive manner.[25]

12.2.2.3   Definition of the VAT Fraud

After almost five years of negotiation, the PIF Directive expressly included VAT fraud within its scope. The offence of VAT fraud is prescribed in two articles in the PIF Directive: Article 2(2) that limits this offence only to serious cases and Article 3(2)(d) that prescribes the elements of the offence. Due to the political compromise, the PIF Directive is not applied to all cases of VAT fraud as was proposed by the Commission[26] and as was prescribed, according to the ECJ, by the PIF Convention but only to cases of serious offences against the common VAT system.[27] The serious offences against the common VAT system exist where the intentional acts or omissions defined in Article 3(2)(d) are connected with the territory of two or more Member States and involve the total damage[28] of at least 10,000,000 euros (Recital 4, Article 2(b)(2)). The directive cites the examples of serious fraud such as carousel fraud, VAT fraud through missing traders[29] and VAT fraud committed within a criminal organization, which create serious threats to the common VAT system and thus to the Union budget (Recital 4).

---

23   Case C-105/14, Criminal proceedings against Ivo Taricco and Others, § 38.
24   *Ibid.*, § 36.
25   *Ibid.*, § 39.
26   COM (2012) 363 final, Brussels 11 July 2012, p. 12, Recital (4).
27   The common VAT system is established by Council Directive 2006/112/EC of 28 November 2006 on the common system of value-added tax (OJ L 347, 11 December 2006, p. 1).
28   The notion of total damage refers to the estimated damage that results from the entire fraud scheme, both to the financial interests of the Member States concerned and to the Union, excluding interest and penalties (Recital 4). Kaiafa-Gbandi is warning that no damage other than that relating to Member States exists and therefore the calculation of total damages that include the losses of both the EU and Member States results in an erroneous double computation. *See* Maria Kaiafa-Gbandi, *op. cit.* at p. 577.
29   Examples of MTIC fraud including missing traders fraud and carousel fraud *see* Eurojust News, Issue No. 11 March 2014.

Additionally, the elements of VAT fraud are not the same as the elements of the classic EU fraud regarding revenue. The introduction of the VAT fraud in the PIF Directive was not only the introduction of a new object of EU fraud comparing to the PIF Convention but an introduction of a new form of EU fraud against the revenue. While the PIF Convention has common forms of fraud against all kinds of EU revenue,[30] the PIF Directive has split the fraud against revenue into: a) fraud in respect of revenue other than revenue arising from VAT own resources (Article 3(2)(c)) that correspond in full to the forms of fraud against revenue in the PIF Convention (Article 1(1)(b)),[31] and b) fraud in respect of revenue arising from VAT own resources (Article 3 (2)(d)). VAT fraud also has three forms of fraudulent behaviour, but they have to be committed in cross-border fraudulent schemes. This additional common element corresponds to the requirement from Article 2(2) that fraud is connected with the territory of two or more Member States of the Union. The difference in the first two forms is that the required effect for the VAT fraud is "the diminution of the resources of the Union budget", while for fraud against other EU revenue it is "illegal diminution of the resources of the Union budget" so the illegality of the diminution of the resources has to be proven. Additionally, the third form of VAT fraud is a new offence committed by "the presentation of correct VAT-related statements for the purposes of fraudulently disguising the non-payment or wrongful creation of rights to VAT refunds".

So, EU VAT fraud has forms that do not correspond to the existing forms of fraud against EU revenue that existed in the PIF Convention, and the Member States had an obligation to transpose them in the national criminal law.

12.2.3   Procurement-Related Expenditure

Public procurement, the largest channel of public spending, constitutes an area that is particularly vulnerable to fraud and irregularities.[32] From 2011-2016, 20 per cent of all

---

30   Art. 1(1)(b) of the PIF Convention: 1. For the purposes of this Convention, fraud affecting the European Communities' financial interests shall consist of:
(b) in respect of revenue, any intentional act or omission relating to:
– the use or presentation of false, incorrect or incomplete statements or documents, which has as its effect the illegal diminution of the resources of the general budget of the European Communities or budgets managed by, or on behalf of, the European Communities,
– non-disclosure of information in violation of a specific obligation, with the same effect,
– misapplication of a legally obtained benefit, with the same effect.
31   The Art. 3(2)(c) of the PIF Directive and Article 1(1)(b) of the PIF Convention are the same. Only difference is that the Convention uses the term 'intentional act or omission' and the Directive 'act or omission'. The reason is that the PIF Directive in Recital 11 has expressly excluded criminal offences which do not require intention from its scope.
However, the act or omission of fraud has to be intentional, so legally and practically there is no difference.
32   Fraud in Public Procurement: A Collection of Red Flags and Best Practices, OLAF, Ref. Ares(2017)6254403 – 20/12/2017, p. 3.

reported irregularities have been related to breaches of public procurement rules, accounting for 30 per cent of all reported irregular financial amounts.[33] Therefore, a large part of the caseload of the OLAF investigators relates to allegations of fraud in public procurement[34] and OLAF cases frequently concern cross-border procurement fraud or corruption in public procurement procedures involving EU financing.[35] The 2016 OLAF report explains the functioning, significance, prevalence and certain cases of fraud in public procurement that OLAF dealt with.[36] The fraud related to public procurement was the focus of the European Commission anti-fraud strategy for years,[37] and the PIF Directive is its significant addition.

The PIF Directive is introducing novelties also on the side of the fraud against EU expenditure related to the fraud in procurement. It establishes a new distinction between non-procurement- and procurement-related expenditure fraud. The non-procurement-related fraud (Article 3(2)(a)) is identical to the fraud against expenditure in the PIF Convention (Article 1(1)(a)).[38] However, the procurement-related expenditure contains new elements of crime (Article 3(2)(b)).

Procurement-related expenditure is any expenditure in connection with the public contracts as determined by Article 101(1) of Regulation (EU, Euratom) No 966/2012 on the financial rules applicable to the general budget of the Union (Recital 6). It prescribes that public contracts are contracted for pecuniary interests, concluded in writing between economic operators and contracting authorities against payment of a price paid in whole or in part from the budget, the supply of movable or immovable

---

33   *Ibid.*
34   Report from the Commission to the European Parliament and the Council, Protection of the European Union's financial interests – Fight against fraud, 2016 Annual Report, Brussels, 20 July 2017. COM (2017) 383 final, 15.
35   The OLAF Report 2017, p. 10. See cases pp. 14-16.
36   *Ibid.*, 15-18.
37   *See* Fraud in Public Procurement: A Collection of Red Flags and Best Practices, OLAF, Ref. Ares (2017) 6254403 – 20 December 2017; Identifying and Reducing Corruption in Public Procurement in the EU, study prepared for the European Commission by PwC and Ecorys, 30 June 2013; Public Procurement: Costs we Pay for Corruption – Identifying and Reducing Corruption in Public Procurement in the EU, PwC and Ecorys, University of Utrecht, 2013; Fraud Indicators, European Commission, SOLID/2012/REV.
38   Art. 1(1)(a) of the PIF Convention: 1. For the purposes of this Convention, fraud affecting the European Communities' financial interests shall consist of:
(a) in respect of expenditure, any intentional act or omission relating to:
– the use or presentation of false, incorrect or incomplete statements or documents, which has as its effect the misappropriation or wrongful retention of funds from the general budget of the European Communities or budgets managed by, or on behalf of, the European Communities,
– non-disclosure of information in violation of a specific obligation, with the same effect,1
– the misapplication of such funds for purposes other than those for which they were originally granted;
The Art. 3(2)(a) of the PIF Directive and Article 1(1)(b) of the PIF Convention are the same. The only difference is that the Convention uses the term 'intentional act or omission' and the Directive 'act or omission'. However, as already mentioned, the PIF Directive, in Recital 11, has expressly excluded criminal offences which do not require intention from its scope.

assets, the execution of works or the provision of services. Such contracts comprise a) building contracts, b) supply contracts, c) works contracts and d) service contracts.[39]

Procurement-related fraud also has three forms, two of which relate to the classic form of EU expenditure fraud as (i) the use or presentation of false, incorrect or incomplete statements or documents (first indents of Article 3(2)(b)) and (ii) non-disclosure of information in violation of a specific obligation (second indents of Article 3(2)(b)). The effect of both forms has to be the misappropriation or wrongful retention of funds or assets from the Union budget or budgets managed by the Union, or on its behalf. The third form of procurement-related fraud is classical fraud against expenditure through the misapplication of funds or assets for purposes other than those for which they were originally granted, which damages the Union's financial interests. The last part of the provision that requires the establishment of the damage to the EU budget represents an additional objective element that was in the PIF Convention removed from the fraud against other types of expenditure.

Furthermore, there are additional elements of crime that do not exist in the description of the expenditure-related fraud in the PIF Conventions. All three forms of procurement-related fraud in the PIF Directive exist "at least when committed in order to make an unlawful gain for the perpetrator or another by causing a loss to the Union's financial interests". An offence committed "in order to make an unlawful gain for the perpetrator, or another" is a subjective element of the offence, part of intention or *mens rea*, and "causing a loss to the Union's financial interests" is the objective element of causing damage. These additional elements are narrowing the field of incrimination of fraud and are prohibited when transposing the non-procurement-related expenditure. Words 'at least' would suggest that these elements are not obligatory and the Member States may leave them out when transposing procurement-related fraud.

12.2.4   Misappropriation by a Public Official

The entirely new offence introduced by the PIF Directive is misappropriation. An offence of misappropriation is the action of a public official who is directly or indirectly entrusted with the management of funds or assets to commit or disburse funds or appropriate or use assets contrary to the purpose for which they were intended in any way which damages the Union's financial interests. The fraudulent behaviour of this offence is similar to the offences of EU fraud through misapplication of funds, assets or benefits[40] as in both cases the perpetrator is using them contrary to the purpose for which they were

---

39   Art, 101(1) of the Regulation (EU, Euratom) No 966/2012 of the European Parliament and of the Council of 25 October 2012 on the financial rules applicable to the general budget of the Union and repealing Council Regulation (EC, Euratom) No 1605/2002.

40   Offences of misapplication are prescribed by Arts. 3(2)(a)(iii)/(b)(iii)/(c)(iii) of the PIF Directive.

intended. However, in case of misappropriation, a perpetrator is not a person who uses EU funds or is obliged to pay duties to the EU budget, but a person that is entrusted with disbursing funds to the final user. In most cases, these are public officials of the Member States or the EU. The other difference is that the damages to the Union's financial interests have to be determined. This objective element of actual damage to the EU budget is introduced in order to differentiate a criminal offence of misappropriation from a mere breach of the terms of use regarding the allocated resources.[41]

The PIF Directive, in relation to the offences of misappropriation and passive corruption needs to expand a definition of public officials covering not only a Union official and a national official, but also any other person assigned and exercising a public service function involving the management of or decisions concerning the Union's financial interests (Article 4(4)(b)). In Recital 10 it is explained that private persons are increasingly involved in the management of Union funds, and therefore there is a need to cover persons who do not hold formal office but who are nonetheless assigned and exercise, in a similar manner, a public service function in relation to Union funds, such as contractors involved in the management of such funds. Therefore, Member States have to extend the definition of public officials also to private persons involved in the management of the EU funds.

12.3   Transposition of the PIF Directive in Croatia

At the end of 2018, on December 19, the Republic of Croatia adopted the amendments of the Criminal Code implementing the PIF Directive. The law came into force on 4 January 2019, and thereby Croatia has fulfilled its obligation from Article 16 of the PIF Directive, which prescribed that the deadline to transpose the PIF Directive into the national law of the Member States was 6 July 2019 (Article 16). However, the only change that was introduced was the reference to the PIF Directive in Article 386 of the Criminal Code. Article 386 of the Criminal Code contains the list of legal acts of the European Union that were transposed in the Croatian Criminal Code, and in point 13, the reference to the PIF Directive was introduced as required by Article 17(1) of the PIF Directive.[42] The Croatian government claimed that the analysis of the PIF Directive revealed that national criminal legislation is already in line with the requirements that the directive places on the

---

41   Kaiafa-Gbandi, *op. cit.* at p. 579.
42   Art. 17(1) of the PIF Directive: 1. Member States shall adopt and publish, by 6 July 2019, the laws, regulations and administrative provisions necessary to comply with this Directive. (...) When Member States adopt those measures, they shall contain a reference to this Directive or be accompanied by such a reference on the occasion of their official publication.

Member States[43] and the Croatian Parliament accepted the same position and adopted the transposition of the PIF Directives with no substantial changes.

The explanation of the Proposal of the Amendments of the Criminal Code given by the Government of the Republic of Croatia from 27 June 2018, cited the offences of the Criminal Code that protect the Union's financial interests. It is asserted that the offences under Article 3 of the PIF Directive correspond in the Croatian law to the following offences: tax or customs duty evasion (Article 256 of the Criminal Code), subsidy fraud (Article 258 of the Criminal Code) and fraud in business dealings (Article 247 of the Criminal Code).[44] As regards the other criminal offences affecting the Union's financial interests under Article 4 of the PIF Directive, an analysis revealed that they correspond to the criminal offences of money laundering (Article 265 Criminal Code), taking a bribe (Article 293 of the Criminal Code), giving a bribe (Article 294 of the Criminal Code), embezzlement (Article 232 of the Criminal Code) and embezzlement at work (Article 233 of the Criminal Code).[45] Furthermore, the analysis of the criminal sanctions of the above-mentioned offences has shown their compliance with Article 7 of the PIF Directive, which provides for a maximum penalty of at least four years of imprisonment. The legislative proposal recognizes and mentions as the only novelty Article 12 of the PIF Directive that prescribes the statute of limitations on criminal prosecution and the statute of limitations for imprisonment for the offences referred to in Articles 3 and 4. The analysis of the time limits in question showed their compliance with Article 81 of the Criminal Code (statute of limitations for prosecution) and Article 83 of the Criminal Code (statute of limitations for the execution of sentence).

Without aspirations to offer solutions to the transposition of the PIF Directive in Croatia and to expose the full analysis of shortcomings of the protection of the Union's financial interests in Croatia, the mere correlation of novelties in the PIF Directive with the provisions of the Croatian Criminal Code expose that the transposition is defective and without any proper content. Just a few arguments related to offences of EU fraud will be given:

– The legislator has just repeated the criminal offences implementing the PIF Convention and its two protocols. Furthermore, without any reference to the PIF Directive, the explanation of the Amendments is referring to the offences that do not mention or refer to the protection of the Union's financial interests and did not serve previously in theory or case law for that purpose. For example, it is not clear why the legislator considered that the offence of fraud in business dealings (Article 247 of the Criminal Code) transpose the offences under Article 3 of the PIF Directive or why the offences of embezzlement (Article 232 of the Criminal Code) and

---

43 The proposal of the Act on Amendments of the Criminal Code, Government of the Republic of Croatia, June 27, 2018, p. 2.
44 *Ibid.*
45 *Ibid.*

embezzlement at work (Article 233 of the Criminal Code) serve as transposition of offences under Article 4 of the PIF Directive. Elements of crimes prescribed by Article 3 and Article 4 of the PIF Directive cannot be recognized in mentioned offences of the Croatian Criminal Code.

–   In the Act of transposition, there are no references, explanations or provisions with regard to new forms of EU fraud such as VAT fraud, procurement fraud or the new offence of misappropriation.

–   It is very dubious that the offence of tax or customs duty evasion (Article 256 of the Criminal Code) can cover the VAT fraud as it refers only to serious fraud involving two or more Member States, cross-border fraudulent schemes and total damage of at least 10,000,000 euros. According to the Croatian transposition of the PIF Directive, the European Public Prosecutor shall have the jurisdiction to prosecute for any tax or customs duty evasion.

–   The third form of the VAT fraud described as "the presentation of correct VAT-related statements for the purposes of fraudulently disguising the non-payment or wrongful creation of rights to VAT refunds" cannot be covered by the fraudulent behaviour of tax evasion from Article 256 of the Criminal Code.[46]

–   The Act on transposition does not mention procurement or procurement-related expenditure. The EU subsidies cannot be equated with the public contract in the procurement procedure. Also the perpetrator of the subsidy fraud is a receiver of the subsidies and aid granted from European Union funds and not the responsible person in contracting authorities or in economic operators concluding public contracts in the procurement procedure.[47]

–   Additionally, the third form of the procurement fraud (iii) requires the establishment of the damage to the EU budget, while the first two forms give the possibility to the state to introduce the elements of damage. The introduction of this element will narrow the area of incrimination of fraudulent behaviour. The criminal law as *ultima ratio* generally should not be used too extensively and over the limits

---

46   Art. 256 of the Criminal Code: (1) Whoever, with the aim that he or she or another person evade paying in full or in part a tax or customs duty, provides false or incomplete information on income, items or other facts of relevance for determining the amount of tax or customs duty payable or whoever, in the case of mandatory declaration, fails, with the same aim, to declare his or her income, items or other facts of relevance to the determination of tax or customs duty payable, which results in a reduction of the tax or customs duty payable by an amount exceeding twenty thousand kuna or to its non-determination in the said amount.

47   Subsidy Fraud: Art. 258 of the Criminal Code (1) Whoever, with the aim that he or she or another person receive a state subsidy, provides a state subsidy provider with false or incomplete information concerning the facts on which the decision on the granting of a state subsidy depends, or fails to inform a state subsidy provider of changes important for making the decision on the granting of a state subsidy.
(5) State subsidies within the meaning of this article shall be equated with subsidies and aid granted from European Union funds.

required by the EU law or at least such overcriminalization requires particular justifications.

–   There is no reference to the new offence of misappropriation. When referring to the offences under Article 4 of the PIF Directive, the legislator does not mention this offence at all. This offence was not transposed at all in the Croatian Criminal Code.

–   Accordingly, a definition of public officials in Article 87(3) of the Criminal Code[48] was not extended to cover private persons involved in the management of the EU funds as required by the PIF Directive.

Finally, the superficial and ignorant attitude to the transposition of the PIF Directive in Croatia is evident from the fact that the list of the transposed legal acts of the European Union in Article 386 of the Criminal Code still contains the PIF Convention and its two protocols[49] although, as it was already mentioned, they are replaced by the PIF Directive, and therefore the Member States are not any more bound by it (Article 16 of the PIF Directive). The transposition of the PIF Convention in Croatia required three subsequent legislative amendments, and we can hope that this will not be the case with the transposition of the PIF Directive. In any case, Croatia was required to immediately communicate to the Commission the text of the main provisions of national law which it adopted in the field covered by the PIF Directive. So, the ball is in the Commission's court. In any case, the PIF Directive requires the Commission to submit a report to the European Parliament and the Council assessing the extent to which the Member States have taken the necessary measures to comply with this directive by 6 July 2021 (Article 18(1)).

12.4   CONCLUSION

The transposition of the PIF Directive in the national criminal law is a very complex and demanding task that should not be underestimated. The legislators have to keep in mind that there are two substantial differences between the transposition of the PIF Directive to the transposition of the PIF Convention. Firstly, the failure of transposition or inadequate transposition of the directive is subject to the infringement procedure that can result in a high monetary penalty. That was not the case with the PIF Convention adopted before

---

48   Art. 87(3): "An official person shall mean a high-ranking or a lower-ranking state official, a high-ranking or a lower-ranking official in a unit of the local or regional self-government, holder of judicial authority, lay judge, member of the State Judiciary Council or the State Attorney Council, arbitrator notary public and public bailiff. An official person shall also mean a person who in the European Union, another state, international organisation of which the Republic of Croatia is a member, international tribunal or arbitration board the jurisdiction of which the Republic of Croatia accepts, performs the duties confided to persons listed in the previous sentence."

49   Art. 386 point 20, 21 and 22.

the Lisbon Treaty. The present analysis shows that Croatia is already under the threat of such a procedure that can endanger already insufficient resources of the Croatian budget. Secondly, the national legislators should be aware that the national transposition act of the PIF Directive will decide on the subject matter jurisdiction of the European Public Prosecutor's Office (EPPO). The EPPO will not apply the PIF Directive in criminal proceedings before the national courts but offences prescribed by national law. In order to respect the principle of legality in criminal law, legal certainty and the division of jurisdiction between the national prosecutor and the EPPO, the national law should precisely define offences under the jurisdiction of the EPPO. For the EPPO it will not be possible to reach some other criminal offence in order to prosecute fraudulent behaviour outside of the PIF offences. Furthermore, it is not probable that the national legislators will opt for the provisions that allow the EPPO to prosecute for more extensive fraudulent behaviour than required by the PIF Directive. This would lead to the overburdening of the EPPO, uneven treatment of the EU citizens and forum shopping. Therefore, the national legislator should strictly abide by the requirements of the PIF Directive and follow the elements of crimes prescribed in it, clearly establishing the field of prosecution for the EPPO.

13 SELECTED CASE STUDIES: THE CASE STUDY OF ITALY (IT)

*Giovanni Grasso & Fabio Giufreddi**

13.1 INTRODUCTION

European criminal law is a fast-evolving area of the European Union (EU) law. Especially after the Treaty of Maastricht, the number of EU instruments concerning the field of criminal justice has steeply increased. The EU legislator has adopted several measures of both substantive and procedural criminal law, which span from mutual recognition instruments to pieces of legislation providing for the definition of some criminal conducts and setting out the penalties thereof. At the same time, the Court of Justice of the European Union (CJEU)[1] has played a key role in shaping EU criminal law, by supporting national courts in the interpretation of EU legislation and clarifying the extent to which the European Union is allowed to regulate matters of criminal justice. Finally, some EU bodies have been created to enhance the cooperation of police, judicial and prosecuting authorities throughout the EU (Europol and Eurojust) and, more recently, even to investigate and prosecute the perpetrators of, and accomplices to, criminal offences affecting the financial interests of the Union (the European Public Prosecutor's Office, EPPO).

This contribution focuses on the position of Italy vis-à-vis EU criminal law, and on the impact of the latter on the Italian criminal justice system. Section 13.2 of this chapter provides an overview of the matter and describes the overall Italian approach to EU criminal justice. Section 13.3 discusses two key issues concerning the protection of the Union's financial interests (PIF)[2] in Italy, namely the application of the *ne bis in idem* principle in case of concurrent administrative and criminal proceedings on the same facts (Section 13.3.1) and the implementation of the EPPO Regulation[3] (Section 13.3.2). Section 13.4 delves into the implementation of the directive on the fight against fraud

---

* This paper has been jointly conceived by the authors, who have co-authored section 13.5 and have taken the lead of different parts. Sections 13.1, 13.4.3 and 13.4.4 shall be attributed to Giovanni Grasso, whereas sections 13.2, 13.3, 13.3.1, 13.3.2, 13.4, 13.4.1 and 13.4.2 shall be attributed to Fabio Giuffrida.
1 The acronym CJEU will be used to refer to the Court of Justice for both the pre-Lisbon and the post-Lisbon periods.
2 PIF stands for '*protection des intérêts financiers*'.
3 Council Regulation (EU) 2017/1939 of 12 October 2017 implementing enhanced cooperation on the establishment of the European Public Prosecutor's Office ('the EPPO') [2017] OJ L283/1 ('EPPO Regulation').

to the Union's financial interests by means of criminal law ('PIF Directive')[4] in Italy, by looking at the challenges it may raise with regard to four different aspects: definition of, and penalties for, the crimes listed in the directive (Section 13.4.1); inchoate offences and liability of legal persons (Section 13.4.2); prescription (Section 13.4.3) and freezing and confiscation (Section 13.4.4). Section 13.5 sums up the findings of the analysis.

13.2   Italy and EU Criminal Law: A History of Stops and Goes

The chequered role of Italy in the history and development of EU criminal law can be summed up by considering two different levels, namely the judicial and the legislative.

At the *judicial* level, Italian courts have on average been committed to ensuring Italy's compliance with EU legislation and principles. It is not a coincidence that the CJEU handed down some leading judgments in the field of criminal law upon requests for a preliminary ruling that had been lodged by Italian tribunals. To mention only two of them: in *Berlusconi*, the Court acknowledged that the *lex mitior* principle "forms part of the constitutional traditions common to the Member States";[5] in *Pupino*, the principle of consistent interpretation with EU law was extended so as to apply to Framework Decisions.[6] More recently, Italian law and its (controversial) relationship with EU law have been again in the limelight thanks to the *Taricco* saga, which will be discussed in Section 13.4.3 below.

Turning to the *legislative* level, the scenario is more complex. Up until 2015, Italy was lagging behind in the implementation of several EU criminal law instruments, but in 2015 and 2016 it largely repaired its delays and failures.[7] Among others, in these two years, Italy has implemented the Framework Decision on Joint Investigation Teams,[8] which dated back to 2002, as well as the Framework Decisions on the mutual recognition of both confiscation orders[9] and orders freezing property or evidence.[10]

Italy has instead not implemented – nor it is expected to do so anytime soon – the Council Framework Decision 2008/841/JHA on organized crime.[11] While the Framework Decision aimed to achieve "greater consistency of approximation in order to tackle organized crime more effectively at EU level",[12] the Commission itself noted that "[t]he

---

4   [2017] OJ L198/29.
5   Joined Cases C-387/02, C-391/02 and C-403/02 *Berlusconi et al*, EU:C:2005:270, para. 68.
6   Case C-105/03 *Pupino*, EU:C:2005:386.
7   Information on the implementation of EU instruments concerning the field of criminal justice can be found on the website of the European Judicial Network, available at: www.ejn-crimjust.europa.eu/ejn/EJN_Library_StatusOfImpByCou.aspx?CountryId=295, accessed 19 August 2019.
8   [2002] OJ L162/1. *See* Legislative Decree No 34/15.
9   [2006] OJ L328/59. *See* Legislative Decree No 137/15.
10   [2003] OJ L196/45. *See* Legislative Decree No 35/16.
11   [2008] OJ L300/42.
12   Commission, 'Report based on Article 10 of Council Framework Decision 2008/841/JHA of 24 October 2008 on the fight against organised crime' COM(2016) 448 final, 2.

outcome of the negotiations was less ambitious than the initial proposal".[13] Backed by Italy (and France), the Commission issued a declaration "questioning the added value of the instrument from the point of view of achieving the necessary minimum degree of approximation".[14] Due to historical and sociological reasons, Italian legislation on the crime of participating in a criminal organization is in fact rather advanced, and already compliant with the EU obligations set out in the Framework Decision.[15] In the field of environmental crime, the European Parliament even considered the Italian legislation as an example to follow.[16] In a resolution of 2011, it called on the Commission

> to develop innovative instruments for the prosecution of those who commit environmental offences in which organised crime plays a role, for example by submitting a proposal to extend to the EU Italy's positive experience with the offence of 'organised illegal waste trafficking', since 2011 classed as an offence with a major social impact (and thus dealt with by the District Anti-mafia Bureau).[17]

By the same token, the impact of two further Framework Decisions on the Italian system has been very limited and, curiously, Italy seems to have been more influenced by the Council of Europe instruments dealing with the same matters than by those adopted within the (former) third pillar.

On the one hand, while Italy adopted a new law concerning cybercrime in 2008 with the aim to define and punish further criminal conducts,[18] the Italian legislator expressly chose to implement the 2001 Council of Europe Convention on Cybercrime ('Budapest Convention') rather than Framework Decision 2005/222/JHA.[19] Given the large similarity between the two texts, this choice does not seem very problematic per se.[20] After all, Directive 2013/40/EU on attacks against information systems, which repealed

---

13   *Ibid.*
14   *Ibid.*
15   For some remarks on Italian legislation on organized crime, *see* Section 4.1 below.
16   Reference is meant to previous Art. 260 Legislative Decree No 152/06 ('organised illegal waste trafficking'), which has been 'moved' to the Italian Penal Code in 2018 and it is now Art. 452 *quaterdecies* of this Code. For a comprehensive analysis of the position of Italy vis-à-vis (European) environmental criminal law, *see* G. M. Vagliasindi, 'Environmental Crime in Italy', in A. Farmer, M. Faure, and G. M. Vagliasindi (eds.), *Environmental Crime in Europe*, Hart, 2017, pp. 119-157.
17   European Parliament resolution of 25 October 2011 on organized crime in the European Union (2010/2309 (INI)), para. 42.
18   Law No 48/08. This Law introduced some new provisions in the Italian Penal Code, such as Arts. 635*ter* ('Damaging information, data and informatic programmes used by the State or other public entity or of public utility'), 635*quater* ('Damaging information or telematic system') and 635*quinquies* ('Damaging information or telematic system of public utility').
19   [2005] OJ L69/67. *See* L. De Matteis, 'Art 635*bis*', in G. Lattanzi and E. Lupo (eds.), *Codice Penale. Rassegna di Giurisprudenza e di Dottrina*, Vol XII (Giuffrè 2010) 270.
20   *Ibid.*

Council Framework Decision 2005/222/JHA,[21] acknowledged that the Budapest Convention is the "legal framework of reference for combating cybercrime, including attacks against information systems' and that Directive 2013/40/EU itself 'builds on that Convention".[22]

On the other hand, Italy has aligned, with some delay, its internal legislation on terrorism with the European requirements set out in Framework Decision 2002/475/JHA.[23] In 2005, the Italian Parliament passed Law No 144/2005 that, *inter alia*, introduced some new crimes related to terrorism in the Italian Penal Code (CP for *'Codice Penale'*).[24] Again, the adoption of this law seems to have been mostly influenced by the 2005 Council of Europe Convention on the Prevention of Terrorism ('Warsaw Convention') than by the obligation to implement the above-mentioned EU instrument. Law No 144/2005 provides indeed for the new crimes of recruitment and training for terrorism, which are not mentioned in the 2002 Framework Decision but only in the Warsaw Convention.[25] Nonetheless, the same law also defines the meaning of the 'aim of terrorism' (*'finalità di terrorismo'*), which is an expression used in various provisions of the Italian CP concerning terrorism.[26] The definition of 'aim of terrorism' is inspired by the 2002 Framework Decision: the Italian legislator refers to

> those conducts that, for their nature or context, may seriously damage a country or an international organisation and are committed with the aim of intimidating the population or compelling a Government or international organisation to perform or abstain from performing any act, or destabilising or destroying the fundamental political, constitutional, economic or social structures of a country or an international organisation.[27]

These words replicate almost verbatim the first part of Article 1(1) of Framework Decision 2002/475/JHA.

Finally, a few remarks on Council Framework Decision 2002/584/JHA on the European Arrest Warrant (EAW) are necessary.[28] Italy was the last Member State to

---

21 [2013] OJ L218/8.
22 Recital No 15 Directive 2013/40/EU. As a consequence, '[c]ompleting the process of ratification of that Convention by all Member States as soon as possible should be considered to be a priority' (*Ibid.*).
23 [2002] OJ L164/3.
24 See Arts. 270 *quater* ('recruitment for terrorism, also international' – in Italian, *'Arruolamento con finalità di terrorismo anche internazionale'*) and Art. 270*quinquies* ('training for terrorism, also international' – in Italian, *'Addestramento ad attività con finalità di terrorismo anche internazionale'*). These provisions have been further amended in February 2015, in the aftermath of the terrorist attack to the premises of the French magazine *Charlie Hebdo*.
25 Arts. 6 and 7 Warsaw Convention.
26 *See* n 24 above for some examples.
27 Art. 270*sexies* Italian CP. Translation of the authors.
28 [2002] OJ L190/1.

implement the EAW Framework Decision. Law No 69/2005 provides for a long list of *mandatory* grounds for refusal (20 in total), many of which are not mentioned in the Framework Decision. Law No 69/2005 includes, among those grounds, the risk that the person whose surrender is sought may be subject to the death penalty, torture or other inhuman and degrading penalties.[29] In the aftermath of *Aranyosi and Căldăraru*,[30] the Italian Court of Cassation has relied on this ground to halt the surrender of individuals to countries where their right not to be subject to inhuman and degrading penalties might be violated, requiring the competent national courts to collect more information on the detention conditions that individuals were expected to face in the requesting countries.[31]

Surrender should also be refused if the requesting Member State does not have time limits for pre-trial detention.[32] Given the diversity of national legislation on the matter, this provision does not sit well with the principle of mutual trust that underpins EU mutual recognition instruments. It is thus to be welcomed that the Italian Court of Cassation and the Italian Constitutional Court have interpreted such provision as meaning that surrender shall *not* be denied if in the executing Member State there is at least a judicial procedure ensuring a periodic review of pre-trial detention, which would allow persons under detention to be immediately released should the conditions for their deprivation of liberty not be compelling or sufficient anymore.[33]

A similar pattern, according to which the Italian legislator has envisaged a ground for refusal or a rule that risks jeopardizing the very same functioning of the EAW, and the national judiciary has then interpreted it in a way that is more consistent with the essence of mutual trust, has come to the fore with respect to other provisions of Law No 69/05. This is the case, for instance, of the lack of motivation of the decision upon which the EAW has been issued, which should lead to the non-execution of the EAW as well.[34] The Court of Cassation has clarified that this 'motivation' cannot be understood as and equated with the motivation of national decisions, and it is instead sufficient for the requesting judicial authorities to mention the factual evidence against the suspect that justifies their request.[35]

---

29   Art. 18(1)(h) Law No 69/2005.
30   Joined Cases C-404/15 and C-659/15 PPU *Aranyosi and Căldăraru*, EU:C:2016:198.
31   This case law has been inaugurated by the decision of the Italian Court of Cassation, Sixth Chamber, 1 June 2016, No 23277.
32   Art. 18(1)(e) Law No 69/2005.
33   G. De Amicis, 'Mandato d'Arresto Europeo. Profili Processuali', in *Libro dell'Anno del Diritto 2012*, Treccani, 2012, www.treccani.it/enciclopedia/mandato-d-arresto-europeo-profili-processuali_%28Il-Libro-dell%27anno-del-Diritto%29/, accessed 19 August 2019. *See* the decisions of the Italian Court of Cassation, United Chambers, 30 January 2017, No 4614, and of the Italian Constitutional Court, 14 April 2008, No 109.
34   Art. 18(1)(t) Law No 69/2005.
35   Court of Cassation, United Chambers, 30 January 2007, No 4614, and several following judgments have confirmed this principle. For further examples *see* G. De Amicis, *op. cit.*

13.3   THE PROTECTION OF THE UNION'S FINANCIAL INTERESTS IN ITALY: FOCUS ON
        NE BIS IN IDEM AND THE EPPO

Italy has traditionally been committed to the protection of the Union's financial interests on multiple levels. On the academic side, it is worth mentioning that one of eight experts who drafted the *Corpus Juris*, which represents the birthplace of the current EPPO, was Italian.[36] Carried out in the 1990s under the supervision of Mireille Delmas-Marty, this study was part of the 'European Legal Area Project' that was strongly supported by the XX Directorate General of the Commission, which was at the time led by Francesco De Angelis.[37] Extensive debates followed the adoption of the *Corpus Juris* in Italy, and several Italian practitioners and academics gave their contribution to the consultation launched by the Commission with the 2001 Green Paper.[38] In addition to this noteworthy doctrinal dimension, the prominent role of Italy vis-à-vis the protection of the Union's financial interests can be once more analysed by looking at the judicial and the legislative level, as both of them are of essence in this context. As for the former, the following section briefly outlines the issues related to the application of *ne bis in idem* in case of concurring administrative and criminal proceedings (Section 13.3.1), while Section 13.3.2 focuses on the support that Italy gave to the establishment of the EPPO and on a few challenges that this new body may raise in Italy.

13.3.1   The Judicial Level: Ne Bis In Idem and the 'Double-Track' System

One of the most debated issues in Italy is currently the applicability of the *ne bis in idem* principle to concurrent administrative and criminal proceedings concerning the same conduct (the so-called 'double-track' system).[39] The issue is extremely relevant in the

---

36 *See* more in G. Grasso, '*Prefazione. Il Corpus Juris e le Prospettive di Formazione di un Diritto Penale dell'Unione Europea*', in *Verso uno Spazio Giudiziario Europeo. Corpus Juris Contenente Disposizioni Penali per la Tutela degli Interessi Finanziari dell'Unione Europea* (Giuffrè 1997); R. Sicurella, 'Il *Corpus Juris*: Elementi per una Procedura Penale Europea', in G. Grasso (ed.), *Prospettive di un Diritto Penale Europeo*, Giuffrè, 1998, pp. 63-86. The eight experts that composed the group responsible for drafting the *Corpus Juris* were: Enrique Bacigalupo, Mireille Delmas-Marty, Giovanni Grasso, John Spencer, Dionysios Spinellis, Klaus Tiedemann, John Vervaele, and Christine van den Wyngaert.

37 *See* the foreword to Corpus Juris *Introducing Penal Provisions for the Purpose of the Financial Interests of the European Union*, under the direction of M. Delmas-Marty (Economica 1997).

38 Commission, 'Green Paper on criminal-law protection of the financial interests of the Community and the establishment of a European Prosecutor' COM (2001) 715 final. The reactions to this Green Paper are available at: https://ec.europa.eu/anti-fraud/about-us/legal-framework/green_paper/items/contributions_ date, accessed 19 August 2019.

39 *See*, for instance, M. Böse, 'The Consecutive Application of Different Types of Sanctions and the Principle of *Ne Bis in Idem*: The EU and the US on Different Tracks?', in K. Ligeti and V. Franssen (eds.), *Challenges in the Field of Economic and Financial Crime in Europe and the US,* Hart, 2017, p. 219.

field of the protection of the Union's financial interests.[40] The CJEU and the European Court of Human Rights (ECtHR) have already handed down a number of judgments on the matter,[41] and many of them concern Italian legislation.

In Italy, Article 649 of the Code of Penal Procedure (CPP) states that a person who has been finally acquitted or convicted cannot be subject to further criminal proceedings concerning the same fact ('procedural *ne bis in idem*'). Due to its wording, this rule does *not* apply when the first proceedings are formally of administrative – rather than criminal – nature. Italian legislation on tax crime also clarifies that, when the same fact triggers both administrative and criminal liability, the same person can be subject to both proceedings. Such legislation prohibits, however, the duplication of penalties ('substantive *ne bis in idem*').[42] In other words, competent administrative authorities may issue administrative penalties when administrative violations occur, but, if the same facts are also punished by criminal legislation and the person is being prosecuted, the administrative penalties are temporarily not executed while the criminal trial takes place. If the person is convicted, these penalties will not be executed as the criminal sanctions will prevail; otherwise, in case of acquittal, he or she would be subject to the administrative penalties that were previously issued.[43]

An Italian court doubted whether these rules on tax crime were compatible with the *ne bis in idem* principle as interpreted by the European Court of Human Rights, and escalated the issue to the Italian Constitutional Court. In *Grande Stevens v. Italy*,[44] which concerned the Italian rules on market manipulation, the ECtHR ruled out the compatibility of the duplication of administrative and criminal proceedings with the right to *ne bis in idem*, when the administrative procedure can be considered as concerning a 'criminal charge' in accordance with the *Engel* criteria. Had the Constitutional Court followed the request of the national court, the remit of the 'procedural *ne bis in idem*' enshrined in Article 649 CPP would have been extended so as to bar further criminal proceedings concerning the same facts on which an administrative authority had already decided by means of a final decision and in accordance with proceedings having, in essence, a criminal nature. While the case was pending before the Constitutional Court, however, the ECtHR issued the *A & B v. Norway* judgment. In this decision, the ECtHR changed its approach and decided that the duplication of criminal and administrative proceedings does not breach the *ne bis in*

---

40   For an overview, *see* V. Mitsilegas and F. Giuffrida, '*Ne Bis in Idem*', in R. Sicurella, V. Mitsilegas, R. Parizot, and A. Lucifora (eds.), *General Principles for a Common Criminal Law Framework in the EU. A Guide for Legal Practitioners,* Giuffrè, 2017, pp. 237-241.

41   The *ne bis in idem* principle is enshrined in Art. 50 of the Charter of Fundamental Rights and in Art. 54 of the Convention Implementing the Schengen Agreement (CISA), as well as in Art. 4 of Protocol No 7 to the European Convention on Human Rights (ECHR).

42   Arts. 20 and 21 Legislative Decree No 74/00.

43   Art. 21(2) Legislative Decree No 74/00.

44   *Grande Stevens et al v. Italy*, App Nos 18640/10, 18647/10, 18663/10, 18668/10 et 18698/10, Judgment of 4 March 2014.

idem principle if there is a sufficient connection in time and substance between these proceedings.[45] *A & B v. Norway* lists in detail the criteria to follow in the evaluation of whether such sufficient connection exists in a given case.[46]

In light of this judgment of the ECtHR, the Italian Constitutional Court sent the case back to the referring court, which will then have to assess whether, in that specific case, the sufficient close connection in time and substance exists or not.[47] If it does, and thus the *ne bis in idem* principle does not apply, Italian legislation would already be compliant with the case law of the ECtHR. The Italian Constitutional Court clearly states that *A & B v. Norway* makes it less likely that the duplication of criminal and administrative proceedings violates the *ne bis in idem* principle as interpreted by the ECtHR. Nonetheless, the Court adds, such duplication may eventually turn out to violate the right to *ne bis in idem* in the field of a tax crime or other fields if the sufficient close connection in time and substance is lacking in a specific case because of the way in which proceedings have been handled.[48]

The Italian rules on *ne bis in idem* were also suspected to be at variance with EU law. The Court of Justice of the European Union has endorsed the case law of the Strasbourg Court to a large extent. Upon request of an Italian court, in *Menci* the CJEU has clarified that Article 50 of the Charter is compatible with the issuing of both administrative and criminal sanctions against the same person for the same facts (in that case, failure to pay due value-added tax within the time limits provided by the law), upon compliance with some strict conditions though.[49] The duplication of penalties and proceedings thus represents a limitation – rather than a violation – of *ne bis in idem*.[50] In the case of value-added tax (VAT) offences, the objective of general interest justifying such duplication is combating these crimes and ensuring the collection of due VAT.[51] Administrative and criminal proceedings and penalties should, however, be

---

45 *A & B v. Norway*, Apps Nos 24130/11 and 29758/11, Judgment of 15 November 2016.

46 *Ibid.*, paras 132-134. Among them, the overall proportionality of penalties is of the utmost importance, as national courts should evaluate whether 'the sanction imposed in the proceedings which become final first is taken into account in those which become final last, so as to prevent that the individual concerned is in the end made to bear an excessive burden' (*Ibid.*, para. 132).

47 Italian Constitutional Court, decision of 24 January 2018, No 43.

48 *Ibid.*

49 Case C-524/15 *Menci*, EU:C:2018:197.

50 F. Consulich, 'Il Prisma del *Ne Bis in Idem* nelle Mani del Giudice Eurounitario' (2018) *Diritto Penale e Processo* 949, 951. *See* Case C-524/15 *Menci*, para. 39.

51 In accordance with Art. 52(1) of the Charter, "Any limitation on the exercise of the rights and freedoms recognised by this Charter must be provided for by law and respect the essence of those rights and freedoms. Subject to the principle of proportionality, limitations may be made only if they are necessary and genuinely meet objectives of general interest recognised by the Union or the need to protect the rights and freedoms of others."

complementary, i.e., they should relate to "different aspects of the same unlawful conduct at issue".[52]

After *Menci*, the same Italian court which requested the preliminary ruling from the CJEU did not take a decision on the merits of the case, but it raised a further question before the Italian Constitutional Court.[53] The Italian court asked the Constitutional Court to rule once more on whether Article 649 CPP is compatible with the *ne bis in idem* principle as interpreted by the ECtHR, and now also by the CJEU. The Italian court underlines that, when it comes to the failure to pay due VAT within the time limits set out by the law, there is no complementarity at all between administrative and criminal proceedings, as they both have the very same aim, i.e., the punishment of the identical conduct. Besides, there is no real coordination among these proceedings as each of them follows its own rules and, at the most, there are some rules on the coordination of penalties issued at the end of these proceedings.[54] The Italian Constitutional Court has not yet decided on the matter. The intense dialogue between European and Italian courts nonetheless demonstrates that the latter is committed to avoiding disproportionate punishment for the offenders and to balancing the effective protection of the Union's budget with adequate protection of the right not to be tried or punished twice for the same facts.[55]

It is worth adding that, beyond the PIF sector and the issues connected to the 'double-track' system, the attention Italian courts pay to the *ne bis in idem* principle and its interpretation by the ECtHR and the CJEU is further witnessed by a recent judgment of the Italian Constitutional Court. With decision No 200/16, the Constitutional Court

---

52   Case C-524/15 *Menci*, para. 44. Like the ECtHR, the CJEU emphasizes the importance of proportionality, as there would be no violation of Art. 50 of the Charter if, inter alia, national legislation "contains rules ensuring coordination which limits to what is strictly necessary the additional disadvantage which results, for the persons concerned, from a duplication of proceedings" (*Ibid.*, para. 63).

53   *See* the decision of Tribunal of Bergamo of 27 June 2018, available at: www.giurisprudenzapenale.com/wp-content/uploads/2018/11/qlc-menci-2.pdf, accessed 19 August 2019.

54   *Ibid.*

55   On the same day of *Menci*, the CJEU handed down two further judgments that dealt with the duplication of administrative and criminal proceedings in Italy, although they concern the different field of market manipulation (Case C-537/16 *Garlsson Real Estate and others*, EU:C:2018:193; Joined Cases C-596/16 and C-597/16 *Di Puma and Zecca*, EU:C:2018:192). *See* more in F. Consulich, *op. cit.* at 949, 951. *See* Case C-524/15 *Menci*, 949ff; M. Luchtman, 'The ECJ's Recent Case Law on *Ne Bis in Idem*: Implications for Law Enforcement in a Shared Legal Order' (2018) 55 *Common Market Law Review* 1717; S. Mirandola and G. Lasagni, 'The Principle *Ne Bis in Idem* at the Crossroads between Administrative and Criminal Law: Current Landscape and Future Challenges', *eucrim*, forthcoming. The Court of Appeal of Milan has recently ruled that, as the criminal and administrative penalties provided for by Italian legislation on insider dealing respect the proportionality principle, there is no violation of the *ne bis in idem* principle as interpreted by the CJEU and the ECtHR (*see* Court of Appeal of Milan, Second Chamber, 15 January 2019, No 284, available at: www.penalecontemporaneo.it/upload/1220-appello-milano-cremonini.pdf, accessed 22 August 2019, together with a commentary by C. Pagella).

partially overturned its previous jurisprudence on the '*idem*' element ('same offence')[56] of the right at hand.[57] In Italy, Article 649 CPP applies when two criminal proceedings concern the very same facts, i.e., when the conduct, event, and causation are the same.[58] This is in line with the stance of the European Courts, which have repeatedly stated that the *ne bis in idem* principle applies when the second proceedings concern the same "set of facts which are inextricably linked together, irrespective of the legal classification given to them or the legal interest protected".[59] At the same time, however, established Italian case law did not prohibit further proceedings on the same facts in case of the so-called '*concours idéal d'infractions*'. In other words, when the same action or omission entails two (or more) different crimes, and the defendant has been prosecuted for one of those crimes, he or she should also be prosecuted for the other(s), and the right to *ne bis in idem* would not apply.

In the proceedings that led to the judgment No 200/16 of the Italian Constitutional Court, 200 people, employees of the multinational company Eternit and residents in the surrounding zone, died because of their exposure to asbestos.[60] This gave rise to two sets of criminal proceedings. In the first, the owner of the company had been prosecuted for crimes such as the omission of protective measures against work accidents and the so-called 'unnamed disaster'.[61] The charges were dropped because the crimes had become time-barred. After that, the second set of proceedings ('*Eternit-bis*') dealt with the same facts, yet the owner was in this case prosecuted for murder. There was, therefore, no apparent breach of *ne bis in idem*: the second set of proceedings was set in motion with respect to a crime – 'murder' – which was formally different from the offences that were dealt with in the first set of proceedings ('omission of protective measures against work accidents' and 'unnamed disaster'). However, the court that was handling the *Eternit-bis* proceedings required the Constitutional Court to rule on the compatibility of Article 649 CPP with the *ne bis in idem* principle as interpreted by the ECtHR.

The Constitutional Court overturned its well-established interpretation of Article 649 CPP. In the light of the ECtHR case law, it declared this provision to be unconstitutional when it is interpreted so as to exclude the violation of *ne bis in idem* when there is a *concours idéal* between the crime on which a court has already decided a final judgment and the crime that is dealt with by another judicial authority in a new set of proceedings.

---

56 Art. 50 of the Chapter, like Art. 4 of Protocol No 7 to the ECHR, provides for the '[r]ight not to be tried or punished twice in criminal proceedings for the same criminal offence', while Art. 54 CISA refers to 'same acts'.

57 Italian Constitutional Court, decision of 21 July 2016, No 200.

58 Italian Court of Cassation, United Chambers, 28 June 2005, No 34655, *Donati*.

59 Case C-436/04 *Van Esbroeck*, EU:C:2006:165, para. 42. For the very similar stance of the ECtHR, *see Zolotukhin v. Russia*, App No 14939/03, judgment of 10 February 2009, para. 84.

60 V. Mitsilegas and F. Giuffrida, *op. cit.* at p. 236, upon which the following remarks on decision No 200/16 build.

61 Art. 434 Italian CP criminalizes the conduct of whoever commits a fact that is directed at causing the collapse of a building or any other disaster, if this fact creates a danger for public safety.

In both proceedings, the facts were indeed the same, while there is only a formal difference in their classification. By recognizing that the *ne bis in idem* principle also applies in case of a *concours idéal d'infractions*, the Italian Constitutional Court has thus strengthened the level of protection of the right not to be tried or punished twice for the same criminal offence and has shown a clear willingness to align itself with the case law of the European courts.

13.3.2   The Legislative Level: The EPPO Regulation and Its Implementation

Italy was among the most vocal supporters of the establishment of the EPPO. This commitment of the Italian government has led it not to sign the letter with which 16 Member States established the enhanced cooperation on the EPPO in April 2017.[62] This was meant to show deep dissatisfaction with the outcome of the negotiations: the text agreed was considered by the Italian government a too low-profile compromise.[63] Once having obtained some amendments to the draft Regulation, Italy finally joined the other 19 (now 21) countries of the enhanced cooperation. Nonetheless, the then Italian Minister of Justice, in his speech at the Justice and Home Affairs (JHA) Council meeting of June 2017, where the Regulation was eventually agreed upon, declared once more that the text does not entirely meet the Italian expectations.[64] While the current EPPO has a collegiate structure (a College with one European Prosecutor from each Member State and then a number of Permanent Chambers steering the investigations),[65] Italy would have favoured the establishment of a more hierarchical EPPO.[66] Furthermore, the same Minister strongly supported the extension of the EPPO's competence to other serious cross-border crimes, and especially terrorism.[67]

The implementation of the EPPO Regulation is still ongoing in Italy. By means of the so-called '*legge di delegazione europea*' ('European delegating law'), which should in principle be adopted every year, the Parliament delegates the government to adopt one

---

62   *See* Council doc 8027/17.
63   *See* N. Nielsen, 'EU Backs Setting up Prosecutor's Office', *euobserver*, 17 March 2017.
64   A. Orlando, Speech at the JHA Council of 8 June 2017, available at: http://video.consilium.europa.eu/en/webcast/c52f2355-f9ab-4a62-ac0e-d12825ef02c8, accessed 19 August 2019.
65   Arts. 9 and 10 EPPO Regulation.
66   *See* L. Salazar, '*Habemus* EPPO! La Lunga Marcia della Procura europea' (2017) *Archivio Penale* 1, 14.
67   'Guardasigilli Orlando: Estendere la Procura Europea anche ai Reati di Terrorismo' (2017) *Diritto e Giustizia*. On the extension of the EPPO competence beyond the PIF domain, *see* the following contributions in G. Grasso, G. Illuminati, R. Sicurella, and S. Allegrezza (eds.), *Le Sfide dell'Attuazione di una Procura Europea: Definizione di Regole Comuni e Loro Impatto sugli Ordinamenti Interni*, Giuffrè, 2013: F. Bianco, 'Tutela dell'Euro e Competenza della Procura Europea nel Futuro Scenario dell'Unione', 149ff; A. Lucifora, 'I Reati Connessi all'Immigrazione Irregolare Quale Futuro Ambito di Competenza del Pubblico Ministero Europeo', 167ff; and G.M. Vagliasindi, 'Istituzione di una Procura Europea e Diritto Penale Sostanziale: L'Eventuale Estensione della Competenza Materiale della Futura Procura alla Criminalità Ambientale' 189ff.

or more legislative decrees ('*decreti legislativi*') implementing EU legislative instruments. According to the Italian Constitution, legislative decrees have the same legal value as any other law of the Parliament ('*legge*'). In the 'European delegating law', the Parliament sets out clear principles and criteria that the government shall follow in the adoption of legislative decree(s). At the end of September 2018, the government put forward a bill for the European delegating law that should delegate to it the implementation of the EPPO Regulation and of the PIF Directive (the 'Government's bill').[68] In November 2018, the lower chamber of the Parliament (Chamber of Deputies) approved the text, which was then discussed by the Senate.[69] At the end of July 2019, the text was then sent back to the Chamber of Deputies with the amendments suggested by the Senate ('draft European delegating law').[70]

On a general level, three points can be made when discussing the implementation of the EPPO Regulation in Italy. First, some of the key principles of the Regulation are already part of the Italian legal tradition; hence, it should not be difficult to accommodate them within the Italian system. This is the case, for instance, of the independence of the EPPO[71] and of the principle of mandatory prosecution,[72] which implies that

> the investigations of the EPPO should, as a rule, lead to prosecution in the competent national courts in cases where there are sufficient evidence and no legal ground bars prosecution, or where no simplified prosecution procedure has been applied.[73]

Both these principles – independence of public prosecutors from other powers of the State and their obligation to prosecute all cases, unless the elements collected during the investigations are not sufficient to support the accusation – are even enshrined in the Italian Constitution, respectively in Articles 104 and 112.

Second, a number of provisions of the Regulation may instead raise some questions of compatibility with the Italian system. Just to mention a few of them, the Regulation allows the EPPO, namely the Permanent Chamber, to dismiss the case without any involvement of a court.[74] In Italy, on the contrary, public prosecutors require the

---

68 *See* Arts. 3 (PIF Directive) and 4 (EPPO Regulation) of the Disegno di Legge (bill), Act of the Chamber of Deputies, No 1201 (the 'Government's bill').

69 *See* Arts. 3 (PIF Directive) and 4 (EPPO Regulation) of the Disegno di Legge (bill), Act of the Senate, No 944, which are very similar to Arts. 3 and 4 of the Government's bill (above n 68).

70 *See* Arts. 3 (PIF Directive) and 4 (EPPO Regulation) of the Disegno di Legge (bill), Act of the Chamber of Deputies, No 1201-B ('draft European delegating law'), which do not substantially alter the previous versions of these two provisions. The research for this contribution has been finalized in August 2019.

71 Art. 6(1) EPPO Regulation.

72 Recitals Nos 66 and 81 EPPO Regulation refer to it as 'legality principle'.

73 Recital No 81 EPPO Regulation.

74 Art. 39 EPPO Regulation.

competent court to dismiss the case if they have not collected sufficient evidence to bring the case to trial.[75] This is often considered as a further guarantee of the principle of mandatory prosecution: if public prosecutors were allowed to drop the case without involving a court, the obligation to prosecute enshrined in the Constitution would be deprived of any effective control. Despite the public prosecutors' request to dismiss the case, the court can order them either to carry out further investigations or to bring the case to judgment altogether.[76]

Albeit relevant in a systematic and constitutional perspective,[77] there are no details nor remarks on the matter in the explanatory memorandum to the Government's bill, apart from a generic reference to the fact that rules on the dismissal of the case need to be aligned with those of the EPPO Regulation. Likewise, the explanatory memorandum does not delve into an issue that is at the time discussed in the literature, namely the compatibility of the rules of the Regulation on the choice of a forum with the principle of the 'natural judge'.[78] In accordance with Article 25(1) of the Italian Constitution, no one can be 'detached' from the natural judge pre-established by the law; in other words, any person should always be in a position to know which court will be competent to rule on a given crime he or she may commit. As the Regulation allows the EPPO to bring the case to judgment in a different Member State than that where the crime was committed, the right to the natural judge may be jeopardized. However, the criteria for the choice of the forum are spelled out and hierarchically listed in the Regulation,[79] so that it may be argued that, all in all, the Regulation does not run counter to the Italian Constitution in that respect.

At any rate, as anticipated, the Government's bill and the draft European delegating law do not touch upon the issue, while the explanatory memorandum to the former makes a number of remarks on the fact that Italian legislation needs to be coordinated with the Regulation so as to ensure that the central level of the Office will be in a position to steer the investigations on PIF offences, both in individual cases (the Permanent Chambers) and on a more strategic level (the College).[80] Further amendments of national legislation will also be necessary to ensure that the European Chief Prosecutor

---

75   Cfr Arts 408ff Italian CPP.

76   Art. 409 Italian CPP.

77   Cfr S. Ruggeri, 'Indagini e Azione Penale nei Procedimenti di Competenza della Nuova Procura Europea' (2018) *Processo Penale e Giustizia* 602, 611ff.

78   *See*, for instance, S. Allegrezza, 'National Report No 2 on the Italian Criminal Justice System', Annex to E. Sellier and A. Weyembergh, 'Criminal Procedural Laws across the European Union – A Comparative Analysis of Selected Main Differences and the Impact They Have Over the Development of EU Legislation' (2018) *Study for the European Parliament* 228.

79   The criteria to be taken into account in the choice of forum are, in order of priority, "the place of the suspect's or accused person's habitual residence; ... the nationality of the suspect or accused person; ... the place where the main financial damage has occurred" (Art 26(4) EPPO Regulation).

80   *See* the Explanatory memorandum to Disegno di Legge, Act of the Chamber of Deputies, No 1201 (the 'Government's bill'), 10-13; Art. 4(3)(d)–(f) Disegno di Legge (bill), Act of the Chamber of Deputies, No 1201-B ('draft European delegating law').

is involved in the disciplinary procedures concerning the European Delegated Prosecutors, as required by the Regulation.[81]

Third, as far as some practical details are concerned, it seems that Italian European Delegated Prosecutors in Italy will be placed within the ordinary public prosecutor's offices of the first instance, but not within the special divisions dealing with terrorism and mafia cases.[82] While some countries are inclined to provide that their European Delegated Prosecutors will have to work full-time for the EPPO, although the Regulation would allow them to 'exercise functions as national prosecutors'[83] while being members of the EPPO, the draft European delegating law does not take a clear stance on the matter.

13.4 THE IMPLEMENTATION OF THE PIF DIRECTIVE IN ITALY: A FEW CHANGES EXPECTED

A further and fundamental testament to the Italian commitment to the fight against PIF crimes on the legislative level is the fact that Italy, with Law No 300/00,[84] has implemented the 1995 Convention on the protection of the European Communities' financial interests ('PIF Convention')[85] and its first Protocol,[86] which have now been replaced by the PIF Directive.[87] As the PIF Directive does not substantially depart from the PIF Convention,[88] the legislative amendments that this new instrument would

---

81 Explanatory memorandum to the Government's bill (above n 80), 13-14; Art. 4(3)(g) draft European delegating law (above n 80). Art. 17(4) EPPO Regulation provides that "[i]f a Member State decides to dismiss, or to take disciplinary action against, a national prosecutor who has been appointed as European Delegated Prosecutor for reasons not connected with his/her responsibilities under this Regulation, it shall inform the European Chief Prosecutor before taking such action. A Member State may not dismiss, or take disciplinary action against, a European Delegated Prosecutor for reasons connected with his/her responsibilities under this Regulation without the consent of the European Chief Prosecutor. If the European Chief Prosecutor does not consent, the Member State concerned may request the College to review the matter".

82 Explanatory memorandum to the Government's bill (above n 80) 11-12.

83 Art. 13(3) EPPO Regulation.

84 Law No 300/00 also implemented the 1997 OECD Convention on Combating Bribery of Foreign Public Officials in International Business Transactions and the1997 Convention against corruption involving officials [1997] OJ C195.

85 [1995] OJ C316/49.

86 [1996] OJ C313/1.

87 Art. 16 PIF Directive.

88 See R. Sicurella, 'A Blunt Weapon for the EPPO? Taking the Edge Off the Proposed PIF Directive', in W. Geelhoed, A. Meij, and L. Erkelens (eds.), *Shifting Perspectives on the European Public Prosecutor's Office*, TMC Asser Press & Springer-Verlag, 2018, pp. 116-120. On the limited innovations that the PIF Directive has brought about in the PIF *acquis see also* L. Picotti, 'La Protezione Penale degli Interessi Finanziari dell'Unione Europea nell'Era Post-Lisbona: La Direttiva PIF nel Contesto di una Riforma "di Sistema"', in G. Grasso, R. Sicurella, F. Bianco, and V. Scalia (eds.), *Tutela Penale degli Interessi Finanziari dell'Unione Europea. Stato dell'Arte e Prospettive alla Luce della Creazione della Procura Europea,* Ius Pisa University Press, 2018, p. 47, in the framework of a more detailed analysis of the PIF Directive's provisions.

require in the Italian system are limited,[89] as confirmed by the draft European delegating law.[90] The sections below will discuss in more detail some issues that the implementation of the PIF Directive may raise in Italy,[91] and namely those concerning: definition and penalties of PIF offences (Section 13.4.1); inchoate offences and liability of legal persons (Section 13.4.2); prescription of PIF crimes (Section 13.4.3) and freezing and confiscation (Section 13.4.4).

13.4.1   Definition and Penalties of PIF Offences

Before looking at the offences mentioned in the PIF Directive, the rules on sanctions laid down therein can be summed up as follows.[92] In general, criminal sanctions shall be effective, proportionate and dissuasive, and the maximum penalty shall provide for imprisonment.[93] In serious cases, i.e., when considerable damage or advantage is involved,[94] or when serious circumstances defined in national law occur, the maximum penalty shall be of at least four years of imprisonment.[95] Apart from VAT-related fraud, for which the PIF Directive provides some distinctive rules,[96] in minor cases of fraud, i.e., when the damage or advantage does not meet the threshold of €10,000, the Member States can opt for non-criminal sanctions.[97] Furthermore, if the offence is committed within a criminal organization, the Member States shall ensure that this represents an aggravating circumstance.[98] They are not obliged to provide for such circumstance if domestic legislation criminalizes the participation in a criminal organization "as a separate offence, and this may lead to more severe sanctions".[99] In Italy, Article 416 of the Italian CP criminalizes the participation in a criminal organization in general, while

---

89   For a similar instance, see also E. Basile, 'Brevi Note sulla Nuova Direttiva PIF. Luci e Ombre del Processo di Integrazione UE in Materia Penale' (2017) 12 Diritto Penale Contemporaneo 63, 72; S.M. Ronco, 'Frodi "Gravi" IVA e Tutela degli Interessi Finanziari dell'Unione Europea' (2017) 3 Archivio Penale 1, 2; L. Salazar, 'La Situazione Italiana', in M. Fidelbo (ed.), La Cooperazione Rafforzata per l'Istituzione dell'Ufficio del Procuratore Europeo, Fondazione Basso, 2018, 108ff.

90   See also the explanatory memorandum to Disegno di Legge, Act of the Chamber of Deputies, No 1201 (the 'Government's bill') 66.

91   The deadline for implementation was 6 July 2019 (Art. 17(1) PIF Directive).

92   The following remarks and those of the next section build on F. Giuffrida, 'The Protection of the Union's Financial Interests After Lisbon' in Sicurella, Mitsilegas, Parizot, and Lucifora (eds.) (above n 41) 251ff.

93   Art. 7(1) and (2) PIF Directive.

94   "The damage or advantage ... shall be presumed to be considerable where the damage or advantage involves more than 100 000 euros. The damage or advantage resulting from [serious cross-border VAT fraud] shall always be presumed to be considerable" (Art. 7(3) PIF Directive).

95   Ibid.

96   See immediately below in the text.

97   Art. 7(4) PIF Directive.

98   Art. 8 PIF Directive.

99   Recital No 19 PIF Directive.

Article 416*bis* provides for slightly different rules if the organization is a mafia-type one.[100] For the mere participation in a criminal syndicate, the maximum penalty is five years of imprisonment.[101] Nonetheless, the draft European delegating law seems to be considering the option of introducing an *ad hoc* aggravating circumstance for PIF offences,[102] but the matter has not yet been decided at the time of writing.

As for the PIF crimes that the directive requires the Member States to criminalize, 'fraud' is the most emblematic, as it represents the offence that par excellence affects the Union budget. 'Fraud' traditionally refers to criminal conducts concerning either the revenue side (e.g. customs duties) or the expenditure one (e.g. EU funds distributed to natural and legal persons in the framework of EU projects). Article 3 of the PIF Directive upholds such dualism and distinguishes, within fraud in respect of revenues, between fraud concerning revenues arising from VAT own resources and fraud concerning all other revenues. As for the expenditure side, the directive refers to 'non-procurement-related' and 'procurement-related' expenditure.[103] Focusing on fraud concerning 'non-procurement-related' expenses for the sake of analysis, three conducts fall within this category, and the Member States are required to penalize them when committed intentionally:[104]

i. the use or presentation of false, incorrect or incomplete statements or documents, which has as its effect the misappropriation or wrongful retention of funds or assets from the Union budget or budgets managed by the Union, or on its behalf;

ii. non-disclosure of information in violation of a specific obligation, with the same effect; or

iii. the misapplication of such funds or assets for purposes other than those for which they were originally granted.[105]

Considerable legislative amendments do not seem necessary in Italy to comply with the obligation to criminalize the above conducts and introduce the above penalties.[106] Article 640*bis* of the Italian CP specifically deals with fraud concerning public contributions or funds, including that of the Union. This provision was introduced in the Italian Penal

---

100 Further provisions of the Italian CP deal with specific cases of organized crime: *see*, for instance, the above-mentioned Art. 452*quaterdecies* on waste trafficking and Art. 270*bis* on terrorist criminal organizations.

101 Art. 416(2) Italian CP.

102 Art. 3(1)(g) Disegno di Legge (bill), Act of the Chamber of Deputies, No 1201-B ('draft European delegating law'). *See also* the explanatory memorandum to Disegno di Legge, Act of the Chamber of Deputies, No 1201 (the 'Government's bill') 9 and 68.

103 Arts. 3(2)(a) and 3(2)(b) PIF Directive.

104 Art. 3(1) PIF Directive.

105 Art. 3(2)(a) PIF Directive.

106 *See also* the explanatory memorandum to the Government's bill (above n 80) 4; F. La Vattiata, 'La Nuova Direttiva PIF. Alcune Riflessioni in Tema di Adattamento dell'Ordinamento Italiano' (*eurojus.it*, 8 June 2018), http://rivista.eurojus.it/la-nuova-direttiva-PIF-alcune-riflessioni-in-tema-di-adattamento-dellordi namento-italiano/, accessed 22 August 2019; L. Salazar, 'La Situazione Italiana', *op. cit.*

Code already in 1990, i.e., five years before the adoption of the PIF Convention.[107] It represents an aggravating circumstance of the ordinary crime of fraud, which is regulated by Article 640 of the CP and is defined as the conduct of "whoever gains advantage for himself or for a third party to the detriment of others, with tricks and deceptions, by misleading someone else".[108] Article 640*bis* provides for a maximum penalty of seven years of imprisonment.

Article 316*bis* of the Italian CP penalizes instead the misapplication of public funds (including the Union's) for purposes other than those for which they were originally granted, and the maximum penalty is four years of imprisonment. Finally, Article 316*ter*, which was introduced by Law No 300/00,[109] criminalizes the conduct of whoever unduly gains, for himself or a third party, contributions or other public funds (including the Union's) by using or presenting false statements or documents, or by not disclosing information in violation of a specific obligation. The text of this provision clearly recalls the PIF Convention (and now the PIF Directive). Moreover, like the two EU instruments, Article 316*ter* CP provides for a *de minimis* exception: when the amount of money unduly gained is below €3,999,96, only administrative sanctions apply. Article 2 (2) of the PIF Convention already included such a threshold, which has now been raised to €10,000,[110] so that the Italian provision may be modified accordingly.[111] Article 316*ter* provides for a maximum sanction of three-year imprisonment; if the crime is committed by a public official by abusing his or her powers, the maximum penalty is four years. In accordance with the PIF Directive, the maximum sanction should be at least four years of imprisonment for everybody in cases where there is considerable damage or advantage.[112] The amendment of Article 316*ter* may not be mandatory, at least as far as the hypotheses of considerable damage are concerned, since Italian law already provides for an aggravating circumstance that applies to any crime involving considerable economic damage.[113] It ought to be added, however, that Article 316*ter* has a 'very

---

107 A. Venegoni, 'La Definizione del Reato di Frode Nella Legislazione dell'Unione. Dalla Convenzione PIF alla Proposta di Direttiva PIF' (2016) *Diritto Penale Contemporaneo*, available at: www.penalecontemporaneo.it/upload/1474711704VENEGONI_2016b.pdf, accessed 19 August 2019, 6.

108 Art. 640 Italian CP (translation of the author).

109 Law No 300/00 also implemented the 1997 OECD Convention on Combating Bribery of Foreign Public Officials in International Business Transactions and the1997 Convention against corruption involving officials [1997] OJ C195.

110 Art. 7(4) PIF Directive.

111 The Italian legislator may also decide to keep this threshold unchanged, as Art. 7(4) PIF Directive only provides for an option rather than an obligation: where any PIF offence, with the only exception of VAT fraud, 'involves damage of less than €10,000 or an advantage of less than €10,000, Member States *may* provide for sanctions other than criminal sanctions' (emphasis added).

112 Art. 3(1)(f) Disegno di Legge (bill), Act of the Chamber of Deputies, No 1201-B ('draft European delegating law') requires that PIF crimes from which a considerable damage or advantage derives are punished with a maximum penalty of at least four years of imprisonment. *See also* the explanatory memorandum to Disegno di Legge, Act of the Chamber of Deputies, No 1201 (the 'Government's bill') 8.

113 Art. 61(7) Italian CP. In accordance with Art. 64 Italian CP, when there is only one aggravating circumstance, the penalty may be increased up to one-third.

limited scope of application'[114] since it does not apply when Article 640*bis* comes to the fore, on the one hand.[115] On the other hand, Italian courts have adopted an interpretation that makes Article 316*ter* applicable only in a few circumstances.[116]

Looking at fraud on the revenue side, a few remarks on VAT fraud are appropriate as well. After heated debates and in the aftermath of the *Taricco* case of the Court of Justice,[117] the Member States agreed that the directive applies to – and thus obliges the Member States to harmonize the definition and penalties of – VAT fraud which is connected with the territory of two or more Member States and involves a total damage of at least €10 million.[118] In the frame of 'fraudulent cross-border schemes',[119] three conducts should, therefore, be regarded as amounting to VAT fraud, namely:

i. the use or presentation of false, incorrect or incomplete VAT-related statements or documents, which has as an effect the diminution of the resources of the Union budget;

ii. non-disclosure of VAT-related information in violation of a specific obligation, with the same effect; or

iii. the presentation of correct VAT-related statements for the purposes of fraudulently disguising the non-payment or wrongful creation of rights to VAT refunds.[120]

In Italy, Legislative Decree No 74/00 deals with VAT fraud. While an in-depth analysis of this piece of legislation is not possible in this contribution, three remarks need to be made. First, as also posited by the explanatory memorandum to the Government's bill,[121] Articles 2, 3, 4 and 5 of Legislative Decree No 74/00 already criminalize the three above-mentioned conducts.[122] Second, those articles provide for maximum penalties that are equal to, or higher than four years of imprisonment,[123] with the only

---

114 G.F. Perilongo, 'Much Ado About Something? The PIF Directive Proposal and Its Impact on the Italian Legal System' (2016) 6 *European Criminal Law Review* 264, 277.

115 The text of Art. 316*ter* expressly states that this provision applies if the fact does *not* amount to the crime laid down in Art. 640*bis*.

116 G. Fiandaca and E. Musco, *Diritto Penale. Parte Speciale*, Vol. I, Zanichelli, 4th edn, 2008, pp. 204-206.

117 Case C-105/14 *Taricco et al.*, EU:C:2015:555. *See* more in Section 4.3 below. For the impact of this ruling on the negotiations of the PIF Directive, *see* R. Sicurella, 'A Blunt Weapon for the EPPO? Taking the Edge Off the Proposed PIF Directive', *op. cit.* at 108ff.

118 Art. 2(2) PIF Directive.

119 Art. 3(2)(d) PIF Directive.

120 *Ibid.*

121 Explanatory memorandum to Disegno di Legge, Act of the Chamber of Deputies, No 1201 (the 'Government's bill') 4-5.

122 *See also* G. F. Perilongo, *op. cit.* at pp. 264, 277-280. Art. 2 deals with the fraudulent declaration by means of invoices or other documents for non-existing operations and Art. 3 with fraudulent declaration by means of other tricks. Art. 4 concerns instead all the other cases of untrue declaration falling outside the field of application of Arts. 2 and 3. Art. 5 criminalizes the conduct of failing to present mandatory VAT-related declarations.

123 G.F. Perilongo, (above n 114) 281.

exception of Article 4.[124] While the implementation of the PIF Directive may lead to increasing the penalty provided for by this provision, it is instead more controversial whether it *should* have this effect.[125]

Third, Legislative Decree No 74/00 deals not only with VAT fraud but also with fraud concerning income taxes ('*imposte sui redditi*'), which affects the national – rather than the EU – budget. The Italian legislator has sometimes decided to regulate the two matters in a different way. For instance, the failure to pay correctly declared VAT is punished with criminal sanctions,[126] and the same goes for the failure to pay withholding tax owed or certified.[127] However, while the first conduct shall be regarded as a crime when the amount of VAT that is not paid is equal to or higher than €250,000,[128] the threshold for the equivalent crime at the national level is lower (€150,000).[129] In line with the above-mentioned trend of Italian courts to ensure the maximum compliance possible of this country with EU obligations, the CJEU has been required to rule on whether the difference between these two thresholds is justified or whether it breaches the assimilation principle provided for by Article 325(2) TFEU.[130] In *Scialdone*, the Court did not find any violation of EU law, and it submitted that failure to pay correctly declared VAT is not comparable to the allegedly similar Italian offence concerning direct taxation, as they "can be distinguished by both their constituent elements and the difficulty involved in their detection".[131]

Moving on to Article 4 of the PIF Directive, it first requires the criminalization of money laundering involving property derived from PIF offences. Like the First Protocol

---

124 Explanatory memorandum to the Government's bill (above n), 8. See also Art. 3(1)(f) Disegno di Legge (bill), Act of the Chamber of Deputies, No 1201-B ('draft European delegating law'), which is mentioned in n 113 above.

125 Note that, on the one hand, the provision of Art. 4 of Legislative Decree No 74/00 applies also to VAT fraud that does not have transnational scale and that escapes the high threshold provided for by the PIF Directive (damage of €10 million). On the other hand, in cases of serious VAT fraud, the application of Italian rules on aggravating circumstances may already ensure that the maximum penalty reaches the threshold of four years of imprisonment. Finally, cross-border fraudulent schemes, such as those to which Art. 3(2)(d) of the PIF Directive refers, are commonly to be found in the frame of criminal syndicates; should this be the case, the application of the domestic provisions on the participation in criminal organizations – together with the provisions on VAT fraud – is likely to lead to penalties that can be much higher than four years of imprisonment.

126 Art. 10*ter* Legislative Decree No 74/00. This conduct does not however fall within the notion of 'VAT fraud' of Art. 3(2)(d) PIF Directive.

127 Art. 10*bis* Legislative Decree No 74/00. This refers to the conduct of whoever 'fails to pay, within the period fixed for the filing of the withholding agent's annual tax return, the withholding tax resulting from that return or from the certification issued to the taxpayers in respect of whom tax is withheld'. This translation can be found in Case C-574/15 *Scialdone*, EU:C:2018:295, para. 14. On *Scialdone*, see immediately below in the text.

128 Art. 10*ter* Legislative Decree No 74/00.

129 Art. 10*bis* Legislative Decree No 74/00.

130 In accordance with Art. 325(2) TFEU, 'Member States shall take the same measures to counter fraud affecting the financial interests of the Union as they take to counter fraud affecting their own financial interests'.

131 Case C-574/15 *Scialdone*, para. 57. *See* more *Ibid.*, paras 58-60.

to the PIF Convention, the Directive does not define this conduct but rather refers to another EU instrument, namely the Anti-Money Laundering (AML) Directive. Whereas the Protocol recalled Council Directive 91/308/EEC (the first AML Directive),[132] the PIF Directive refers to Directive (EU) 2015/849 (the fourth AML Directive),[133] but the conduct described in both the AML Directives is identical. Italian domestic legislation on money laundering seems already compliant with the obligations set out at the European level.[134] This was already argued at the times of the *Corpus Juris*,[135] which laid down a provision on the issue that did not significantly depart from the current notion of money laundering,[136] and has been confirmed by the explanatory memorandum to the Government's bill.[137] In addition, penalties are much higher than those laid down in the Directive, as money laundering is punished with a maximum penalty of 12 years of imprisonment.[138]

Article 4(2) of the PIF Directive requires the Member States to criminalize also passive and active corruption when committed intentionally. In particular, 'passive corruption' is the conduct of the public official who "[acts] or [refrains] from acting in accordance with his duty or in the exercise of his functions in a way which damages or is likely to damage the Union's financial interests",[139] in exchange of money or advantages of any kind. Once more, the expected impact of this provision on Italian domestic legislation is limited. Article 318 of the Italian CP, as amended in 2012, penalizes the conduct of a public official who is unduly remunerated to exercise his or her functions, without any specific reference to an act or an omission, which is admittedly not always easy to detect during the investigations. Article 318 also applies when the public official works for the European Union, as a member of the institutions or as an EU *fonctionnaire*.[140] Article 319 criminalizes instead the conduct of the public official, including an EU public

---

132 [1999] OJ L *166/77*.

133 [2005] OJ L 141/73. This Directive has been recently amended by Directive (EU) 2018/843 [2018] OJ L156/43.

134 *See* Arts. 648 to 648*quater* Italian CP.

135 R. Sicurella, 'Criminal Law Special Part: Articles 1-8 *Corpus Juris*', in M. Delmas-Marty and J.A.E. Vervaele (eds.), *The Implementation of the* Corpus Juris *in the Member States*, Vol. 1, Intersentia, 2000, pp. 230-231.

136 *See* Art. 3 of the *Corpus Juris* 2000 ('Money laundering and receiving'). The conclusion on the Italian system's compliance with EU obligations seems even more valid nowadays, since Italy has recently penalized also self-laundering (Art 648*ter*.1 Italian CP). The new directive on money laundering expressly requires the Member States to criminalize self-laundering as well (*see* Art. 3(5) of Directive 2018/1673 of 23 October 2018 on combating money laundering by criminal law [2018] OJ L284/22).

137 Explanatory memorandum to Disegno di Legge, Act of the Chamber of Deputies, No 1201 (the 'Government's bill') 5.

138 Art. 648*bis* Italian CP.

139 Art. 4(2)(a) and (b) PIF Directive.

140 Art. 322*bis* Italian CP. This provision extends the field of application of some – exhaustively listed – crimes against the public administration (such as corruption or embezzlement) so as to include those cases where the public official works for the EU, for the International Criminal Court or for the public administration of other EU countries and for other international organizations. This provision was introduced by Law No 300/00.

official,[141] who receives money or other advantages to act against his duty or to refrain from acting in accordance with his duty.[142] Again, maximum penalties for (the different types of) corruption are higher than four years of imprisonment.[143] Until January 2019, the two provisions at hand did not apply when the public official who was corrupted was a *fonctionnaire* of other international organizations or of third countries.[144] Law No 3/2019 bridged the gap with regard to public officials working for international organizations, while the implementation of the PIF Directive could extend the provisions on passive corruption of a *fonctionnaire* of third countries, as long as this conduct damages or is likely to damage the Union's financial interests.[145]

Furthermore, the PIF Directive introduces the crime of misappropriation, which the PIF Convention did not address. Article 4(3) defines misappropriation as the intentional

> action of a public official who is directly or indirectly entrusted with the management of funds or assets to commit or disburse funds or appropriate or use assets contrary to the purpose for which they were intended in any way which damages the Union's financial interests.

In Italy, this conduct may fall within the remit of two different provisions, i.e., Article 314 ('*peculato*' – embezzlement) and Article 323 ('*abuso d'ufficio*' – abuse of office) of the Penal Code.[146] The first concerns the case of unlawful appropriation by a public official of funds entrusted to him; the offence is also punished when committed by Union officials.[147] Other hypotheses of illegally diverting public funds fall within the scope of application of Article 323. This provision criminalizes the conduct of the public official who, in the exercise of his or her functions, intentionally either gains an unjust advantage

---

141 Art. 322*bis* Italian CP.
142 Corruption related to, or impacting on, the administration of justice is expressly dealt with in a separate provision (Art. 319*ter* Italian CP).
143 The current maximum penalties are, without taking into account possible aggravating circumstances, eight (Art. 318), 10 (Art. 319) and 12 (Art. 319*ter*) years of imprisonment.
144 Cfr Art. 322*bis*(2) Italian CP. On the limited amendments to Italian legislation that are likely to be required to comply with the PIF Directive's provisions on corruption, *see also* L. Salazar, 'La Situazione Italiana', *op. cit.* at p. 109. For an in-depth analysis of corruption crimes in the framework of the PIF Directive, *see* V. Scalia, 'La Corruzione nel Quadro della Direttiva sulla Protezione degli Interessi Finanziari dell'Unione Europea', in G. Grasso, R. Sicurella, F. Bianco, and V. Scalia (eds.), *Tutela Penale degli Interessi Finanziari dell'Unione Europea. Stato dell'Arte e Prospettive alla Luce della Creazione della Procura Europea*, Ius Pisa University Press, 2018, pp. 75-130.
145 Cfr Art. 3(1)(d) Disegno di Legge (bill), Act of the Chamber of Deputies, No 1201-B ('draft European delegating law'), which calls for the punishment of passive corruption to be extended to public officials of third countries, when their illegal conduct affects or can affect the Union budget. *See also* L. Salazar, 'La Situazione Italiana', *op. cit.* at p. 109.
146 *See* the explanatory memorandum to the Disegno di Legge, Act of the Chamber of Deputies, No 1201 (the 'Government's bill') 5, which mentions the equivalence between misappropriation and 'embezzlement' (*peculato*).
147 *See* Art. 322*bis* Italian CP.

for himself or herself or for a third party, or causes an unjust damage to others, by violation of laws or regulations or by omitting from abstaining when such an abstention is prescribed by law. The 'abuse of office' is punished less seriously than 'embezzlement', yet the maximum penalty is four years of imprisonment. For the time being, Article 323 does not apply to Union officials,[148] and the implementation of the PIF Directive may bridge this gap.

13.4.2   Inchoate Offences and Liability of Legal Persons

The PIF Directive also lays down some rules concerning the so-called general part of (substantive) criminal law. Among others, it regulates inchoate offences and liability of legal persons for PIF crimes.

Like the PIF Convention and its Protocols, the PIF Directive obliges the Member States to criminalize 'incitement, aiding and abetting, and attempt' to commit PIF offences,[149] but it does not define to which conducts these notions refer. Italy will continue to apply its ordinary rules concerning incitement, aiding and abetting,[150] and attempt to commit crimes.[151] The implementation of the PIF Directive may nonetheless represent the opportunity to amend Article 6 of the Legislative Decree No 74/00, which currently prohibits from punishing an attempt to commit VAT fraud with criminal sanctions.[152]

Furthermore, the PIF Directive introduces some rules concerning the liability of legal persons for PIF offences. In Italy, the liability of legal persons, which is regulated by Legislative Decree No 231/01, is historically interwoven with the protection of the Union's financial interests. The Government adopted Legislative Decree No 231/01 upon delegation of the Parliament, which was given with Law No 300/00. As noted above, Law No 300/00 aimed at the implementation of the PIF Convention and its First Protocol, as well as some other conventions, such as the 1997 OECD Convention on

---

148 See also M. Romano, I Delitti Contro la Pubblica Amministrazione. Commentario Sistematico, Giuffrè, 2nd ed., 2006, 243.

149 Art. 5 PIF Directive.

150 These three conducts fall within the scope of application of the rules concerning complicity ('concorso di persone nel reato'), which are to be found in Arts. 110ff Italian CP. Also Arts. 378 and 379 Italian CP may come to the fore in this context, as they lay down the definition of the crime of aiding and abetting ('favoreggiamento'): in the first case (Art. 378), the crime is that of helping someone who has committed a crime to elude the investigations, while Art. 379 criminalizes the conduct of whoever helps the offender to secure the proceeds of crime. See the explanatory memorandum to Disegno di Legge, Act of the Chamber of Deputies, No 1201 (the 'Government's bill') 6.

151 Art. 56 Italian CP.

152 See Art. 3(1)(c) Disegno di Legge (bill), Act of the Chamber of Deputies, No 1201-B ('draft European delegating law'). In addition, Art. 9 of Law No 74/00 forbids the application of the ordinary rules on complicity with regard to some tax crime, including that mentioned in Art. 2 (above n 114), so that the implementation of the PIF Directive could lead the legislator to remove this exception (Art 3(1)(c) draft European delegating law).

Combating Bribery of Foreign Public Officials in International Business Transactions. While the 1997 OECD Convention provides for a generic obligation for State Parties to introduce the liability of legal persons for the corruption of a foreign public official, it is in the Second Protocol to the PIF Convention that more detailed rules on the matter can be found. Yet Law No 300/00 does not formally implement the Second Protocol, as the latter had not yet been ratified at the time; nonetheless, it is clear that the rules of this Protocol have influenced Legislative Decree No 231/01.[153]

The PIF Directive defines a 'legal person' as "an entity having legal personality under the applicable law, except for States or public bodies in the exercise of State authority and for international public organisations".[154] In Italy, the State is not subject to criminal liability either and, more broadly, Legislative Decree No 231/01 does not apply to bodies carrying out functions of constitutional interests, local public authorities and non-economic public entities.[155] Therefore, Italy seems to comply with the definition of the PIF Directive, although it may be desirable to clearly spell out the exclusion of international public organizations as well.

The Member States shall ensure that legal persons can be held responsible for any PIF offence "committed for their *benefit* by any person, acting either individually or as part of an organ of the legal person, and having a leading position within the legal person".[156] When it comes to subjects who do not hold a leading position,

> legal persons can be held liable where the lack of supervision or control by a person [having a leading position] has made possible the commission, by a person under its authority, of any [PIF offence] for the benefit of that legal person.[157]

Legislative Decree No 231/01 already provides that the liability of legal persons should follow from a crime that is committed for the benefit of the legal person.[158] As for the natural person's liability, Italian legislation complies with the directive since it lays down two different rules for the attribution of the crime to the legal person, according to

---

153 The ministerial report accompanying the adoption of Legislative Decree No 231/01 notes that, with this piece of legislation, Italy complies with the obligations of the 1997 OECD Convention and other instruments that were on the verge of being ratified; among the latter, it expressly (and only) mentions the Second Protocol to the PIF Convention (*see* 'Relazione Ministeriale al D. Lgs. n. 231/2001').

154 Art. 2(1)(b) PIF Directive.

155 Art. 1(3) Legislative Decree No 231/2001. See more in G. Grasso and F. Giuffrida, 'Ai Confini tra il Giudice Contabile e il Giudice Penale: I Rapporti tra le Giurisdizioni e la Problematica Nozione di "Ente Pubblico"' (2016) *L'Indice Penale* 894.

156 Art. 6(1) PIF Directive (emphasis added).

157 Art. 6(2) PIF Directive.

158 Art. 5 Legislative Decree No 231/2001 ('*nel suo interesse o a suo vantaggio*').

whether the natural person holds a leading position or whether he or she is a subordinate.[159]

In Italy, the law lists exhaustively the crimes for which legal persons can be held responsible. Among them, Legislative Decree No 231/2001 does not include misappropriation (*'peculato'*, Article 314 CP, and *'abuso d'ufficio'*, Article 323 CP), arguably because these crimes are typically committed by a natural person for his or her own benefit, rather than for that of the company. The exclusion of tax crimes, including VAT fraud, from the scope of Legislative Decree No 231/2001 is instead more contentious, and the implementation of the directive could bridge this gap.[160] Article 3(1)(e) of the draft European delegating law expressly requires that the list of crimes from which the liability of legal persons may derive shall include crimes affecting the Union's financial interests; as noted, this includes cross-border VAT fraud causing total damage of at least €10 million.

Finally, the PIF Directive requires penalties for legal persons to be 'effective, proportionate and dissuasive',[161] and in any case, they shall 'include criminal or non-criminal fines'.[162] The directive lists, as an example, six sanctions that may be provided, such as the 'exclusion from entitlement to public benefits or aid'[163] or the 'judicial winding-up'.[164] Legislative Decree No 231/2001 already provides for all those six penalties, as well as for further financial fines.[165]

13.4.3   Prescription of PIF Offences

Another key provision of the PIF Directive is Article 12, which – for the first time in EU criminal law – introduces some rules to harmonize the statute of limitation (or 'prescription') of PIF crimes. The (allegedly unsatisfactory) limitation period of serious VAT fraud in Italy was the key issue addressed by the CJEU in one of the most debated judgments it issued over the last years, i.e., *Taricco*.[166] In this ruling, the CJEU argued in

---

159 *See*, respectively, Arts. 6 and 7 Legislative Decree No 231/2001.

160 Similar views are expressed by G.F. Perilongo, *op. cit.* at pp. 264, 279 and 281; E. Basile, *op. cit.*; S.M. Ronco, *op. cit.* at pp. 8-9; L. Salazar, 'La Situazione Italiana', *op. cit.* at pp. 109-110. *See also* the explanatory memorandum to Disegno di Legge, Act of the Chamber of Deputies, No 1201 (the 'Government's bill') 7.

161 Art. 9(1) PIF Directive.

162 *Ibid.*

163 Art. 9(1)(a) PIF Directive.

164 Art. 9(1)(e) PIF Directive.

165 Sanctions for legal persons are extensively regulated in Arts. 9-23 Legislative Decree No 231/01. For similar remarks, *see* the explanatory memorandum to the Disegno di Legge, Act of the Chamber of Deputies, No 1201 (the 'Government's bill') 7, which however would not exclude the introduction of further sanctions, should they be considered necessary to ensure effective, proportionate and dissuasive penalties for legal persons that have benefitted from PIF crimes. *See* Art. 3(1)(h) Disegno di Legge (bill), Act of the Chamber of Deputies, No 1201-B ('draft European delegating law').

166 Case C-105/14 *Taricco*.

essence that, *if* national rules on the limitation period of PIF offences prevent "the imposition of effective and dissuasive penalties in a significant number of cases of serious fraud affecting the financial interests of the European Union",[167] or provide for longer limitation periods in respect of cases of fraud affecting the financial interests of the Member State concerned than in respect of those affecting the EU budget, national courts should disapply such national rules.[168] This disapplication would follow from the incompatibility of national legislation on the limitation period with Article 325 TFEU, which represents the key EU constitutional provision concerning the protection of the Union's financial interests.[169]

Taricco wreaked havoc in Italy,[170] as the disapplication of national law envisaged by the CJEU would amount to a violation of the principle of legality. The latter is enshrined in the Italian Constitution and is the cornerstone of the Italian criminal justice system. The principle of legality encompasses different sub-principles, such as that of non-retroactivity, which implies that substantive criminal laws do not apply to the offences committed before these laws entered into force if they aggravate the position of the defendants. Courts have to apply the substantive criminal laws that were in force at the time of the commission of the fact unless the subsequent ones are more favourable to the defendant.[171] According to the well-established case law of the Italian Constitutional Court, this regime also applies to the rules on the limitation period of crimes, which are considered as forming part of substantive, rather than procedural, criminal law.[172] Consequently, when a new law prolongs the limitation period of a crime, the new regime does not apply to the facts committed before the entry into force of that law. The obligation to disapply national law in accordance with the *Taricco* ruling of the CJEU would have the same – unacceptable, from the Italian perspective – effect of extending the limitation period beyond the maximum time limit that was provided by the law in force at the time when the facts were committed.

---

167 *Ibid.*, para. 58.

168 *Ibid.*

169 *Ibid.* Art. 325(1) TFEU reads as follows: '1. The Union and the Member States shall counter fraud and any other illegal activities affecting the financial interests of the Union through measures to be taken in accordance with this Article, which shall act as a deterrent and be such as to afford effective protection in the Member States, and in all the Union's institutions, bodies, offices and agencies'. As for Art. 325(2) TFEU, *see* n 131 above.

170 This contribution cannot delve into the multifarious and complex issues that this decision raised, which are addressed in more detail in G. Grasso, 'Evoluzione del Diritto Penale Europeo e Tutela dei Diritti Fondamentali alla Luce della «Saga Taricco»' (2018) *La Legislazione Penale* 1-30, available at: www.lalegisl azionepenale.eu/wp-content/uploads/2018/10/Grasso-Studi.pdf, accessed 19 August 2019.

171 F. Giuffrida, 'The Limitation Period of Crimes: Same Old Italian Story, New Intriguing European Answers– Case Note on C-105/14, *Taricco*' (2016) 7 *New Journal of European Criminal Law* 100, 109-110. For the principle of legality in Italian constitutional and (substantive) criminal law *see*, *e.g.*, G. Fiandaca and E. Musco, *op. cit* at pp. 47-111.

172 *See*, for instance, the decisions of the Italian Constitutional Court of 23 October 2006, No 393, and of 30 July 2008, No 324.

The Italian Constitutional Court thus required further clarification from the CJEU, which, in *MAS, MB*, acknowledged that national courts may refrain from disapplying national legislation if they believe that such disapplication entails a breach of the legality principle

> because of the lack of precision of the applicable law or because of the retroactive application of legislation imposing conditions of criminal liability stricter than those in force at the time the infringement was committed.[173]

In *MAS, MB*, the Court of Justice, therefore, paid more attention to the (national) principle of legality than in *Taricco*.[174] Applying in essence Article 53 of the Charter, without mentioning it though, the Court recognized that the respect of such a principle may even trump the protection of the Union's financial interests in some instances, as is the case when the principle of legality is enshrined in a national constitution and covers – unlike the principle of legality at the EU level – also the regime of the statute of limitation.[175]

After the decision in *MAS, MB*, the Italian Constitutional Court has brought to an end the *Taricco* saga with a decision where it stresses the importance of the principle of legality, which is "both a supreme principle of the Italian constitutional system and a foundational pillar of EU law".[176] The Court argues that the '*Taricco* rule' – i.e., disapplication of national law that allegedly violates Article 325 TFEU – suffers from a clear lack of certainty. Even more, Article 325 TFEU is vague per se because "its text does not allow persons to foresee whether or not the '*Taricco* rule' will apply".[177] It is even 'intuitive', the Italian Court continues, that

> a person, despite full awareness of Article 325 TFEU, *could not* (and cannot today, on the basis of that article alone) *imagine* that a rule would be

---

173 Case C-42/17 *MAS, MB*, EU:C:2017:936, para. 62.
174 *See* more in R. Sicurella, 'Effectiveness of EU Law and Protection of Fundamental Rights: The Questions Settled and the New Challenges After the ECJ Decision in the *M.A.S.* and *M.B.* Case (C-42/17)' (2018) 9 *New Journal of European Criminal Law* 24.
175 In *Taricco*, the CJEU held that, according to the case law of the ECtHR, "the extension of the limitation period and its immediate application do not entail an infringement of the rights guaranteed by Article 7 [ECHR], since that provision cannot be interpreted as prohibiting an extension of limitation periods where the relevant offences have never become subject to limitation" (Case C-105/14 *Taricco*, para. 57). As the Court points out, Art. 7 ECHR, where the principle of legality is enshrined, corresponds to Art. 49 of the EU Charter of Fundamental Rights ('Principles of legality and proportionality of criminal offences and penalties').
176 Italian Constitutional Court, decision of 10 April 2018, No 115.
177 *Ibid.*

extrapolated from it obliging courts to disapply a particular aspect of the legal framework governing limitation periods, under truly peculiar conditions.[178]

This runs counter to the essence of the (constitutional) principle of legality, which in Italy also applies to the statute of limitation, i.e., "an institution that impacts the liability of persons to punishment, by linking the passage of time with the effect of blocking the application of a punishment".[179]

It is interesting to note that, although the CJEU seems to imply the opposite,[180] the PIF Directive does not take a stance on the nature – i.e., substantive or procedural – of the prescription of crimes. It only aims to harmonize – and in a limited way[181] – the regime of the limitation periods of PIF offences. In more detail, Article 12(1) requires Member States to take the necessary measures to provide for a limitation period that is sufficient in order for PIF offences to be tackled effectively. According to Article 12(2), the limitation period shall be at least 'five years from the time when the offence was committed'[182] when the PIF crimes defined in the PIF Directive are punishable by a maximum sanction of at least four years of imprisonment.

In Italy, when it comes to serious crimes ('*delitti*'),[183] the limitation period is generally equal to the amount of the maximum imprisonment penalty; in any case, it cannot be shorter than six years.[184] Furthermore, Legislative Decree No 74/00 provides that the limitation period of VAT fraud is equal to the amount of the maximum imprisonment penalty increased by a third.[185] The limitation period runs from the day the offence has been committed and is interrupted in a number of cases listed in Article 160 of the Italian CP. Once interrupted, it starts to run anew from the day of the interruption but, in principle, it cannot exceed the amount of the maximum prescribed period, extended by a quarter.[186] Therefore, for instance, if the limitation period amounts to six years, the

---

178 *Ibid.* (emphasis added).

179 *Ibid.*

180 In *MAS, MB*, the CJEU argues that, at the time of the proceedings in *Taricco*, "the limitation rules applicable to criminal proceedings relating to VAT had not been harmonized by the EU legislature, and harmonization has since taken place only to a partial extent by the adoption of [the PIF Directive]". Hence, Italy was "at that time, free to provide that in its legal system those rules, like the rules on the definition of offences and the determination of penalties, form part of substantive criminal law, and are thereby, like those rules, subject to the principle that offences and penalties must be defined by law" (Case C-42/17 *MAS, MB*, paras 44-45). For some remarks on this – admittedly unclear and contentious – statement, *see* Grasso, 'Evoluzione del Diritto Penale Europeo' (above n 170), 25-27.

181 Notably, Recital No 22 of the PIF Directive clarifies that the rules of the Directive on the limitation period "should be without prejudice to those Member States which do not set limitation periods for investigation, prosecution and enforcement".

182 Art. 12(2) PIF Directive.

183 PIF offences are '*delitti*' according to Italian law; hence, the rules concerning petty offences ('*contravvenzioni*') are not addressed in this contribution.

184 Art. 157(1) Italian CP.

185 Art. 17 Legislative Decree No 74/00.

186 *See* Arts. 160 and 161 Italian CP.

crime becomes time-barred after seven years and six months if the prescription period has been interrupted.[187]

A reform approved in June 2017 has however changed the rules for corruption and fraud (Article 640*bis* of the Italian CP), as well as for different crimes against the public administration when committed by Union or foreign officials. The reform provides that, for these crimes, the extension of their limitation period due to interruptions cannot exceed the maximum prescribed period of imprisonment, extended by a half (rather than simply a quarter, as provided for the other crimes).[188] The 2017 law has also introduced new rules that will make the limitation period longer for all crimes, and these rules have been further amended in 2019 by means of a contentious reform.[189] From 1 January 2020, the limitation period of a crime will be 'suspended' after the decision issued by the first-instance judge up until the moment when the decision becomes final (Article 159(2) of the Italian CP). Although the wording of Article 159(2) formally refers to 'suspension', which would imply that the limitation period starts to run again at some point, this new rule provides, in essence, for a definitive ban on prescription; after the court of the first instance has delivered its judgment (acquittal or conviction), the crimes at stake can no longer become time-barred. In the light of the foregoing, no amendment of the Italian rules on prescription is likely to follow from the implementation of the PIF Directive, as can also be inferred from the absence of any reference to Article 12 of the Directive in the draft European delegating law.[190]

13.4.4   Freezing and Confiscation

Article 10 of the PIF Directive requires the Member States to take the necessary measures to enable the freezing and confiscation of instrumentalities and proceeds from PIF offences. If the Member States are bound by Directive 2014/42 on freezing and confiscation,[191] as is the case with Italy, they should adopt such measures in accordance with that directive. Italy introduced few rules to implement Directive 2014/42,[192] as its system was (and still is) already largely compliant with the EU obligations on the matter. Hence, it seems unlikely that the PIF Directive will lead to any change in domestic

---

187 F. Giuffrida, 'The Limitation Period of Crimes: Same Old Italian Story, New Intriguing European Answers–Case Note on C-105/14, Taricco' *op. cit.* at pp. 100, 101, 109-110.
188 Law No 103/17.
189 Law No 3/19.
190 Only a few words on the matter are to be found in the explanatory memorandum to the Government's bill, as Art. 12 of the PIF Directive is briefly described without further details on its implementation in Italy (see the explanatory memorandum to Disegno di Legge, Act of the Chamber of Deputies, No 1201 (the 'Government's bill', 68-69).
191 Directive 2014/42/EU on the freezing and confiscation of instrumentalities and proceeds of crime in the European Union [2014] OJ L127/39.
192 *See* Legislative Decree No 202/16.

legislation on freezing and confiscation, as noted in the explanatory memorandum to the Government's bill.[193] No provision of the draft European delegating law mentions Article 10 of the PIF Directive.

As for freezing of instrumentalities and proceeds of crime, Article 321 of the Italian CPP on the so-called 'preventive seizure' (*'sequestro preventivo'*) will apply. Already when implementing Directive 2014/42, the regime of the *'sequestro preventivo'* was considered sufficient to abide by the provisions of the directive and it was not amended.[194] The 'preventive seizure' is a 'preventive measure on things' (*'misura cautelare reale'*), and it can be adopted during the investigations on two grounds (either separately or together). First, things that are connected with a crime can be seized when there are both sufficient elements to suspect that a crime has been committed (*fumus boni iuris*) and the risk that those things may be used to exacerbate the consequences of the crime or to commit other crimes (*periculum in mora*).[195] Second, the *'sequestro preventivo'* can also concern things that – at the end of the trial – will be subject to confiscation; the seizure thus aims to avert the risk that those things will disappear once the proceedings come to an end.[196] This kind of seizure requires the existence of a specific and structural link between the things to be frozen and the crime under investigation.

In accordance with Article 321 CPP, it is usually the public prosecutor who requires the competent judge (the judge for the preliminary investigations) to order the seizure; however, in case of urgency, the public prosecutor can order the seizure himself or herself and then ask the judge to confirm it within 48 hours.

While the rules on freezing of instrumentalities and proceeds are mostly to be found in a single provision of the code of criminal procedure, those on confiscation are instead fragmented.[197] Nonetheless, they already cover the remit of the PIF Directive. In more detail, the *mandatory* confiscation of *proceeds* is provided for by Article 322*ter* of the Italian CP, with regard to corruption, misappropriation and some hypotheses of fraud;[198] Article 640*ter* of the Italian CP, for the case of fraud punished by Article 640*bis* of the same code;[199] Article 648*quater* of the Italian CP, for money laundering; and Article 12*bis* of Legislative Decree No 74/00, with regard to VAT-related offences.[200] All these provisions allow for value confiscation as well. Furthermore, when a person is

---

193 Explanatory memorandum to the Government's bill (above n) 9.
194 *Ibid.*
195 Art. 321(1) Italian CPP.
196 Art. 321(2) Italian CPP.
197 For a detailed and extensive analysis *see* A.M. Maugeri, 'Confisca (Diritto Penale)' in *Enciclopedia del Diritto*, Annali VIII (Giuffrè 2015), 185-225.
198 Namely, fraud as defined in Arts. 316*bis* and 316*ter* Italian CP. *See* more in Section 4.1 above.
199 *See* Section 4.1 above.
200 Art. 12*bis*(2) Legislative Decree No 74/00 however clarifies that the confiscation does not extend to the amount of money that the offender agrees to pay even in case of seizure.

convicted, the court *may* always order the confiscation of *instrumentalities* of that crime, on the one hand.[201] On the other hand, in case of conviction issued for most PIF offences, the judge shall also order the confiscation of money or goods of the convicted person, if the latter cannot justify their origin and if such goods are disproportionate when compared to the income of the convicted person or his or her economic activity.[202]

13.5   CONCLUSION

If the trends singled out in this contribution will not change in the years to come, Italy is expected to (continue to) play a key role in the development of EU criminal law. While the Italian legislator has not always been a model to follow when it comes to the implementation of EU criminal legislation, Italian courts have been very proactive in ensuring that the national system is in line with EU principles and obligations (Section 13.2). Especially bearing in mind that current university curricula now provide for more and more modules on EU (criminal) law,[203] the familiarity of national judges with EU matters is likely to increase in the future and may further ensure Italy's alignment with EU obligations.

Section 13.3 has discussed two main issues concerning the role of Italy vis-à-vis the protection of the Union's financial interests. On the judicial level, the application of *ne bis in idem* to concurrent administrative and criminal proceedings concerning the same facts is one of the most debated issues in Italy. For the time being, administrative proceedings, albeit having a criminal nature, cannot bar further criminal proceedings on the same facts. The Constitutional Court has, however, been recently required to rule on whether this approach is compatible with the *ne bis in idem* principle as interpreted by the ECtHR and, more recently, by the CJEU. Although the Constitutional Court has not yet issued its decision on the matter, it has been noted that this Court has already shown its willingness to align itself with the case law of the European Courts, as was the case with the *Eternit-bis* proceedings (Section 13.3.1). On the legislative level, Italy has been among the most vocal supporters of the EPPO and called for the extension of the Office's competence over serious crimes having a cross-border dimension. As for the implementation of the EPPO Regulation in Italy, the legislative procedure has just started at the time of writing, although few issues of compatibility between the regulation and (constitutional and/or criminal) law may already be envisaged (Section 13.3.2).

Section 13.4 has analysed the expected impact of the PIF Directive in Italy, arguing that only a few amendments of domestic legislation seem necessary to implement the

---

201 Art. 240(1) Italian CP. *See* more in G. Grasso, 'Art 240' in M. Romano, G. Grasso and T. Padovani (eds.), *Commentario Sistematico del Codice Penale*, Giuffrè, 2nd ed., 2011, 614ff.

202 Art. 240*bis* Italian CP, which allows value confiscation as well.

203 In Italy, the first course on EU criminal law was held at the University of Catania back in 2004.

directive. As for the definition and penalties of PIF offences, no groundbreaking amendments are expected, apart from slightly elevating both the maximum penalty of the conducts provided for by Article 316*ter* of the Italian CP (when committed by persons who are not public officials) and Article 4 of Legislative Decree No 74/00.[204] It may also be worth considering to extend the field of application of Article 323 of the Italian CP ('abuse of office') so as to include those cases where the fact is committed by EU officials (Section 13.4.1).

With respect to the general part of criminal law, the implementation of the directive may lead to the criminalization of the attempt to commit VAT fraud. It is to be welcomed that the PIF Directive confirms the obligation for the Member States to regulate the liability of legal persons, which can admittedly play a relevant role when it comes to fraud, especially VAT-related cases. The provisions of the directive are quite far-reaching, but the Italian system is already compliant with the obligations thereof to a large extent. The implementation of the directive can, however, allow bridging some existing gaps, as the notable lack of tax crimes (including VAT fraud) among the crimes for which a legal entity may be held liable in accordance with Legislative Decree No 231/2001 (Section 13.4.2).

Likewise, it is important (also) on a symbolic level that the EU legislator has finally laid down some rules aimed at the harmonization of national provisions on the statute of limitation. Yet the Italian system should not undergo any amendment in that respect either, as it already provides for limitation periods of PIF offences that are much longer than those set out in the PIF Directive. Besides, although the words of the CJEU in the *MAS, MB* case seem to imply that the PIF Directive requires the Member State to treat the prescription of crimes as a matter of procedural law, there is no indication that this is the goal of the directive. Hence, Italy is likely to continue to consider the statute of limitation as forming part of substantive criminal law, at least until the Constitutional Court will change, if ever, its established approach to the matter (Section 13.4.3).

Finally, the PIF Directive includes some rules on freezing and confiscation of instrumentalities and proceeds of PIF crimes. Once more, Italian legislation already abides by the provisions of the directive. On the one hand, the Code of Penal Procedure provides for a general rule on freezing of assets that also applies to crimes affecting the Union's financial interests. On the other hand, albeit scattered throughout the Penal Code and other pieces of legislation, Italian rules on confiscation are already sufficient to comply with the obligations stemming from the PIF Directive (Section 13.4.4).

---

204 As for Art. 316*ter* Italian CP, also the *de minimis* threshold provided therein could be increased.

14 SELECTED CASE STUDIES: THE CASE STUDY OF LATVIA (LV)

Jelena Agranovska

14.1 THE IMPLEMENTATION OF CRIMINAL EU LAW IN LATVIA

The aim of this report is to describe and provide an analysis of the implementation and enforcement of the EU criminal law norms in the criminal law of Latvia regarding certain fields, particularly in the area of fraud and corruption affecting the financial interests of the EU.

14.1.1   Overview

Criminal law in Latvia is regulated by the two acts: the Criminal Law (hereafter 'LCL') and the Criminal Procedure Law (hereafter 'LCPL').[1] There are also a number of further acts which contain legal norms regulating criminal law and criminal procedure – the Law on the Prevention of Money Laundering and Terrorism and Proliferation Financing,[2] the Office of the Prosecutor Law[3] and the Operational Activities Law.[4]

Latvian Criminal law is one of the branches of law most susceptible to change. It has continuously evolved in sync with Latvia's move from one Union towards the other. Basically, LCL has the Criminal Code of the Latvian SSR at its foundation.[5] The new LCL came into force on 1 April 1999 replacing the old Latvian Criminal Code. This was the first significant criminal law reform, and since then the LCL has constantly been changing. To a great extent, the change has been dictated by Latvia's aspiration in joining the EU; in accordance with Article 69 of the Association Agreement, Latvia had to ensure that its legislation will be gradually made compatible with that of the Community.[6] Since its implementation and until Latvia joined the EU, the LCL was

---

1 Latvijas Vēstnesis, 74 (3232), 11 May 2005.
2 Latvijas Vēstnesis, 116 (3900), 30 July 2008.
3 Latvijas Vēstnesis, 65 (196), 2 June 1994.
4 Latvijas Vēstnesis, 131, 30 December 1993.
5 U. Krastiņš, Kriminālikumam 10 gadi: tapšana, attīstība, perspektīva, Žurnāls Juridiskā zinātne, Nr 1, 2010, pp. 5-24, University of Latvia.
6 Europe Agreement establishing an association between the European Communities and their Member States, of the one part, and the Republic of Latvia, of the other part L 26 (2 February 1998).

amended 15 times. Since Latvia's accession to the EU and until today,[7] the LCL has been amended 48 times.

Before restoration of independence, all of the Latvian criminal law norms were found only in the Criminal Code – the situation prevailing in all Soviet Republics' legal systems. The judiciary and academia had long got accustomed to the exclusive and central position of the Criminal Code in both legal theory and practice, where any international agreements or treaties were annexed via one-provision laws. Upon signing the Association Agreement with the European Community, Latvia engaged in 'the approximation of Latvia's existing and future legislation to that of the Community' in the sphere of criminal law through an already-established process – all new penalties and crimes were incorporated into the country's Criminal Law.

The working group entrusted with the task of developing a new criminal law draft had to comply with Article 69 of the Association Agreement by including the measures required by the acts of the third pillar of the European Union. Before the new LCL of 1999 came into force, the Latvian Parliament (Saeima) took into account the Joint Actions[8] and the Conventions by adding to the norms: (a) criminal liability for cruelty towards and violence against a minor (now Article 174 LCL), (b) kidnapping (Article 153 LCL) and (c) infringement of copyright and neighbouring rights (Article 148 LCL). The new part in the draft law which aimed at combating corruption by state officials and public servants had been influenced by the Convention on the fight against corruption involving officials of the European Communities or officials of Member States of the EU.[9] It could be concluded, therefore, that the impact of EU criminal law on the LCL has been a significant one.

The influence of EU criminal law on procedural criminal law has also been significant. This is evident from the implementation of the Criminal Procedure Law, which was implemented on 21 April 2005 and entered into force on 1 October 2005. At the time of its implementation, Latvia was already a Member State; hence, the drafters had to comply with all of the acquis, ECHR as well as the decisions of the ECtHR. Since its entry into force, the LCPL was amended 38 times. In Latvia, the EU criminal law had a significant impact on the rights of a victim in criminal proceedings, rights of the accused as well as significant influence on the substantial scope of criminal offences and inter-state cooperation (Joint Investigation Teams, European Arrest Warrant and recognition and enforcement of foreign decisions through EU instruments).

---

7   July 2019.

8   Joint Action of 24 February 1997 adopted by the Council on the basis of Art. K.3 of the Treaty on European Union concerning action to combat trafficking in human beings and sexual exploitation of children.

9   The Convention of 26 May 1997 drawn up on the basis of Art. K.3(2)(c) of the Treaty on European Union on the fight against corruption involving officials of the European Communities or officials of Member States of the European Union, 97/C 195/01.

The following sections analyse the impact of EU criminal law legislation on the Latvian criminal justice system. In particular, the EU provisions on terrorism, cybercrime, money laundering and participation in a criminal group will be looked into.

14.1.2   Impact of EU Law (Framework Decisions 2002/475/JHA and 2008/919/JHA) on the Criminalization of Terrorism in Latvia

Before the implementation of the LCL in 1999, the Criminal Code of the Latvian SSR envisaged criminal liability for 'homeland betrayal' in Article 59 and *'diversija'* (sabotage) in Article 63. The terms of criminal liability in these areas have been preserved and used within a wider norm connected to the term 'terrorism'.[10] The *Saeima* implemented the amendment to the LCL on 18 May 2000 which entered into force on 1 June 2000.[11] The amendment introduced the new Article 88, which defined terrorist acts and established penalties. Crimes relating to terrorism were covered by Articles 88 to 89 of the LCL in Chapter X dealing with crimes against the Latvian State. This chapter covers significant violations of the interests of the state and acts that threaten the security and independence of Latvia (e.g., espionage, sabotage, invitation to destroy the independence of Latvia as a State and invitation to the destruction of the territorial integrity of Latvia).

The EU legislation brought the most recent and significant changes on provisions dealing with terrorism. Council Framework Decisions 2002/475/JHA and 2008/919/ JHA (hereafter 'FD') on the criminalization of terrorism harmonize the Member States' laws in this area. Member States had to comply with these FDs by 31 December 2002 and 9 December 2010 respectively.

The new Article 88 of the amended LCL of 2000 complied with the subsequent EU legislation on the criminalization of terrorism only in part, and further measures had to be implemented. For instance, there were no provisions in the LCL on offences relating to a terrorist group, offences linked to terrorist activities and inciting or aiding or abetting to commit a terrorist attack. Likewise, offences provided for in Article 1(c) to (f) FD 2002/475/JHA[12] were not part of the terrorist act definition and had to be included in further amendments.

Prescribed sanctions for terrorist acts under Article 88 LCL were in line with the subsequent FDs of 2002 and 2008 since, at the time, Latvian criminal penalties were one of the most severe in the Union. At the time, Article 88 of the amended LCL of

---

10   U. Krastiņš, p. 14.

11   Latvijas Vēstnesis, 1 June 2000, Nr. 197/200 (2108/2111).

12   *E.g.* kidnapping or hostage taking; destruction to an information system, seizure of aircraft or ships, manufacture, possession, acquisition, transport, supply or use of weapons, explosives or of nuclear, biological or chemical weapons, as well as research into, and development of, biological and chemical weapons.

2000 provided that terrorist acts are punishable by penalties corresponding to the seriousness of those offences committed – life imprisonment or imprisonment of a term of eight to 20 years with confiscation of property, or between 15 and 20 years with confiscation of property. Article 88 of the LCL was further amended in 2005 to expand the definition of terrorist acts and implement provisions on offences relating to a terrorist group[13] and to include a provision on terrorism financing.[14] Following this amendment, the aim of terrorism shifted from being solely directed against Latvia's interests and society to include also interests of international organizations.

Further amendments to Article 88 LCL, which were influenced by the Council of Europe Convention on the Prevention of Terrorism of 2005, were implemented in 2007.[15] The 2007 amendment introduced three new offences dealing with incitement to terrorism and terrorist threats, recruitment and training for terrorism.[16] The 2007 modifications were sufficient for Latvia to comply with the subsequent FD of 2008; hence, no further reforms were needed.

The latest EU legislation, which requires the Member States to criminalize travelling abroad for the purpose of terrorism, is the Directive (EU) 2017/541 of the European Parliament and of the Council of 15 March 2017 on combating terrorism. Member States had to comply with the directive by 8 September 2018. Latvia had complied with the directive on 23 May 2018 when the new amendments to the LCL were implemented. Now, the new Chapter IX of the LCL entitled 'Crimes connected to terrorism' contains further new types of terrorism-related offences that have so far not been criminalized at the national or international level, namely, providing or receiving recruitment and training for terrorism, involvement in a terrorist group, public praise or justification of terrorism, travelling for the purposes of committing or aiding terrorism, the incitement to terrorism and terrorist threats.[17]

Essentially, the drafters have aligned the definitions of terms relating to terrorism found in Article 79(1) to (6) of the current LCL with the ones provided for by the EU legislation.

---

13 Latvijas Vēstnesis, 22 December 2005, Nr. 205 (3363).
14 Latvijas Vēstnesis, 18 May 2005, Nr. 78 (3236).
15 Latvijas Vēstnesis, 29 December 2007, Nr. 208 (3784).
16 Report from the Commission to the European Parliament and the Council on the implementation of Council Framework Decision 2008/919/JHA of 28 November 2008 amending Framework Decision 2002/475/JHA on combating terrorism, SWD (2014) 270 final, Brussels, 5 October 2014.
17 I. Kucina and L. Medina, 'Būtiskākās izmaiņas tiesu sistēmā un tiesību politikas jomā', 29 January 2019 /NR. 4 (1062).

14.1.3   *Impact of EU Law (Framework Decision 2008/841/JHA) on the Criminalization Participation in a Criminal Organization in Latvia*

The Latvian legislator has criminalized participation in a criminal organization in the LCL of 1999. Article 21 LCL defined a criminal organization as

> a stable association formed by *more than two persons* which have been created for the purpose of jointly committing a criminal offense or a serious or very serious crime, and the participants of which in accordance with the *previous agreement have divided responsibilities.*

Acts such as formation and leadership of a group, and participation in preparation for a serious or especially serious crime or in the commission of a crime, irrespective of the role of the person in the jointly committed offence, all fall under acts punishable under Article 21 LCL on organized groups.

The Latvian legislator amended Article 21 LCL in 2002[18] to exclude the element of 'stable' from the definition of an organized group. It seems that this reference to the stability of an organization could have limited the scope of the definition, which was later provided in the EU criminal law. The FD 2008/841/JHA provides that a criminal organization has to be 'established over a period of time', which arguably presupposes a less significant element of continuity than a 'stable' organization under the Latvian definition would. Therefore, the definition of an 'organized group' found in the LCL (as amended in 2002) has been in line with the FD by the deadline allocated for the transposition thereof falling on 11 May 2010.

Interestingly, the Commission Report on the implementation of the FD 2008/841/JHA asserts erroneously that Latvian legislation "restricts the scope of application to groups formed by at least five persons" and has, therefore, narrowed the scope of the EU definition in respect to membership of a criminal organization which refers to "more than two persons acting in concert".[19] Nevertheless, there are three discrepancies in how the 'criminal organization' is defined in the EU and national provisions. First, the Latvian definition does not have the criterion of *benefit* which has been provided for in FD Article 1(1) as 'to obtain, directly or indirectly, a financial or another material benefit'. The purpose of forming a criminal organization in Latvia is limited to jointly committing one or several crimes, and *not* to obtain a material gain. As a result, Article 21 LCL has a broader definition of an 'organized group', which is applicable to non-profit driven

---

18   Latvijas Vēstnesis, 69 (2644), 9 May 2002.
19   Report from the Commission to the European Parliament and the Council based on Art. 10 of Council Framework Decision 2008/841/JHA of 24 October 2008 on the fight against organized crime, Brussels, 7 July 2016, COM (2016) 448 final, p. 4.

criminal organizations, unlike Article 1(1) FD.[20] Secondly, in contrast to FD Article 1(1), the definition found in Article 21 LCL does not make any reference to a 'structured association', also potentially making the Latvian definition applicable to organizations that lack any structure. Thirdly, national legislature includes the element of 'division of responsibilities in accordance with previous agreement', which is not expressed in Article 1(1) FD, and with Article 1(2) FD providing that a 'structured association' does not have to define roles for its members. As a result, the national definition would have a narrower scope of application.

As regards penalties for natural persons, it should be observed that basic penalty levels in LCL are higher than envisaged by Article 3 FD.

14.1.4 Impact of EU Law (Framework Decision 2005/222/JHA) on the Criminalization of Attacks Against Information Systems in Latvia

In 2004 Latvia became a party to the Budapest Convention on Cybercrime,[21] and on 18 May 2005,[22] a number of new substantive offences have been introduced into the amended LCL to criminalize attacks against information systems. By the time when the Member States had to comply with the provisions of FD 2005/222/JHA (16 March 2007), the LCL already covered the acts delineated therein.

Article 177(1) LCL criminalizes computer fraud, which includes the act of 'the knowingly entering of false data'. Article 241 LCL deals with arbitrary access to an automated data processing system, making it an offence in paragraph 1 to intentionally access an information system without lawful authority *if* it is related to breaching of system protective means *and* causing substantial harm thereby. Arbitrary access to such systems is covered by Article 2 of the FD which provides that such an act must be 'punishable as a criminal offence, *at least for cases which are not minor*'. It could be argued that there is a minor discrepancy in definitions contained in Article 241(1) LCL and Article 2 FD insofar as national provision requires that there must be substantial harm caused. It also could be argued that the Latvian legislature opted to include the element referring to 'substantial harm', in order to reflect on the Article 2 FD which limits the application of its provisions 'for cases which are not minor'. If such is the explanation, then there is not much discrepancy between the Latvian and the EU definitions of what constitutes an offence. Still, in the Commission's view, the concept

---

20 Report from the Commission on FC 2008/841/JHA, at p. 4.
21 Council of Europe Convention on Cybercrime of 23 November 2001.
22 Latvijas Vēstnesis, 78 (3236), 18 May 2005; available in Latvian at: https://www.vestnesis.lv/ta/id/108357-grozijumi-kriminallikuma.

'minor case' refers to "cases where instances of illegal access are of *minor importance* or where an infringement of information system confidentiality is of *a minor degree*"[23] and is, therefore, inconsistent with Latvia's concept of the 'substantial harm'. It is questionable whether the Commission's argument holds, given that illegal access of minor importance would inevitably be liable for causing harm that is not substantial and does, therefore, falls outside of the scope of Article 241(1) LCL definition.

Article 243(1) LCL makes it an offence to interfere without authorization with *information* stored in an automated data processing system; this offence corresponds with Article 4 FD. Article 243(2) LCL makes it an offence to unlawfully interfere in the *operation* of an automated data processing system; this offence corresponds with Article 3 FD. However, for both these provisions of the LCL, there is a discrepancy of the kind present in Article 241(1) LCL which requires that for the act to be criminalized there must be substantial harm caused.[24] The Latvian interpretation of the offence has a much narrower scope of application if compared to the provisions of FD, and this poses a serious risk to the objective of harmonizing national laws in the area of cybersecurity.

In compliance with Article 7 FD, Articles 177(1) and 243 (3) LCL provide that when an offence is committed within the framework of a criminal organization, it will be an aggravating circumstance. In contrast, Article 241 LCL does not provide for such aggravating circumstances; hence, there is a discrepancy between the EU and national provisions. With regard to penalties, it should be noted that, in contrast to Article 7 FD, the LCL lays down the more severe minimum penalties.

14.1.5   Impact of the Commission Proposal for a New Directive on Cybercrime (COM (2010) 517 Final) and Subsequent Directive 2013/40/EU on Attacks Against Information Systems in Latvia

Directive 2013/40/EU on attacks against information systems (hereafter the 'Cybercrime Directive') amended and expanded the provisions of the FD 2005/222/JHA which established minimum rules concerning the definition of criminal offences and sanctions in the area of attacks against information systems. Indeed, the EU criminal law provisions have changed; however, the national definition of criminal offences in the area of attacks

---

23 Report from the Commission to the Council based on Art. 12 of the Council Framework Decision of 24 February 2005 on attacks against information systems, Brussels, 14 July 2008, COM (2008) 448 final p. 4, emphasis added.

24 Art. 243(1) LCL: "For a person who commits unauthorised modifying, damaging, destroying, impairing or hiding of information stored in an automated data processing system, or knowingly entering false information into an automated data processing system, *if substantial harm has been caused thereby*" (emphasis added).

against information systems discussed above have not, save for the introduction of three new offences.

Following the amendments of the LCL, two new Articles 244[25] and 244(1)[26] were added to the list of attacks against information systems which had to be criminalized by the Member States. Article 244 LCL criminalizes illegal operations with automated data processing system resource influencing devices. This offence corresponds with Article 7 of the Cybercrime Directive, which covers tools used for committing offences. In its report, the Commission erroneously notes[27] that there are discrepancies between Article 7 and the Latvian measures insofar that some of the possible acts listed in the directive were not transposed into the national law. However, after analysing the concerned provisions, one could certainly confirm that Article 244 LCL covers an even greater number of acts when compared to Article 7 of the Cybercrime Directive.

Article 244(1) LCL criminalizes acquisition, development, alterations, storage and distribution of data, programmes and equipment for illegal activities with electronic communications network terminal equipment

> *if* such activities have been committed for the purpose of acquiring property or
> *if* it has been committed by a group of persons according to a prior agreement,
> or *if* it has caused significant damage.[28]

Article 6 of the directive introduced a new act – interception – that must qualify as a criminal offence. Criminal liability for such acts in Latvia is provided for in LCL Part XIV on Criminal Offences against Fundamental Rights and Freedoms of a Person, specifically in Article 144 on violations of the confidentiality of correspondence and information to be transmitted over telecommunications networks.[29] This article was in line with the requirements of the directive, but a number of conceptual changes were necessary, and these were implemented in 2014.[30]

The penalty for failure to comply with cybersecurity regulations depends on the crime and its gravity. For natural persons, the penalty is usually a fine or imprisonment for up to seven years. For legal persons, the court may order the confiscation of property or a fine. The discrepancies between EU and national legislative provisions which were identified in the previous section (Articles 241 and 243 LCL) simultaneously apply to

---

25 (Art. 244 LCL), Latvijas Vēstnesis, 78 (3236), 18 May 2005.
26 (Art. 244(1) LCL), Latvijas Vēstnesis, 90 (4076), 10 June 2009.
27 Report from the Commission to the European Parliament and the Council assessing the extent to which the Member States have taken the necessary measures in order to comply with Directive 2013/40/EU on attacks against information systems and replacing Council Framework Decision 2005/222/JHA, Brussels, 13 September 2017, COM (2017) 474 final, p. 8.
28 Latvijas Vēstnesis, 208 (3784), 29 December 2007.
29 Likumprojekta "Grozījumi Krimināllikumā" sākotnējās ietekmes novērtējuma ziņojums (anotācija).
30 Latvijas Vēstnesis, 204 (5264), 15 October 2014.

the new provisions insofar as Article 245 LCL requires that there must be an element of 'significant damage' present, while Article 244(1) encompasses two concurrent elements for an act to become a criminal offence.

All in all, given that the discrepancy in the correlation between the EU provisions referring to 'minor cases' and Latvia's provisions referring to 'substantial harm' is of minor and questionable validity, it should be noted that the Latvian legislature transposed both the FD and the directive in a satisfactory and effective manner.

14.1.6   The Impact of EU Measures Facilitating the Exchange of Personal Data Between National Police and Judicial Authorities on the Legal Orders of EU Member States

The FD 2008/977/JHA on the protection of personal data processed in the framework of police and judicial cooperation in criminal matters is a general EU legislative instrument that sought to facilitate a high level of protection of the fundamental rights and freedoms of natural persons when processing personal data in the framework of police and judicial cooperation in criminal matters, while also providing a guarantee of a high level of public safety.[31] The Member States had to implement the FD by 27 November 2010. The relevant national law which regulated the area covered by the FD was the Latvian Personal Data Protection Law of 2000 – the country's general data protection legislation which protected the fundamental human rights and freedoms of natural persons, in particular, the inviolability of private life, with respect to the processing of data regarding natural persons.[32] It has been amended and updated eight times in order to comply with the FD before it was finally repealed and substituted with the Personal Data Processing Law of 2018 which sought to give effect to the General Data Protection Regulation[33] by creating legal preconditions for setting up of a system for the protection of personal data of a natural person at a national level by providing for the institutions necessary for such purpose, determining the competence and basic principles of operation thereof, as well as regulating the operation of data protection officers and provisions of data processing and free movement.[34] The Personal Data Processing Law had been criticized for contributing to the fragmentation of the regulatory framework,

---

31   Report from the Commission to the European Parliament and the Council the European Economic and Social Committee and the Committee of the Regions of 27 November 2008, assessing the extent to which the Member States have taken the necessary measures in order to comply with the Council FD 2008/977/ JHA on the protection of personal data processed in the framework of police and judicial cooperation in criminal matters, Brussels, 25 January 2012 COM (2012) 12 final.

32   Latvijas Vēstnesis;123/124 (2034/2035); 6 April 2000.

33   Regulation (EU) 2016/679 of the European Parliament and of the Council of 27 April 2016 on the protection of natural persons with regard to the processing of personal data and on the free movement of such data, and repealing Directive 95/46/EC (General Data Protection Regulation).

34   Latvijas Vēstnesis, 132 (6218), 4 July 2018.

while also being the source of a number of irregularities.[35] Therefore, the Ministry of Justice sought to draft a new law which would maintain the basic principles of the data processing included in the Personal Data Processing Law, while adapting the regulatory framework to the specific area.

In 2019, this law was supplemented with the special Law on the Processing of Personal Data in Criminal and Administrative Offenses[36] which sought to give effect to the Directive (EU) 2016/680 on the protection of natural persons with regard to the processing of personal data by competent authorities for the purposes of the prevention, investigation, detection or prosecution of criminal offences or the execution of criminal penalties, and on the free movement of such data, and repealing FD 2008/977/JHA.[37] The aim of the national law is to protect the fundamental rights of individuals to privacy, including personal data protection, when personal data are processed by the competent authorities with the aim of preventing, investigating and detecting criminal offences and administrative infringements, to enforce the penalties as well as to protect from threats to public and national security.

Article 11 of the special law implements the provisions of Article 16[38] of FD 2008/977/JHA on the right to access information on the processing of the data subject's personal data – paragraphs 1 and 2 provide a non-exhaustive list of information which the controller shall make available to the data subject.[39] The provision lists at least nine pieces of information which the controller has to disclose. These generous rights to data access granted to data subjects go in stark contrast to practices employed in some other Member States.[40]

Articles 12 and 13 of Law on the Processing of Personal Data in Criminal and Administrative Offenses are another two exemplary demonstrations of effective transposition of the EU legal provisions. These articles mirror the provisions of Article 14[41] and Article 16[42] of the Directive (EU) 2016/680 dealing with the right of access of data subjects and the right to rectification or erasure of personal data and restriction of processing respectively.

The Latvian legislature had promptly implemented the given EU laws, while at the same time, meticulously following the structure of the EU legal provisions with exceptional due diligence, which resulted in a satisfactory transposition. It could be

---

35 Ministry of Justice of the Republic of Latvia, A separate regulation that will protect the fundamental rights of individuals to privacy is drawn up, 12 October 2017, available at: https://www.tm.gov.lv/en/news/a-separate-regulation-that-will-protect-the-fundamental-rights-of-individuals-to-privacy-is-drawn-up.
36 Latvijas Vēstnesis, 147 (6486), 22 July 2019.
37 https://eur-lex.europa.eu/legal-content/EN/TXT/PDF/?uri=CELEX:32016L0680&from=EN.
38 Now Art. 13 of the Directive (EU) 2016/680.
39 There are nine instances listed.
40 For example France and Denmark do not provide data subjects with information on the processing of their personal data, see Report from the Commission on implementation of FD 2008/977/JHA, see above, at p. 5.
41 Art. 17 of FD 2008/977/JHA.
42 Art. 18 of FD 2008/977/JHA.

concluded, therefore, that the relevant EU laws should have a significant influence on the exchange of personal data between national police and judicial authorities with the other Member States.

14.1.7   *Application of the European Arrest Warrant Framework Decision*

Among all the EU criminal law instruments, the European Arrest Warrant (EAW),[43] which was created with the purpose of combating the serious criminal offences and the organized crime, is the most widely applicable. On 21 April 2005, the Latvian legislature implemented the FD 2002/584/JHA on the EAW by including the legal basis for the EAW in Chapters 65 and 66 of the LCPL, making it much easier to arrest and surrender persons for the purposes of conducting a criminal prosecution, execution of a custodial sentence or detention order. Despite the fact that there are some minor divergences between the EU and national provisions, and the fact that the Latvian legislature failed to transpose some of FD provisions,[44] the overall functionality of the system is not impaired, and the Commission was satisfied with the end result of the national implementation exercise.

The EAW system is based on the principle of mutual recognition, which essentially relies on mutual trust between the Member States. Despite its increasing popularity, this EU criminal law instrument has often been criticized[45] for inappropriate or *disproportionate* use, in particular, because of an increasing number of cases where it has been issued for the surrender of persons sought in respect of not serious crimes, but rather for minor and often very trivial offences. Such misuse of the EAW has a negative impact on mutual trust between the Member States as a result.

When recognizing an arrest warrant, Member States apply the so-called 'proportionality test' by comparing whether the offence in question is punishable under national criminal law or whether it is included in the offence list, and since there is no harmonization for some offences, the arrest warrant will sometimes be refused (or misused). In Latvia, the proportionality test is found in Article 682(3) of the LCPL which provides that a request for the extradition of a person may not be submitted if the seriousness or nature of a criminal offence is *disproportionate* in comparison with the expenses of the extradition. The Latvian Prosecutor General's Office relies on Article 682

---

43   Council Framework Decision of 13 June 2002 on the European arrest warrant and the surrender procedures between Member States – Statements made by certain Member States on the adoption of the Framework Decision, 2002/584/JHA.

44   J. Groma and S Kaija, *Mediterranean Journal of Social Sciences*, Vol 4, No 11, October 2013, MCSER Publishing, Rome-Italy, pp. 310-315, p. 314.

45   Report from the Commission to the European Parliament and the Council On the implementation since 2007 of the Council Framework Decision of 13 June 2002 on the European arrest warrant and the surrender procedures between Member States, Brussels, 11 April 2001, COM (2011) 175 final, p. 3.

(3) of the LCPL to refuse to issue around 20 per cent of EAWs.[46] According to the Commission, non-application of the proportionality test in the issuing Member State undermines the confidence in the EAW as the instrument of mutual recognition.

Therefore, the Council of the European Union called upon Latvian authorities to identify factors which would facilitate adopting a decision to issue an EAW in accordance with the proportionality test.[47]

The International Cooperation Division of the Prosecutor's Office responded by providing a list of seven factors which would have to be assessed before the decision to issue an EAW is adopted. For example, some factors to take into account are the amount of damage caused, seriousness and nature of the criminal offence, the method and motive of its perpetration and analysis of the administrative costs related with the extradition.[48]

In order for the EAW to work smoothly, the mutual trust must be significantly reinforced by improving the national standards of respect for fundamental rights and fundamental legal principles enshrined in Article 6 TEU.[49] In order to address these issues, Latvia moved in the right direction by improving, for example, the fundamental right to trial within a reasonable time.[50] The legislator has amended the LCL by introducing a new Article 49(1) dealing with the determination of punishment if the rights to termination of criminal proceedings in reasonable time have not been observed.[51] Essentially, Article 49(1) LCL provides that if the fundamental right in question is violated, the court may mitigate the punishment.

Additionally, since Latvia is facing certain challenges as regards its judicial system, including the rule of law and the independence of the judiciary, in order to improve the mutual trust required by the EAW it has to improve the effectiveness of its judicial system.[52]

---

46   Prosecutor's Office of the Republic of Latvia, Observing the principle of proportionality upon issuing the European arrest warrant, available in English at: www.prokuratura.gov.lv/en/starptautiska-sadarbiba/proporcionalitates-principa-ieverosana-pienemot-eiropas-apcietinajuma-lemumu.
47   The Council of the European Union in 7th Recommendation of its Report on the fourth round of mutual evaluations 'The practical application of the European Arrest Warrant and corresponding surrender procedures between Member States' (17220/1/08 REV 1), Brussels, 23 January 2009, p. 39, at p. 35.
48   Prosecutor's Office of the Republic of Latvia, Observing the principle of proportionality upon issuing the European arrest warrant, available in English at: www.prokuratura.gov.lv/en/starptautiska-sadarbiba/proporcionalitates-principa-ieverosana-pienemot-eiropas-apcietinajuma-lemumu.
49   FD 2002/584/JHA Article 1(3) and 2.
50   J. Rozenbergs, 'On Some Developments in Latvian Criminal Law and Criminal Procedure', available in English at: www.ecba.org/extdocserv/conferences/geneva2012/recdevRozenbergsLatvia.pdf.
51   Latvijas Vēstnesis; 10 November 2010, Nr. 178 (4370), available in Latvian at: vestnesis.lv/ta/id/220966-grozijumi-kriminallikuma.
52   The 2019 EU Justice Scoreboard, as above p. 6.

14.1.8   Main Challenges for the Legal Systems of EU Member States in Implementing the EU Acquis?

Even though initially intra-state cooperation in criminal matters was not mentioned in detail in Latvian legislation, today cross-border cooperation is a crucial part of the criminal justice system. When the principle of mutual recognition was adopted at the Tampere European Council in 1999, it kick-started the development of EU's justice and home affairs policies, while simultaneously changing the traditional view of cross-border cooperation in criminal matters. Although the national implementation of EU criminal law affects everyone involved in criminal proceedings, at times EU legislative instruments are only formally adopted into the Latvian criminal justice system since the exact terminology and nature of those instruments and their incorporation into Latvian provisions and application in practice are rarely considered.[53] Therefore, the old cooperative practices still prevail over innovative instruments provided for in the EU *acquis*.[54]

Another crucial link that is missing from the puzzle of effective cross-border cooperation in criminal matters is mutual trust, which has not yet reached the sufficient levels required. Quite naturally, this can be explained by the fact that the investigating authorities of the Member States have different tactics when conducting their work.[55] The representatives of each Member State thus are inclined to conduct investigations in accordance with a nationally established practice.

14.2   CRIMES AGAINST THE FINANCIAL INTERESTS OF THE EU

14.2.1   Protecting the Financial Interests of the EU in Latvia

Latvia is fully supportive of the EU's initiatives and innovative instruments created for combating fraud and protecting the EU's financial interests. Latvia has signed and ratified the Convention on the protection of the European Communities' financial interests[56] (the 'PIF Convention') and its three protocols. However, as is often the case, ratification alone hasn't triggered a flawless and effective implementation into national judicial

---

53   Strada-Rozenberga K. Savstarpējās atzīšanas princips starptautiskajā kriminālprocesuālajā sadarbība Eiropas Savienības telpā – teorija un prakse. Grām.: Meikališa Ā., Strada-Rozenberga K. Kriminālprocess. Raksti 2005-2010. Rīga: Latvijas Vēstnesis, 2010, 828. lpp.

54   E. Krutova, 'Joint Investigation Teams as One of the Forms of International Cooperation in Criminal Proceedings', PhD thesis, Law Faculty of the University of Latvia, 2013.

55   *Ibid.*, p. 67.

56   Council Act of 26 July 1995 drawing up the Convention on the protection of the European Communities' financial interests, OJ C 316, 27 November 1995, pp. 48-57, available at: https://eur-lex.europa.eu/legal-content/EN/TXT/PDF/?uri=CELEX:31995F1127(03)&from=EN.

systems. There was a pressing need to strengthen the protection of the Union's financial interests established by the PIF Convention as this instrument suffered from great ambiguity. As a result, the Convention failed to achieve adequate harmonization of applicable definitions, penalties and prescription periods (active/passive corruption and fraud).[57] Many Member States struggled with proper transposition and application of the PIF Convention, and there were multiple discrepancies and irregularities across jurisdictions. For example, in contrast to the requirements of the PIF Article 1(1)(a), the provisions of the LCL applicable at the time required that the element of intent is present for an act to fall under the definition of an offence.[58]

The PIF Convention has been replaced by the Directive on the fight against fraud to the Union's financial interests (hereafter 'the PIF Directive'). The aim of the directive is to ensure further approximation of the Member States' provisions by further harmonization of the definitions and penalties for criminal offences affecting the Union's financial interests.

The Latvian legislature approached the implementation of the PIF Directive in the same way it used to transpose all EU instruments discussed in the previous sections, namely, by amending the existing national provisions and by introducing new ones into the LCL and the LCPL. By following this familiar approach of transposing the EU criminal law, there was no need to introduce a separate special law on the protection of the financial interests of the EU. Nowhere in its provisions does the LCL refer specifically to the protection of the EU's financial interests, so that the protection of such interests would fall under the general definitions of the LCL, such as bribe, misappropriation and fraud. In terms of procedural norms, it should be noted that the LCPL refers to cooperation in criminal proceedings with other Member States – which is crucial for effective cross-border investigations.

However, still, prompt implementation of EU criminal measures alone is not enough for the Latvian system of criminal justice to be effective at protecting the EU's financial interests. Effective and proactive investigative and monitoring authorities on the ground are necessary.

The following national key players are entrusted with the task of dealing with financial crimes and concurrently, with the protection of the EU's financial interests: the Ministry of Finance, the Office for Prevention of Laundering of Proceeds Derived from Criminal Activity (hereafter the Control Service) and the Latvian Bureau for Prevention and Combating of Corruption (KNAB). KNAB combines tasks related to prevention and investigation and also acts as a pre-trial investigatory body endowed with traditional police powers. The Control Service is a specially established top local anti-money laundering institution under the supervision of the Cabinet of Ministers. It receives,

---

57   C. Stefanou, S. White, and H. Xanthaki, *OLAF at the Crossroads: Action against EU Fraud*, Hart Publishing, p. 24.
58   *Ibid.*, p. 25.

processes and analyses reports on suspicious financial transactions and provides this information to a pre-trial investigatory body (Finance Police and KNAB), court authorities as well as to the Prosecutor's Office. The Financial Police would then make decisions on commencing criminal procedures.

However, the question remains: how effective are these Latvian authorities? Firstly, over the years the Control Service has been criticized as ineffective, and recently it has been criticized by the Minister of Finance as "the weakest link among the country's safeguards against the funnelling of illicit proceeds".[59] Secondly, the State Audit Office indicates that more than 45 per cent of criminal proceedings in financial crimes are terminated due to limitation periods of criminal liability entering into effect.[60] As the chief of the Criminal Police Department for Economic Crimes (ENAP) P. Bauska clarified, many criminal cases under his authority could not be successfully transferred to the prosecution because the cases are complex and this particularly applied to cases where a cross-border element is present.[61] P. Bauska gave an example of a foreigner arriving in Latvia with fraudulent identification documents and committing a large-scale money laundering which is covered by the limitation period of 15 years. When, after conducting all the necessary investigatory steps, it becomes apparent that the person cannot be identified, the authorities simply wait for the limitation period to enter into effect. However, on a positive note, a new remuneration system established a bonus scheme for employees entrusted with the investigation and detection of economic crimes, which is very motivating. In 2017, ENAP initiated five criminal proceedings for improper use of the EU structural funds, which resulted in unlawfully obtained support from the European Union Structural Funds to the amount of €7,581,802. These criminal proceedings involved four cases of large-scale fraud or committed in an organized group. Eventually, three cases have been transferred for prosecution. As a result of these crimes, the Rural Support Service and the Latvian Investment and Development Agency suffered material losses of €474,970.

14.2.2   Latvian Participation in the Institutions and Bodies Entrusted in the Fight Against Crimes Against the Financial Interests of the EU

A need for the PIF Directive and the establishment of the European Public Prosecutor's Office (EPPO) is dictated by a pressing need to ensure that EU financial interests are duly protected. This need stems from the fact that the Member States themselves do not feel

---

59   https://eng.lsm.lv/article/society/society/finance-minister-anti-money-laundering-office-has-been-the-weakest-link.a289869/.

60   I. Helmane, Ekonomisko noziegumu apkarošana: likumu netrūks, bet tie jāievieš, available in Latvian at: https://lvportals.lv/norises/296381-ekonomisko-noziegumu-apkarosana-likumu-netruks-bet-tie-jaievies-2018.

61   Ibid.

the loss following from the fraud that affects the EU's financial interest. The European Anti-Fraud Office (OLAF) together with the Latvian Ministry of Finance, will usually oversee if there are any fraudulent actions with EU funds. So OLAF and the Ministry of Finance, instead of the EU itself, would see whether there is a need to investigate. And because it is all done in a very passive way (unless significant damage is suffered concurrently by the local authorities), the Regulation on EPPO[62] seeks to rectify the status quo.

Latvia was among the 17 EU Member States that signed a letter addressed to the chairman of the European Council, asking to include the matter regarding the project on the EPPO Regulation to the agenda of the 9 March 2017 meeting of the European Council.[63] Latvia's national position on this matter was supported by *Saeima*'s European Affairs Committee on 19 April 2017.[64] Generally, the EPPO project is seen as a positive step towards the protection of the EU's financial interests, since EPPO will dedicate itself fully towards the protection of those interests, whereas the Latvian procurator also has a hefty caseload to deal with. In order to be in line with the EPPO Regulation, the Latvian legislature is currently working on changes in the LCPL and other laws.[65] However, there are some concerns about the inclusion of the EPPO into Latvia's criminal justice system.[66]

Latvia is represented in the European Union's Judicial Cooperation Unit (Eurojust), and it also has supported and actively participates in the European Judicial Network (EJN).

14.2.3   Legal Actions Taken to Fight Corruption and Fraud

Currently, Latvia is experiencing one of its worst reputational crises. In 2018, the long-tolerated 'money laundering capital of Europe' came under fire and the scrutiny came not from the EU, but from the USA's Treasury's Financial Crimes Enforcement Network (FinCEN). Pursuant to Section 311 of the USA PATRIOT Act, FinCEN confirmed that the Latvian ABLV Bank is liable for multiple instances of institutionalized money laundering which catered for subjects engaged in transnational organized crime,

---

62 Council Regulation (EU) 2017/1939 of 12 October 2017 implementing enhanced cooperation on the establishment of the European Public Prosecutor's Office ('the EPPO') L 283/1, available at: https://eur-lex.europa.eu/eli/reg/2017/1939/oj.

63 Ministry of Justice of the Republic of Latvia, '20 member states confirm the creation of an European Public Prosecutor's Office' (12 October 2017). Available at: https://www.tm.gov.lv/en/news/20-member-states-confirm-the-creation-of-an-european-public-prosecutor-s-office.

64 Baltic News Network, Latvia and other EU member states will form European Public Prosecutor's Office, 20 April 2017, Ref: 224.109.109.1209, available at: https://bnn-news.com/latvia-and-other-eu-member-states-will-form-european-public-prosecutor-s-office-164093.

65 *Ibid.*

66 Latvijas Satversmes tiesa (Constitutional Court of Latvia) judgment of 7 April 2009 in *Lisbon* Case No. 2008-35-01, pp. 16, 66-67.

corruption and sanctions evasion.[67] This international scandal demonstrates the serious consequences of the lack of effective action in the fight against money laundering, corruption and fraud in Latvia. What is the situation today, and where is Latvia going? The following analysis aims to shed light on this issue.

Latvia is a party to the Council of Europe Criminal Law Convention on Corruption[68] and the Council of Europe Civil Law Convention on Corruption.[69] Latvia has joined all major international anti-corruption treaties such as the United Nations Convention against Corruption (UNCAC)[70] and the United Nations Convention against Transnational Organized Crime (UNTOC or 'Palermo Convention')[71] For example, in line with Article 8 of the Palermo Convention, Latvia adopted legislative and other measures to criminalize corruption. In 2002, the Latvian legislator implemented the Law on Prevention of Conflict of Interest in Activities of Public Officials[72] and the law establishing the Latvian Bureau for Prevention and Combating of Corruption (KNAB).[73] The Conflict of Interest Law contains compatibility provisions, which are among the strictest in Europe.[74] KNAB works closely with the Lithuanian Special Investigation Service, the National Anti-Corruption Agency of the Kyrgyz Republic, the Estonian Security Police, the Polish Central Anti-Corruption Service, the Austrian Federal Anti-Corruption Service and the British Agency for Investigation on Serious Organized Crime.[75] KNAB represents Latvia in the Council of Europe Group of States against Corruption (GRECO) attending meetings five times a year.[76]

However, despite having all the necessary instruments in place, KNAB has long suffered from inefficiency and lack of independence, which has significantly undermined its credibility among the population.[77] In recent years its performance and

---

67 Statement of Assistant Secretary for Terrorist Financing Marshall Billingslea Before the U.S. Senate Committee on Foreign Relations. Available at: https://home.treasury.gov/news/press-releases/sm464.

68 https://www.coe.int/en/web/conventions/full-list/-/conventions/treaty/173.

69 https://www.coe.int/en/web/conventions/full-list/-/conventions/treaty/174.

70 https://www.unodc.org/documents/brussels/UN_Convention_Against_Corruption.pdf.

71 https://www.unodc.org/documents/middleeastandnorthafrica/organised-crime/UNITED_NATIONS_CONVENTION_AGAINST_TRANSNATIONAL_ORGANIZED_CRIME_AND_THE_PROTOCOLS_THERETO.pdf.

72 Latvijas Vēstnesis, 69 (2644), 9 May 2002; Latvijas Republikas Saeimas un Ministru Kabineta Ziņotājs, 11, 13 June 2002.

73 Latvijas Vēstnesis, 65 (2640), 30 April 2002; Latvijas Republikas Saeimas un Ministru Kabineta Ziņotājs, 10, 23 May 2002.

74 Latvia Corruption Report, available at: https://www.ganintegrity.com/portal/country-profiles/latvia/

75 Korupcijas novēršanas un apkarošanas birojs 10 gadi. Pieejams: www.knab.lv/uploads/free/knab_10_gadi_lv.pdf.

76 https://www.knab.gov.lv/en/knab/cooperation/.

77 Country Report Latvia 2018, Assessment of progress on structural reforms, prevention and correction of macroeconomic imbalances, and results of in-depth reviews under Regulation (EU) No 1176/2011, SWD (2018) 212 final/2, p. 47.

the level of independence have improved with the appointment of a new director and a significant restructuration.[78] KNAB has adopted a mid-term report for 2018-2019 on the implementation of the Operational Strategy of the Corruption Prevention based on the new national Anti-Corruption Guidelines for the Corruption Prevention and Combating 2015-2020.[79] These improvements have led to the strengthened independence of KNAB, which led to the increase in prosecution of corruption offences, including a number of high-profile cases.[80] However, there is room to improve KNAB's effectiveness as there are still very few cases opened and even fewer prosecutions.[81]

The Public Procurement Law[82] regulates and strengthens the transparency of public procurement by ensuring the independence of institutions in charge of combating corruption and by providing practical guidance on conflicts of interest and strengthening transparency in public procurement.[83] Latvia has improved efficiency and transparency in public procurement, but not to a great extent.[84]

Latvia has also strengthened its legal anti-corruption framework by adopting (with a considerable delay[85]) the new Whistle-blower Protection Law[86] which entered into force on 1 May 2019. This law is particularly important for tackling corruption, fraud, tax evasion and violations in public procurement.

The LCL does not make explicit reference to fraud against the EU's financial interests, and it contains only general definitions of the offence, with no specific reference to the 'victim' of the crime. There are special systems and guidelines for signalling suspected irregularities.[87]

Legal actions taken by the Latvian state to fight corruption and fraud are many, but their effectiveness is of questionable quality. As recent large-scale scandals demonstrate, money laundering, corruption and trade-in influence is of great concern in Latvia.[88] Even

---

78 Country Report Latvia 2019, Assessment of progress on structural reforms, prevention and correction of macroeconomic imbalances, and results of in-depth reviews under Regulation (EU) No 1176/2011, COM (2019) 150 final, p. 52.
79 Guidelines for the Corruption Prevention and Combating 2015-2020 (approved according to the Cabinet of Ministers Order No. 393 of 16 July 2015).
80 Country Report Latvia 2019, COM (2019) 150 final, p. 52.
81 https://eng.lsm.lv/article/society/society/finance-minister-anti-money-laundering-office-has-been-the-weakest-link.a289869/.
82 Latvijas Vēstnesis, 254 (5826), 29 December 2016.
83 C. Klein and R. Price, 'Improving Public Sector Efficiency for More Inclusive Growth in Latvia' (2015) OECD Economics Department Working Papers, No. 1254, OECD Publishing, Paris, https://doi.org/10.1787/5jrw57p59bxx-en.
84 Country Report Latvia 2018, SWD (2018) 212 final/2, p. 46.
85 Country Report Latvia 2018, SWD (2018) 212 final/2.
86 Latvijas Vēstnesis, 210 (6296), 24 October 2018.
87 Report from the Commission to the European Parliament and the Council on Protection of the European Union's financial interests – Fight against fraud 2014, Annual Report, pp. 16-17.
88 Country report Latvia 2019, COM (2019) 150 final, p. 52.

though the fight against corruption was one of the key campaign issues for the Latvian parliamentary elections of 6 October 2018,[89] Latvia is still considered by many as the money laundering capital of Europe.

14.2.4   *Money Laundering*

The LCL criminalizes money laundering (Article 195, LCL). The Directive (EU) 2015/849 of the European Parliament and of the Council of 20 May 2015 on the prevention of the use of the financial system for the purposes of money laundering or terrorist financing (the fourth AML Directive), is another EU legislation related to combating corruption. At the time when the fifth AML Directive[90] has already been adopted by the EU (transposition deadline 10 January 2020), Latvia still failed to comply with the previous version of this legislation.[91] In July 2017, the Commission started an infringement procedure under Article 258 TFEU for non-compliance, issuing a reasoned opinion in July 2018 and giving Latvian authorities two months to comply.[92] At the same time, in July 2018, the Council of Europe Committee of experts on the evaluation of anti-money laundering measures and the financing of terrorism (MONEYVAL) published its report on Latvia's AML system.[93] The AML Report fell like a bomb, exposing the blatant inefficiencies of Latvia's AML system and demonstrating that AML monitoring, investigations and sanctions essentially worked only on paper.[94] The report listed 15 areas where the Latvian government had to improve. On a positive note, the report noted that Latvia proactively and effectively cooperates with foreign counterparts.[95]

As a result of these external pressures, Latvia has embarked on an ambitious reform for improving its AML/counter terrorist financing system. In 2019, the Latvian

---

89   A. Robert, Latvian elections approach under high tension, 7 September 2018, Latvia: the eurozone thriller, https://www.euractiv.com/section/economy-jobs/news/latvian-elections-approach-under-high-tension/
90   Directive (EU) 2018/843 of the European Parliament and of the Council of 30 May 2018 amending Directive (EU) 2015/849 on the prevention of the use of the financial system for the purposes of money laundering or terrorist financing.
91   Transposition deadline: 26 June 2017.
92   European Parliament Parliamentary questions, 7 January 2019, Question reference: E-005065/2018, available at: www.europarl.europa.eu/doceo/document/E-8-2018-005065-ASW_EN.html.
93   Council of Europe, Committee of experts on the evaluation of anti-money laundering measures and the financing of terrorism (Moneyval), Anti-money laundering and counter-terrorist financing measures Latvia Fifth Round Mutual Evaluation Report, MONEYVAL (2018) 8, available at: https://rm.coe.int/moneyval-2018-8-5th-round-mer-latvia/16808ce61b.
94   Country Report Latvia 2019, COM (2019) 150 final, pp. 52, 25.
95   Anti-money laundering and counter-terrorist financing measures Latvia Fifth Round Mutual Evaluation Report, MONEYVAL (2018) 8.

government has implemented 12 measures, including the amendments to the Law on the Prevention of Money Laundering and of Terrorist Financing of 2008.[96] In essence, the amended law imposed a ban on servicing shell companies.[97] The reform package simultaneously complied with the provisions of the fourth and fifth AML Directives. It has been reported that Latvia has achieved substantial progress in tackling money laundering. For instance, in June 2019, the government has revealed that the Latvian authorities have already frozen €83.2 million in assets to prevent money laundering, which is five times that of the same period in 2018 and eliminated over 17,000 shell companies.[98]

Despite these national legislative developments, the Commission analysis of 2019 on the effectiveness of Latvia's AML/counter terrorist financing legislative framework draws a dire picture. Even though the adequate legal instruments are in place, Latvia is facing the most substantial challenges in view of the substantial length of proceedings. Further significant work is necessary to improve the effectiveness of investigation and enforcement.[99]

14.3 IMPLEMENTATION OF THE PIF DIRECTIVE

14.3.1 Reactions to the PIF Directive and Its Transposition

The preceding PIF Convention was drawn in general terms, and there was no common definition of fraud falling within the scope of the Convention. Likewise, there were no common types and levels of sanctions when the criminal offences affecting the financial interest of the EU are committed. Therefore the Commission sought to implement the directive to ensure a common system in all Member States.

During Latvia's presidency in 2015, the Latvian Ministry of Justice participated in deliberations on the final draft of the PIF Directive together with the European Parliament and the other Member States. Agreeing on the final draft of the Directive

---

96 Latvian AML Law, Latvijas Vēstnesis, 116 (3900), 30 July 2008, available in English at: https://likumi.lv/ta/en/id/178987-law-on-the-prevention-of-money-laundering-and-terrorism-financing, amendments of AML Law: Latvijas Vēstnesis; Number: 129 (6468); Publication date: 2019-06-28, available at: https://www.vestnesis.lv/op/2019/129.7.

97 https://www.mk.gov.lv/en/aktualitates/saeima-imposes-ban-servicing-shell-companies.

98 S. Sabajevs, Press Secretary of the Prime Minister, 'PM: Latvia passes ambitious reforms to fight financial crime', Cabinet of Ministers, 13 June 2019, available at: https://www.mk.gov.lv/en/aktualitates/pm-latvia-passes-ambitious-reforms-fight-financial-crime.

99 EU Justice scoreboard 2019, Communication from the Commission to the European Parliament, the Council, the European Central Bank, the European Economic and Social Committee and the Committee of the Regions, COM (2019) 198/2, available at: https://ec.europa.eu/info/sites/info/files/justice_scoreboard_2019_en.pdf, p. 21.

was very difficult. The most contentious part was to agree on the issue of VAT, which was hotly debated.

The provisions on VAT became a stumbling block in deliberations as both the Commission and European Parliament insisted that it is necessary, yet the many Member States disagreed and resisted including the relevant provisions into the draft text of the directive. All Member States collect VAT, but the part that goes directly to the EU budget is very small, not exceeding 1.5 to 2 per cent of the sums collected. So, many Member States insisted that this amount does not have much influence on the EU's budget. For example, if there are some fraudulent actions with VAT payments, the Member State concerned will be at a loss as it would lose much more by not receiving the VAT payment in its entirety. This situation was contrasted to 2 per cent VAT payments that go to the EU budget, concluding that Member States' interests are affected much more by this issue.

While the European Parliament insisted on including fraud with VAT, the Council of the EU upheld the position of the general approach supported by many Member States. In the draft PIF Directive, the Council provided in Article 2 on the definition of the Union's financial interests that "revenues arising from VAT shall be excluded from the scope".[100] In the Council's view, this was the best compromise aimed to align interests of the Member States, the Commission and the European Parliament. However eventually, the best compromise was the current definition of Article 2 which introduces a threshold to define serious offences against the common VAT system only when total damage is above an established threshold of at least €10,000,000. This was a compromise reached during the negotiations; in order to exclude cases of minor fraud, the threshold was set up, which would trigger the applicability of the directive to the case.

Other matters did not cause much discussion during the negotiation phase. The PIF Directive was seen as a positive step by the Latvian legislator, and since much of PIF provisions are already part of the LCL, no difficulties in implementation have been envisaged.

The institution in charge of the implementation of the Directive is the Criminal Law Department (*Krimināltiesību departaments*) of the Ministry of Justice. The draft amendment project went through the inter-ministerial discussion and has been agreed upon by all the ministries who participated in its drafting and who will eventually be affected by it. There was not a single dissent among the ministers as regards the provisions of the PIF needing implementing. Sometimes it so happens that when a draft law project is under discussion, special committees are formed in order to reach a compromise agreement on the final text. In the case of the PIF Directive, everything went smoothly, and there was no dissent among those participating in its drafting. The draft law could have been implemented in August 2018, when it was finalized.

---

100 Council of the EU, Note, 3 June 2013, 10232/13, at p. 12, available at: http://data.consilium.europa.eu/doc/document/ST-10232-2013-INIT/en/pdf.

However, the progress on implementation of the necessary provisions was put on hold by the outgoing government due to upcoming general elections to the *Saeima* on 6 October 2018. So if the draft law had been sent to the *Saeima* in August 2018, the parliament would not have time to pass it in three readings. Therefore, the newly elected *Saeima* would have to start the process all over again. As a result, following the approval of the new government, the draft law was forwarded to *Saeima,* and there was still sufficient time until the implementation deadline of 6 July 2019. It was anticipated that the law would be passed swiftly, as provisions relating to the PIF Directive do not significantly change or alter the current LCL. In October 2018, Latvia, together with all other Member States, participated in a first meeting organized by the Commission on the implementation of the PIF Directive into national law so as to address any difficulties and questions.

On 23 October 2018, the Latvian government supported the draft law 'Amendments to the Criminal Law', which intended to implement the PIF Directive. The parliament adopted the law on 6 June 2019, which is one month before the implementation deadline.[101] The Amendments to the LCL aimed to strengthen the protection against this type of crime by preventing fraud and other illegal activities in the area of the EU's financial interests.

14.3.2 Issues to be Solved in Legislation Implementing the PIF Directive

In order to evaluate the level of protection provided by Latvian criminal law regarding the EU's financial interests, it is necessary to analyse implementation for the most important articles of the PIF Directive. The following contains a summary assessment. There were *three* major discrepancies between the PIF Directive and the Latvian LCL. Therefore, the Latvian legislature had to implement three amendments in order to be in line with the EU provisions.

14.3.3 Article 12 – Limitation Periods

The first issue was the limitation period. When the directive was deliberated, the limitation period caused a lot of discussion and arguments, since it was a novelty for the EU harmonizing legislation. Never before had an EU Directive had a limitation period coveted in its scope. However, since this directive was so important for the EU in order to guarantee the protection of its own financial interests, the Commission very much insisted that there should be a limitation period implemented. Harmonizing

---

101 Latvijas Vēstnesis, 19 June 2019., Nr. 123 (6462).

national limitation periods would make it possible for the law to apply over a sufficient period of time in order to ensure that the infringements can be effectively addressed.

Essentially, the directive aimed to introduce a limitation period of criminal liability for enforcing the sentence which applies following a final sentence. This limitation period has to be established at a considerable level, allowing for effective prosecution. Article 12 (4) of the directive provides for such a limitation period for enforcing the sentence, obliging the Member States to take the measures necessary to ensure that:

a. penalty of more than one year of imprisonment; *or alternatively*

b. a penalty of imprisonment in the case of a criminal offence which is punishable by a maximum sanction of at least four years of imprisonment, imposed following a final conviction for a criminal offence referred to in Article 3, 4 or 5, *for at least five years from the date of the final conviction*.

There was inconsistency across national laws; in some Member States, limitation periods would apply similarly to Article 4(a) and in others similarly to Article 4(b). However, irrespective of how the limitation periods applied in a given Member State, the PIF Directive required the limitation period to be for at least five years.

The limitation period for the enforcement of a conviction under Article 62 LCL is consistent with the system laid down in Article 12(4)(a) PIF Directive, that is to say, depending on the type and duration of the sentence imposed. In Latvia, the decisive element of the applicable limitation period is the sentence allocated by the court, irrespective of what the LCL proscribes. For example the LCL proscribes penalties between three and ten years, but what is determinative, is the type and duration of the final sentence issued by the court (e.g., three, five or ten years). Since the Latvian system on applicable limitation period is based on the type and duration of the final sentence, it is similar to the system laid down in PIF Directive Article 12(4)(a); there is a correlation between the penalty imposed and the limitation period applicable.

At the same time, under Article 62(1)(2) LCL, the final conviction shall not be executed, if, from the day when it comes into legal effect, it has not been executed *within three years*, if the deprivation of liberty has been adjudged for a period *not exceeding two years*. Therefore, under the previous version of the LCL, if the deprivation of liberty has been adjudged for a period *of two years* it would be subject to a limitation period *of three years*, which did not correspond to the five-year period laid down in Article 12(4) of the directive. So the necessary amendment to the LCL was to eliminate the distinction between the length of the allocated penalty and the limitation period. As a result, Article 62(1)(2) LCL was deleted from the legislative text with the 2019 amendment. Now irrespective of the sentence (whether it is two, three or five years) the limitation period will always be five years.

14.3.4 Article 7 – Penalties for Natural Persons and Article 8 – Aggravating Circumstance

The second and third issues to be solved by the Latvian legislator in order to comply with the PIF Directive related to penalties. In all paragraphs of the LCL, all penalties correlated to penalties established in the PIF Directive, save for the two following discrepancies.

Firstly, Article 7(3) of the PIF Directive on sanctions to natural persons provides that Member States must ensure that the criminal offences referred to in Articles 3 and 4 are punishable by a maximum penalty of at least *four years* of imprisonment when they involve considerable damage or advantage which involves more than €100,000.

Under Article 210 LCL, when a person knowingly provides incorrect information upon obtaining subsidies or during the period of use of the subsidies and if this causes considerable damage to the State or to protected interests of other persons, it constitutes a criminal offence similar to the one provided under Articles 3(2)(a)(b)(c) of the PIF Directive. Pursuant to Article 210 LCL, the penalty provided for the said offence was *one year* of imprisonment or temporary deprivation of liberty or community service or a fine. As a result, here was a discrepancy between the Latvian and the EU penalties, where national provisions provided for a significantly milder penalty. To rectify this discrepancy, the amended Article 210 LCL now provides for four years of imprisonment. The same can be said for Article 217(2) LCL on breach of accounting and statistical information and Article 275 LCL on forgery of documents, which envisaged a maximum penalty of *at least three years*. Therefore, in order to comply with the provisions of Article 7(3), there is a change of increasing the imprisonment *from three to four years*.

Secondly, it should be noted that the Latvian provisions on sanctions could be seen as stricter than those provided in the directive. Article 20 of the Procedures for the Coming into Force and Application of The Criminal Law[102] provides that the considerable damage shall be *not less than* the total of 50 minimum monthly wages (which is equivalent to €21,500).

14.3.5 Article 3 – Fraud Affecting the Union's Financial Interests

The PIF Directive Article 3 contains the definition of fraud affecting the Union's financial interests. The corresponding national provisions are scattered across the LCL, so that that the Latvian legislator had gone through the relevant provisions of the LCL to seek out the inconsistencies with the PIF definition. The drafters concluded that the fraud activities referred to in PIF Article 3 are not only related to classic cases of fraud covered by Article 177 of the LCL but also to other types of offences such as: Article 179 on

---

102 Latvijas Vēstnesis, 331/332 (1392/1393), 4 November 1998.

misappropriation, Article 210 on fraudulent obtaining and use of subsidies, credit and loans, Article 217 on violation of accounting rules, Article 218 on tax evasion, Article 275 on forgery of documents, Article 177(1) on fraud in an automated data processing system and Article 180 on theft, fraud and misappropriation on a small scale. Therefore, the Latvian legislator concluded that there is no need to draft a separate article in the LCL or implement a separate legislative act dealing with actions listed in PIF Article 3. Otherwise, the legislator would have to repeat everything that is already protected by existing articles.

As regards Article 210 on subsidies fraud, it should be noted that the government has established a special European Union Funds Audit Department in the Ministry of Finance which oversees the usage of subsidies and grants by inspecting whether there is any fraud. Prior to the 2012 amendments,[103] there was no reference to subsidies in the LCL, so the Latvian legislator added a specific provision covering subsidies making any fraud relating to subsidies fall under the provisions of the LCL.

As regards VAT fraud, the PIF only applies if considerable damage is caused. If there is no considerable damage, it would not amount to a criminal offence and could potentially be an administrative offence instead. However, this is not the case in Latvia. For example, if one fraudulently claims to have overpaid VAT with the purpose of having the government reimburse it, then it is not treated as tax evasion, but as a classic act of fraud which is criminally punishable under Article 177 LCL.

It is interesting to note that the PIF Directive also envisages in Article 7(4) that when the damage is less than €10,000, then the Member States may provide for other sanctions (e.g., administrative). Still, in Latvia, it is very straightforward – if it is a fraud, then right from the €1 damage, it becomes a criminal liability. Every now and then, there are political discussions stating that small amount frauds should be de-criminalized, but it has not happened yet, as there are no suitable instruments for investigation in the administrative process which do exist in the criminal process.

14.3.6   *Article 4(2) – Passive/Active Corruption*

Most provisions dealing with corruption are found in a new special Chapter XXIV of the LCL on Criminal Offences Committed in State Authority Service. The national provisions on corruption offences fully comply with the requirements of PIF Directive Article 4(2)(3)(4).

---

103 Latvijas Vēstnesis, 27 December 2012., Nr. 202 (4805).

14.3.7   Article 6 – Liability of Legal Persons and Article 9 – Sanctions with Regard to Legal Persons – Criminal Responsibility of Legal Persons

Liability of legal persons is a relatively new concept in the Latvian legal system; before 1999, only factual perpetrators would be punished, while the legal entity would escape any punishment, which could result in future criminal conduct. Amendments to LCL introduced liability of legal persons in 2005.[104] The liability is coercive, and there is no criminal responsibility. In practice, the sanctions are rarely applicable, making it a rather symbolic legislation. Criminal law is not applicable to legal entities on its own due to the subjective side of the criminal offence of legal entities. Articles 4(1)(1) and 12 LCL now provide for liability for legal persons, while Chapter VIII.1 specifically deals with coercive measures applicable to legal persons. It is possible to apply to a legal entity one of the following primary coercive means: liquidation, limitation of rights, confiscation of property and recovery of funds. In addition to these primary coercive means, it is possible to apply the following supplementary coercive means: confiscation of property and indemnification.

14.4   CONCLUSION

This chapter examined the role of the EU criminal law in the Latvian system of criminal justice. The breadth of legislative amendments implemented by the Latvian government in order to comply with the EU criminal law has been a significant one. There was a significant impact on both substantial and procedural law as both Latvian Criminal Law and the Criminal Procedure Law were modified to comply with the requirements of EU law. Other special criminal laws such as, for example, the Law on the Processing of Personal Data in Criminal and Administrative Offenses and the Law on the Prevention of Money Laundering and Terrorism and Proliferation Financing were also implemented to give effect to EU criminal legislation. Liability of legal persons for criminal offences has also been introduced as an element of the Latvian system of criminal justice. By the same token, the protection of the financial interests of the EU has taken centre stage in the puzzle of the Latvian judicial system producing a significant impact on the national substantial and procedural criminal law. It could be argued that the Latvian legislature outperformed many fellow Member States as it has promptly and fully implemented the PIF Directive in its LCL.

However, the analysis of the national provisions has revealed that the practical impact of these changes could be improved by further development and approximation of national provisions. In addition, new legislative measures which aim to enhance the protection of Latvia's financial interests are being constantly developed and

---

104 Latvijas Vēstnesis, 25 May 2005., Nr. 82 (3240).

implemented, such as the Public Procurement Law which has entered into force in 2017.[105] Since the legislative measures aimed at the protection of Latvian financial interests are constantly evolving, the protection of the EU's financial interests is simultaneously evolving with them.

---

105 Latvijas Vēstnesis, 29 December 2016, 254 (5826).

15 SELECTED CASE STUDIES: THE CASE STUDY OF MALTA (MT)

Stefano Filletti

15.1 IMPLEMENTING THE PIF DIRECTIVE IN MALTA

The PIF Directive has been implemented in Malta through sporadic legislative amendments and administrative interventions. When dealing with substantive crimes relating to the protection of the financial interests of the European Union, the Maltese Criminal Code already contains relative provisions referring to various instances of fraud[1] which adequately cover the offences within the PIF Directive. One can identify, *inter alia,* the offence of misappropriation,[2] obtaining money by false pretences[3] and the catch-all 'other fraudulent gain'.[4] The offence is aggravated if the perpetrator is a public officer or a person vested with some form of entrustment as well as aggravated by amount.

Malta also has an established solid anti-corruption legal framework[5] providing for bribery[6] (active and passive bribery of domestic public officials) and trading in influence.[7] The sanction in respect of bribery of public officials is imprisonment for a period of six months to eight years.[8] In the case of a magistrate or judge, the term of imprisonment can range from 18 months to 10 years, and in the case of a member of parliament, the sanction is imprisonment for a term from one year to eight years.[9] In addition to imprisonment, a person convicted of bribery may also be punished with temporary or perpetual interdiction, i.e., disqualification from holding a public office or employment with the public sector.[10] The punishment for trading in influence is imprisonment for a term of three years.

---

1 Section 293 *et seq,* Cap. 9, Laws of Malta.
2 Section 293, Cap. 9, Laws of Malta.
3 Section 308, Cap. 9, Laws of Malta.
4 Section 309, Cap. 9, Laws of Malta.
5 Council of Europe, Group of States against corruption (2009) *Third Evaluation Round: Evaluation Report on Malta, op. cit.,* pp. 18-19, paragraphs 94-95.
6 Chapter 9, Laws of Malta.
7 Arts. 115, 120 and 121A of the Criminal Code.
8 *Ibid.,* Art. 115.
9 *Ibid.,* Arts. 116-118.
10 *Ibid.,* Art. 119.

The Criminal Code contains provisions regarding prescription[11] (statute of limitation rules). The length of prescription varies according to the gravity of the offence, which is generally reflected by the punishment. For example, active/passive bribery of public officials with a maximum punishment of eight years imprisonment[12] has a prescription period of 10 years, and active/passive bribery of judges with a maximum punishment of 10 years imprisonment[13] has a prescription period of 15 years. The Criminal Code provisions on active and passive bribery also apply to corruption in the private sector.[14] Corporate liability for corruption offences is also specifically dealt with in the Criminal Code,[15] which states that where the person found guilty of a bribery offence is the director, manager, secretary or other principal officer of a body corporate or has the power to represent, take decisions or bind the body corporate, and the offence was committed for the benefit of that body corporate, then such person is deemed to be vested with the legal representation of the body corporate, which shall be liable to a fine.

The Code also criminalizes the conspiracy to commit an offence,[16] the attempt[17] and complicity in an attempt[18] of a criminal offence.

15.2 MALTA'S EFFORTS IN COMBATING FINANCIAL CRIME AND PROTECTING THE FINANCIAL INTERESTS OF THE EU

Combating financial crime and protecting the financial interests of the EU requires effective implementation of EU legal norms in the domestic scenario. This requires not only the actual amendment of the law but also an effective implementation by local authorities and a correct application of specialized investigative legal instruments. When dealing with financial crime and more, in particular, the protection of the EU's financial interests, the following local key players can be identified:

The Attorney General (AG)[19] is the designated competent authority within the EJN and Eurojust, which is empowered to facilitate cooperation with other supranational agencies in Malta. The AG is not only formally represented in Eurojust[20] and actively participates in matters of coordination and facilitation of criminal activity of mutual concern, but is also the national contact point within the EJN. Within the AG's office, it is the Criminal Matters Unit, more specifically the International Cooperation Office,

---

11 Chapter 9, Laws of Malta. *See* Arts. 687-694.
12 Art. 115(c) of the Criminal Code.
13 *Ibid.*, Art. 116(a).
14 *Ibid.*, Art. 121(3).
15 *Ibid.*, Art. 121D.
16 Section 48A, Cap. 9, Laws of Malta.
17 Section 41, Cap. 9, Laws of Malta.
18 Section 42, Cap. 9, Laws of Malta.
19 Established in virtue of the Attorney General Ordinance, Cap. 90 Laws of Malta.
20 http://eurojust.europa.eu/about/structure/college/Pages/national-members.aspx.

which is responsible for coordinating activities with the respective contact points within the network.

It is also possible for the Minister for Justice to communicate requests to a Magistrate. Article 649(3) provides that:

> where the Minister responsible for justice communicates to a magistrate a request made by the judicial authority of any place outside Malta for the examination of any witness present in Malta, touching an offence cognizable by the courts of that place, the magistrate shall examine on oath the said witness on the interrogatories forwarded by the said authority or otherwise, notwithstanding that the accused were not present, and shall take down such testimony in writing.

This residual power vested in the Minister for Justice is essential. Whereas the AG is generally the first contact point for such a request it is also clear that for the AG to handle such a request, it must have been issued within the framework of a treaty, convention or agreement based on the principle of mutual assistance as per Section 649 (2) of the Criminal Code.[21]

In all other cases, where the AG is not competent to act, requests for cooperation can be made to the Minister of Justice who would then proceed, if he so accepts and agrees, to forward such a request to a Magistrate in Malta. Procedures under this subsection would also require the consent and political discretion of the Minister for Justice, depending on the case and its circumstances. This power can be seen as an umbrella, or catch-all, provision to allow for incoming requests to be processed even if they do not fall within the strict parameters of a treaty or come from the AFSJ.

The Economic Crimes Unit is a specialized unit within the Maltese Police Force,[22] and it is the special branch or unit which liaises mostly with Europol. The Economic Crime Unit handles all investigations relating *inter alia* to offences against property, corruption, embezzlement, theft, all forms of fraud, money laundering and white-collar crime. The Economic Crime Unit, therefore, is authorized to act as the official interlocutor with Europol. It is empowered to forward and request sensitive and relative data in the course of investigations as well as to request or provide assistance within Europol channels in the course of an investigation.

Since the Economic Crime Unit is the designated national asset recovery office, it is enabled to communicate through the Camden Asset Recovery Inter-Agency Network.[23]

---

21   Cap. 9, Laws of Malta.
22   Established in virtue of the Police Act, Cap. 164, Laws of Malta.
23   This is an informal association of national contact points whose aim is to develop and improve criminal asset recovery or proceeds of crime. This network or association is open to all EU Member States reserving observer status to non-EU Member States. This association is housed within Europol.

The Economic Crimes Unit offers other assistance where requested by other specialized agencies, such as OLAF, in the course of their investigation.

The Internal Audit and Financial Investigations Unit[24] is the official interlocutor of DG OLAF in Malta. The Financial Investigations and European Anti-Fraud Office Related Matters Unit within the IAID has the remit to conduct financial investigations in government departments and in any other public or private entities which are in any way beneficiaries, debtors or managers of public funds, including EU funds, for the purpose of protecting such funds against irregularities and fraud or otherwise to assess public or private entities' liability to contribute to such funds.

Since the IAID is the designated interlocutor of DG OLAF in Malta and is the Anti-Fraud Co-Coordinating Service (AFCOS) for Malta, the IAID Unit can conduct joint investigations with OLAF, the European Anti-Fraud Office, with respect to EU funds availed of by Malta.[25] The Unit reports irregularities to DG OLAF on a quarterly basis with respect to pre-accession funds, transition facility funds, structural funds, cohesion fund and agricultural funds. The Unit also provides substantial contributions, including feedback, to various sub-units within OLAF all in charge of protecting the EU's financial interests under different facets.

- The Permanent Commission Against Corruption (PCAC) is a specialized body dealing exclusively with the investigation of alleged or suspected corrupt practices within the public administration. In 2010, a bill[26] was presented to amend the Permanent Commission Against Corruption Act and widen the scope of the PCAC to include private citizens and legal entities. The bill also provides for the appointment of a Special Prosecutor who will file reports to the police on any act or omission which, if proven, would constitute a corrupt practice; and if the Commissioner of Police fails to take action, the Special Prosecutor will make an application before the competent court. These amendments, however, are not yet in force.

- The Ombudsman is an officer of Parliament and a Commissioner for Administrative Investigations[27] who investigates and resolves citizens' grievances about government departments and public bodies.[28] The Ombudsman reports to the House of Representatives. However, the Ombudsman's recommendations are not binding, and he has no power to enforce them.

---

24 Established in virtue of the Internal Audit and Financial Investigation Act, Cap. 461 of the Laws of Malta.
25 In fact Art. 2 of Cap. 461 of the Laws of Malta defines public funds as including: "funds that Government receives, pays, including funds to local councils, or is required to manage under Malta's international obligations, or under any other public funds arising under any other law".
26 Bill 57 of 2010 – Permanent Commission Against Corruption (Amendment) Act, 2010.
27 Art. 3 of the Ombudsman Act, Chapter 385, Laws of Malta.
28 Ombudsman's Website *Mission Statement* [WWW] Ombudsman. Available at: www.ombudsman.org.mt/index.asp?pg=missionstatement, accessed 12 September 2012.

–   The National Audit Office (NAO) has a mandate to encourage accountability of
    public officers and to contribute towards better management of public funds and
    resources.[29] The Public Accounts Committee (PAC) of the House of
    Representatives is one of the standing committees of Parliament.[30] It is empowered
    to inquire into matters related to public accounts and expenditure, examine the
    accounts of statutory authorities and consider reports by the NAO and ask the
    NAO to investigate and report back to the PAC.

In combating financial crime, including the protection of the financial interests of the EU,
there are several legal tools at one's disposal:

Without a shadow of a doubt, the European Arrest Warrant (EAW) has been
successfully applied in many cases. The EAW has been successful when Malta
requested the surrender or return of a foreign national[31] or the surrender of persons
resident in Malta to a foreign jurisdiction. There is likewise, no doubt, that the EAW,
even from Malta's perspective, constitutes an important investigative and judicial tool in
combating crime. It has aided and facilitated prosecuting officers, to a large extent, in
bringing offenders to justice. With the application of the principles of mutual assistance
and recognition, the EAW is a streamlined, more efficient and less cumbersome version
of the traditional extradition process.

Another instrument of note when discussing European criminal law is that relating to
the European Evidence Warrant (EEW). This EEW is one of the strongest expressions of
mutual recognition and assistance.[32] It actually allows foreign judicial figures to request
and obtain evidence which can be found in other Member States' territory with minimal
scrutiny to be exercised by the executing or requesting State. The EEW was introduced at
the EU level in virtue of the Council Framework Decision 2008/978 JHA dated
18 December 2008. The EEW is a judicial decision in consequence of which data,
documents or any *repertus* may be lifted and obtained from another Member State. The
issuance of the warrant ought to be ordered by a judge, magistrate, court, public

---

29   Nao Website *History of the National Audit Office* [WWW] NAO. Available at: www.nao.gov.mt/page.aspx?
     id=84, accessed 12 September 2012.
30   *See* Kamra Tad-Deputati Malta Website *Parliamentary Committees: Public Accounts Committee* [WWW]
     Kamra tad-Deputati. Available at: www.parlament.mt/publicaccountscommittee, accessed 12 September
     2012.
31   In the case *Police vs Fabio Zulian*, (decided 3 January 2015, Court of Magistrates, per Magistrate Dr
     M. Hayman) a request was made for the return of the accused from Torino, Italy; in the case of *Police vs
     Dimitrios Drossos* (decided 5 September 2012, Court of Magistrates, per Magistrate Dr A. Vella) a request
     was made for the return of a Greek national from Greece; in the case of *Police vs Stephen John Smith*
     (decided 28 December 2012 Court of Magistrates) a request was made for the return of an English
     national from London, United Kingdom.
32   *See* C.C. Murphy, 'The European Evidence Warrant: Mutual Recognition and Mutual (Dis)Trust?', King's
     College London – The Dickson Poon School of Law, 1 September 2010, in Eckes and Konstadinides, eds.,
     Crime Within the Area of Freedom, Security And Justice: A European Public Order, Cambridge University
     Press, 2011.

prosecutor or judicial authority in the issuing State. The warrant would be then transmitted to the competent local authority for onward transmission to the competent local authority of the requested State for execution. This legal instrument has not been successful application-wise and, in fact, few countries have actually implemented it.

Another instrument which generates considerable interest at EU level is the cross-border enforcement of orders for the freezing of assets. Freezing orders are an essential investigative tool aimed at freezing assets in the hands of third parties, allowing for more time to conduct investigations and, more importantly, to secure the confiscation of assets upon conviction. Without such precautionary orders, assets would be dissipated even before a conviction can be secured. This tool has certain draconian effects and can be prejudicial to persons subject to similar orders. Pursuant to the application of the principle of mutual recognition and assistance, a freezing order may be issued upon a request made by a foreign competent authority,[33] pursuant to section 435C of the Criminal Code and Article 10(1) of the Prevention of Money Laundering Act.[34] The effect is similar to a civil garnishee order and is applicable to all offences. This order is governed by Article 4(6) of the Prevention of Money Laundering Act.[35]

Joint Investigative Teams[36] (JITs) are of interest because they offer the possibility for national investigative teams to work together on crimes committed in a number of jurisdictions. This is a matter which is of relevance to the central thesis hypothesis, especially when one considers that the rules of investigation and collection of evidence vary from one jurisdiction to another. There remains a thorny issue as to the probative value of illegally obtained evidence in jurisdictions where such evidence is admissible. JITs were originally envisaged in Article 13 of the 2000 MLA Convention. Given the slow ratification of the Convention, the Commission adopted an FD on JITs.[37] It was

---

33 The Framework Decision on the execution in the European Union of orders freezing property or evidence (2003/577/JHA) was transposed and implemented by means of Subsidiary Legislation number 9.13, Freezing Orders (Execution in the European Union) Regulations made under the Criminal Code, published in Legal Notice 397/07 and subsequently amended by Legal Notice 354/09.

34 Prevention of Money Laundering Act, Cap. 373 of the Laws of Malta.

35 Section 4(6) of the Prevention of Money Laundering Act: "Together with or separately from an application for an investigation order, the Attorney General may, in the circumstances mentioned in sub-article (1), apply to the Criminal Court for an order (hereinafter referred to as 'attachment order'): (a) attaching in the hands of such persons (hereinafter referred to as 'the garnishees') as are mentioned in the application all moneys and other movable property due or pertaining or belonging to the suspect; (b) requiring the garnishee to declare in writing to the Attorney General, not later than twenty-four hours from the time of service of the order, the nature and source of all money and other movable property so attached; and (c) prohibiting the suspect from transferring or otherwise disposing of any movable or immovable property."

36 The FD was implemented in local law in virtue of the Joint Investigation Teams (EU Member States) Regulations.
    Pursuant to these Regulations, the Attorney General is empowered to request the setting up of a JIT with the forces of other Member States. The terms of reference would have to be subject to a specific agreement to that effect. The overall aim would be to request for assistance in any investigation which would need to be carried out in another Member State.

37 2002/465/JHA which had to be implemented by 1 January 2003.

originally envisaged that JITs would be useful to bring together the various law enforcement agencies and forces of the various Member States. However, there was great reluctance by the Member States to actually establish and create JITs. The Hague Programme also called upon States to put forward national experts and also to promote the use of JITs.

Confiscation orders allow the Member States, subject to certain conditions, to seize and confiscate assets of subject persons in another Member State. This is an important tool to combat trans-boundary crime and to ensure the recovery of assets. This having been said, the confiscation of assets is not a matter free from legal difficulty. The FD on confiscation orders (2006/783/JHA) (as amended by FD 2009/299/JHA), the FD on Confiscation of Crime-Related Proceeds, Instrumentalities and Property (2005/212/JHA), together with the Council Directive on return of cultural objects unlawfully removed from the territory of a Member State (Directive 93/7/EEC) were all implemented into Maltese law, by virtue of S.L. 9.15, Confiscation Orders (Execution in the European Union) Regulations made under the Criminal Code, published in Legal Notice 464/10 and amended by Legal Notice 426/12. The implementation of these instruments means that it is possible for local courts to order the confiscation of assets in Malta upon a request by a foreign authority in the execution of a foreign court order to that effect.

More problematic are the ramifications of a directive proposal[38] identifying two main legislative efforts in the field of confiscation, namely,

i.   the non-conviction based confiscation of assets and
ii. third party confiscation of assets,

two areas which were found absent in the EU legal framework.[39] The current legal framework in Malta does not support the confiscation of criminal assets in the absence of a criminal conviction. Therefore, substantial amendments would need to be carried out. Furthermore, such types of confiscation are not even in line with the fundamental principles embraced in the penal code, namely, that there can only be the forfeiture of a *corpus delicti* (in this case being the proceeds of crime) strictly as a consequence of a conviction of a crime. This is so much so that certain alternative modes of punishment such as probation orders, conditional or unconditional discharges cannot order the

---

38 Brussels, 12 March 2012, COM (2012) 85 final, 2012/0036 (COD).
39 In fact the current legal framework on freezing and confiscation envisages the following instruments: Framework Decision 2001/500/JHA13, obliging States to enable confiscation, to allow value confiscation where the direct proceeds of crime cannot be seized and to ensure that requests from other Member States are treated with the same priority as domestic proceedings; Framework Decision 2005/212/JHA15, which harmonizes confiscation laws; Framework Decision 2003/577/JHA17, which provides for mutual recognition of freezing orders; Framework Decision 2006/783/JHA18, which provides for the mutual recognition of confiscation orders; and Council Decision 2007/845/JHA19 on the exchange of information and cooperation between national Asset Recovery Offices.

forfeiture of the *corpus delicti* simply because such judgments are not convictions at law. Even more debatable would be a confiscation order issued against a person who has not been tried or found guilty of any offence.[40] Since it is not possible, under Maltese law, to issue non-conviction-based confiscation orders, this deficiency also extends to foreign-issued non-conviction-based confiscation orders. The position is slightly different with respect to third-party confiscations. It can be argued that actually, we have one example of third-party confiscation. Under the Customs Ordinance,[41] the forfeiture occurs automatically and independently of whether the proprietor is the defendant or a third party who is not involved in the offence.[42] In addition, the forfeiture takes place independently of the knowledge of the commission of the offence in question. Furthermore, it is also possible under Maltese law to confiscate any criminal assets that have been passed on to a third party in bad faith. However, this is only possible in the case that provisional measures have already been implemented against the suspect or accused (i.e., attachment or freezing orders). In this case, by virtue of Article 4(10) and Article 6 of the PMLA, the property transferred would be liable to confiscation, and if the third-party transferee had knowledge of the illicit nature of the transfer, he might be guilty of the offence of money laundering.

There are other additional investigation measures available at the domestic level: financial criminal investigations, surveillance, infiltration and controlled deliveries.

15.3   OBSERVATIONS

There are practical difficulties when implementing and applying these instruments and measures at the domestic level. A first difficulty encountered was how to ensure the correct interpretation and application of certain trans-boundary criminal offences in Malta. Most of the offences introduced, such as money laundering and crimes protecting the financial interests of the EU, are specialized crimes requiring to a certain extent, a uniform interpretation throughout the EU and the AFSJ. Case law has shown, for instance, that there could still be language barriers and translation difficulties in executing instruments of mutual recognition between the Member States. Clearer definitions and judicial training are a must to reduce, as much as possible, wrong application and interpretation of local norms giving effect to Malta's international obligations.

When examining EAWs in Malta, it can safely be concluded that this instrument has worked with success in achieving notable results. However, at both the EU and local level,

---

40   J. Boucht, *Civil Asset Forfeiture and the Presumption of Innocence under Article 6(2) ECHR*, NJEL, 2014/2, Intersentia, 2014.
41   Cap. 37, Laws of Malta.
42   *P. v. Osama Salem Algrig*, Court of Criminal Appeal, 1992.

further action is necessary to limit the legal issues. At the EU level, the application of EAWs raises two key issues: proportionality and fair trials. With respect to proportionality, rules have to be properly streamlined and a balance sought between this procedure and the seriousness of the offence. The EAW should never be used to cover frivolous or minor offences. On the contrary, it should be reserved for the more serious offences, also taking into account the length of the applicable sentence and the cost-benefit of using this mechanism. Equally, EAWs have to lead to the surrender of individuals to legal systems which will guarantee a fair trial. This would tally with minimum rights and minimum defence rights available for every person within the AFSJ applicable with regard to any criminal trial throughout the various Member States.

A basic form of a minimum guarantee of fair trial throughout the Member States would thus be ensured. From a domestic perspective, the application of EAWs has raised issues of unnecessary delays, overstay and, in certain circumstances, lack of proportionality in the application. Regarding proportionality, selected Maltese cases have shown that where a person effectively rectifies his wrong, or even where a person firmly believes that he is unjustly prosecuted, that person would still be subjected to the execution of an EAW and surrendered to the requesting State. It may be alleged that in certain cases, the execution of the EAW was not motivated to bring justice or to vindicate the injured parties who were already satisfied with payment. These circumstances are difficult to contest, if at all, and in most cases, the real reasons to request the issuance of an EAW remain obscure. It is likewise possible that the execution of these instruments may also be affected by political motivations which are hard to detect and identify. Possible solutions, by way of remedy, could be the introduction of an obligation on the competent authority to declare, whenever challenged or requested to do so, the reasons for the return of an individual in cases where it becomes clear that either the facts for which a person was requested have been remedied or where it is abundantly clear that the punishment to be imposed would be such that it would not justify the arrest and return of an individual pursuant to an EAW, thus introducing the principle of proportionality not only at the issuance of an EAW request but also in the committal stage. Possibly a measure could be introduced whereby an individual facing judicial proceedings pursuant to an EAW abroad, would be afforded the possibility to file an application to the Criminal Court in Malta to have the request for the issuance of the EAW reviewed. It cannot be the case that justice must be done at all costs, but rather a balance ought to be struck respecting the need to sanction criminal offences while weighing the overwhelming effects EAWs have on citizens. Equally, from a purely domestic scenario, local case law has shown that EAWs may create unnecessary delays in procedural and physical overstay in Malta to the detriment of the person subject to an EAW.

Another instrument of note is the EEW, which can be considered as one of the strongest expressions of mutual recognition and assistance. It actually allows foreign judicial authorities to request and obtain evidence which can be found in other

Member States' territory with minimal scrutiny to be exercised by the executing or requesting State. This legal instrument has not been successful application-wise, and in fact, few countries have actually implemented it. Many reasons can be adduced for the poor record. At the political level, the cessation of sovereignty and control over things and persons could be considered too much and really invasive. Equally, at the political level, there is still some level of mistrust of other Member States' judicial systems and therefore receiving a judicial order for the production of evidence might not be immediately acceptable from certain jurisdictions. As has been shown, there are further practical complications worth mentioning, such as, but not limited to, the cost involved in the execution of such warrants. The execution of such warrants would additionally require the involvement of local police forces and specialized individuals, where necessary, to identify and collect the documents and data requested. These documents, according to the circumstances need to be preserved, copied or lifted, rendered secure and then transmitted back to the issuing State. All this involves procedures and monies, even more so if a particular State (for example a State specializing in financial services, including Malta) is being served with a multitude of such warrants for companies operating or registered in its jurisdiction. Moreover, such warrants could require specialized procedures given that the powers of search, seizure and retention in most cases, including in Malta, are directly linked with the investigation of a criminal offence. It is unsure whether this instrument will come into effect and whether Malta, in particular, would, if it had the opportunity, implement it. A thorny issue could be the collection of illegally obtained evidence. It is apt to note, however, that it is not clear if the evidence which would otherwise be excluded being illegally collected evidence, can still be adduced in trial simply because in terms of the requested State that is actually collecting the evidence, such evidence is either considered to be legally collected or, in any case, admissible.

A point must also be raised on the general application of instruments of mutual recognition and assistance, which is particular only to Malta. A common ground for the refusal of execution of these instruments is that of *ne bis in idem*. It is the particular definition of *ne bis in idem* which could create difficulties. Whereas the most acceptable definition would be that *ne bis in idem* would offer protection from persons not to be prosecuted twice for the same offence, Maltese law uses the term 'fact' rather than 'offence'. This necessarily means, as has been shown, that there can be cases for the refusal to execute any request even though there is no problem concerning *ne bis in idem* in the issuing State. There is not much which can be done to resolve any conflicts which may arise. The only solution would be to restrict the definition of *ne bis in idem* to bring it in line with its European counterparts. However, from a local perspective, this would go against years of court decisions and interpretation. It must not follow that for the sake of uniformity, and the smooth application of legal instruments, the principle of *ne bis in idem* as embraced in the local judicial and legal field should be narrowed.

Freezing and confiscation orders have proven to be a difficult issue. As has been shown, freezing orders have the effect of freezing all assets of the subject matter indiscriminately. Such wide application can be considered as an interference with the enjoyment of one's property. The issue in Malta is that freezing orders do not conform to any rule or principle of proportionality. Moreover, the problem similarly arises in the execution of foreign requests for the freezing of assets. If and when the Criminal Court issues a freezing order pursuant to a foreign request, all assets of the person or company concerned are frozen indiscriminately, leading very often to various difficulties. A freezing order, being precautionary in nature, has a devastating and deeply prejudicial effect on the person concerned. A person affected by a freezing order cannot operate any business whatsoever and can hardly conduct an ordinary life with access simply to a small sum of money provided for one's maintenance. Such dire consequences arising from freezing orders are untenable. A possible solution could be the introduction of a mechanism whereby it would be possible to afford discretion to the issuing court of criminal jurisdiction to limit the effects of the order. The only reasonable solution would be to allow the court the means to calculate or quantify any rewards received in furtherance of any criminal activity and freeze that amount, rather than indiscriminately and wrongly freezing the totality of assets. This could, however, be a lengthy process involving scrutiny of evidence regarding assets, and possibly the setting up of a specialized asset management unit.

Worse still is the position with respect to foreign freezing orders. In this case, no contestation could legally be presented in a court in Malta. The only way such an order could be removed is if the foreign order would no longer be in force. It is clear that the lack of an effective remedy to challenge the issuance of freezing orders is a serious shortcoming. The effects of a freezing order are far too serious not to afford a remedy where it is alleged that the freezing order is being issued for an offence which does not amount to or rather should not amount to an offence warranting the issuance of a freezing order. The national courts should always retain a residual, albeit very limited, discretion in issuing orders to ensure the proper and correct application of the law. Arguing that a remedy does exist, and yet admit that the remedy to this situation is that challenge proceedings may be brought in the issuing State, cannot be enough.

Confiscation orders usually follow convictions in cases where freezing orders would have been issued. It has been shown that confiscation orders have proven extremely complex to execute, especially in ranking creditors and apportioning revenues between creditors and the requesting State. Legal issues remain in giving effect to the civil liquidation of assets and the remittance of funds to the requesting State.

16   Selected Case Studies: The Case Study of Poland (PL)

Celina Nowak

16.1   Introduction

Poland has expressed interest in joining Western political and economic international organizations right after the democratic transformation and change of regime in 1989. This political declaration set a goal for an entire generation of lawyers, as it was followed by an unprecedented effort of modification of law and implementation of both the Council of Europe standards as well as the EU *acquis*. The process of harmonization of law consisted of the introduction of, on the one hand, human rights and the rule of law, and on the other, free market values and relevant legal instruments into the Polish legal framework.

Criminal law was only one of the spheres of the national legal system affected by this complex and challenging process. From a political point of view, during the EU membership negotiations, criminal law was deemed important, yet less urgent than other fields requiring legal modifications. This was one of the reasons why this chapter of negotiations was closed as one of the last ones, and thus most of the changes to criminal law were introduced just before the accession of Poland to the EU on 1 May 2004.

This chapter aims to examine the role of the EU criminal law in the Polish criminal legal system. The scope of legislative amendments conducted by the Polish legislator in order to implement the EU criminal law instruments has been quite broad. The Penal Code (PC), the Criminal Procedure Code and the Fiscal Criminal Code (FCC) were all modified. Liability of legal persons for offences has been introduced as an element of the repressive Polish law. However, the practical impact of these changes could be improved, as discussed below.

16.2   Substantive Law

Polish criminal law is mainly regulated in two separate legal acts: the Penal Code of 6 June 1997,[1] which provides for general rules of penal responsibility and defines most

---

1   Unified text in O.J. of 2018, item 1600, as amended. Hereinafter referred to as 'the PC'.

common offences, and the Fiscal Criminal Code of 10 September 1999,[2] which covers a specific area of crime, i.e., behaviours detrimental to the public financial interests. Due to this duality, the reform of the substantive criminal law related to the Polish accession to the EU had to be twofold and referred both to the Penal Code and the Fiscal Criminal Code. The scope of the changes originally made before 2004 was not broad, although subsequent amendments were made in the following years, along with the development of the EU criminal legal framework.

Before 2004, Polish criminal law had been parochial, domestically oriented and protected only the interests of Polish entities and of the Polish state. After the accession, this approach had to change, and the process of Europeanization of the Polish criminal law which stemmed from the accession has led to enlarging the scope of criminal law protection in order to cover interests of the EU and of the other EU Member States. It should be emphasized that the protection of the EU's interests is particularly important in the context of PIF offences.

The extension of the scope of the Polish criminal law protection, necessary to criminalize EU fraud, was far easier with regard to the PC, as the features of offences have been formulated in such a general manner that they may have been applied to prohibited behaviours related to all types of funds. In most cases, a change of the interpretation of the law sufficed to apply the PC provisions to EU fraud.[3] However, in some cases, a reference to national interests as protected legal goods had to be removed from definitions of financial offences in the PC (such as the definition of financial fraud in Article 297 PC), hence extending their scope to the interests of the EU.

On the other hand, prior to the Polish accession to the EU, the FCC had operated as a separate legal act referring to the financial offences against the financial interests of the Polish state and the Polish local government entities only. Therefore, the application of the FCC to EU funds was far more problematic than with regard to the PC.[4] However, before 2004, a set of amendments to the FCC was adopted to provide the EU funds with the same protection as the funds of national origin.[5] In particular, the definition of public due, together with a tax due, which are the main objects protected by the fiscal criminal law, was extended to include "the revenue of the European Union's budget or budgets managed by the Union or on its behalf" (new Article 53 paragraph 26a FCC). In addition, the definition of a taxpayer as a perpetrator of fiscal offences was extended to cover crimes against the EU's revenue (new Article 53 paragraph 30a FCC). These

---

2   Unified text in O.J. of 2018, item 1958, as amended. Hereinafter referred to as 'the FCC'.
3   Cf. E. Zielińska, 'Polskie prawo karne a ochrona interesów finansowych Wspólnot Europejskich – w przeddzień akcesji', in M. Hudzik and C. Nowak (eds.), *Instytucje i instrumenty prawne w walce z przestępczością przeciwko interesom finansowym Unii Europejskiej – prawo krajowe i perspektywa europejska. Materiały z konferencji, Warszawa, 4–7 grudnia 2003*, Warsaw, 2005, p. 36.
4   *Ibid.*, pp. 36-37.
5   The Act amending the Fiscal Criminal Code of 24 July 2003, OJ No 162, item 1569, effective from the day of Poland's accession to the EU, *i.e.*, 1 May 2004.

amendments contributed to a significant shift in the hierarchy of legal goods protected by the Polish criminal law, which has henceforth become more internationalized. This change was further confirmed by the amendments to the general provisions on public funds. Pursuant to Article 5 (1) paragraph 2 of the Act of 27 August 2009 on public finance,[6] the EU funds are considered public funds.

As a result of the legislative modifications examined above, as well as of a pro-European interpretation of the features of offences which had not been amended, one can safely say that the scope of criminalization of PIF offences under Polish criminal law had fulfilled the requirements set forth in the EU criminal law in force at the time, in particular, the 1995 PIF Convention and its Protocols. The Polish legislator did not introduce PIF offences as new types of offences per se, and so one would not find a PIF offence in the Polish Penal Code or in the Fiscal Criminal Code, but instead the legislator adjusted the already existing provisions of domestic criminal law to those provided for in EU legal instruments, by enlarging the definition of protected legal goods – as it had been done in the case of fraud, or the definition of prospective perpetrators – as it had been done with regard to corruption.[7]

As it is known, in 2017, the EU adopted the so-called PIF Directive,[8] which replaced the Convention on the protection of the European Communities' financial interests of 26 July 1995, including the Protocols thereto of 27 September 1996, of 29 November 1996 and of 19 June 1997, with effect from 6 July 2019. The Polish legislator has not undertaken any actions in order to implement this new legal instrument. One can argue this is mainly related to the fact that indeed, at this point, no additional modifications of the elements of offences set forth in the Polish law are necessary, as all the offences set forth in the 2017 directive are already criminalized in the Polish criminal law. Some other aspects of the directive, such as the effectiveness of sanctioning, would require an intervention on the side of the Polish authorities, but for political reasons, they do not constitute a priority for the current government.

It is, however, interesting to note that parallelly the fight against VAT fraud has recently become an important part of the political agenda in Poland. The current government drafted a law amending the PC which was adopted by the Parliament in 2017.[9] The new provisions aim to reinforce the fight against VAT fraud, notably by introducing several new types of invoice frauds to the PC – Article 270a PC penalizing forging, counterfeiting or altering an invoice and Article 271a PC penalizing issuing an invoice stating untrue facts. In addition, if the invoices refer to overall sums exceeding

---

6   Unified text in O.J. 2019, item 869.
7   C. Nowak, 'PIF Offences in Poland', in C. Nowak (ed.), *Evidence in EU Fraud Cases*, Warsaw, 2013, pp. 137-169.
8   Directive (EU) 2017/1371 of the European Parliament and of the Council of 5 July 2017 on the fight against fraud to the Union's financial interests by means of criminal law, OJ L 198, 28 July 2017, pp. 29-41.
9   The Act of 10 February 2017 amending the Penal Code and other statutory acts, O.J. 2017, item 244, entered into force on 1 March 2017.

five million Polish zlotys, the prohibited acts may be subject to very severe sanctions of imprisonment for a period from five up to 25 years (Article 277a PC).

It seems important to emphasize, though, that the protection of the financial interests of the EU had not been mentioned as a reason for the 2017 reform. These amendments have been focused on the internal situation and the protection of the national financial interests exclusively. Despite this generally positive opinion on the harmonization of the Polish criminal law with the EU criminal law with regard to criminalization, in particular of the PIF offences, as mentioned above, there are other deficiencies in the Polish criminal law system that leave much room for improvement. These deficiencies are both legislative and practical in nature.

Article 7 of the 2017 directive stipulates that the EU Member States should ensure that the individuals who commit criminal offences covered by the directive are punished with effective, proportionate and dissuasive criminal sanctions, including imprisonment and a maximum penalty of at least four years of imprisonment when they involve considerable damage or advantage.[10] As examined above, the criminalization of EU fraud and related offences remains divided between the Penal Code and the Fiscal Criminal Code, just like it is divided in relation to fraud against Polish public funds. Yet, the sanctions for fiscal offences are considerably lower compared to the sanctions for offences set forth in the PC. Not only is the deterrent impact of the FCC thus weaker, but also, in my view, this solution may be questionable from the point of view of the dissuasive character of these sanctions, required in the directive. A legislative intervention would be necessary in this regard.

Practical hindrances related to the protection of the EU's financial interests refer, firstly, to the recovery of assets. The Polish Penal Code provides for a set of measures allowing to forfeit benefits coming directly or indirectly from the commission of a crime. As a part of the 2017 Penal Code modifications, a new instrument extending the scope of forfeiture was added to the PC. At present, pursuant to the newly formulated Article 45 PC, in cases of serious crime and organized crime, forfeiture may apply to any assets acquired by the perpetrator five years prior to the commission of the offence which is considered benefits from crime, unless the perpetrator may produce proof otherwise. This particular measure is also applicable to assets owned by other entities (individuals, legal persons) who acquired it from the perpetrator unless they could not have suspected while acquiring the assets in question that they had come from crime (Article 45 paragraph 3 PC). In addition, the law allows to forfeit an enterprise (e.g., a company) owned by the perpetrator if this enterprise had been used in the commission of the offence.

---

10   The damage or advantage resulting from the criminal offences referred to in points (a), (b) and (c) of Art. 3(2) and in Art. 4 shall be presumed to be considerable where the damage or advantage involves more than €100,000. The damage or advantage resulting from the criminal offences referred to in point (d) of Art. 3(2) and subject to Art. 2(2) shall always be presumed to be considerable.

Not only are these measures questionable from the constitutional point of view due to a reversed burden of proof required, but also they are hardly applied in practice. Sometimes the courts lack knowledge on the material situation of perpetrators, and often the perpetrator formally possesses no assets whatsoever. In result, whereas asset recovery should be a priority in proceedings referring to PIF offences as well as any financial crime, the practical observations indicate otherwise. Only small amounts of funds are recoverable, hence the weakness of the Polish system of asset recovery. The practical implementation of EU criminal law in these matters has not been fully achieved.

As mentioned elsewhere,[11] the overall annual number of cases of PIF offences detected in Poland is rather low. On top of that, in many of those cases, the proceedings are discontinued due to a failure to qualify the alleged criminal behaviour as an offence. Most of the notifications on a suspected PIF offence are made by administrative authorities, which seem compelled to submit such a notification in case of any irregularity they come across in their activities.[12] On can argue that they do it out of convenience – it is easier to delegate the problem to law enforcement agencies, or precaution – the administrative officials do not want to be held liable for not reporting a crime in the rather unlikely event the unreported irregularity actually constitutes an offence. In any case, it seems desirable that law enforcement agencies increase their efforts in order to improve the investigation of PIF crimes.

It must be noted that the modifications of the Polish criminal law stemming from the EU law also referred to other issues than the protection of the financial interests of the EU and the fight against EU fraud. Other third pillar legal instruments were implemented in the Polish criminal law as well. For instance, new types of offences were introduced into the Polish PC, which covered corruptive behaviours (Articles 228-229 PC on the corruption of foreign public officials[13]) and cybercrime (sexual cybercrimes and non-sexual cybercrimes introduced in a series of amendments to the PC between 2004 and 2008[14]). In 2004, a new definition of an offence of terrorist character was provided for in the general part of the PC (Article 120 paragraph 20 PC[15]), but as an aggravating

---

11   *See* C. Nowak, 'PIF Offences in Poland', *op. cit.* at p. 164.

12   *Ibid.*

13   *See* more in C. Nowak, *Korupcja w polskim prawie karnym na tle uregulowań międzynarodowych*, C.H. Beck, Warszawa, 2008.

14   *See* more in C. Nowak, *Wpływ procesów globalizacyjnych na polskie prawo karne*, wyd. Wolters Kluwer, Warszawa, 2014, 332ff.

15   Which stipulates as follows: "A terrorist offence is a prohibited act subject to the penalty of deprivation of liberty with the upper limit of at least five years, committed in order to: 1) seriously intimidate many persons; 2) to compel public authority of the Republic of Poland or of the other State or of international organization agency to undertake or abandon specific actions; 3) cause serious disturbance to the constitutional system or to the economy of the Republic of Poland, of the other State or international organization – and a threat to commit such an act."

circumstance, not a separate type of an offence. Regrettably, the said provision is not fully harmonized with the EU law, as stated by the European Commission in 2007.[16]

The accession to the EU also required amending the rules on jurisdiction. The general provisions in this regard are set forth in the PC. The Polish jurisdiction applies, of course, to acts committed within the territory of the Republic of Poland, or on a Polish vessel or aircraft. It also covers actions committed by Polish citizens abroad, and applies to aliens who have committed an offence abroad against the interests of the Republic of Poland, a Polish citizen, a Polish legal person or a Polish organizational unit not having legal personality and to aliens who have committed a terrorist offence abroad, provided these acts are likewise recognized as an offence by a law in force in the place of its commission (Article 111 paragraph 1 PC). Also, pursuant to Article 112 PC, notwithstanding the provisions in force in the place of the commission of the offence, the Polish penal law applies to a Polish citizen or an alien in case of the commission of: 1) an offence against the internal or external security of the Republic of Poland; 2) an offence against Polish offices or public officials; 3) an offence against essential economic interests of Poland; 4) an offence of false deposition made before a Polish office; 5) an offence from which any material benefit has been obtained, even indirectly, within the territory of the Republic of Poland. The latter provision covers acts of economic character detrimental to the EU.

The Polish jurisdiction with regard to Polish citizens was also expanded in order to cover tax and customs offences that they commit abroad against the financial interests of the EU (new Article 3 Section 3a FCC). In addition, the FCC was to be applied to Polish citizens as well as foreigners who while sojourning in the territory of the Republic of Poland instigate or aid or abet the commission of a tax or customs offence against the EU's financial interests abroad (new Article 3 Section 5 FCC).

16.3 LIABILITY OF LEGAL PERSONS

Criminal responsibility of legal persons has been a subject of doctrinal debate in Poland since at least the 1990s. But the concept as such has been rejected, due to a theoretical premise that legal entities cannot be found guilty. However, the accession of Poland to the EU and other international organizations made the Polish legislator show more flexibility in this matter and to comply with the obligation to provide for responsibility of legal persons for offences. Hence a new statutory act, adopted in 2002, entered into force in 2003. The law in question[17] provided for the responsibility of legal persons (collective

---

16 Report from the Commission based on Article 11 of the Council Framework Decision of 13 June 2002 on combatting terrorism, COM (2007) 681 final, 6 November 2007, 5.

17 The Act of 28 October 2002 on Liability of Collective Entities for Acts Prohibited under Penalty, unified text in O.J. 2019, item 628 as amended.

entities) committed to their benefit by individuals. It has been constructed as a repressive, not criminal, liability, and therefore, it does not constitute a part of criminal law.

According to the law, the liability of a legal person depends upon a prior final and valid conviction of an individual linked to this legal person. Also, the liability may only be established with regard to some offences (enumerated in Article 16 of the Act) and when there has been a fault in choosing or supervising the individual who committed the crime, or the internal organization of the legal person did not prevent the offence from being committed. Sanctions include a financial penalty, forfeiture of assets and additional measures, for example, prohibition from taking part in public procurement procedures.

These conditions – in particular, the mechanism of consecutive liability (first an individual must be tried, and only then a legal person) – contributed to the fact that this piece of legislation has hardly ever been applied in practice. This has just been a symbolic statutory act.[18] Yet, these deficiencies have recently encouraged the government to elaborate a draft law amending the 2002 Act. The purpose of the reform, which has been submitted to the Parliament in 2019, is to modify the rules of responsibility entirely in order to make the liability of legal persons independent from the liability of individuals. The proceedings with regard to legal persons will be parallel to proceedings with regard to individuals who committed an offence to the benefit of the legal person in question. The draft foresees a possibility to open proceedings with regard to a legal person even if the authorities are unable to identify the individual within the organization who actually committed the crime. Also, according to the draft, sanctions applied to legal persons are to be increased, and they will include dissolution of a legal person (as a form of capital punishment for legal persons). The draft law may still be subject to modifications at the Parliament, but in any case, it shows that the current government is politically very committed to this reform and to making the rules of liability of legal persons effective and dissuasive, which would certainly be more in line with the EU law and in particular Article 9 of the 2017 PIF Directive.

16.4   PROCEDURAL ISSUES

Concerning the harmonization of Polish law with the EU legal framework with regard to procedural aspects of criminal law, several issues deserve particular attention. At the outset, it should be noted that the Polish legislator has consequently implemented all instruments of the cooperation in criminal matters in the EU, before and after the accession of Poland to the EU. The amendments of the Polish law were quite extensive, up to the point that the Polish Constitution of 1997 had to be amended in order to

---

18   Cf C. Nowak, *Odpowiedzialność podmiotów zbiorowych – praktyka stosowania przepisów*, in *Rola urzędów administracji państwowej w identyfikowaniu nieprawidłowości w zamówieniach publicznych. IV Międzynarodowa Konferencja Antykorupcyjna. Materiały pokonferencyjne*, Warszawa, 2014, pp. 36-47.

introduce the European Arrest Warrant (EAW) into the domestic legal order.[19] In consequence, the Polish Criminal Procedure Code of 1997[20] is generally in line with the EU instruments. There are, however, some elements of the national legal system that may require modification, especially in order to improve the detection and prosecution of EU fraud. For instance, in the Polish legal system, criminal and administrative proceedings are two separate types of proceedings. Therefore, evidence collected by OLAF within administrative proceedings could not have been upheld by Polish law enforcement authorities as such, and OLAF's report was considered just a notification of crime. For this reason, the principle *ne bis in idem* is not applicable to overlapping administrative and criminal proceedings. Furthermore, practical difficulties with investigating financial crimes have made it hard for the Polish law enforcement authorities to focus on the PIF offences committed at the domestic level.

Furthermore, Poland has been one of the EU Member States actively involved in the development of the European Public Prosecutor's Office (EPPO) and in advocating for its establishment. Despite some legislative and practical obstacles, the commitment of Poland to fight against crime, in particular, EU fraud, alongside the other EU Member States, could have never been questioned. Sadly, only recently, the situation changed. The new government which had emerged after the parliamentary elections in Fall 2015 decided not to take part in the enhanced cooperation on the establishment of the EPPO.[21] Poland is thus a non-participating Member State and will be left outside the group of Member States closely cooperating in combating PIF offences through the intermediary of this new institution. The rationale for this decision, as one may assume, has been political – the government has been quite vocal about the need to protect national sovereignty.

Furthermore, the changes made under the current government related to the organization of courts as well as the independence of the judiciary have also contributed to the weakening of the position of Poland in the EU and the hindering of the procedural cooperation in criminal matters between Poland and the other EU Member States. The CJEU preliminary ruling in case C-216/18 PPU[22] of 25 July 2018 is a very good example of how these institutional modifications might affect the cooperation between the other EU Member States and Poland. The case referred to a Polish national against whom Polish courts issued three EAWs, in order for him to be arrested and surrendered to those courts for the purpose of conducting criminal prosecutions, *inter alia*, for trafficking in narcotic drugs and psychotropic substances. The person concerned was subsequently arrested in Ireland on the basis of those EAWs

---

19 Act of 8 September 2006 amending the Constitution of the Republic of Poland, O.J. No 200, item 1471.
20 Act of 6 June 1997, unified text in O.J. 2018, item 1987, as amended.
21 *See* Council Regulation (EU) 2017/1939 of 12 October 2017 implementing enhanced cooperation on the establishment of the European Public Prosecutor's Office ('the EPPO'), OJ L 283, 31 October 2017, pp. 1-71.
22 ECLI:EU:C:2018:586.

and brought before the High Court. He informed that court that he did not consent to his surrender to the Polish judicial authorities and was placed in custody pending a decision on his surrender to them. In support of his opposition to being surrendered, the person concerned submitted, *inter alia*, that his surrender would expose him to a real risk of a flagrant denial of justice in contravention of Article 6 of the ECHR since the legislative reforms of the system of justice in the Republic of Poland deny him his right to a fair trial. In his submission, those changes fundamentally undermine the basis of the mutual trust between the authority issuing the EAW and the executing authority, calling the operation of the European arrest warrant mechanism into question.

In its decision, the Court shared the views of the person concerned and stated that "systemic or generalised deficiencies so far as concerns the independence of the issuing Member State's judiciary" have to be taken into account when executing the EAW.[23] Therefore, it must be noted that the recent transformations of the system of the judiciary in Poland put into jeopardy the effective application of EAWs issued by Polish courts and undermine the cooperation in criminal matters between Polish authorities and authorities from the other EU Member States. The available statistical data on EAW indicate that the number of warrants issued by Polish authorities and implemented by the other EU Member States has significantly decreased in recent years, noting the lowest number in 2018 in the last 10 years.[24]

16.5   COOPERATION

Concerning the horizontal aspect of cooperation, i.e., the cooperation between different Polish agencies and institutions from other EU Member States, it should be noted that in Poland there are many bodies responsible for investigating and prosecuting PIF offences,

---

23   The Court concluded as follows: "Article 1(3) of Council Framework Decision 2002/584/JHA of 13 June 2002 on the European arrest warrant and the surrender procedures between Member States, as amended by Council Framework Decision 2009/299/JHA of 26 February 2009, must be interpreted as meaning that, where the executing judicial authority, called upon to decide whether a person in respect of whom a European arrest warrant has been issued for the purposes of conducting a criminal prosecution is to be surrendered, has material, such as that set out in a reasoned proposal of the European Commission adopted pursuant to Article 7(1) TEU, indicating that there is a real risk of breach of the fundamental right to a fair trial guaranteed by the second paragraph of Article 47 of the Charter of Fundamental Rights of the European Union, on account of systemic or generalised deficiencies so far as concerns the independence of the issuing Member State's judiciary, that authority must determine, specifically and precisely, whether, having regard to his personal situation, as well as to the nature of the offence for which he is being prosecuted and the factual context that form the basis of the European arrest warrant, and in the light of the information provided by the issuing Member State pursuant to Article 15(2) of Framework Decision 2002/584, as amended, there are substantial grounds for believing that that person will run such a risk if he is surrendered to that State."

24   See table: ENA – Europejski Nakaz Aresztowania w latach 2004-2018, available at: https://isws.ms.gov.pl/pl/baza-statystyczna/opracowania-wieloletnie/, accessed 22 August 2019.

and, on the other hand, many institutions responsible for the administrative proceedings with regard to irregularities affecting the EU's financial interests.

Criminal investigations are usually conducted by the Police, under the supervision of the public prosecutor. However, other law enforcement agencies also have jurisdiction over the PIF cases, provided they detected such a case in the course of their operational activities or where informed thereof while conducting their regular activities. These bodies include the Central Anti-Corruption Bureau, Military Police, Border Guard. They are also supervised by prosecutors, but there is no direct and permanent coordination between them – information exchange, if any, can only go through a higher-level body that is the office of the coordinator of special services, in the rank of a secretary of state. In practice, these different law enforcement agencies compete with each other, and therefore are hesitant to share information with colleagues from other institutions.

Prosecutors working in a unified and hierarchically structured public prosecutors' office are overwhelmed with work and also encounter difficulties sharing information. Furthermore, the public prosecutor's office has recently lost its autonomy and since 2016 has been again managed by the Minister of Justice who at the same time, by law, is the Prosecutor General. Also, the position of the individual prosecutor has been diminished, as they are no longer independent in their procedural decisions, but controlled by supervisors and obligated to follow their superiors' instructions.

Regrettably, in Poland, there is no entity responsible for the prevention of financial crimes, including PIF offences, not to mention a body in charge of the coordination of multi-agency preventing actions. The Central Anti-Corruption Bureau conducts some preventive activities, but since this is not its primary task, contrary to the investigation of crime, it is not a priority. This complex picture of many law enforcement agencies, enjoying overlapping jurisdiction with regard to financial crime, is further complicated by the administrative authorities conducting their own proceedings with regard to irregularities. The main focus when it comes to the protection of the financial interests of the Polish state and the EU lies within the National Revenue Administration (NRA), established in 2017, which is a **merger of previously autonomous tax administration, fiscal control and customs service. One of the main tasks of the NRA is to** control and combat economic crime by means of eliminating the grey market and reducing offences and irregularities. The impact of this new body on the actual level of irregularities is yet to be assessed.

Concerning the vertical cooperation between Polish and European institutions, it must be noted that Poland has been very open to cooperation until the new government took over in late 2015. Due to a lack of political will, cooperation with European institutions has ceased to be a priority for the current public administration. As mentioned above, Poland is not participating in the enhanced cooperation to establish the EPPO, so the investigating and prosecuting of PIF crimes, especially those of a transnational character, will naturally become more challenging. Poland still maintains cooperation with OLAF, although after the reorganization of the internal structure of the Ministry of Finance, a separate department previously responsible for performing the tasks of an AFCOS has been abolished. The AFCOS tasks, as well as audit and control of funds originating from the EU, are now assigned to a new Department for Audit of Public Funds, and constitute just a part of the Department's agenda. This organizational decision constitutes a symbolic gesture, sadly summarizing the diminished importance of EU issues for the current Polish administration.

16.6   CONCLUSION

The challenging process of implementation of the EU legal framework into Polish criminal law has been ongoing for the last two decades. The Polish legislator does not always succeed in obtaining a desirable level of harmonization of the national law with the EU law. The methods used to transpose the EU criminal legal framework are not thought through, but rather used randomly. The new provisions are often inconsistent with the already existing ones, and the European legal transplantations are not always well received by the bodies enforcing the provisions. Yet, despite the deficiencies of this process, it has been conducted in an overall pro-European spirit.

The enforcement of the new harmonizing provisions has been the most problematic. Some of the provisions aimed at implementation of the EU legal instruments are not enforced at all – for instance, provisions on the corruption of foreign public officials and officials of international organizations. And when the new implementing provisions are actually enforced, for instance, with regard to credit and subvention fraud, the practical aspects are questionable – for instance, the duration of the criminal proceedings exceeds any reasonable delay. These practical difficulties make one wonder if the proceedings and the eventually imposed sanctions fulfil the criteria of effectiveness and deterrence, as required by the EU criminal instruments. The sanctions with regard to legal persons are also inefficient, as they are hardly ever imposed, due to a systemic lack of application of responsibility of legal persons for offences.

In conclusion, however, one has to express a general concern regarding the future of the EU criminal law in Poland as well as the Polish commitment to protect the financial interests of the EU. Sadly, for over the past three years, in political debate, more often than ever, the EU has been presented as an organization limiting Polish sovereignty. Some politicians do not consider the EU a common platform enabling to strengthen the position of Poland in the world together with other partners, but a foreign body undermining Polish interests. Thus the political will to protect the EU's financial interests has decreased accordingly. Having in mind this populist political climate both in Europe and in Poland, it is hard to say at this point what the future will bring.

17 COMPARATIVE ANALYSIS

Ivan Sammut & Jelena Agranovska

17.1 INTRODUCTION

The European Union has, in the past years, developed criminal legislation to protect its financial interests. The focus of the legislation has been on public spending, fraud, bribery and cybercrime. Despite the desire by the Union to establish a harmonized legal framework to curb crimes in these areas, the transposition of these measures in the Member States has faced a series of challenges. Equally, the legal basis in the Treaty of the Functioning of the European Union (TFEU) has contrasted the legal philosophy in some Member States. In understanding the trends and challenges faced by the Member States in both the implementation and the transposition of EU criminal law protecting the Union's financial interests, this study performs a comparative analysis on practices employed in 11 selected Member States. The countries are Malta, Latvia, Ireland, France, Estonia, Croatia, Greece, Poland, Spain, Italy and Germany. The focus will then be on examining the issues arising from the implementation of the PIF Directive, which was adopted in July 2017 after extensive negotiations by the Member States, to further protect the financial interests of the EU.

17.2 COMMON TRENDS AND CHALLENGES IN THE IMPLEMENTATION OF THE EU CRIMINAL LAW IN THE MEMBER STATES

There is variance in how the EU criminal law is implemented in Member States, and this depends on the national legislative approach of each Member State. Visible commonalities also exist in methods of some jurisdictions, especially those in which judicial systems have been influenced by one another, such as the civil law systems in Germany and the Baltic States. Like Germany, the two Baltic States – Estonia and Latvia – similarly dealt with the implementation of the EU criminal law in their national judicial structures. For example, the effect of EU's criminal law became apparent when these countries drafted their penal codes in anticipation of Union membership. At the time when the Estonian Penal Code (EPC) and the Latvian Criminal Law (LCL) were drafted and implemented, both countries were on their way to becoming EU Member States. Therefore, to comply with the requirements of the Association Agreements, both the Baltic States had to make their legislation compatible with the legal framework and philosophy of the EU, and this included the development of new criminal law provisions, comprising the measures that the acts of the third pillar of the European Union required.

The drafters of the EPC and the LCL managed to ensure compliance in some critical areas of EU legislation on criminal law, by introducing new offences into their national criminal laws such as offences against a person, family and minors. When drafting the provisions covering fraud, the EPC promulgators also ensured compliance with the Convention on the Protection of the European Communities' Financial Interests and Article 209a of the Maastricht Treaty. Likewise, in line with the Convention on the fight against corruption involving officials of the EU or officials of Member States of the EU, the drafters of the EPC took into account the EU legal position on active and passive corruption. In addition to compliance in these areas, the drafters of the EPC also ensured that the country aligned its laws to accommodate the Council of Europe Recommendations by criminalizing offences committed by legal persons and also by introducing a new penalty of community service.

Despite these efforts, Estonia was still unable to fully integrate its legal system and introduce all offences that would warrant its full compliance with the European Union law at the time of its accession to the Union. With these adoptions, it is evident that Estonia had to rearrange its legal philosophy and attempt to reconcile its criminal justice system to the demands of EU criminal law regime. However, the country has systematically introduced the doctrines found within the EU legal framework in its penal code, striving to achieve full compliance. Latvia has taken a similar approach in this regard.

The influence of the EU criminal law on the procedural criminal law of Estonia and Latvia has also been significant. At the time when both countries adopted their laws on the criminal procedure (entered into force on 1 July 2004 and 21 April 2005 respectively), they had already become members of the EU. Therefore, the national legislators sought to draft the laws that would be in full compliance with the requirements of the EU, the Council of Europe conventions, the ECHR as well as the decisions of the ECtHR. However, the original criminal procedure laws did not comply with the EU *acquis* in their entirety, as Estonia complied with the European Arrest Warrant (EAW) Directive only after the original law on criminal procedure was amended on 28 June 2004, that is, before the original law entered into force on 1 July 2004.

In contrast to the two Baltic States, whose legal systems proved to be rather susceptible to change and influence stemming from the Union's law, the situation in Germany – a judicial system that had itself significantly influenced the criminal law systems of the Baltic States – has been different. Due to the existence of well-developed and long-established criminal law concepts, the degree of EU criminal law influence on German criminal law varies from area to area. At the same time, the influence of EU law on Germany's procedural rules has been quite limited. Like many other Member States considered in this study, the German legislator had to adjust its penalties to comply with EU provisions. However, there are a number of discrepancies between the EU and national provisions that still remain. For instance, Germany has been less cooperative in the efforts to adjust its penalties to correspond to EU provisions.

The challenges on compliance witnessed by the two Baltic States were not posed to all countries that sought membership with the EU. However, there are also challenges that exist in those Member States which initially formed the foundation of the EU in Europe. In practice, such countries have determined the trajectory of the overall development of the EU and dominated the ways in which it has implemented its policies. Generally, they have had minimal challenges in implementing the legal requirements dictated by the EU. For instance, in the case of France, it has not had difficulty in complying with the provisions of the EU *acquis* because of its leadership role in drafting new instruments required for the development of the EU legislation, or its influence in directing the choices that are made within the EU. It will not be an overstatement to say that most of the EU convention decisions, new laws and directives in the area of EU criminal law would almost always be compatible with the criminal law regime of France. Despite this, there are legal experts and criminal lawyers in France who have expressed concern on the difficulty to implement some legislative proposals of the EU because of their effect on the fundamental principles to which the French procedural criminal law is predicated. Two of the concerns are the French approach to the European Public Prosecutor's Office (EPPO) and the legal framework implementing the PIF Directive.

Even with this reservation, France has often been supportive of EU legal considerations that would make the Union more efficient in its operations. However, in the past, France has shown reluctance to accept centralized options fronted by the EU. This is different from Estonian and Latvian approaches since these Member States showed no resistance to the effective national implementation of new criminal law provisions according to the third pillar of the European Union. A report commissioned by the European Parliament and released in 2018 on procedural criminal law highlighted France as one of the countries that were not ready to fully introduce changes to its legal regime that would significantly alter its legal system. However, legal experts explain the highlight of the report by pointing to the compatibility that EU legal instruments have with the fundamental principles of French procedural law.

There are instances where France has shown the challenges it has in implementing EU criminal law. It has been noted that sometimes the legislative intervention to implement new secondary law is insufficient, while the supreme courts of France show a lack of enthusiasm to interpret the EU instruments and to assess the appropriateness of national implementation. French courts have reacted in dismissive ways to legislative interventions of the EU through its directives to provide a secondary law that the country can use when determining its cases.

The challenges exhibited in France in the implementation of the EU's criminal law are different from those exhibited in Ireland. First, it should be noted that together with the UK and Denmark, Ireland has opted out from the entire Area of Freedom, Security and Justice (AFSJ). Likewise, the CJEU's jurisdiction interpreting any provision of the Area of Freedom, Security and Justice would not apply to it. However, having opted into many of the legislative measures adopted by the EU, Ireland actively participates in their application, specifically in the areas where there is a distinctive need for cross-border cooperation, such as money laundering, terrorism and cybercrime. Unlike the Member States that habitually implement EU criminal law provisions by systematically adopting amendments to their penal codes (i.e., Greece, Estonia, Latvia and Germany), the Irish legislature complies with the EU law by implementing separate Criminal Justice Acts covering special areas. Such Criminal Justice Acts remain the only necessary reference points for specific types of offences. In line with the EU criminal law and the requirements of the PIF Directive, Ireland established criminal liability for legal persons. Of note is a creative way in which Ireland has given extraterritorial effect to cybercrime, promoting a cross-border approach in this area. Ireland has opted to participate in the Directive (EU) 2015/849 on the prevention of the use of the financial system for the purposes of money laundering or terrorist financing. However, it has not yet implemented the relevant national law.

The implementation of the EU criminal law in Greece is relatively different from the approach of some other Member States. Unlike Ireland, which has separate Criminal Justice Acts covering offences such as terrorism, the Hellenic Republic has placed all the provisions of EU criminal law within the Hellenic Criminal Code. In this respect, the Hellenic approach is similar to the one adopted by the two Baltic States. However, while Greece strongly relies on the Criminal Code, Article 29 of the Constitution of Ireland governs the adoption and application of EU law in the country. Moreover, Ireland's steps towards collaborating with the EU is closely related to the approach of other states such as Germany and France. Arguably, like these jurisdictions' efforts, the Constitution of Ireland mainly supports its international relations such as becoming a member of the EU. However, despite this legal practice, it protects the way EU law operates in Ireland to ensure that laws enacted, acts accomplished and measures implemented by the country corresponds to EU membership requirements. In this regard, the European Communities Act 1972 was introduced to give both domestic effects to EU law and to permit the government to implement EU law in the form of secondary regulations.

Unlike in the other Member States, the legislative and juridical arms of the government have significantly influenced Italy's EU law implementation process. While other states rely on the Criminal Code and the Constitution, only Italian courts have actively participated in the adoption of EU law. This standoff implies a stalemate between the Italian courts and their relationship with EU law. The situation has been worsened by the complexity at the legislative level. For instance, in 2015 and 2016, Italy managed to implement only two important EU criminal law instruments namely, the Framework Decision on Joint Investigation Teams and the Framework Decisions on the mutual recognition of both confiscation orders. These back and forth issues in Italy directly derail the efforts of other Member States such as France and Spain, which have readily complied with the EU legal instruments. In Spain, for instance, there is a positive attitude towards implementation of the EU criminal law. Like Italy, Spain is successful at both the judicial and legislative levels. Therefore, the country is likely to benefit from implementing EU criminal law compared to Italy, which still drags out the process because of different legal issues.

Most of the national reports have commented on the limits of mutual trust in the execution of EAWs, the major culprits being the non-application of the proportionality test when EAWs were issued for minor offences and the issue of interaction between the application of EAW Framework Decision and fundamental rights. It should be emphasized that even though there are some well-developed EU measures aimed at enhancing the Member States' cooperation, the lack of trust and inefficiency both undermine the effective and smooth cooperation in all instances.

For instance, Malta has a strict policy on fairness and some of the reasons that EAWs contain do not fall within the fairness and proportionality trials that Malta's legal framework demands. This has led to the country having challenges in actualizing EAWs, but has effectively discharged its mandate at the local level through its legal framework.

In Poland, there were challenges as well, just like in Malta. Poland had to change its Constitution to allow for EAWs to be enabled in the country. Subsequently, this aligned the Polish Criminal Procedure Code with the EU legal instruments on administrative proceedings that protect the EU's financial interests through the PIF Directive. Apart from the introduction of the EAW, the amendment to the Constitution was also to establish rules of jurisdiction. Poland's Constitution was strict and lacked flexibility in granting of jurisdiction to external bodies and countries. Despite the efforts made by Poland, there are provisions within the EU legal framework that still contradict the national legal regime. One of those provisions is the forfeiture of assets of a suspect that were acquired five years before the crime was committed unless the suspect can show proof that the assets were acquired in a legal process. Poland's Penal Code does not allow for this provision, and it makes it impossible to implement this provision by EU law where an EAW is made within Poland. Equally, perpetrators can successfully adjudicate their cases in Polish courts against forfeiture of their assets acquired years before an offence was committed. The effect is a setback to the PIF Directive in Poland.

Although Poland is new to the Western political influence due to its democratic transformation only in 1989, the country is geared towards unprecedented developments in terms of law modification and enforcing the Council of Europe

Standards. The adoption of the EU Criminal law is progressive since the Polish legislator's process of implementation has been broad. Poland and Malta have robust and specific EU criminal laws. For instance, in Malta, the PIF Directive has been enforced based on the speedy legislative amendments and other administrative interventions. Like the Hellenic Republic, Malta strongly relies on its Criminal Code to implement some of the EU criminal law against crimes such as fraud, bribery and financial corruption.

All the reports highlighted that generally, the Member States have successfully implemented in their criminal laws the EU legislative norms dealing with offences of terrorism, organized crime and cybercrime. Several new substantive offences have been introduced in all countries. However, there are still a number of discrepancies in definitions of what constitutes an offence. For example, the Estonian definition of an act that constitutes a 'terrorist offence' does not contain all of the terrorist activities listed in Article 1(1)(f) of the Framework Decision 2002/475/JHA.

The national reports have revealed that not all implementation and transposition were smooth, as some elements of the definitions of offences found in EU provisions were not duly implemented; in some instances, the scope of the EU measures has been widened, while in others it has been narrowed. For instance, in Germany, the traditional definition of the term 'organization' would have a more formal structure, which inevitably narrows the definition provided for in the EU Framework Decisions on the criminalization of terrorism. Similarly, the Latvian definition of an 'organized group' appears to have a wider scope, since it does not have the criterion of benefit, which could be found in Article 1(1) of the Framework Decision FD 2008/841/JHA. Likewise, the Estonian legislature has narrowed the scope of the definition of 'criminal organization', since the national measure has an additional element of 'division of tasks and functions in the criminal organization'. Another criticism of the German transposition of EU criminal law relates to Framework Decision 2005/222/JHA on the criminalization of attacks against information systems, where under the national rules some acts covered by the EU law would not be covered by the relevant national provisions.

Like the rest of the EU Member States, Greece, Spain, and Italy have also encountered issues during the implementation of EU criminal law. In Greece, the idea of incorporating the new EU instruments into the Criminal Code did not meet the expectations of the EU. In effect, the EU reacted negatively to such a proposition because, in its opinion, it was inadequate. In other words, EU standards demand criminal law instruments to entail non-criminal elements. However, this can only happen if the offence is included in the national legal order and a state introduces administrative measures to ensure the efficiency of the substantive criminal provision, which the Hellenic legislators failed to observe. Similarly, Spain has encountered uneven legal connotations. Although this country has had a positive attitude towards its implementation task, it postpones enforcing critical legal issues. For instance, most of the mutual recognition instruments that were adopted during The Hague Programme (i.e., before the entry into force of the Treaty of Lisbon in December 2009) were not accomplished till December 2014 when Act 23/2014 came into force. Based on these delays, the Spanish legislature often refers to EU law notions, which are alien to the legislators. The situation is similar in Italy. Although the administrative structure has made efforts to ensure the country complies with the EU criminal law, the legislative arm of the government still lags in the implementation process. For instance, these drawbacks at the legislative level have thwarted efforts to implement the Council Framework Decision 2008/841/JHA on organized crime and the PIF Directive. Therefore, these countries have encountered issues with the EU criminal law implementation.

Some discrepancies were eventually cured by subsequent amendments to the national provisions; however, other discrepancies and lacunas remain. It should be noted that there is a lack of effective prosecution in some areas. For example, there are barely any significant prosecutions under money laundering legislation in Latvia and no prosecutions of cybercrime in Ireland. Therefore, it should be concluded, that in order for the EU legislative measures to reach their full potential, Member States have to further amend their applicable legislation and implement all of the necessary provisions found in the EU legislative measures.

The implementation of the EU criminal law in the Member States discussed above express the different trends and challenges that the national legislators have in adopting and accommodating the EU criminal law. In the case of Estonia and Latvia, the challenges presented are reflective of the trends that countries who were not EU members face when they decide to become EU members. The requirement for compliance with the criminal law system of the EU significantly alters the legal regime of a country and the fundamental principles to which the legal justice system of a country is predicated upon. The cases of Germany and France represent a situation where Member States which have a dominant influence of the EU legislative agenda face resistance to change in its national criminal justice systems. In the case of Ireland, there is representation of a country that has opted out of participating in the entire Area of Freedom, Security and Justice, while at the same time, chose to opt into many EU criminal law measures. These countries broadly represent the trends and challenges that the Member States are facing when implementing the EU criminal law.

17.3   COMMON TRENDS AND CHALLENGES IN THE TRANSPOSITION OF EU LAW ON THE CRIMES AGAINST THE FINANCIAL INTERESTS OF THE EU

It has been confirmed that all Member States participating in this study are fully involved in the EU's action to protect its financial interests and combat fraud. However, some reports ascertained that corruption and money laundering is of great concern in some

Member States (e.g., Ireland and Latvia). Both Ireland and Latvia faced infringement actions under the enforcement procedure of Article 258 TFEU for non-implementation of the fourth AML Directive. This situation reflects the fact that even though the adequate legal instruments could be in place, further work needs to be done in order to effectively investigate and enforce them. Additionally, in some instances, the Member States have failed to implement the necessary national measures in a timely manner, as for example, Estonia in the case of Directive (EU) 2016/680 on the protection of natural persons with regard to the processing of personal data by competent authorities.

One of the issues relevant to the application of EU law in practice is the efficiency of national monitoring processes, as well as the independence of national agencies and bodies engaged in investigations and prosecutions. In some instances, the multitude of agencies creates a situation where it is literally impossible to discern the responsibilities and obligations of the authorities at hand. The effectiveness of investigation and prosecution is also of concern.

Transposition of EU law in protecting the financial interests of the Union depends on the national legal regimes of Member States. In the case of Italy, the country has used its governance platform and influence within the EU to ensure the protection of the Union's financial interests. On the academic front, Italy contributed a member to the eight-member experts team that drafted the *Corpus Juris*. *Corpus Juris* is synonymous with the existence of the current EPPO. The EPPO enables the EU to effectively adjudicate on offences committed against its financial interests. *Corpus Juris* was carried out in the 1990s as part of the European Legal Area Project aimed at identifying how Member States can contribute to the legislative framework of the Union with the aim of protecting the EU's financial interests. Several experts and practitioners from Italy made their contributions, specifically in the establishment of the EPPO. This is the academic contribution that Italy made. However, there is the legal contribution through Italy's judicial system in the confines of 'double-track' system and *ne bis in idem*.

The present legal debate in Italy is how the principle of *ne bis in idem* can be applied concurrently in administrative and within criminal proceedings on issues on a 'double-track' system. 'Double-track' system is a sentencing system that provides measures of prevention and penalties for offenders. It considers the criminal capacity of offenders and the prevention measures for dangerous offenders. *Ne bis in idem* on the other hand follows through with the provisions of Article 649 of Italy's Code of Penal Procedure (CPP) that eliminates subjecting a person who has been acquitted or convicted from further criminal proceedings on the same facts. The wording of the principle makes it inapplicable to situations where first proceedings are of an administrative nature, and not of a criminal nature. The clarification in the country's tax crime laws is that when the same fact enables both criminal and administrative liability, then a person can be subjected to the two proceedings. The tax crime legislation, however, prohibits providing similar penalties to the individual. This is in consideration of the substantive principle of *ne bis in idem*. In practice, where an individual has administratively been found guilty of misappropriation of funds, administrative penalties can be issued by competent administrative authorities, but, if criminal legislation also punishes the same facts and the person found guilty is undergoing prosecution, then the penalties issued are not executed during the period when the criminal trial is taking place. If the legal system finds the person guilty and he or she is convicted, then the administrative penalties are not executed. However, if there is an acquittal through the criminal justice system, then the person is subject to the previously issued administrative penalties.

The debate between *ne bis in idem* and 'double-track' system is central to protecting the financial interests of the EU in Italy. There are already judgments that have been handed down by both the European Court of Human Rights (ECtHR) and the Court of Justice of the European Union (CJEU) on the matter. The ECtHR had determined that the principle of *ne bis in idem* was compatible with the rules on tax crime. The consequence was an escalation of the same to the Italian Constitutional Court. One of the cases that ECtHR had to rule in recognition of *ne bis in idem* was the case of *Grande Stevens v. Italy*. The case concerned the rules on market manipulation in Italy. ECtHR ruled that there was no compatibility of the duplication of criminal and administrative proceedings where the right to *ne bis in idem* was to be considered if the administrative procedure which the facts are subjected to is deemed to be similar to a 'criminal charge' using the Engel criteria. The Constitutional Court in Italy failed to follow a request made by the national Court, which proposed an extension of Article 649 CPP to bar further criminal proceedings through procedural *ne bis in idem* on the same facts that had been decided upon by an administrative authority and a final decision made, which in accordance to the proceedings, had a criminal nature.

When the matter was still under consideration by the Constitutional Court, the ECtHR, through its decision on *A & B v. Norway*, changed its approach on the issue and ruled that duplication of administrative and criminal proceedings does not breach the principle of *ne bis in idem*, where there is sufficient time and a substantial connection between the two proceedings. The ruling also provided a criterion to be followed in determining the existence of adequate time and substance connection in a case. The implication of this development led the Constitutional Court of Italy to send the case back to the national Court for a determination on whether there were sufficient substance and time connection between the administrative and the criminal proceedings on the matters of the case. The statement by the Constitutional Court of Italy meant that the ruling in *A & B v. Norway* made it less likely to subject violation of the principle of *ne bis in idem* where duplication of administrative and criminal proceedings take place.

However, the Constitutional Court added that if there is lack of sufficient time and substance connection in a specific case due to the handling of the proceedings of matters in the case, whether in the field of tax crime or any other field, then the duplication is adduced to have violated the principle of *ne bis in idem*.

Apart from the ECtHR, the CJEU also suspected that there was variance in the way the Italian rule was applied in relation to EU law. In its ruling that was an endorsement to a large extent of the Strasbourg Court, the CJEU determined in the case of *Menci*, upon an Italian court's request, that Article 50 of the European Charter was compatible to issuing both criminal and administrative sanctions for the same facts against the same person. The facts of the case were a failure to pay Value-Added Tax (VAT) that was due as provided for by law within certain time limits. According to the ruling by the CJEU, duplication of proceedings and penalties represents a limit and not a violation of *ne bis in idem*. In VAT offences, the justification for enabling duplication of penalties and proceedings is the general interest objective of combating such crimes and ensuring that collection of due VAT is not hampered through legal means. There are experts who point to a complementary approach to the application of both criminal and administrative proceedings since they consider different aspects of the unlawful conduct.

Once the CJEU had pronounced itself in the *Menci* case on what it perceived as applicability of *ne bis in idem* in tax laws and its compatibility to EU law, the Italian Court that had requested the direction of the CJEU on the case failed to take a decision on the case merits, but raised a question to the Constitutional Court of Italy. The Italian Court wanted the Constitutional Court of Italy to make a determination on how the *ne bis in idem* principle applies in relation to its compatibility to Article 649 of Italy's Code of Penal Procedure given the two rulings by the ECtHR and the CJEU. The dilemma that the Italian Court needed clarification on is that on tax laws, specifically on failure to pay VAT in a timely manner within the specifications of the law, there is a lack of complementarity between criminal and administrative proceedings since they both aim at punishing identical conduct. Subsequently, the Court pointed to a lack of real coordination between the two proceedings since they are predicated upon different rules. The Constitutional Court of Italy is still seized of the matter and is yet to make a determination. This further fuels speculation on the intent of the Italian and European courts, with the Italian courts committed to ensuring that there is no disproportionate punishment of persons who are at fault of tax laws. The aim of the Italian courts is also to balance the protection of the EU's budget with the protection of the right not to undergo punishment twice for an offence on the same facts.

The metrics of protection of the EU's financial interests do not measure favourably to Spain as they do to Italy. However, Spain still does not stand out, whether positive or negative, on the subject. There have been doubts raised on Spain's accuracy in calculating fraud, specifically tax fraud, but EU's usual reports do not single out Spain negatively or positively on the same. The areas that Spain has made contributions on are dealing with the crimes against the EU's financial interests using Spain's criminal justice system, and its application of both the *ne bis in idem* principle and the stature of limitations. The 2004 report by the European Commission on compliance of Member States to the legal framework on fraud and other financial interest cases rates Spain as compliant. Despite this, there were doubts raised on the intensity by Spain's criminal justice system to evenly prosecute all instances of money laundering without focusing only on serious cases. A similar report in 2008 by the European Commission was equally positive about Spain with a single issue raised on how Spain was going to treat liability of legal persons. At the time, the problem was still under consideration by Spain's judicial system.

Unlike in Italy, where the principle of *ne bis in idem* is yet to be concluded by the Italian Constitutional Court given the reference by the national Court on clarification of compatibility to Article 649 given the rulings made by both the CJEU and ECtHR, the Court of Justice in Spain has given a verdict on how the principle applies with relation to laws in Spain. The Court of Justice in Spain had previously made a ruling, even in the absence of the secondary legislation of the EU that requires compliance of EU criminal law by all Member States, to the effect that Article 325 of TFEU obligates Member States to protect the EU's financial interests. The Court of Justice added that such support has in recent and immediate cases taken a narrative of ensuring punishment of a criminal nature to offenders. After its ruling in the *Akerberg Fransson* case, Spain's Court of Justice lowered its exigencies that it made in its judgment on *Luca Menci* where it stated that the Member States may impose both a formal administrative sanction and a criminal penalty where conditions under the Engel criteria are met. This is despite Spain having one of the strongest adherences to the principle of *ne bis in idem*. Spain does not allow the cumulative imposition of both criminal and administrative penalties in a single case. An individual case in this context means a case where there are identical facts, legal ground, and subjects. In such a situation, it is only criminal law that has priority.

Unlike the situation in Italy and Spain on the continued debate on *ne bis in idem*, there are other countries that do not have many controversies in their transposition of EU criminal law on the protection of financial interests of the Union. Estonia represents the countries that operate with minimal legal controversies with the EU criminal legislation of cybercrime, fraud and public spending. Estonia is one of the countries that has fully transposed Directives 2014/25/EU, 2014/24/EU and 2014/23/EU. It did this through the Public Procurement Act of 2017, which meant that all information and communication exchange relating to public procurement would be done in the e-procurement system. This includes exchanges between an economic operator and the contracting entity or authority, availability of procurement documents, submission of tenders, clarifications on procurement issues and requests to participate in procurement opportunities. Apart from the Public Procurement Act of 2017, Estonia had also adopted a new Customs Act in 2017 that made its customs laws compliant with the EU Customs Code. Some of the changes that the Customs Act introduced were the use of x-ray images and establishing an image database for customs check purposes and collecting information. Subsequently, such information shall be used in the prevention of tax fraud and smuggling. The new Customs Act also added a requirement to collect information about all international train and bus passengers and their carriages as well.

Just like Estonia, Latvia has also aligned its laws with the requirements of the EU laws on the protection of the Union's financial interests. For instance, Latvia had enacted a law that sought to protect the right of its citizens against the usage of personal data by unauthorized and third-party entities. The rights were captured in the Latvian Personal Data Protection Law of 2000. However, this law made it difficult to enact the requirements of information sharing between the Member States on individual information of persons in Latvia. Subsequently, the law was a barrier to the fight against cybercrime and other fraud-related cases. This forced Latvia to make a series of amendments to the law and later substituted the law in 2018 with the Personal Data Processing Law. The law set preconditions for sharing of personal data with other agencies both at a national and international level. Just like the previous law, the 2018 law received criticism from EU members on its contribution to fragmentation of the EU's regulatory framework. This led Latvia's Ministry of Justice to draft a new law that would enable the effective sharing of data within the EU to curb fraud and cybercrime. The Personal Data Processing Law was then effectively supplemented with the 2019 special law on the Processing of Personal Data in Criminal and Administrative Offenses.

The transposition of EU law on the crimes against the financial interests of the EU has created specific challenges to the principles of Member States. For instance, in the case of Italy and Spain, both countries have had to rethink their application of the principle of *ne bis in idem* to conform to the rulings made by both the CJEU and the ECtHR. In the case of Italy, the Constitutional Court is yet to determine whether its protection of double penalty on an offence liability is against the provisions of EU law. Likewise, in Spain, the Court of Justice had to make a ruling in support of the EU law, while locally, the courts still firmly hold to a strong *ne bis in idem* principle. This means that transposition of EU law has not been smooth in some of the dominant countries within the EU. However, in countries such as Estonia and Latvia, the legal justice systems have acted to conform to the EU Directives with minimal resistance. Transposition of EU law has had a negative effect in some EU countries with respect to changing their legal principles on fundamental issues.

17.4   ISSUES ARISING FROM THE IMPLEMENTATION OF PIF

Implementation of some provisions of the PIF Directive has proved to be a challenge to some Member States, same as participation in the EPPO. In contrast to a relatively conflict-free implementation of the PIF provisions into the national systems in Estonia and Latvia, other Member States, such as France and Germany, had some challenges to overcome. Likewise, the participation in the EPPO has been a hotly debated (and resisted to) issue in some Member States such as Ireland, Germany and France, while at the same time being wholeheartedly accepted and committed to by others, such as Latvia and Estonia.

Like the other EU Member States, Malta had to change its penal codes and criminal justice frameworks to enable compliance to the requirements of the PIF Directive. In dealing with crimes that relate to protecting the EU's financial interests, the Maltese Criminal Code has numerous provisions that tackle offences in the PIF Directive. Some of such offences are obtaining money by pretence, misappropriation of funds and use of resources for fraudulent gains. The implementation of PIF in Malta also faced issues arising from the inadequate application of the specialized investigative legal instruments. These are not the only problems that characterize the PIF Directive in Malta. Arguably, the field of determining confiscations present two issues, namely, the non-conviction-based confiscation of assets and third-party confiscation of assets. Ideally, these two elements were absent from the critical EU legal framework. Locally, other issues exist, such as the use of EAW to cover frivolous offences, which should not be the case. Arguably, another problem has been about freezing and confiscation, which may interfere with the freedom of one's property. However, the primary issue in Malta regarding enforcing the PIF Directive is that the process can significantly lead to freezing of all assets of the subject matter indiscriminately. In effect, such actions can lead to interference with the freedom of an individual. In other words, the problem of freezing orders in Malta does not meet any proportionality principle.

In the case of Greece, the country has used a different approach than other countries who prefer the copy-paste method in establishing a legal framework to support the PIF Directive. Greece chose to tackle the cases within the PIF Directive on an issue-by-issue basis, and where possible, align them to the existing legal framework in Greece. This meant that the legal framework in Greece on topics such as tax fraud, cybercrime and public expenditure are different from the laws on the same problems in other countries. There have been calls for Greece to align its laws to mirror similar laws around Europe. One area that the European Commission has shown its displeasure with the Hellenic Republic is in the decision by Greece to opt for a criminal code as the basis for directives on money laundering rather than having a particular criminal law on the same. A criminal code has a limited scope of application and implementation as opposed to a full special criminal law that covers extensive areas of law regarding a crime. Greece attributes their insistence to adopting a different approach to the dormant and ineffective laws that other countries have concerning the implementation of the PIF Directive.

A similar but more drastic approach to the PIF Directive was taken by Germany as well. As of 2018, Germany had not enacted any laws or revised any of its criminal codes to support the implementation of the PIF Directive. Unlike for Greece, there has not been any criticism of Germany for its failure to enact a legal framework and instruments in support of the PIF Directive. However, the country has indicated its support through verbal pronouncement on the need to have a more comprehensive way of protecting the rights of suspected persons. Germany has also proposed the establishment of a link to which the financial interests of the EU can be protected in legislations where it is eminent that an expansion of substantive criminal law must occur. The difference in applicability and implementation of the PIF Directive reveals the issues that the EU faces in protecting its financial interests among the Member States.

Latvia has already implemented the necessary measures to comply with the PIF Directive. Ireland has also implemented parts of the required amendments to comply with the PIF, and further measures are anticipated to be implemented by the end of 2019. For both Latvia and Ireland, one of the issues that needed tackling with regards to compliance with the PIF Directive was the limitation periods. While the former had to amend its criminal law provisions relating to limitation periods, the latter does not have prescription periods, so the Recital 22 of the PIF directive would apply to it.

Estonia is currently in the process of drafting the relevant legislation to comply with the PIF Directive provisions, yet there are no drafts available at the moment. The German limitation periods were in line with the provisions of the directive, so no action was required on that front.

Similarly, France and Poland have encountered issues arising from the implementation of PIF. On the one hand, the PIF Directive first featured in the French Official Journal in July 2017. Despite this achievement, the implementation measures did not take place at the time of writing. Secondly, the *verrou de Bercy* has been incompatible with the EPPO's elements as stipulated in the EPPO Regulation and the PIF Directive. Another crucial shortcoming relates to the criminal liability of legal persons – in France the offence must be committed on behalf of a legal person. However, this has proven challenging since the criterion in the PIF Directive dictates that an offence must be committed for the benefit of a legal person. On the other hand, Poland has had issues in harmonizing the EU legal instruments. These problems remain unsolved. For instance, enforcement remains an issue, as some of the provisions aimed at implementation of the EU legal instruments, such as provisions on corruption of foreign public officials and officials of international organizations, are not enforced. The practical aspects of enforcement, for instance with regard to credit and subvention fraud, are questionable since the duration of the criminal proceedings is excessively long. As a result, one is not certain if the proceedings and the eventually imposed sanctions fulfil the criteria of effectiveness and deterrence, as required by the EU criminal instruments. In this way, there is a systematic lack of effective legal measures regarding criminal liability of legal persons, as the criminal sanctions are hardly ever imposed. Additionally, there is significant difficulty in ensuring effective asset recovery. Therefore, in practice, the effective implementation of EU criminal law in these matters has not been fully achieved. On the other hand, Poland has not actively participated in the adoption of the PIF Directive because an intervention of authorities is necessary to officiate the effectiveness of sanctioning.

Like France and Poland, Spain and Italy have also faced challenges concerning the implementation of the PIF Directive. Although Spain has introduced a new criminal offence of misappropriation and inclusion of VAT fraud, it has lagged behind its other national counterparts in fulfilling some of the directive's requirements. Arguably, the highly volatile Spanish political landscape has thwarted the implementation of PIF Directive.

On the face of it, Croatia appears to be one of the few Member States that has already successfully adopted the amendments necessary for implementing the PIF Directive into the national criminal justice system. However, the Croatian national compliance measures could be said to be of dubious quality, as the only change that was introduced is the reference to the PIF Directive in Article 386 of the Criminal Code. The Croatian Government claimed that national criminal legislation already complies with the PIF Directive and there is no need for any additional substantive changes. Nevertheless, a number of shortcomings highlighted in the report prove that the transposition is defective and without any proper content. It is evident that Croatia has failed to fully transpose the directive. For instance, elements of crimes prescribed by Article 3 and Article 4 of the directive cannot be aligned with the national offences found in the Croatian Criminal Code.

17.5 CONCLUSION

The EU seeks to ensure the adoption of its criminal legislation by its Member States. The countries considered in this study have successfully managed to adapt their legal systems to the demands of the EU criminal legislation on the protection of the EU's financial interests. Countries such as Spain and Italy had sought to offer support to the EU criminal legislation, but their attempts raised a discourse on the viability of their principles in the context of applying a different principle in the EU cases while having a separate legal application in the local context. One such area of variance is in the application of the *ne bis in idem* principle. There have also been issues in the implementation of the PIF Directive, and this largely informs the definitions of offences in the national judicial systems. Malta, for instance, has had to change its laws to achieve conformity to the requirements by the EU on data sharing in curbing of fraud. Poland, on the other hand, had difficulties in allowing the implementation of the forfeiture principle of the accused where assets acquired five years before a crime is committed had to be confiscated as well. While other countries tried to align their laws to the requirements of the PIF Directive, there were others such as Germany that had not enacted any laws in support of the implementation of the PIF Directive. The EU has faced significant challenges in its desire to implement criminal legislation and make it effectively implemented and applied by the Member States. This jeopardizes the aim of securing the financial interests of the Union.

CONCLUSION

Ivan Sammut & Jelena Agranovska

The Lisbon Treaty has provided the tools to further European policies through criminal law. European criminal law has become a proper area of European law even if it was not traditionally linked with the Internal Market. This work has examined the tools which have been provided through the Lisbon Treaty on European criminal law, using which crimes are criminalized because they negatively affect the financial interests of the European Union. After introducing the legal basis and crimes against the financial interests of the EU, the study looked at inter-agency cooperation and cybercrime. This was followed by several case studies from 11 Member States selected based on their size, geographical position and legal tradition.

From all the discussions, one can conclude that while considerable effort is being taken to harmonize or to deal with the Europeanization of criminal law in order to protect crimes against the financial interests of the EU as well as the public at large through cooperation between the national authorities, a lot of work is still needed for Europeanization to work properly. As it has been outlined throughout this study, it is very clear that the difference between national substantive law is often difficult to break. An offence may be a crime in one Member State but not an offence in another, or it may be classified differently. From one particular Member State perspective, an EAW may make sense; from another, it may be an overkill. We have seen examples where individuals subjected to European criminal law may have suffered, or even fundamental rights may have been breached as a result of a ticking-the-box exercise in enforcing European criminal law. Europeanization of criminal law cannot work without mutual recognition between Member States. Yet mutual recognition is essential as European criminal law is based on the assumption that Member States are the ultimate sovereign states and so criminal law is in their domain and Europeanization of criminal law is accepted on the grounds of mutual benefit and that it will make the EU function better. However, with so many different states of different legal cultures, languages and history, one cannot assume that states have the same standards; different standards may well result because of these differences. Hence, the marriage between mutual recognition and respecting the national tradition may be very challenging, for even if it is similar, it may be interpreted differently.

Because of the above, the smooth Europeanization of criminal law may be more of a pipe dream than reality and unless Member States are careful, not only will some agreed objectives not be achieved, but the opposite may be achieved and the EU citizen would be worse off. There is no quick or easy solution to this. The above study shows that a good approach to the Europeanization of criminal law is to respect the balance between what may work smoothly and what may create more problems. Europeanization cannot be an end, and it may not be the appropriate tool for some objectives. Respecting and acknowledging diversity is essential, and mutual respect should not be forced down the throats of Member States' legal systems. Often cooperation between the Member States may work but often it may not. Going down the path of Europeanizing all the objectives that look nice on paper without realizing the day-to-day, practical implications may be self-defeating and may lead to possible breaches of fundamental rights. A good way of approaching European criminal law is a balance of respecting theory and practice and keeping this to a minimum. Unless the Member States opt into a unified system, which in the current situation is much more of a pipe dream and is not desired, achieving better results may also mean doing less than what appears attractive on paper. With the current and foreseeable state of fragmentation and diversity of European criminal law, respecting the Member States' legal traditions and individuality may be a more appropriate position in the interests of EU citizens.